Fashion, Work, and Politics in
Modern France

Fashion, Work, and Politics in Modern France

Steve Zdatny

First published in 2006 by
PALGRAVE MACMILLAN™
175 Fifth Avenue, New York, N.Y. 10010 and
Houndmills, Basingstoke, Hampshire, England RG21 6XS
Companies and representatives throughout the world.

PALGRAVE MACMILLAN is the global academic imprint of the Palgrave Macmillan division of St. Martin's Press, LLC and of Palgrave Macmillan Ltd. Macmillan® is a registered trademark in the United States, United Kingdom and other countries. Palgrave is a registered trademark in the European Union and other countries.

ISBN-13: 978–1–4039–7217–0
ISBN-10: 1–4039–7217–6

Library of Congress Cataloging-in-Publication Data is available from the Library of Congress.

A catalogue record for this book is available from the British Library.

Design by Newgen Imaging Systems (P) Ltd., Chennai, India.

First edition: May 2006

10 9 8 7 6 5 4 3 2 1

Printed in the United States of America.

To Sophie

Contents

Illustrations

Abbreviations

AN	Archives Nationales, Paris
AP	Administrateur provisoire (of a confiscated Jewish business)
CATC	Cercle des arts et techniques de la coiffure française
CCIP	Archives of the Chambre de Commerce et d'Industrie de Paris
CDROS	Commission départementale de reconstruction des organisations syndicales
CGQJ	Commissariat général aux questions juives
CGT	Confédération générale du travail
CNE	Conseil national économique
CNR-Coiffure	Comité national de répartition des produits rationnés aux coiffeurs
CNROS	Commission nationale de reconstitution des organisations syndicales
CO	Comité d'organisation
CPC	Confédération patronale des coiffeurs de France et des colonies
CPO	Commission provisoire d'organisation de la famille professionnelle en hygiène
CSO	Chambre syndicale ouvrière des coiffeurs de Paris
CSP	Chambre syndicale des patrons coiffeurs de Paris
FNC	Fédération nationale des maîtres-artisans et patrons coiffeurs de France, d'Algérie, et des colonies
FNCEP-FO	Fédération nationale de la coiffure, de l'esthétique et de la parfumerie -Force Ouvrière
FNSOC	Fédération nationale des syndicates d'ouvriers coiffeurs de France et des colonies
FO	Confédération générale du travail-Force Ouvrière
HWJS	*Hairdressers' Weekly Journal Supplement*
ICD	Institut des coiffeurs de dames

INSEE	Institut national de la statistique et des études économiques
OCRPI	Office central de répartition des produits industriels
PCF	Parti communiste français
PP	Archives of the Prefecture de Police, Paris
SCAP	Service de contrôle des administrateurs provisoires
SCP	Syndicat des coiffeurs de Paris
SOC	Syndicat des ouvriers coiffeurs de Paris
SVRP	Société de vente et représentation publicitaire
UF	Union fédérale des maîtres-coiffeurs de France, d'Algérie et des Colonies
UNS	Union nationale syndicale des coiffeurs de France

Preface

France began the twentieth century as a place where the huge majority of people worked long hours for low wages, inhabited tiny dwellings without amenities and, since almost the whole of their earnings went to life's necessities, had little to spend on looking beautiful. By the end of what the French call *les trentes glorieuses* (1945–1975), in comparison, virtually the whole of the population had entered the market for mass fashion, spending billions of francs on clothes, make-up, and the other elements of social propriety and personal vanity. Standing at the confluence of commerce, beauty, and discretionary income, the history of coiffure reflects the enormous changes in French society as it became richer, more urban, more concerned with being clean and well turned-out.

The story is all the more remarkable since at the end of the nineteenth century, hairdressing was a miserably paid corner of the economy, where men mostly served other men in tiny barbershops. This began to change with the extraordinary expansion of ladies' hairdressing, discernible before 1914 and accelerating thereafter. There was, of course, nothing new about women dressing their hair. What was new was its increasing commercialization and the way it moved steadily down the social scale. The effect was dramatic. The number of hairdressing salons exploded, and young women poured into them as both workers and clients. At the same time, technology and sales—from shampoos and dye-jobs to permanent waves—boosted revenues and helped to ameliorate working conditions. By the end of the 1960s, the weekly visit to the beauty salon had become a national habit. Women now comprised a substantial majority of hairdressers, with a decent standard of living, and the barbershops that had defined the *métier* a hundred years earlier had disappeared almost entirely.

The consumer revolution that frames the history of coiffure has lately received increasing attention from historians, who have greatly expanded our understanding of commodity culture.[1] But it is only one of the concerns that crisscross this account, which pivots around three major themes: working life in the salons, the opportunities and perils of *petite enterprise*, and the evolution of hairstyles as both social process and professional environment.

The chapters that follow are structured as a series of essays that trace the development of coiffure from the end of the nineteenth century into the 1960s. They are linked by the continuity of characters and issues, yet each focuses on a different element of that history. This material points both inward and outward. On the one hand, it describes a venerable trade being remade in the course of a tumultuous century, on the other, it roots that story in the larger context of French history, always keeping an eye on the century's most important historiographical issues: from the construction of the "New Woman" to revolutionary syndicalism, from the collapse of the Blum experiment to the temptations of Pétainism, from the communist takeover of the CGT to the full flowering of mass consumer society. There is nothing parochial about hairdressers' story.

In addition to the many specific historiographical questions it addresses, the history of coiffure begins to compensate for an enormous disproportion in the historical literature. Almost our entire sense of social history in urban, industrial France derives from work on Big Labor and Big Business, while the world of bakers, truck drivers, hairdressers, and the rest of petty commerce remains all but unknown.[2] To be sure, hairdressers lack the socioeconomic weight of heavy industry or the strategic importance of foreign policy. Nevertheless, with 50,000 *établissements* and a *population active* three times as large, coiffure constituted a considerable sector of economic activity. Particularly in a country whose economy retained such a large proportion of *petites entreprises*, and where the urge to set up as an *indépendant* held on so tenaciously, we ought to know more about life among the *classes moyennes* and those who worked for them.

Hairdressers' close dependence on popular taste and the structures of consumption also brings exceptionally good grist to the mill of social history of fashion. Until recently, serious historians had little to say about fashion, which remained the province of memoirs, puffy biographies, and glossy catalogues.[3] But in fact, the history of coiffure allows us to see fashion, not chiefly as art or celebrity, but as social practice. Above all, it points to the fundamental importance of women's spending habits, especially those of nonelite young women. Whether they wore bobs or bouffants hardly matters, compared to the revolution of consumption reflected in the ascent of ladies' hairdressing.

What follows then is an intimate portrait of a profession populated with struggling small businessmen and *grands artistes*, with poky barbershops and gleaming *instituts de beauté*, with young women who cropped their hair to look like Mary Pickford and window-smashing barbers' assistants, with platinum blondes and victims of "aryanization," with hot-running water, electrical appliances, and changing hygienic sensibilities. In a word, from a history of coiffure, this book constructs a history of modern France.

*   *   *

I have many people to thank. Among the librarians and archivists who welcomed me to collections are Emmanuelle Montet, at the Union française des arts du costume; Madame Hausser at the offices of the Société d'Editions Parisiennes modernes; Henri Sinno and Colette l'Hôpital-Navarre at the CGT's Institut social; Anne Goulet and Jean-Louis Glénisson at the Paris Chamber of Commerce; Jacqueline Aknine and Christine Colas at Editions S.E.I.D.; Didier Naudin and Madame Martin at the *Eclaireur des Coiffeurs*; Chantal Bonazzi, Roger Cousin, and Jean Pouessel at the Archives nationales; Brigitte Lainé and Philippe Grand at the Archives de Paris; Jacques de Closet and François Princivalle of the École parisienne de la coiffure; Erika Cialoni of the Association nationale des salaries de la coiffure-Force Ouvrière; Pierre Séassari, Robert Maréchal, Madame Benoît, Josiane Bayard-Jarige and Alain Chantalat of the *Fédération national de la coiffure*; Alandria Holly of the New York Public Library. I profited enormously from conversations with Alexandre de Paris; François Magnien; Georges Nogarède and Georges Méry, Meilleurs ouvriers de France; Pierre Simon and Ivan Beauchemin of the Confédération nationale de la coiffure; Guillaume Sénéchal of Salon Desfossé; Maxime Kant of Intercoiffure; Marcel Haggaï, president of the Paris Chambre de métiers; Jérôme Bédier and Sophie Sayanoff-Lévy, at the Direction de l'Artisanat; Georges Braud and Alexis Govciyan, of the Institut supérieur des métiers. I owe a particular debt to Michel Bourlon, general secretary of the Fédération nationale de la coiffure, de l'esthétique et de la parfumerie-Force Ouvrière, who opened his superb archives to me. I also want to thank colleagues and friends: Herrick Chapman, Kyri Claflin, Michel David, Kathryn Earle, Patrick Fridenson, Robert Frost, Sylvie Gillet, Jacques Girault, Jean-Pierre Le Crom, Claudine Marenco, Michelle Perrot, Mary Lou Roberts, Henry Rousso, Michèle Ruffat, Christian Topolov, and Dominique Veillon. Kolleen Guy made crucial suggestions about the manuscript. Rice University, Augustana College, West Virginia University, and the Fulbright Commission helped finance many trips to France. Melissa Nosal has been a wonderful editor. Finally, I want to thank Billie, Kelly, and Edward McNally for their boundless hospitality, my children Isabelle and Sam for putting up with my absences, and my wife Sophie for lending me her excellent research skills and loving support. This book is dedicated to her.

Author's Notes

A note about page numbers for journals

You will notice that not all journal selections have page numbers. That is particularly true for most of the hairdressers' trade and syndical journals. That is because these journals were very short and did not have page numbers. Where I was able to get those numbers, I included them. Where they are not included, they are not available.

Country "hair harvest" at the beginning of the century

The Rise of *Coiffure pour Dames*

Under any circumstances, hair is a richly "privileged" site from which to survey a society. Hairstyles resemble clothes in that respect; they are both filled with symbolic meaning and rooted in tangible structures of production and consumption. This was truer than ever in the Belle Epoque, as the profession of coiffure began to leave old styles and practices behind. It was especially true of the sector of ladies' hairdressing, which was to lead coiffure headlong into the consumer society of the twentieth century.

Coiffure pour dames was a venerable *métier*, with its roots in the fashion excesses of the Old Regime, whose outsized coiffures have become a convenient cliché of the period. The premier artist-coiffeur of the baroque period, a former shepherd, called himself Champagne. He was followed in the eighteenth century by the renowned court hairdressers, Frédéric, Larseneur, and Legros de Rumigny, author of *L'art de la coiffure des dames françaises* (1768) and founder of the Académie des Coiffures, whose career came to an abrupt end when he was crushed in the Place Louis XV during the marriage celebrations for the Dauphin's marriage to Marie Antoinette.[1]

The most famous of the rococo hairdressers was Léonard, who became Marie-Antoinette's favorite. Indeed, the unfortunate queen so trusted her personal coiffeur that she charged him with a number of crucial political tasks. The most important of these was to prepare the relays of horses and to forward a case of jewelry to Brussels, in anticipation of the royal family's flight to Varennes in 1791.[2]

It was not his doubtful talent for intrigue, however, but the audacity of his coiffures that made Léonard a figure of significance in the court of Louis XVI. He had no monopoly on immoderation, however. As historian Fernand Braudel observed, "The coquette easily took five or six hours to dress, in the hands of her servants and even more under the care of her hairdresser, chatting with her priest or lover." The result of these efforts was hair "built up so high that the eyes of the beauties seemed to start out from the middle of their bodies."[3] Wendy Cooper related the tale of "a certain Madame de Lauzun [who] reached perhaps the most absurd extreme by wearing an enormously high headdress of hair and artificial hair, on top of which were modeled ducks swimming in a stormy sea, scenes of hunting and shooting, a mill with a miller's wife flirting with a priest, and a miller leading an ass by its halter."[4]

These colossal headdresses often became a sort of discourse, where creations like the "Spaniel's Ears," the "Drowned Chicken," "Mad Dog," and "Sportsman-in-the-Coppice" evoked nature or some historical motif. Currency and excess reached their apex with the legendary hairstyle, the "Belle Poule," which celebrated the victory of the British warship Arethusa with "seas of hair, with model ships, fully rigged and manned with toy sailors."[5] More architect than hygienist, the eighteenth-century hairdresser constructed his hairdos largely from whatever material came to hand. Bill Severn described coiffures wadded with "bushels of cotton wool, shreds of rope, horsehair, bran, or straw [and] almost every dressing table was equipped with a 'scratcher,' a long-handled stick with a hooked end for stabbing through the hair to give some relief from itching."[6]

Surely the destruction of such hairdos was one of the more benign effects of the Revolution. Yet fashionable women in the 1800s continued to wear big, complicated coiffures: the intricate knickknacks and hanging curls of the "1830s" style, or the hairstyles of 1863 recorded in Godey's Lady's Book. The magazine counted "two rats, two mice, a cat, and a cataract"—terms that referred not to small mammals but to the kinds of cushions used to create the huge coiffures.[7] Even the relatively sober Victorian woman à la mode sported a surfeit of curls and postiches piled high on top of the head and low down the neck— en poire, it was called.[8]

Despite its antiquity and importance to the expression of fashion, there were surprisingly few practitioners of coiffure pour dames in turn-of-the-century Paris. René Rambaud, an icon of haute coiffure, wrote that at the time of the Universal Exposition of 1889 Paris counted only a dozen salons de coiffure that were solely for women. Hardly fifty "ladies hands" worked therein.[9] The scarcity of beauty salons reflected not relative disinterest in the hairdresser's art but the social and commercial structures of the consumption of fashion in the nineteenth century. The fashionable Victorian *dame* had her hair "done" every day—several times a day in most cases. She simply did not leave the private space of the home for her toilette. Rather, the lady of leisure met her day-to-day requirements for a *coiffure du jour* in her boudoir, depending on her ladies' maid "who came in the morning to perpetrate the edifice that [she] carried around during the day."[10] Indeed, the ability to dress hair was one of the skills an excellent ladies' maid needed to acquire, and a young woman who was also a talented *coiffeuse* became a valuable asset in the market of social distinction.

Even for most evening occasions, the *bourgeoise* and her ladies' maid would put together something elegant but comparatively simple at home. Only for the most special affairs did the average lady of fashion call on the high-class coiffeur. He would arrive at her home "garbed in a frock coat, white tie, and silk hat" and work his magic there.[11] At the top of the *beau monde*, women might see their hairdressers more frequently, even daily. Yet none of this would have involved a trip to a *salon de coiffure*.

At the turn of the century, fashion in France still belonged, as it had traditionally, to the elite. It remained dominated by the search for "distinction" guided by the principle that "the more useless and hemmed about the wearer, the more incapable of free and easy movement, the more genteel he or she must be."[12] So far as fashion circulated, it still tended to trickle down, although the limits of imitation were closely circumscribed by the masses' lack of disposable income. The leisure class hobnobbed at Auteuil and Longchamps during the racing season. In the heat of the summer, they escaped to the Channel resorts of Deauville and Trouville or the southwest town of Biarritz, once made chic by Napoleon III and his Empress Eugénie. In the winter they gathered at *stations thermales* of Vichy and Aix-les-Bains. Wherever they assembled, the countesses, princes of the blood, *hautes bourgeoises*, actresses, and the rest of French high society occupied "themselves with every aspect of their wardrobes—primary criteria in establishing social status and wealth," served by "a large and highly-trained staff."[13] They gambled, flirted, gossiped, danced at *soirées* and masquerade balls. Done up in the latest creations from the finest *couturiers*—Worth, Paquin, Lanvin, Vionnet—they jostled for position along the social hierarchy.[14]

It was in Deauville, in the summer of 1904, that one of the singular careers of twentieth-century fashion was born: that of Antoine de Paris, "the one and only author of the modern coiffure." By his own account, Antoine, *né* Antek Cierplikowski, had developed his ethereal sensibilities amidst the flowers and music of his small village church in his native Siedradz, Poland. He then learned his trade and refined his artistic genius in Lodz, as an apprentice to his uncle Pawel. The ambitious young esthete left Poland and arrived in Paris in 1901. His talent must have been plain, because his first position brought him not to some grotty salon on the periphery but to the Galeries Lafayette. He soon began to work the "season" in the Channel resorts.

There, in September 1904, Antoine seized his big break. In his autobiography, he recalled getting the opportunity to dress the hair of Lily de Moure, mistress of a Prince of the Blood, for an evening in Deauville Society. Poor Mademoiselle de Moure suffered a *crise* when she lost the hat that was to have finished her extraordinary *toilette*. Soothing her, Antoine convinced de Moure that she could take the unheard of step of going hatless on such a magnificent occasion, and he set about creating a suitably fabulous coiffure. The prince himself was sitting admiringly in the boudoir, watching the performance, when a maid arrived with the missing hat. But Antoine did not want his *chef d'oeuvre* ruined, and he prevailed upon Mademoiselle de Moure to leave it home and to spend the evening *sans chapeau*. The bareheaded Lily de Moure on the arm of a prince stirred up a sensation, and the next morning a line of fashionable ladies gathered at the door of the Maison Decoux, where Antoine worked, begging to be served by "*le petit rousse*" [*sic*].[15]

From his luxurious salon on the rue Cambon just behind the Ritz Hotel, with its plush red carpeting and Modiglianis on the walls, which he opened in 1910, Antoine became the best-known hairdresser of the age. Among the famous women who passed through the rue Cambon over the years were Coco Chanel, Pola Negri, Josephine Baker, Elizabeth Schwartzkopf, Simone Signoret, Arletty, Jane Auber, Simone Simone, Danielle Darieux, Lily Pons, and Sonja Hennie. Antoine coiffed Louis Brooks for Loulou. He invented Claudette Colbert's famous *frange* (bangs) and, many years later, the "sex-kitten" hairdo for Brigitte Bardot. After the World War I, he pioneered the export of French coiffure, taking his talents to New York, where he opened a boutique in Saks Fifth Avenue.[16]

Whether she enjoyed the privilege of an Antoine coiffure or not, no lady of any social pretension would venture into high society in a *couturier* gown, coifed by her ladies' maid. As *Votre Beauté* warned its readers, "the most beautiful dress, worn with untidy hair, loses fifty-percent of its value."[17] The *grande dame* therefore required an elegant hairstyle at the hands of one of the great coiffeurs of the epoch: Dupuy, Perrin, Dupont, Dondel, Long. These paragons were invariably ready to advance their reputations and fortunes by weaving intricate patterns into a woman's hair and by placing in it any number of baubles and other items: flowers, combs, pearls, fabric, and feathers "which would turn the last of the Redskins green with envy."[18] When Jourliac recommended the "Directory" and "Modern Empire" styles for 1909, he imagined them full of *postiches*, chignons, plaits, and *torsades* (braids). Paul Gerbod described the reigning styles of 1903. They were wavy and puffy, with long braids, ornamented with feathers, tortoise-shell combs, and huge pins, bearing such grandiose names as "Queen of Spades" and "Bird Charmer."[19]

The cost of such "extravagant femininity" was enormous. It was not unusual for a woman to spend five hours or more in the hands of her coiffeur before a grand ball. For an important society occasion, the excited demand for exquisite hairstyles might oblige those slightly lower on the social scale to have their hair done two days before the big event, which might compel them to spend a couple of nights "sitting up in a chair in order not to crush the elaborate coiffure."[20] At the summit of society, an actress like Caroline Otéro, or a courtesan like Liane de Pougy, might pay up to 1,600 francs for a ball gown, "a good deal more than their maid's annual wages."[21] The accompanying coiffure might cost almost as much.

"To each generation its type," wrote Antoine, and the type that defined the Edwardian beauty was tall, full-figured—"a glorification of mature womanhood," as Jane Mulvagh expressed it—and well-covered. Thinness, according to Valerie Steele, was despised. Experts compared the debutante's figure unfavorably with her mother's, as conventional wisdom found the younger woman's "paucity of curves and contours" not very sexy. "Cover some of [your] angles," she was rudely advised.[22]

Clothing naturally expressed this ideal of mature womanhood. When *Vogue* magazine looked back from the vantage of 1924 at the preceding twenty years its depiction of Edwardian styles betrayed a sort of bemused horror. at the "edifice" of hair and the "ridiculous" hats, at the corset that deformed the body's natural lines, the number of petticoats, the pointed shoes with very high heels, and tiny gloves that squeezed the hands.[23]

"The sum of [these] garments," wrote historian Bonnie Smith, "testified to female imprisonment, to an unliberated ego, and were voluntarily worn to testify to this aspect of their lives."[24] We should be careful, however, about seeing this ideology reflected too literally in fashions, as if those who thought women naturally fanciful and child-like necessarily entombed them in corsets and petticoats. In the 1920s, when *couturiers* and coiffeurs continued to dish out the same nonsense about "*l'éternel féminin*," they designed radically different styles to suit it.

In any event, the engineers of "female imprisonment," would have disagreed heartily. Those in the *industries de la mode* saw themselves rather as the servants of women's inescapable predilection for beauty and superfluity. "A woman," wrote Antoine, "is a work of art and creation"—especially the French woman, whom "the whole world recognized [for her] innate taste . . ."[25] Emile Long, the president of the prestigious Institut des coiffeurs de dames (ICD), concurred: "The more civilized and cultured a woman becomes," he wrote, "the more she resembles the savage of the Pacific Islands in her taste for showy colors and glittering ornaments."[26] Indeed, Long considered "hair vanity" a law of nature: "Irrespective of her social and financial posi-tion," he wrote, "every woman who has the slightest respect for her-self must look after her hair."[27] Happily, reflected René Rambaud, women's "congenital coquetry is a sure and inexhaustible source of profits."[28]

Hairdressers were fortunate that while Edwardian hairstyles required long, luxurious tresses, most women's hair lacked the quali-ties necessary to a first-class coiffure. Even the most exquisite orna-ments and skill could not rescue a hairstyle made with thin, limp hair. Hence, the liberal deployment of prestyled hairpieces that allowed hairdressers to compensate for deficient nature and give new life to the hair of "those women who are no longer young,"[29] *Postiche*, at least before the coming of the permanent wave, was a coiffeur's principal source of added value, the item that lifted *coiffeurs pour dames* above their poor barbering cousins. No weapon in a hairdresser's arsenal, thought Emile Long, was more essential to art and profits.

One glance at the price of *postiches* would explain Long's enthusi-asm. At the high end of the market, the creations of the great *maisons* of Cuverville, Calou, Jourliac, François, Croizier-Noirat, and Antoine could fetch hundreds of francs "in the prettiest up-to-date tints, and at much higher prices if the hair is grey or of rare color."[30] True, demand for *postiches* fluctuated with the fashion of the moment. Yet women's desire for *postiches* always seemed to return. In August 1913, Long wrote that the styles favored light *postiches*—but not cheap, at 300 francs—whereas in June 1914, the *Coiffure Française Illustrée* regretted that "if current coiffures are all the more elegant for their high forms and ornaments, they are not profitable for the sale of *postiches*." Two years later the new models exhibited by Cuverville and Calou featured big *postiches*, some the size of full wigs. Even the developing partiality for short hair did not kill women's appetite for *postiches*, which could serve both originality and convenience.[31]

The manufacture of these hairpieces rested on an extensive world market in raw hair. In France, according to A. Coffignon, 80,000 kilograms of raw hair reached the market every year in the 1880s. An especially strong demand for *postiches* in the first decade of the twentieth century doubled the imports of raw hair between 1902 and 1906, when they reached a third of a million tons.[32] Every year, agents from the Maison Patte and other *négociants* fanned out to the poorest regions of France: Brittany and the Auvergne in the nineteenth century, moving to the Savoie and Haute-Savoie in the twentieth. They especially favored districts where girls drank a lot of beer and cider, because it was said that these beverages made hair longer and thicker.[33]

The *Journal de la Coiffure* set the scene: A man arrives at some central spot in a town or village. The women circle around him while he unwraps the merchandise that he has brought to exchange, usually some sort of trinkets, costume jewelry, or even a religious icon. A woman steps forward. The merchant examines her hair, as she unfastens whatever headdress covers it, looking at color, length, thickness, and proposing a price. Buyer and seller quickly come to an agreement, and the woman is shorn. "If the spectacle was sometimes amusing," the reporter remarked, "it was also pitiable for the great sacrifice and the great poverty it revealed."[34]

This hair often found its way to Limoges, where once a year wigmakers and *posticheurs* "from all of Europe flocked to the Café de France . . . to attend [the big auction at] its Bourse aux Cheveux."[35] The hair gleaned from European peasants then traveled to New York, London, and Paris, where it soon appeared on the heads of ladies of fashion.

In 1903, the New York *Sun* reported a drastic rise in the price of hair: 30 to 50 percent since the beginning of the year. The *Sun* attributed this inflation to growing sophistication of peasants in France and Germany. Less isolated and better informed, they now demanded to be paid in something more valuable than handkerchiefs and religious knickknacks. Moreover, as an awareness of fashion began to penetrate into the countryside, peasant women began to wear hats, "which leads them to want to keep their hair." The shortage was compounded by the Anglo-Saxon distaste for "foreign" hair; that is for hair *not* from Europeans. "Worse yet," the *Sun* continued, Norway and Sweden had passed laws that substantially constrained the traffic in hair, which undoubtedly inflated the price of rare and valuable blonde hair.[36]

The hair harvest survived and the manufacturers of *postiche*s continued to prosper well into the twentieth century. The last woman in Pierre-Jakez Hélias's Breton village of Pouldreuzic to sell her hair "out of need" reportedly died during the Battle of the Marne.[37] And the *Coiffure de Paris* reported in January 1937 that Max Factor spent $1.5 million in Europe buying up hair to be used in Hollywood spectaculars, adding that blonde hair commanded three times the price of other colors.

This remunerative commerce in raw hair and the *postiche* business that drove it found themselves threatened by the appearance of the Marcel wave, which burst upon the trade in the mid-1880s and almost instantly revitalized it. Marcel's wave quickly acquired a mythical quality, but the truth seems to go something like this. Born in 1852, the hairdresser Marcel Grateau began his career inauspiciously. Finishing his apprenticeship in the provincial town of Chauvigny, Marcel came to Paris, bringing his widowed mother with him. During his initial years in the capital, he struggled. Fired by several employers for "insufficient attention to cleaning up, professional incapacity" and other misdemeanors, he installed himself in a small shop on the rue Dunkerque, not far from the Gare du Nord. During the day, Marcel coifed "tarts" for half a franc. At night he made wigs for theater. He must have done well enough, because a few years later he bought a salon closer to the center of town, on the rue de l'Echelle, where the rue St.-Honoré meets the Avenue de l'Opéra. But Marcel remained unknown to elegant *parisiennes* and continued to work in anonymity until 1882, when his experience and observations let him to his "genial" invention.[38]

The key to Marcel's method lay in his use of a new type of curling iron. It had two branches, one hollow and the other round, which he used upside down—that is, with the cylinder on top—which produced a soft, supple, and relatively durable wave. Marcel, incidentally, never actually dressed his clients' hair. He left that to others. The Master, as he was known among his acolytes, merely provided the inimitable waves.

Celebrity did not arrive overnight. But one evening in 1885 Marcel waved the hair of actress Jane Hading for her triumph in the play,

Le Maître des Forges: "not a single hairpin, not a single piece of false hair," just a wave from top to bottom. Marcel's success was phenomenal, and stories abound of his conquest of *le tout Paris*. No one had ever seen, wrote the *Hairdressers' Weekly Journal*, "such a prolific patronage that lady clients of wealth and social distinction formed a long and eager queue, awaiting their 'turn' for his services like outpatients at a hospital or 'first nighters' at a theater . . ."[39] According to one story, the Baroness de Buire discovered one morning that her bath had "gravely compromised" her coiffure. She headed off to Marcel, only to find a big crowd ahead of her. The baroness declared she was going ahead of everyone and that she would pay the price, 500 francs: " 'Six hundred!' shouted a charming little vicomtesse. 'Seven hundred!' said a marquise. 'Eight hundred!' " the baroness raised her bid. The *grande dame* who finally bought the right to be next paid 1,000 francs for it.[40]

The enormous popular appeal of the Marcel wave opened up a bounteous new source of income for ladies' hairdressers. "We cannot recall," wrote the *Hairdressers' Weekly Journal*, "any fashion or device in hair which has ever produced so much revenue to hairdressers as the Marcel wave." Waving caused a simplification and lightening of hairstyles, which pleased hygienists. But it displeased the crusty old traditionalists, whose skill lay in the construction of elaborate (and very expensive) coiffures.[41] "Down With Waving!" was the title of an 1893 article by Georges Dupuy, president of the Ecole française de coiffure and editor of *La Coiffure Française Illustrée*, that likened the "marcel" to the anarchist bombs that were then exploding around Paris.[42] And he prepared a counterattack, launching a volley of curls and *postiches*, piled high on the head and hanging low down the neck.

Such criticism could not hold back a determined public opinion, however, and waving quickly became the essential element in virtually all hairstyles, bringing expansion and prosperity to a profession that had been lagging in the 1880s. Eventually, even Dupuy ran up the white flag: "Long live the 'marcel!' " he recanted in 1907. Waving ruled coiffure "*de manière quasi-absolue*" until well into the 1920s, and students in *écoles de coiffure* continued to learn the "marcel" into the 1960s.

The chief beneficiary of the "marcel" was the Master himself, who made a fortune out of it. While most coiffeurs could charge their customers between 10 and 20 francs to wave their hair—and this was already a great boon to business—Marcel commanded 500. Thus, at a time when a hand in a decent ladies' salon could count on barely 500 francs a month, and an assistant in a barbershop, 100 to 200 francs, Marcel was earning 10,000 francs a month. By 1897, having saved well over a million francs, Marcel retired to his chateau in Normandy. He died in 1936.

Many of Marcel's colleagues resented him because he jealously guarded the secrets of his system while he practiced. He neither taught them at the *écoles de coiffure* nor demonstrated them for his colleagues at competitions. Only when he left the profession in 1897 did he allow the trade journal *La Coiffure Illustrée* to publish a short article laying out the general lines of his method, and he finally agreed to sell his protégé, Emile Long, a private lesson—for 300 francs. It then fell to Long, acting with his retired patron's permission, to introduce the "marcel" into the curriculum of the École parisienne de coiffure in 1904, which is where the talented and ambitious young René Rambaud first learned it in the winter of 1906. Long went on to publish the *Traité complet et illustré de l'ondulation artificielle des cheveux*, in 1909, where in he generously shared with his colleagues the techniques that had brought Marcel such wealth and fame.[43]

Since Marcel had kept his method to himself for so long, other coiffeurs were compelled to find their own way to softer, more natural waves. Edmond Perrin, future president of the Institut des coiffeurs de dames, came up with something called the *peigne onduleur* [comb waving], which he showed off to the Académie de coiffure in 1890. Whereas Marcel had used his fingers to produce his waves, which took a long time, the *ondulation à peigne* could be accomplished much more quickly. Emile Long's judgment was that, although it looked bad and did not last well, it was "acceptable to those ladies who are not very exacting, when they are in a hurry or not desirous of paying a high price."[44] *Ondulation* quickly became the most important skill learned by young *coiffeurs* and *coiffeuses pour dames*. Indeed, Long noted ruefully, it was often their only skill. Producing "waves [that were] as straight and rigid as train rails," semiskilled labor threatened to replace art in the salons.

More than bad taste, these cheap, ugly waves point to a seminal development in the social history of coiffure. For it was not only the elites, or even the upper-middle classes, who wanted to be "marceled." The taste for *ondulation* began to percolate through the popular classes as well. The snob in Long recoiled at the women who emerged from "the cheaper class of establishment" with "curls that are too frizzy and waves which are much too pronounced"—waves that, as

Antoine put it, resembled "the general lines of the rougher part of a washboard." But he saw clearly the tremendous impact it had on the trade. By 1909, Paris had some 300 *maisons pour dames* and 1,800 *maisons mixtes*. And the numbers continued to climb steadily up to 1914.[45]

In a series of articles stretching from the Belle Epoque to the doorstep of the "roaring twenties," Emile Long furnished an immensely rich guide to the evolution of the hairdressing profession implicit in these figures. His reports not only provide an archive of coiffures, hat styles, and clothing designs, they also add up to a brilliant social and cultural history. The changes in hairstyles he recounts were neither dramatic nor regular. One description of 1907 fashions noted that "curls obtained by frizzing the hair are far from enough; we also add pegs of false curls, of *chichis* [chignons]; then clusters, garlands, wreaths, baskets, heaps of curly *postiches*." In 1909 a reduced version of the "Belle Poule" made a brief reappearance. A year later, the "Casque Normande" reigned supreme, temporarily dethroning the "marcel." It returned for the spring of 1912, when it battled for preeminence among coiffures "en boule" and "en oeufs." In July 1913, fashionable women favored the Phrygian Bonnet hairstyle, with its playful allusion to the bloody days of the Revolution. Chignons went up and came down. Feathers came in and went out. Some styles required large *postiches*, some small, and some none at all. Some heads began to sport curls or coiffures with double partings. Others dared to uncover the ears, only to cover them again the next month. At Auteuil, in April 1911, Long saw hair colored mahogany red and brown. A year later, the most fashionable *dames* were to be seen sporting powdered gray coiffures. By the following spring, blonde had come in and gone out, replaced by dark hair, colored with henna. And so on. Even the war could not halt the march of fashion. In 1916, as *poilus* huddled in their shell holes at Verdun, the "1830s style" captured the fancy of Parisian women. Two-and-a-half years later, as Allied troops breached the Hindenburg Line, *les parisiennes* preferred the "Japanese Bonnet."

The profusion and the circularity of coiffures cannot completely hide the steady movement in the direction of smaller, simpler hairstyles. At the same time, the profession began to divide into two distinct schools. Long called them alternatively "classicists" and "modernists," or the "academic style" and the "public style." In effect, the profession split between tradition-bound doyens of *haute coiffure* and a group of young men looking to effect "radical changes" in the aesthetics of hairdressing:

> [T]he moderate, cautious section . . . model their ideas and methods on judgment and good taste [and] are nearly all established for themselves in a suite of rooms; they have clienteles who appreciate their professional talent and are faithful to them, but who are added to with difficulty; whereas the other section, those who are more daring and enterprising, nearly all occupy shops with imposing frontages on the street, where they display not the current fashions, but those which they wish to introduce purely for commercial ends.[46]

The "classicists" had more fixed notions about what was becoming and appropriate on a woman's head and generally refused to style hair in ways that offended their inbred sense of proportion. The "modernists" brought fewer preconceptions to their art. They were willing to satisfy, even to encourage any public whim, however outlandish. Long's aesthetic sympathies generally lay with the "classicists," whose training he shared, and he often disapproved of the "modernists' " handiwork. For example, in 1912, reviewing the work of François, the most prominent of the avant garde, Long found the young man's creations excessively simple, "destitute of knots, curls, interlacings and all kinds of details"—more like a "Dervish's bonnet" or a "bundle of hay" than anything else.[47]

At the same time as he failed to appreciate their art, however, Long admired the "modernists' " commercial acuity. They appealed particularly to younger women anxious to break away from the "wedding-cake" look of their mothers. Long, the traditionalist, had to admit that the "modernists' " openness and innovation presented hairdressers with their most profitable opportunities. In effect, these qualities carried the day, and by the end of the war, the "public style" had completely eclipsed the "classical."

In its general outlines, hairdressing in the Belle Epoque followed the broader drift of fashion toward lighter and less constricting forms. Hat styles changed season by season but were inclined, like the hairstyles they obscured, to get smaller as the years passed. More comfortable and convenient clothes had become available for women by the end of the nineteenth century, tied to an ethic of youthful activity and made particularly imperative by the passion of the French for bicycle riding, which affected all social classes and especially promoted the simplification of underwear.[48]

The chief exponent of the new shape was the *couturier* Paul Poiret, who exploited a trend that had already crept into private and semipublic clothing, such as nightgowns, chemises, and tea-gowns.[49] In the dresses he introduced in 1906 and 1908, Poiret self-consciously "waged war" on the "Gache Sarraute," the Edwardian fashion that, in the designer's words, "divided its wearer into two distinct masses— bosom pushed forward and rear-end forced back—so that she looked "as if she were hauling a trailer."[50]

It is easy to read too much significance into clothing styles, as Modris Eksteins does in his much-acclaimed book, *Rites of Spring: The Great War and the Modern Age*. In one of those grand generalizations common to the genre, Eksteins writes that the "Poiret Revolution . . . offered women freedom from corsets and a new glittering, slouching sensibility" and that it represented a "quest for liberation, a break in aesthetic and moral terms, from central authority, from patriarchy, from bourgeois conformity . . . ."[51] This is hyperbole, delivered in the service of a historical theory based primarily on intuition and a few literary/cultural sources. The fact is that Poiret was no feminist; his styles, lighter in some respects than their predecessors, promoted not liberation but fashion. For example, the "hobble skirt" he designed, very narrow at the bottom, made it difficult for the wearer to walk. It was with some truth that Poiret later claimed: "Yes, I freed the bust, but I shackled the legs."[52]

Meanwhile, as the wheel of fashion revolved, ladies' hairdressers continued to chase it around. They naturally sought hairstyles that flattered their clients. Even more, they coveted coiffures that put money in the till. These two interests did not always fit together seamlessly, and Long regretted that women almost inevitably wanted one thing for their hair and coiffeurs another. The former wanted to spend as little as possible, while the latter pursued the greatest profit. It was only every fifteen years or twenty years, when voluminous and complex coiffures came into fashion, that this tension subsided for a time. Long advised his readers that this conflict was best resolved through accommodation. Coiffeurs should cede to customers' wishes, he reasoned, even if those wishes did not suit their immediate interests. Smaller profits were better than fewer customers, and the woman who did not get what she wanted from one hairdresser would certainly leave him for another.

At the same time, Long was convinced that other *marchandes de modes*—*couturiers* and *modistes*, especially—were able to manipulate their clients "by continually varying their creations and making their seductiveness overpowering . . . pandering to [a lady's] tastes for coquetry and incidentally extracting all her available money." Long pointed specifically to the leading Parisian milliners, all situated in the rue de la Paix or the rue Royal, where they occupied apartments whose rent could run from 25,000 to 100,000 francs a year, and sold hats for as much as 1,500 francs a piece. "The models at 1,000 francs are quite ordinary," he observed, "and should a client's request be for a 'morning hat' at 150 francs, the saleswoman will not even trouble to serve her."[53]

Given that hairdressers similarly stood to benefit from the "right" hairstyles and suffer from the "wrong" ones, it made sense for them to organize so as to nudge women's modish instincts along the proper course. This motive lay behind the formation of a Fashion Committee, composed of Paris's most influential hairdressers. The committee aimed to impose discipline on the profession and encourage its members to set an example by exhibiting only the most lucrative styles. To this end, each month it prescribed the hairstyles members ought to display in their store windows, so as to influence both clients and passersby more effectively.

If there was one thing that the purveyors of fashion regularly discovered, however, it was that customers did not always do as they were bidden. Hairdressers tried for years, for example, to revive the "Grecian" fashion for hanging curls, without results: "Fashionable ladies," they found, "obstinately refuse to cover up their necks."[54] Long, who was a founding member of the Fashion Committee, waxed ambivalent about its purpose. He accepted that the trade needed more coordination and discipline. But he could never fully convince himself that it would work. For one thing, he doubted that women's preferences could be controlled so easily, for while fashion was powerful, it was also capricious. "We can no more resist the on-coming of Fashion," he wrote, "than we can stop the impetuous torrent of a mighty river." Fashion could not be dictated, "only seized at the moment of its appearance."[55] For another, with so many hairdressers at work, the profession was incorrigibly anarchic, with "moderates" pulling hairstyles in one direction and "radicals" in another.

Moreover, hairdressers, dispersed and dependent for their art on clothes and hats, were in no position to govern hairstyles in the way that the powerful manufacturers could dominate *couture*. Finally, even when it decided to feature a certain style, the Fashion Committee could not count on the cooperation of its own associates. In the fall of 1911, for example, the committee voted strongly "in favor of the low chignon, combined with locks of false hair for day wear and curls on the neck for the evening." As Long toured his colleagues' salons, however, he discovered that not a single one of them was exhibiting the styles that "the committee wishe[d] to impose on the bulk of their colleagues."[56]

Hairdressers could never know what accident or random event, such as the discovery of King Tut's tomb that set off a vogue for "Egyptian" styles in 1923, would toss fashion this way or that. To illustrate this principle, Long began his reports from Paris in 1910 with a cautionary tale about Madame Letellier, "the handsomest woman in Paris," whose portraits nearly ruined the hairdressing profession. In the summer of 1907 at Trouville, a member of the so-called modern school had undertaken to paint a portrait of Letellier. These "modern" painters, according to Long, hated heavily waved hair because they lacked the talent and patience to paint the necessary detail. The portrait of *la belle Letellier* therefore showed her with straight hair. This artistic short cut subsequently became a convention, when the celebrated artist Hellenu began to compose portraits of many of France's most fashionable young women—once again, with absolutely straight hair, whereas all of them in reality wore wavy coiffures. Life then proceeded to imitate art as the fashion magazine, *Fémina*, following Hellenu, spread the impression, first, among the "upper circle" and, as a consequence, among "the great public . . . that it was not necessary to wave so much—that, in fact, waving was no longer the fashion." It was this impression, so circuitously produced, that incited women to wear the "turban headdress" and other straight styles, thus suppressing for a time the Marcel wave that had been putting money in hairdressers' pockets for thirty years.[57]

The genesis of the "turban" illustrates a fundamental law of fashion. While its outlines were to some degree determined by technological possibilities and the historical moment, in a more immediate way the kingdom of fashion was ruled by serendipity. Consider what Long learned in November 1910 when he visited the leading Parisian *modistes* (milliners) in the company of his "eminent colleague" Edmond Perrin. Long sought out the milliners because he believed they had been especially successful in channeling public taste, thereby assuring their prosperity. He wanted to find out how. He also understood that, from season to season and for obvious reasons, hats set the effective limits for hairstyles. The famous *cloche* hat of 1909, for example, did not merely "dominate" coiffures, it completely "overwhelmed" them.[58] If his readers could know what milliners had in store, he inferred, they would be in a position to exploit it.

Long and Perrin approached the capital's greatest *modistes* and asked what they were preparing for the coming season. The reply they received everywhere was "toques*—toques in velvet and furs of all kinds."[59] "Why," Long inquired, "are you giving a preference to toques?" No doubt he expected an answer that combined sociological insight and marketing genius. What he got was something else. "We do not make toques out of preference," the *grands modistes* told him, "but simply because our hat shapers have been on strike for four months, and we cannot procure felt shapes." So much for a semiotics of hat styles.

However mercurial the fashions and fickle the customers, whatever the barriers that stood between ladies' hairdressers and their profits, there can be little doubt that those who took care of women's hair enjoyed an immense commercial advantage over their barbering *confrères*. In part, this reflected the different forms of competition within the two distinct worlds of coiffure. Most barbershops offered simple and largely standard operations for men whose fashion demands usually amounted to little more than a clean chin and a clipped head. Competitors who could not distinguish themselves with quality did so by dropping their prices. Conversely, if the barbershops were about neatness, which was cheap, the *salons pour dames* were about beauty, which was almost never cheap and was often very expensive. One man's skill with the *tondeuse* was about the same as any other man's. But skill with a curling iron was a very different matter, and women proved willing to pay for the difference.

A barber could normally count himself fortunate if the customer agreed to have a bit of tonic, worth perhaps a franc, poured on his scalp. Meanwhile, a *coiffeur pour dames* could sell dozens of ornamental add-ons, in addition to the intricate designs he might weave and wave into a client's own hair. In the 1880s, when a day of haircuts and shaves could earn a barber eight or ten francs—and the majority of *assistants* earned less than two francs a day, plus bad food and woeful accommodations—a ladies' hairdresser could pocket five francs for a regular evening hairstyle. For a more formal coiffure, employing flowers or feathers, he might get fifteen or twenty francs; up to thirty for a powdered coiffure. At the top, a "coiffure de genre pour transvestissement"—that is, for a costume ball—might fetch forty or fifty francs.[60]

There existed a small band of elite ladies' hairdressers who could count on lucrative commissions no matter what, and therefore enjoyed the luxury of worrying about "art." But the ordinary coiffeur's opinion of any particular hairstyle depended on the income it was to generate, which varied in direct proportion to the amount of value it allowed him to add to a head of hair. It was precisely the vast increase in the possibilities of added value that brought such a windfall in the wake of the Marcel wave.

At the end of the nineteenth century, the cause of added value received another terrific boost from the new technology that was beginning to creep into hairdressing salons, as well as from the evolution of public sensibilities. The appearance in homes and business of hot, running water, one of the most important and most overlooked revolutions of modern times, illustrated perfectly the reciprocal relationship between technology and sensibility, and its impact on coiffure. Most suburbs did not get running water until after World War I. Baths and water closets came even later to the countryside. Before that, the expense and general inconvenience of making hot water meant that in France "washing was rare and bathing rarer." "Most women die without having once taken a bath," noted Georges Vacher de Lapouge.[61] This was true even at the heights of French society. "No one in my family took a bath," Pauline Laure Marie de Broglie, the Comtesse de Pange recollected. "We washed in a tub with five centimeters of water, or we sponged ourselves down in large basins, but the idea of plunging into water up to our necks seemed pagan, even sinful."[62]

Hair care did not diverge from the normally low standard of hygiene. Alain Corbin described the practice in the mid-nineteenth century, where "hair hygiene consisted of periodic untangling with a fine comb, brushing and plaiting before bed . . . The head was not washed."[63] Conventional wisdom warned women that water would leave their hair brittle and make it fall out sooner. "Out of a hundred bald people," warned a Professor Larbalétrier, "eighty-eight had [washed their hair] since their youth."[64]

It was taboo, wrote Caroline Cox, to wash hair during menstruation, "as it was believed to be harmful for women to be in contact with too much water when the body was in such a weakened state."[65] On the eve of the twentieth century, even privileged ladies of fashion mostly avoided washing their hair. The Comtesse de Pange recalled, "At seventeen, I had very long hair which, when loosened, wrapped around me like a mantle. But these beautiful tresses were never washed. They were stiff and filthy. The word shampoo was ignored. From time to time they rubbed my hair with quinine water."[66]

Antoine recounted the following story. In 1904 he was called to the residence of the Comtesse de Farge to dress her hair for a special occasion and was taken aback by the state of the Countess's hair: "So greasy," he remembered, "that one could have made a bad soup from it." Antoine strongly suggested to his client that he wash her hair before dressing it. The Countess was aghast. "No," she replied imperiously. "Never. Understand that I *never* shampoo. *J'ai horreur de ça*!" To which Antoine replied in turn: "The truth, Madame, is that I would not touch your hair in such a filthy state," and he turned to leave, accompanied by a hail of insults "that would have done credit to a fishmonger."[67]

Yet as the old century came to a close, shampooing was becoming more common. Hairdressers in the early 1890s began offering something called *shampooing sec*, a sort of dry cleaning for hair that used *éther de pétrole*—in effect, kerosene. This method had the advantage of allowing hair to dry immediately, and left it very soft to the touch. The problem was that *éther* was extremely flammable stuff that many coiffeurs used without sufficient knowledge or precautions. Small *salonniers* filled the air with its fumes or poured it down their sinks, endangering sewer workers. Even the best salons occasionally fell victim to its dangers. One ether explosion caused the death of the 28-year old French actress, Mademoiselle Pascoline. Another shook the upscale shop of Gaston Boudou ('Monsieur Emile') in London. Concerned public authorities regularly tried to ban these dangerous chemicals, but coiffeurs ignored the regulations and the enforcement was lax. Accidents continued to endanger public health.[68]

As indoor plumbing and hot-water heaters worked their way through the urban landscape, *shampooing sec* fell out of favor (although *éther de pétrole* continued to be used for other purposes). Coiffeurs installed *accumulateurs* and *chauffes-eau instantanés* (*à pression*—out of a small hose) in their salons for washing hair, as hot water and soapy shampoos became the rule. Like the earlier taste for waved hair, the predilection for capillary hygiene began to spread across the French population. Even working-class young women increasingly wanted clean hair. Shampooing, an article in the *Hairdressers' Weekly Journal* observed with some exaggeration in 1913, until recently a rarity, is now an "everyday requirement."[69]

By the end of the century, Eugen Weber concluded, "the threshold of shame and disgust—what Norbert Elias describes as civility—had been raised another notch." We can measure the distance between nineteenth- and twentieth-century sensibilities in the advice experts dished out on how often people should shampoo their hair. If the Comtesses de Pange and de Farge scorned clean hair at the turn of the

century, by 1923, professors Kauffmann and Barth of the hairdressers'
training facility in Strasbourg were prescribing at least one shampoo a
month, depending on whether hair was dry or oily. A decade later,
Dr. Georges-Lévy stressed the importance of keeping hair and scalp
clean. Those who worked in grimy conditions needed to shampoo
daily. Individuals with dry hair and scalps could afford to wash them
less often: every two weeks for men, three or four weeks for women
with *cheveux courts*, four or five weeks for women with long hair.
These prescriptions might fall short of contemporary practices, but
they clearly marked an enormous advance from the practices of the
previous era.[70]

Better personal hygiene no doubt improved the nation's health, and
it brought coiffeurs a double benefit. Cleaner hair made for more
pleasant work. It was also good business, and coiffeurs' appreciation
of shampooing grew along with the public's fondness for it, which
boosted their income. René Rambaud calculated that the average
française before the war visited her coiffeur for twenty shampooings a
year, at five francs apiece. By 1925, she indulged herself in thirty-six
shampooings a year, at eight francs per treatment—a threefold increase
in receipts.[71]

Advances in the science of hair color, and in the public's appetite for
it, made an additional contribution to hairdressers' revenues. Long's
articles chronicled its rising popularity among *parisiennes*: peroxide
blonde, black henna, gray powders, and Antoine's "Bulgarian" colors
that went so well, he remarked ghoulishly, with black hats and mourning veils. There was nothing very novel in this. Hair coloring was an
ancient practice, and it had been far from extraordinary in nineteenth-
century France. In the 1870s, wrote Theodore Zeldin, "egg yolk" and
"cow's tail" were the fashionable colors. Yet the sense that there was
something vaguely naughty about a woman who dyed her hair
restrained the market for hair coloring, even in the Belle Epoque. "It
goes without saying," wrote Mrs. Mallon in the *Ladies' Home
Journal*, "that a well-bred woman does not dye her hair."[72]

More to the point, many women hesitated because, in an era of
uncertain chemistry, *teinture* could produce some unfortunate effects
on hair and scalp. This began to change with the appearance of new
chemical formulas. The *Journal de la Coiffure* in 1902 praised the new
dyes, based on para-phenaline-diamine, generically known as "para,"
for their sharper and more durable color. But critics complained that
"para" was a powerful, potentially lethal poison. In the worst cases, it
produced nervous system and blood disorders. Less seriously, but

more commonly, it caused serious allergic reactions: "pimples or puostules . . . accompanied by intolerable itchings [and] eczema . . . skin . . . violent red, inflamed, damp and oozing . . . swelling underneath the eyes and eyelids . . . so that the patient is unable to open them," among other problems. Actress Caroline Otéro suffered serious burns in 1909 when several drops of the "para" lotion she was putting on her head came into contact with a hot-water heater. In 1902 alone, the public prosecutor of the Seine Department registered 142 complaints relating to hair-coloring torts, and the fear of burns, rashes, and defoliation remained endemic.[73]

The status of *teinture* began to improve dramatically in the twentieth century, favored by two separate developments. First, dyes made from vegetable matter, especially henna, made hair coloring much less risky. At the same time, a rising "cult of youth" made gray hair seem less distinguished, and therefore less inevitable. Taking the utmost advantage of the new value accorded to youthfulness was the great pioneer of *teinture*, Eugène Schueller. In 1907, the young chemist began to brew synthetic hair dyes in his kitchen laboratory and sell them to hair salons under the name of Auréole. Within two years he had established his own company, which soon became L'Oréal. By 1912, Schueller was selling his products in Austria, Holland, and Italy; by 1920 the market for L'Oréal extended from the Americas to the Soviet Union and the Far East. Working with only three research chemists and ten sales representatives, Schueller developed a host of new products for the elite and popular markets, built a fashion and publishing empire, and poured millions of francs back into advertising, professional *concours*, and subsidies for the coiffeurs on his payroll.[74]

From a commercial point of view, Schueller was without question the most important single figure in the hairdressing profession until the outbreak of World War II, and the basis of his fortune was the safe, long-lasting hair coloring he had been selling since before World War I. L'Oréal became a fixture on millions of heads and a dependable source of income for thousands of coiffeurs. The sale of cheap dyes expanded fivefold by the early 1920s, and recourse to *teinture* penetrated even the countryside, where only the old women still left their hair gray; the others, it was said, had all "gone Hollywood." One coiffeur from a provincial town explained to readers of *Hebdo-Coiffure* why his clients colored their hair: "Twelve older domestics want to look younger." As for the six *commerçantes*, seven *jeunes femmes*, and five *bourgeoises*, they use *teinture* not just for *coquetterie* but for business: "An old-fashioned cashier," they told him, "doesn't attract clients."[75] It was with justice that Raul Patois observed in 1920: "*Teinture* is not the most agreeable work in the profession," he added, "but it is without comparison the most lucrative."[76]

Other technologies emerged that made a greater or lesser impact on the hairdressing trades. The electric curling iron made its appearance in France in 1897. With the diffusion of shampooing, ladies' hairdressers began to install hairdryers in their salons. Antoine claimed to have been the first when his sumptuous *maison* opened on the rue Cambon in 1910. Gas-fired apparatuses pioneered the market. They were cheap to run but tended to suffer from carbon monoxide leaks. Electric hairdryers, more dependable and more expensive, soon became the *secheurs* of choice.[77]

The marriage of science and hair also pointed down some *fausses pistes*. For instance, *Figaro-Mode* in 1904 carried a story about a fellow who claimed to have found relief for those not naturally blessed with a full head of hair. Pursuing his insight that "hair is vegetal," he proposed to "plant" hair on people's heads, adding that, if you did not like your hair color, he could take it all out and plant a new *chevelure* of a different tint. Another "breakthrough" promised to treat facial imperfections, such as acne or wrinkles, using steam and colored light: blue for the lightest treatment and red for tougher cases of greasy skin or mild disease. Or take the case of a Dr. Brown-Séquart, who tried to build his reputation on a technique for rejuvenating patients using juices from the sexual glands of monkeys, and who likewise developed a lotion to cure baldness—made from female urine.[78]

One technological innovation that did not miss the mark was the permanent-wave machine, the *machine à l'indéfrisable*. The "permanent," as it came to be called, had its roots in the deficiencies of Marcel waves. Fine and soft or cheap and frizzy, all *ondulations* shared the same shortcoming: at the end of a humid evening or after a couple of weeks, even the most exquisitely waved hair would return to its natural state.[79] The future Mrs. Robert Henrey recorded her "marcel's" encounter with the London fog: "This evening, with curling tongs and a spirit lamp," she remembered, "I would have to redo all the curls in my hair. Damp weather and bus stops were not good for homemade waves."[80] French hairdressers were naturally intrigued, therefore, by a new invention attracting attention on the other side of the English Channel, the work of Charles Nestlé. Nestlé, born Karl Ludwig Nessler, son of a German shoemaker, had learned the Marcel wave in Paris and then gone to London to set up his own salons.

In September 1906 he placed a notice in the *Hairdressers' Weekly Journal* inviting his colleagues to come to his shop on Oxford Street to "examine . . . an undulation obtained by his new process, which resists the action of water, shampooing, and all atmospheric influences."[81]

The technique for *frisure forcée* was an old recipe of the *posticheur*'s trade. Hair was divided into locks (*mèches*), soaked in alkaline solution, and boiled. For obvious reasons, this process was impractical for hair that remained attached to a client's head. Nestlé's breakthrough invention was a machine—it looked like a sort of electric jellyfish—that could boil a woman's hair *without* scalding her scalp, more or less. He did this by rolling the locks into curlers (*bigoudis*)—thirty or fifty would cover a head—which were then wrapped and subjected to heat from an electric current. The hair could then be washed out and dressed.

Emile Long was the first in France to see the potential of the "permanent," and he invited Nestlé to France for a demonstration of his new apparatus. There, in Long's salon on the rue Moscou in September 1909, Nestlé showed off his device to some of the most eminent coiffeurs from Europe and America. Reports of the event recorded the audience's disappointment, apparently with some reason, with the outcome. It required up to ten hours to complete the process and, because of the size of the *bigoudis*, could not wave hair close to the head. Besides, it produced waves that, in Rambaud's words, had a "truly repulsive look" to them.[82]

If coiffeurs were put off by the dubious results of Nestlé's process, would-be customers were scared off by the ordeal it involved. As the *Hairdressers' Weekly Journal* described it, a woman's hair was,

> encased in asbestos and baked for ten minutes by means of a specially and ingeniously devised electrical heater hanging from a well-conceived bracket . . . Each of the heaters—and there are a number—require as much electricity as an eight-candle powerlamp. A double layer of brown paper was placed near the head to keep as much heat from the head as possible, *and an assistant with a small bellows was kept occupied for a similar purpose.*[83]

Hair had to be heated to over 200 degrees Fahrenheit, and severe burns were a constant danger. So was electric shock, or the possibility that the rods might overheat, leaving the client with a head full of melted rubber. The entire procedure left women, in Caroline Cox's words, "stuck under an extremely weighty mechanical contraption for hours at a time, looking and probably feeling as if they were undergoing some particularly nasty form of futuristic torture." It perhaps explains why, in its first year, only seventy-four women exposed themselves to treatment.[84]

Demand for permanent waves remained weak, as women took a look at Nestlé's machine, figured that discretion was the better part of valor, and opted to stick with their "marcels." Nonetheless, Nestlé had surmounted a significant technological barrier, and those who were intrigued by the stylistic and commercial possibilities of the permanent wave continued to tinker with the machine. Within a few years, as happens to so many pioneers, Nestlé's work was surpassed by new, improved *machines à l'indéfrisable* that offered women the pleasure of permanent waves without the thrill of perching on the technological precipice. The real take-off of the "perm," however, had to wait through the social and cultural upheaval unleashed by the war.

Yet even as Nestlé's permanent-wave machine sat intimidating and largely idle in his salon, it stood as a monument to the transformation of ladies' hairdressing in the preceding thirty years, itself a reflection of the changes overtaking French society as it settled into the twentieth century. Deconstructed, in a manner of speaking, the *machine à l'indéfrisable* suggests much more than the robust demand for wavy hair. It points to the application of new technology to an old art, to the budding appetite for fashion among the unfashionable classes, to women's growing comfort in public spaces. Above all, it indicates a profession poised for its great leap forward.

"Old Jules": Barber on the Paris quais, 1908

2

The Poorest of Trades

The sparkle of these new machines and the glamour attached to fashion tend to obscure the way cultural practices really changed lives. Yet it is critical to remember that one person's hairstyle was another's business and still another's labor, and that the advance of ladies' hairdressing was also a social revolution that transformed life in the salons. In order to measure the impact of new tastes and new technologies on an old trade, it is useful to take stock of life in the hairdressing profession in the period before *coiffure pour dames* began to turn it upside down.

"Perhaps in no city in the world is there such a vast and variegated category of tonsorial establishments," wrote the Paris correspondent of the *Barbers' Journal* in 1902.[1] The huge majority of these were barbershops, where men served men in tiny establishments. Of the 47,640 hairdressers found in the 1896 census, 90 percent were male and almost all of them worked either alone or with one or two *assistants*. In the entire country, only fifty-three hairdressing salons had more than five *ouvriers*. Two alone engaged more than twenty *garçons coiffeurs*, both of them in Paris.[2]

Data on the age structure and marriage status of hairdressers in 1896 help to paint a more detailed picture, dividing the profession into two distinct elements: patrons and *ouvriers*. Almost 90 percent of *chefs d'établissements* were married, divorced, or widowed, and under 5 percent were younger than twenty-five. *Garçons coiffeurs* made up a completely different slice of the population. Sixty-eight percent were younger than twenty-five; almost 30 percent had not yet reached their eighteenth birthday. Considerably younger than their employers, *ouvriers coiffeurs* were also notably more footloose. Seventy-eight percent of these boys and 56 percent of the girls were *célibataires*.

It took time to acquire the skill, clientele, and financial wherewithal to open one's own shop, modest as it might be. A young coiffeur of any energy or ambition either found a way to climb into the *petit patronat* or left the trade entirely. The alternative was a lifetime of near-poverty and semidependency.

That *ouvriers coiffeurs* tended to be young and unattached also accounted for their combustible mixture of feeble union membership and spirited readiness for action. Conversely, it suggests why patronal syndicalism inclined toward more organization and less volatility. It was not only that the working class in the hairdressing trade was desperately underpaid and overworked, it was also that *garçons coiffeurs* were eighteen-years old and single, while their patrons, who were in many cases similarly poor and exhausted, were thirty-five and *pères de familles*.

This large population of coiffeurs worked under a great diversity of conditions, from the wretched to the sumptuous. In the villages, café chairs and tables could be easily enough adapted to clipping and shaving, while grocers and ironmongers also fit the bill as the village barber. Even in Paris, the correspondent for the *Barber's Journal* found Old Jules, who worked "at the foot of a stone stairway leading from the Quai de Conti down to [the edge of the river Seine], nearly under the arches of Pont Neuf," shaving customers en masse with river water and an old straight razor.[3]

At the other end of the profession were the deluxe salons, where "hairdressers, in uniform, elegant and reserved, gladly serve[d] as confidants and advisors in a refined, urbane setting."[4] In 1906, the Paris daily *Le Journal* estimated that the city contained four or five hundred of them, situated in the better-off western districts and along the *grands boulevards*, serving "une clientele riche." The rest of the city's 2,500 barbershops, tucked into those parts of the *center-ville* that still belonged to the working classes or—more and more—in the outlying arrondissements, catered to a less pampered "clientèle ouvriere."[5]

A considerable part of business in all salons derived from mustaches and beards.[6] These remained the measure of manliness into the twentieth century, when opponents of facial hair began to argue that a clean chin was not just more comely, but more sanitary as well. In one "experiment,"

> . . . a group of men decided to conduct a scientific test of the danger of beards to young ladies who were kissed. One man who was bearded and one who was not bearded were walked through the crowded

streets, stores, and museums of Paris, and were then brought back to a laboratory where each kissed a girl, in the interests of science. After each kiss a sterilized brush was passed over the girl's lips, and was dipped in a sterile solution, which was sealed and left standing for four days. Proof was offered that the lips of the shaven man carried only harmless germs, but that the kiss of the bearded man "literally swarmed with malignant microbes."[7]

Sanitary or not, in Belle-Epoque France, beards were still the mainstay of the barber's trade. In the *salons populaires*, barbers scratched out a living providing the most rudimentary and cheapest service: a shave and a haircut, the former at twenty centimes and the latter at forty. Some barbers sold shaves by subscription, which squeezed their meager income even further.[8] Indeed, it was hairdressers' singular misfortune that the most poorly compensated element of their labor, shaving, was the most commanded. It could be said with some justice that barbers found themselves enslaved by their skill with a razor, for it led not only to penury but to the exaggerated hours that barbers spent in their shops. If barbershops stayed open until midnight on Saturday and on the eve of important holidays, it was not because people required haircuts but because everyone wanted to be clean-shaven for the *jours des fêtes*.

The invention of the safety razor by the American, King Gillette, in 1895—"so easy to use a man could shave with his eyes closed"[9]— promised to kill the demand for barbers' principal activity. This would reduce their income in the short run. In the long run, however, it would probably mean fewer barbershops with better incomes, which is more or less what happened when Gillette's ingenious device penetrated the French market after World War I. In the meantime, the hairdressing profession continued to sag under the inconvenient and unremunerative demand for shaves.[10]

With the exception of the smartest bourgeois salons, French barbershops remained technologically primitive affairs, especially compared to the growing number of *salons pour dames*. It would have been rare to find one that matched the ideal described by Kauffmann and Barth, instructors at the Strasboug École de Perfectionnement: marble-topped sinks in front of reclinable chairs, two porcelain spittoons, umbrella-coat-and-hat rack, four electric lamps, and a linoleum floor for easy cleaning. "In the usual Paris shop," according to Richard Corson's Paris observer, "the customers sat in cane-seated armchairs . . . in front of mirrors and wash basins."[11] There is no reason to think that provincial barbershops offered more lavish accommodations.

These small poorly ventilated spaces became especially dangerous when pervaded with the chemicals often used in the barber's trade. On their feet all day, working bent over in suffocating shops, in close contact with customers who smoked continuously, coiffeurs frequently complained of the "maladies professionnalles" that plagued them: eczema, asthma, varicose veins, tuberculosis. Constrained "to work only thirty or forty centimeters from a client's face," complained the first congress of hairdressing workers' unions in 1894, "[the coiffeur] is forced to inhale [his client's] breath, which often bears some sort of disease, either because of rotten teeth or some *maladie des musqueuses*, or other repugnant condition."[12]

Barbershops were widely considered to be "dens" of promiscuity and infection. One source reported that "the same lather was used for several customers, and towels might be used on both face and hair of a dozen men before being discarded. When the shave was finished, the gentleman customarily washed his own face."[13] A Dr. Larroussinie scolded a group of *patrons coiffeurs* in 1903 that hardly any of them bothered to clean or sterilize their instruments from one customer to the next. He admonished them to attend night courses in hygiene and rudimentary biology.[14] Other experts advised barbers to maintain clean spittoons—or better yet, to do as cafés had done and get rid of them entirely, since, as master barber Alfred Spale wrote, *crachoirs* only encouraged customers to spit.[15]

Apparently, coiffeurs remained skeptical of "modern" opinion and were slow to adjust their notions and customs. An article in the *Alliance des Coiffeurs* in 1904, for example, explicitly rejected a "stupefying circular" from the local conseil d'hygiène et de salubrité that recommended sterilizing razors, combs, and the rest in a hot chemical "bath." In fact, the writer contended, it had been proved that an antiseptic effect could more easily be obtained from a strong solution of cinnamon or thyme oil or from perfume.[16]

In sum, the man who walked into his neighborhood barbershop and laid down his sixty centimes or so for a shave and a trim could hardly expect to be pampered. He was willing, in effect, to accept shabby conditions in exchange for very low prices. For barbers themselves, the terms of this exchange lay at the root of their generally woeful professional circumstances.[17] Official and unofficial wage rates placed *garçon coiffeurs* among the lowest paid of French workers. It is easy to imagine that colleagues of the barber Deschamps in Paris's third arrondissement shared his outrage at *ouvriers coiffeurs*, who had invested three years of

Table 2.1   Average Wages in Hairdressing and other Trades, 1896 (in francs per day)

City	Avg.	Coiffeur	Glazier	Day Laborer	Laund-ress	Dress-maker	Sewing Maid	Vest Maker
Bordeaux	4.79	1.20**	3.00	2.50	2.00	2.00	1.50	2.50
(30f/month)								
Nice	4.32	1.20**	3.50	4.00	2.50	2.50	2.50	2.50
(50f/month)								
Lille	4.62	1.58*	3.60	2.50	2.20	2.50	1.25	2.50
(40f/month)								
Cahors (Lot)	3.19	2.50	3.00	2.50	1.50	2.00	1.75	2.00
Paris	4.02	0.83**	6.00	3.50	3.50	4.00	2.50	4.00
(35–50f/month)								

* *plus* board.
** *plus* room and board.

Sources: Ministère du Commerce, de l'Industrie, des Postes et des Télégraphes. Office du Travail, *Salaires et durée du travail dans l'industrie française, tome IV: Résultats généraux* (Paris: Imprimerie Nationale, 1897), 341–7; and Ministère du Travail et de Prévoyance Sociale. Statistique générale de la France, *Salaires et coûts d'existence à diverses époques, jusqu'en 1910* (Paris: Imprimerie Nationale, 1911), 22–5. The 1911 study examined "average wages" in thirty-four *métiers masculins* in various regions, 1896–1911. The 1897 study covered approximately one hundred seventy municipalities. The results of the two surveys have been combined to yield Table 1:1.

apprenticeship and five years as *assistants* and earned 150 francs a month for 360 hours' work.[18]

Two government studies of 1896 and 1911 suggest that in the middle of the 1890s, hairdressing workers in every region of France earned wages below those of an average male laborer (table 2.1). The extent to which *garçons coiffeurs* were *nourris* and *logés* outside Paris makes precise comparisons difficult.[19] It appears, nevertheless, that *ouvriers coiffeurs* earned less than the modestly paid glaziers and perhaps a bit more than unskilled *journaliers*. On the whole, employees in the barbershops seem to have had wages closer to those in the feminine trades than to *salariés* among semiskilled men.[20]

Outside Paris, upwards of three-quarters of barber's assistants were *nourris* and *logés*, often in terrible conditions. They deplored the "miserly portions" of food and wine watered to oblivion, and denounced the many patrons who "lodged their workers in humid, stuffy garrets," on mattresses hard as the ground and dirty, disease-ridden linen.[21] They objected to the "corvées" of *nettoyage* and *frottage*, of having to scrub the floor and sweep the sidewalk in front of the salon, clean the shop window when they were not serving customers. "Instead of being able to leave work peacefully [at the end of a fourteen- or seventeen- hour day]," one worker told the inaugural congress of the Fédération nationale des syndicats d'ouvriers coiffeurs

(FNSOC) in 1894, "we are obliged to wash and scour for another hour or two and to go off, bathed in sweat . . . which results in chills and colds."[22]

There nonetheless existed areas of the hairdressing trades where even an employee could make a decent living. The few hundred "extras," who worked only one or two days a week during the busiest times, could earn fifteen or twenty francs for a day-and-a-half's work.[23] Wages in posh salons of the city centers stood considerably above the average for the trade, precisely what might be expected when services that cost a working man twenty centimes in Belleville could set a gentleman back six francs on the Boulevard St-Germain. In addition to his superior *salaire*, moreover, a young man with a talent for selling tonics, pomades, and lotions might add a 10 percent commission to his income. That handful of *garçons* who worked in the era's *salons pour dames* also stood to earn a better-than-average living. At the top of this pyramid, a small, privileged group could claim wages up to 500 francs a month. But even ordinary *assistants* serving ladies were making ten to twelve francs a day, compared to the seven-and-a-half francs earned by the most fortunate barber's assistants who were neither *nourris* nor *couchés*.[24]

For the majority of hairdressing workers, the sharp edge of poverty was also blunted by the tips they received. In a better shop, a barber with an engaging manner, while he might be paid a weekly wage of only twenty francs, could pocket an additional twelve francs a day in tips. At the low-wage end of the profession, *ouvriers coiffeurs* relied almost entirely on tips to keep body and soul together.

Yet calls for the abolition of the *pourboire* were among the standard *revendications* of the *chambres syndicales* and the FNSOC. Critics attacked the custom from two angles. They argued first that the tip was an undependable source of essential income, since customers could tip or not, as they pleased; second, that some patrons confiscated tips intended for their *assistants*.[25] More than that, hairdressers found this form of "begging" degrading, an insult to their status as *hommes de métiers*.[26] It was to raise both their income and their self-esteem that hairdressing workers sought to eliminate the *pourboire* and establish a new, profession-wide minimum wage.

Miserable incomes, however, tell only half the story. For if *ouvriers coiffeurs* were paid like unskilled women, they were worked like slaves. No trade worked more; given the constraints of physiology, it is difficult to conceive how any could have.[27] Indeed, although the sources do not say so explicitly, it is likely that young barbers were driven out of the profession as much by sleep deprivation as by inadequate pay.

At the end of the nineteenth century, the Commerce Ministry found that barbers' assistants commonly worked eighty to ninety hours a week.[28] What is more, they put in considerably more days than any other tradesmen. In all but a handful of the 170 cities examined in 1901, *ouvriers coiffeurs* worked more than 300 days a year. In over half they worked more than 325 days a year, and in about a quarter they enjoyed not a single day entirely off "to smell the country air" or to enjoy a tranquil dinner "en famille."[29] *Garçons coiffeurs* worked every Sunday, as well as Christmas, Easter, Pentecost, and all the other holidays. In fact, they worked harder on a holiday because barbershops inevitably stayed open late the evening before.[30] The turn of the century was famously a moment for the expansion of commercialized working-class leisure: dance halls, amusement parks, sporting events.[31] But it is hard to imagine how *garçons coiffeurs* could have had any of this.

Albert Goullé summed up the sad career of the *garçon coiffeur*: yelled at incessantly by his clients, dependent on tips, most of which accrued to the patron, fired for the slightest reason. Having joined the profession at fifteen, a barber's assistant was old by the time he reached thirty. At thirty-five he could no longer find anyone willing to hire him. Those who had managed to save a little in their youth set up on their own. Then they waited for customers. Usually, such *petits patrons* could earn their bread, but not enough for meat. And for everyone who succeeded, wrote Goullé, three others "shrivel up in misery."[32]

In conventional labor histories, such distress among employees is the flip side of employers' comfort. But that was decidedly not true in coiffure. Petty enterprise by reputation exacts a high price in self-exploitation, and coiffure provides a case in point. Thus, while *garçons coiffeurs* worked the most murderous schedules, their employers were hardly better off. In virtually all *petits salons*, when the *ouvrier* was at work, thirteen hours a day and more, the patron could be found at the chair beside him. And with few exceptions, if the *garçons* worked every day, so did the masters. So many hours for so small a return, mused Gustave Blavy, "that no one—neither workers nor patrons—earns a decent living, which is why coiffure is considered 'le dernier des métiers.' "[33]

Patrons defended their labor practices by noting that a hairdresser's workday might be long, but it was also very porous. Fourteen or fifteen hours of *présence* might mean only ten hours of real work, and bursts of intense activity would normally punctuate extended periods of waiting around for customers to show up. They argued further that service businesses such as barbershops needed to cater to the convenience of their customers. We can agree on a nine o'clock closing time, the patron Constant told a group of *salonniers* and employees in the eighth arrondissement. But if a client walks through the door at 8:59, we can hardly throw him out. Alphonse Mornot, president of the Paris Chambre syndicale des ouvriers coiffeurs (CSO), claimed that if customers knew the schedule beforehand, they would adjust to it. But he failed to convince his interlocutors.[34]

Especially in working-class neighborhoods, it simply was not feasible to close early. Downtown, where everybody worked but nobody lived, business clustered during the day and during the week. In the outlying arrondissements, however, barbershops had to wait for people to return home from work, and that meant keeping their doors open every weekday well into the evening and on Sundays. And if they needed to stay open until ten o'clock on Wednesday and Friday, or until midnight on Saturday, it was not to squeeze more profit out of employees but *"en raison de la clientèle."*[35]

These awful work conditions and a sense that things ought to be better inexorably led hairdressing workers to organize. Besides, living in working-class districts and talking to their proletarian customers, as most of them did, barbers could not have failed to absorb the sentiments that were fueling the labor movement in *fin-de-siècle* France. Barbers had a long history of corporate organization reaching back to the barber-surgeons of the Old Regime, who had jealously guarded their corporate right to cut hair, pull teeth, and bleed their unlucky clients. Barbers retained their sense of solidarity even after they lost their corporate privileges and continued to organize through the nineteenth century, both for mutual aid and political advantage. Only with the legalization of trade unionism in 1884, however, did these efforts prove durable.[36]

Perhaps their most enduring achievement was the École parisienne de coiffure, created by the CSO in 1887. Floated with subsidies from the municipal authorities, the École parisienne recruited an initial class of 200 students and, within a few years, boasted forty-three professors and forty "honorary members," who taught classes and organized *concours* and exhibitions. The growth of *coiffure pour dames*, involving more difficult technical skills, helped solidify the École's importance within the profession. It has functioned continuously since its inception and trained some of the century's most successful hairdressers.[37]

Efforts to build trade unions of *ouvriers coiffeurs* never succeeded as well. The CSO was founded in 1887 in Paris, with the primary aim of raising wages, shortening work schedules, and battling exploitation by private *bureaux de placement* (employment agencies). Its energetic campaign for a nine o'clock closing time in 1891 led to larger membership, which reached 1,200 that year. But dues and participation remained a problem.[38] Similar organizations of hairdressing workers sprang up around the country in the 1880s and 1890s, all with comparable problems. In Lyon in 1894, a dozen or so of these local *chambres syndicales* joined forces to form a national federation, the FNSOC.[39]

The FNSOC and the CSO attracted the most class conscious and militant *ouvriers coiffeurs*, and, despite the mandate that trade unions should not engage in politics, their program of professional reform acquired a radical political aspect.[40] A police spy reporting on the meeting of March 27, 1903, for example, not only heard speeches denouncing excessively long workdays and parasitical placement agencies, he also listened to a delegate, Jacoby, give a long speech on the inevitable decline of bourgeois society and its fundamental enmity to workers' interests. Such meetings often combined practical discussions of bread and butter issues with calls for a general strike and the "expropriation de la classe capitaliste."[41]

These sentiments naturally drew the FNSOC to the national labor movement. Led by its fiery new general secretary, Alexandre Luquet, the fourth congress of the FNSOC in 1900 affirmed its commitment to a general strike "as a means of revolution" and voted to join the Confédération générale du travail (CGT). Born in Bourges in 1874, Luquet had come to Paris as a teenager. A coiffeur by training and a socialist by inclination, he left the salon and embraced the life of a professional syndicalist. Luquet quickly became the principal figure among the *ouvriers coiffeurs syndiqués* of Paris, where he surrounded himself with such able lieutenants as the young René Rambaud.[42] The FNSOC secretary always remained what one police report called "a warm partisan of direct action." He consistently declared himself against collaboration with employers and the state, and regularly condemned military service as "the surest rampart of the bourgeoisie and the ruling elite."[43]

"Thin, shrill, with a short moustache and a musketeer's goatee," Luquet quickly came to play an important role within the CGT. He became a deputy secretary in 1903, working closely with his friend Victor Griffuelhes. He served on the confederal committee that organized the direct-action campaign for the eight-hour day, and, in 1908, when Griffuelhes was in prison, Luquet served a short term as acting general secretary. On the other hand, despite his fierce rhetoric of an earlier period, in 1914 Luquet followed the CGT majority, led by Léon Jouhaux and Alphonse Merrheim, in supporting the Union Sacrée.[44] When the confederation split after the war, he stuck with Jouhaux against the communist secession.

The story of the FNSOC's role in the CGT is worth recounting because it sheds light on the most contentious issue that was confronting the confederation in the Belle Epoque: proportional representation. At its Limoges congress of 1895, the CGT had agreed to statutes that allowed each federation the greatest measure of autonomy and accorded each an equal vote on the *comité confédéral*, no matter how many members it had. Thus the FNSOC, one of the smaller federations within the CGT, with 2,500 to 3,500 members in twenty or so *chambres syndicales*, wielded as much formal power over CGT policy as the federation of railroad workers, with some 50,000 adherents.[45] The fairness of this arrangement aside, it raised a policy issue, since the bigger industrial unions leaned toward reformism and feared being dragged in a more dangerous direction by such "minorités agissantes" as the hairdressers.

The issue came to the floor of the congress of 1904 in Bourges. Delegates from the smaller unions naturally opposed proportional representation, which would "enable the bigger unions to 'crush' the smaller fry." Luquet, generally considered one of the "anarchists" in the confederation, rose to address the congress and argued that smaller unions deserved a *stronger* voice because they served as "a vanguard . . . and guide to the proletariat." The motion to adopt proportional representation went down: 825 votes for; 369 against. Two years later, the CGT enshrined its commitment to revolutionary syndicalism in the Amiens Charter, of which Luquet was one of the principal architects.[46]

In truth, rather than being a "vanguard," *ouvriers coiffeurs* practiced an idiosyncratic sort of syndicalism. It was only logical that a workforce scattered among thousands of small barbershops could never provide a workable model for miners, navvies, or metallurgists. Mobilizing fifty or a hundred young *garçons coiffeurs* to squeeze a few centimes or a couple of hours' rest out of their individual employers was clearly a different order of business from mustering several thousand men against one or two big companies.[47]

Consider the prospects for strike activity. Only in Paris did hairdressing workers outnumber their employers. In Bordeaux, only a third of the 1,823 hairdressers counted as *ouvriers*, while the deeply rural Lot department had only thirty-nine employees out of 208 coiffeurs.[48] Strikes were thus apt to be small, local, short-lived affairs. Moreover, even though *assistants* could withhold their own labor, and this could have left a certain number of untended chairs in town, they could not by this means force their patrons to stop serving clients. They could not, in other words, close the salons down the way that a strike of *métallos* could shut down a factory.

Garçons coiffeurs' structural disadvantage was compounded by the weakness of the syndical impulse among them. Full of "youth and insouciance," they were at once ripe for action and short on discipline.[49] Their syndicats consequently never managed to attract more than a small part of the labor force, and even those who joined the syndicats proved unreliable when it came to coming out and paying dues.[50] The strength of syndicalism in coiffure was further sapped by the relative ease of social promotion in the world of petty commerce. *Ouvriers coiffeurs* who managed to hoist themselves into the *patronat* might maintain their support for labor reform even as they crossed from the proletariat to the petty bourgeoisie. But their leadership abilities were lost to the labor movement.

All these factors helped to deplete the syndical movement in coiffure and made strikes, the apotheosis of revolutionary syndicalism, a more-than-normally undependable vehicle of social struggle. *Grévistes* seldom won any significant concessions from their employers. It is important to recall, moreover, that the proliferation of small, poor shops made for a pretty anarchistic business climate. Even when the leaders of the *salonniers* signed an agreement, therefore, there was no guarantee that the mass of *petits patrons coiffeurs* would respect them.[51]

The relative uselessness of strikes in coiffure inclined workers toward more direct forms of action. When the CSO launched a campaign for "9–7" (9 p.m. closing during the week, 7 p.m. Sunday) in 1899, for example, it did not declare a strike but began to organize *comités de vigilance*—often in concert with sympathetic patrons. Sources often commented on the disappointing turnout for these vigilante squads, but numbers evidently served for the task.[52] Predictably, these confrontations sometimes turned nasty. One police agent described a particularly dramatic scene on the rue de Ménilmontant that led to an investigation of police brutality. The trouble began with an angry demonstration against several shops open late on a Sunday evening. The demonstrators had rubbed excreta on the storefronts and otherwise defaced them. In front of Henri Piétu's salon they began to yell at his *assistant* and throw rocks into his shop. A crowd of local merchants and residents gathered, some five or six hundred people increasingly hostile to the *ouvriers coiffeurs*. When Louis Chausseude threw a stone at Piétu, the crowd went after him. He ran down the block and grabbed a chair in front of Morissel's shoe store in order to defend himself and finally took refuge in the hallway of a building a bit further down the street. Two cops stepped in and arrested Chausseude and, while shielding him from the crowd, brought him back to Piétu for identification. The letter from Alphonse Mornot, general secretary of the CSO, that inspired the investigation, alleged that the cops then held Chausseude, while Piétu punched him a couple of times. The police denied this and the investigation, for what it is worth, confirmed their version of events with affidavits from witnesses.[53]

The *comités de vigilance* often found themselves in conflict with the authorities, and arrests were common. But they seem to have worked, for Mornot told a big meeting of workers and patrons in August 1899 that adherence to "9–7" was virtually universal.[54]

The intimidation, even the violence, necessary for progress in the class struggle perhaps helps to explain the complete absence of women from syndical activity in the hairdressing trade. Reports on strikes *never* recorded the participation of a single *coiffeuse*. None of the five hundred or so *ouvrières* in Paris ever surfaced at CSO meetings or joined the "patrols" that roamed the *quartiers*, enforcing earlier closing times.

The labor movement's ambivalence about women's appropriate role in the battle for social justice is a familiar one. Women made up 36 percent of the *population active* in 1911, but only 9.8 percent of *syndiqués*.[55] "The CGT," wrote Patricia Hilden, "had only minimal success in mobilizing most working women for their cause."[56] And no wonder, since the confederation could not make up its mind on the woman question, despite a formal commitment to "equal wages for equal work." It seems clear that the majority of male syndicalists believed both that women could be important allies in the class struggle and that the socialist future would restore the "natural" division of labor in the family that capitalism had destroyed.[57] Women consistently found themselves underrepresented and "ghettoized" in the confederation and the individual trade federations, which inevitably subordinated gender issues to class concerns.[58]

The situation in coiffure fit the general rule. Maybe *ouvrières coiffeuses* avoided the *syndicats* for the same reasons that women traditionally hesitated to become involved in predominantly male unions: they felt unwelcome; they shared a sense that politics was men's business; they simply did not like the unions' confrontational approach to issues.[59] In any event, the labor movement made no detectable effort to bring *coiffeuses* into the fold. Perhaps they calculated that the comparatively small number of *coiffeuses* and their likely aversion to militant action made attempts to organize them unprofitable. There is also evidence, however, that *ouvriers coiffeurs* shared the widespread fear of competition from *ouvrières*. Barbers at the founding congress of the FNSOC did not mince words. In the midst of calls for improved conditions and social justice, the congress voted to close its *écoles professionnelles* to "young women desiring to become *coiffeuses*," in order to put an end to this "concurrence redoutable." Indeed it went further, unanimously adopting the rule that "any *patron* or worker who gave [haircutting] lessons to a woman, excepting his wife and daughters, would be *mise à l'index*." President Mornot told a meeting of the CSO in 1896 that a woman's principal syndical duty was to allow her husband to attend more meetings.[60] Even in the new century, as women began to pour into the hairdressing trades, they always remained strangers to the labor movement.

Hairdressers might have shared the CGT's ambivalence toward *ouvrières* and its formal commitment to revolutionary syndicalism. Yet in other respects, their universe of *petites enterprises* represented a very unconventional case of the well-studied combat between workers and employers. To be sure, even in the most modest barbershop, patron and *ouvrier* must have clashed over pay, work time, and dividing up the tips in the *tronc*. On the other hand, little would have separated them with respect to training and social background.[61] Both would have come from a popular milieu. The patron would have come only a little farther. Evidence suggests that income differentials in the small-shops between employers and workers were very low. And there can be no doubt that, the small-shop owner worked the same long hours as his employees—sometimes more, as new laws granted employees time off without forcing salons to close.

The comparative ease of mobility from *ouvrier* to *patron coiffeur* further reduced the distance between barbers and their *assistants*. In the suburbs especially, wrote Albert Goullé, you do not need to be "luxueusement installé," and it cost little enough to become "un commerçant patenté."[62] It was no great rarity even for former trade-union militants to find themselves with a *petite affaire* and workers of their own. Alphonse Mornot, president of the workers' CSO in the 1890s, became president of the Chambre syndicale des patrons coiffeurs

(CSP) only a few years later and in the 1930s finished as honorary president of the FNSOC.[63] Likewise René Chauvin, whose career stretched from *garçon coiffeur* to successful entrepreneur, by way of the marxist Parti ouvrier français and a seat in the National Assembly, where he became the first socialist deputy from Paris and the only hairdresser deputy from anywhere.[64] This was by any standard an extraordinary itinerary, but in coiffure it was far from unique.

Inevitably, some employees who joined the *patronat* sometimes forgot what life was like on the other end of the wage. The *Coiffeur Confédéré* told the story of an ex-secretary of his *chambre syndicale des ouvriers* who had set himself up in a little salon. The journal regretted that this fellow soon forgot everything he had always fought for and became a most disagreeable and exploitative boss. He fired five old comrades when they refused to work illegal hours, and ended up with a disciplinary visit from the *inspecteur du travail*.[65] But Mornot and Chauvin appear to have been more typical, bringing with them to the *patronat* a genuine sympathy for the workers' plight and a keen sensitivity to the ways in which all the interests within a barbershop fit together. "We are as one," Mornot believed, and under his leadership, the CSP generally cooperated with the CSO's efforts to raise wages and reduce the long hours in the salons.[66]

Whatever the *petits patrons'* sense of solidarity with their workers, however, everyone realized that goodwill did not translate automatically into decent wages and humane schedules. Together barbers and their *assistants* searched not for the will but for the way. This proved very difficult to locate, however, for most patrons' slim margin of existence left little over for their employees. In a word, it was the barbershops' meager revenue, rather than any capitalist miserliness, that most relentlessly depressed living standards at the modest end of the trade.

The basic problem lay in the limited commercial opportunities presented by barbering. Men's hairstyles through the second half of the nineteenth and into the twentieth century tended to be simple, practical and cheap: short hair, parted simply on the right side, [sometimes] supplemented with moustaches, beards, and mutton-chops, "to guarantee the masculinity of the wearer."[67] Besides fashion, revenue depended on prices, which varied considerably by neighborhood. In the stylish sixteenth arrondissement in Paris, even unpretentious salons charged between thirty and fifty centimes for a shave and between seventy-five centimes and one franc for a haircut.[68] This was roughly twice what barbershops without a *bourgeois* clientele could ask. Moreover, while the better class of customers might indulge themselves with tonic or cologne,[69] most customers from the popular classes who walked into a barbershop asked for only the simplest services: *barbe et taille*, shave and trim. A Monsieur Ghest, who had once had the good fortune to work as a barber on the cruise ship *Provence*, recounted his disgust with country folk who came to town once a week for a shave. "These week-old beards take more time to soap up than to shave. And for 20 centimes! A haircut with scissors and clippers costs the client another 40 centimes." Who can make a living doing that?[70] The journalist for *Le Rappel*, who wrote the occasional column, "Chez les Coiffeurs," calculated that in order to produce a living wage of eight and a half francs a day in 1900, a worker in an average barbershop had to shave thirty or thirty-five beards at twenty centimes a piece, since many customers did not bother to have their hair cut, which in any case cost only thirty centimes. He concluded that, at the end of a long day, little was left for the patron.[71]

Meanwhile, the costs of doing business continued to rise. Shop owners needed to keep their salons comfortable and clean, and to install electricity and hot, running water as these became available. At the same time, rent, taxes, *patente*, and labor costs increased. The obvious remedy was to raise prices, "more or less equal, if not below, what they were fifty years ago."[72] Yet this was not easy, as coiffeurs' repeated and unavailing attempts to do so demonstrated.

Hairdressers cited two barriers to a remunerative price structure. First, they labored in an overcrowded trade, where businesses competed principally by way of prices. Across the mass of neighborhood barbershops that met the poor man's minimal fashion demands, low prices became the way that coiffeurs chased customers. Ask clients to pay five centimes more for a shave, ten for a haircut, and they would simply take their business elsewhere.

Second, every time patrons proposed a general rise in *tarifs*, the workers objected, reasoning that clients would react by cutting back on tips—that a price increase would, in effect, transfer income from employees to shop owners rather than lifting the entire *métier*. Workers did not oppose higher prices in principal. They insisted, however, that any new price regime guarantee them a share of the new revenues and generally seized on any proposal to raise *tarifs* as an opportunity to campaign for a *salaire minimum* in the profession.

Those who gave advice to hairdressers offered other ways out of the trap of low prices, low profits, and low wages. Monsieur Bussy, writing in the *Journal de la Coiffure* wanted a law to forbid the creation of new *salons de coiffure*; that is, to fight competition with strict regulation. The renowned barber Alfred Spale proposed that coiffeurs should pay closer attention to selling tonics, lotions, combs, razors, colognes, and the like. Sales, not shaves and haircuts, would make the barbershop a profitable enterprise. Indeed, these two prescriptions— corporatist protectionism and vigorous commerce—served throughout the twentieth century as the yin and yang of the trade's salvation. For obvious reasons, the first tended to appeal to the *petits patrons* with a working-class clientele, the second to the more fashionable shops.

As a matter of fact, of all the lines that divided hairdressers— workers from owners, Paris from the provinces, *coiffure-dames* from barbers—the one that separated the profitable *maisons* of the *grands boulevards* from the small, struggling barbershops of the periphery was perhaps the most consequential. It made perfect sense, therefore, that as *patrons coiffeurs* built their own organizations these would reflect the conflicts of interest between *petits* and *gros salonniers*.

The CSP, the main group of hairdressing employers in the capital, became the vehicle of those looking to buoy up prices and reduce the excessive number of hours that most employers were forced to spend in their shops.[73] They found organizing the *patrons coiffeurs* of Paris to be hard going. As it grew, moreover, a rift developed between hairdressers who were *artisans* and those who were *commerçants*. The former looked at the economy as self-employed craftsmen whose prosperity depended on their skilled labor, the latter saw the world as businessmen.[74]

When the CSP ruptured in 1904, however, it was not because of a clash of general perspectives but out of a sharp disagreement over the question of *bureaux de placement*, the labor exchanges that helped *ouvriers coiffeurs* find work. A widespread movement against private *bureaux* "that accepted and even demanded bribes" had broken out in Paris in 1885, and virtually every subsequent list of hairdressers' *revendications* included a call for their suppression. By the end of the century, they had become among the most detested institutions said to be exploiting workers, especially during periods of high unemployment, when those seeking jobs could be shaken down, in effect, by exorbitant fees.

Discontent with the exchanges extended well beyond coiffure, and the National Assembly began to respond to popular sentiment. As a bill passed through the Chamber of Deputies and awaited action by the Senate, however, coiffeurs lost patience with the legislative process that one *ouvrier* called "nothing but a swindle."[75] The affair reached its violent *dénouement* on the afternoon of October 29, 1903. According to *Le Temps*, a crowd of hairdressers and *ouvriers en alimentation* had gathered at the Palais Bourbon, the parliament building, to demand the immediate suppression of the *bureaux*. It then moved on to the Bourse du Travail, where Luquet at his most volatile told his listeners not to wait for the National Assembly but to rid themselves forthwith of the parasitical *placeurs*. The throng spilled out into the street to cries of "vive l'action directe." About half the meeting, 1,500 strong, headed off to the Place de la République. Lepine, the despised prefect of police, had anticipated trouble but not taken sufficient precautions in the face of a huge crowd singing the *Internationale* and screaming of, "Death to the *placeurs*!" Suddenly, *Le Temps* reported, somebody threw a stone, and this sparked off a general mayhem. A pitched battle ensued between the "forces of order" and hundreds of workers armed with stones, sticks, canes, and knives. Some of the demonstrators ducked into surrounding cafés, emerging with broken bottles, chairs, and tables, which they proceeded to fling at police. The police charged the crowd several times, temporarily breaking the onslaught. The wounded lay where they fell. This confrontation lasted several hours, after which fighting began to spread to other locations. At the end of the day, a second, smaller battle occurred at the Bourse du Travail, as police entered to clear it out.[76]

With a different perspective and in purpler prose, *La Voix du Peuple*, described the day as a police riot:

> You had to see the scenes of monstrous savagery that took place to believe them. Saber blows and gunshots cutting down the workers, shattering skulls; the cops advanced in groups of six, knocking down and kicking those poor souls that they managed to grab, behaving no better as they desecrated the [Bourse du Travail] like a troop of savages in a conquered village.[77]

Le Temps recorded only arrests and police casualties: thirty-one of the former and thirty-three of the latter. One policeman had his eye put out. Another was stabbed in the back. The paper wrote nothing about any injuries to the demonstrators. However, according to Charles Desplanques, who had been arrested the previous week for a *sortie* against a placement office, one demonstrator was killed.[78]

Four days after the battle at the Place de la République, the chamber passed a new version of the law dissolving *bureaux de placement* (with compensation) and the Senate followed suit in early January 1904.

For another year there were complaints that *placeurs* were "continuing to exercise their odious commerce." But the gradual if incomplete application of the new law must have had some effect, for the issue faded from the top of the workers' agenda, although it did not disappear entirely.[79]

Ouvriers coiffeurs soon turned their primary attention to other issues, but the battle over *bureaux de placements* left a deep mark on the organized *patronat*. Paris authorities officially closed the placement offices in March 1904. A number of these labor exchanges simply reconstituted themselves as employers' syndicats, this allowed them to continue to charge for placing workers in some of the "better" salons. The most important of these became the Syndicat Amical des patrons coiffeurs, which replaced the big *bureau* on the rue Villedo and represented many of the *gros patrons coiffeurs* who had become disenchanted with the CSP's sympathy for the workers' campaign against the *bureaux*. A second new group of *Indépendant* patrons joined the Fédération des commerçants-détaillants de France—"the retrograde fraction of the *patronat*," according to the *Reveil des Figaros*.[80] Committed to the cause of employers' freedom of action, the Amical and Indépendant groups engaged in a systematic opposition to the application of new labor laws in the hairdressing trades.

These same issues divided *artisans coiffeurs* from *gros* salonniers all across the country. They took institutional form in 1909, when the CSP joined in 1909 with similar groups of *petits patrons* to form the Fédération nationale des patrons coiffeurs de France. With a membership of some 8,000 members, the Fédération nationale stood more or less for the strict application of labor legislation, which it obviously believed would also benefit small-shop owners.[81] The "dissident" employers soon responded. In 1910, they created the Fédération française des patrons coiffeurs, whose primary interest was to see that new laws were applied in ways most favorable to business. Under its founder and president, Ulysse Boucoiran, the Fédération française grew rapidly. By 1911, it claimed to have thirty-one syndicates in fifteen cities, representing 10,000 *patrons coiffeurs*—although this was a gross exaggeration.[82]

It was no coincidence that the second round of organizational activity followed the passage in July 1906 of the *repos hebdomadaire* law, which required employers to give their employees one full day of rest per week.[83] In a profession like coiffure, where days off had been exceedingly rare, the new law received a very warm welcome. *Ouvriers coiffeurs* hailed the "moral and social benefits" it was bound to deliver.[84] *Petits patrons* were sympathetic because they also hoped to benefit from its provisions. Most bigger employers, meanwhile, were already giving their employees a weekly day off. They stayed open by rotating the staff and employing so-called extras.

Supporters of the *repos hebdomadaire* quickly discovered that the devil was in the details, for while most coiffeurs agreed in principle, they fell out over the modalities of application. For example, proponents of the *repos hebdomadaire* had imagined a universal Sunday closure. This did not coincide, however, with the patrons' view on the matter, most of whom wanted Tuesday to be the day of *repos*. As one patron explained to the newspaper *Eclair*: "If workers don't work Tuesday, that was a lost day anyhow. We couldn't even cover our expenses. So [now] the workers won't come in and won't get paid."[85]

Not surprisingly, a patron's preference for *repos* depended on the nature of his business. Jules Guignardat, representing salons in the city center and on the *grands boulevards*, explained that a Sunday closing would pose no difficulty for his constituents, since they did most of their business during the week, when people had reason to go downtown. In contrast, he continued, the *fermeture dominicale* would spell ruin for his colleagues in the neighborhoods. The 70 percent of barbershops that served a working population needed to stay open on Sunday because that was the only day when most of their customers could come in. This incidentally bears out Gary Cross's remark that the worker's weekend implied a weekend of work for those who depended on his business.[86]

In the end, the downtown *maisons* went one way, while the mass of *salons populaires* went another. Formally, the *repos hebdomadaire* meant Sunday off, but the public authorities either tolerated or granted *dérogations* allowing *patrons coiffeurs* to shift the weekly day off to Monday or Tuesday in those neighborhoods where it made sense. This was true not only in Paris but in the cities and towns across France. In Marseille, for example, 90 percent of salons adopted a Monday *repos*—which pointed obliquely to the marginal situation of most Marseillais barbers.[87]

The application of the *repos hebdomadaire* posed another question, which again separated the worlds of business and work. This concerned the reciprocal practices of *roulement* and *repos collectif*. *Roulement* referred to a system where employers could give employees their day off, but not all at the same time. For example, if a barber employed three workers, he could allow each one a different day of *repos* and therefore keep his shop open every day of the week, while respecting the new law. *Repos collectif* denoted a regime that obliged all shops to grant their workers the *same* day off. This was often paired with *fermeture obligatoire*, which required not only that a patron give his *ouvriers* the time off, but that he close his salon entirely.

In the small shops, workers and employers joined in demanding that the government apply the *repos collectif* with *fermeture obligatoire*. But their motives diverged. Workers worried first about protecting their incomes, which would be at risk if employers could keep their shops open while their employees were off. *Petits patrons* reached the same conclusion from a different angle. They were concerned about cheating that would cost them money, or even put them out of business entirely. Take the case where, on one side of the street, a hairdresser worked alone or with only his wife and son and on the other side, a bachelor or widower employed two *assistants*. The first coiffeur could keep his shop open as he liked, since the law on *repos hebdomadaire* did not apply to immediate family members. Meanwhile, the second patron would have to give his workers a *repos hebdomadaire*. He then faced the choice of either closing his shop for the day, which would cost him money, or working by himself, so as not lose customers to his rival, while his employees enjoyed the day off. Such practical considerations taught small-shop owners that without a *fermeture* that was both *obligatoire* and *universelle*, they might *never* enjoy a day off for themselves.

The more substantial *salonniers*, however, saw *repos collectif* and *fermeture obligatoire* as an unwarranted interference with *liberté de commerce*. Their reasoning was simple: as long as hairdressing salons respected each worker's legal right to a *repos hebdomadaire*, why deprive customers of *their* right to be served or the *commerçant's* right to make money? Besides, as Rouger, general secretary of the Syndicat des indépendants, argued to labor minister René Viviani, "The most elementary rules of health and hygiene demand that the public have access to our establishments every day."[88]

These same interests lined up over the issue of *extras*—occasional hairdressers who worked one or two days a week for different salons. Clearly, for those shops wishing to operate normally while some of their workers were off for the day, *extras* were a great asset, even a necessity. The Syndicat amical, successor to a *bureau de placement*, regularly provided *extras* to its members—different *extras* for each salon every week, so as not to fall afoul of the law that forbade their use "d'une manière habituelle."[89]

Conflicting viewpoints sometimes bred violence, and refractory salons occasionally found themselves the target of *comités de vigilance* that roamed the neighborhoods, policing the *repos hebdomadaire* by *badigeonnage*; that is, by throwing acid or whitewash at the storefronts of patrons who violated their sense of the law. One victim, a Monsieur Chesnais, complained to the Paris prefect of police that troublemakers in the nineteenth arrondissement were preparing a campaign of "energetic measures" against so-called *refractaires* such as himself. "This anarchy cannot go on," he protested. And he promised the prefect that he would sleep on a mattress in front of his store, "revolver in hand," lest anyone try to throw acid on *his* store front. He added for emphasis that, "at 30 meters I'm not likely to miss."[90]

There is no evidence that Chenais ever got the chance to test his skill with a pistol, or that anyone was ever seriously hurt in these confrontations. In general, the *repos hebdomadaire* seems to have established itself in the *salons de coiffure* with surprising speed, and the vast majority of hairdressing workers began to feel its benefits. Public authorities, a certain confusion over the rules notwithstanding, showed both firmness in defending the principle and suppleness in applying it, allowing *derogations* where they looked likely to help the majority, and denying them strictly to those seeking individual gain. The 365-day work year soon disappeared from the profession.[91]

Unfortunately, hairdressers achieved no similar breakthrough in the other principal item on their agenda, raising incomes. A *garçon coiffeur* might now have a day off, but he was not apt to spend it doing anything that cost much money. The mass of *petits patrons* probably found themselves in the same position. If they usually had slightly higher incomes than their employees, as *pères de famille* and *hommes d'affaires*, they were also likely to carry heavier obligations. No one had to guess at the problem . . . or the solution. Prices needed to rise; incomes would inevitably follow.

This simple calculation led a coalition of patrons' groups in Paris to launch a campaign for higher prices in the spring of 1907, just as the profession was getting used to the *repos hebdomadaire*.[92] All sides understood that a durable increase in *tarifs* required that all salons apply them. Any significant number of *gâcheurs*, undercutting the new price schedule, would inexorably drive prices back down. In March 1907, therefore, a Union intersyndicale, representing the four principal groups of *salonniers* in the capital, announced that, as of May 1, customers would pay ten centimes more for a shave and twenty more for a haircut. They also agreed to start charging customers for such supplementary services as moustache curling and shaping.

The patrons started trouble, though, when they posted 10,000 leaflets around the capital linking the rise in prices to the disappearance of the tip. The CSO reacted immediately, seeing in the patrons' initiative both an opportunity and a danger. The workers recognized that higher prices could lay the foundation for better wages and appreciated the chance to get rid of the tip, which they found at once degrading and insufficiently remunerative. At the same time, they worried that if the patrons decided not to share the spoils, a new price structure would only make employers richer and employees poorer. To make sure that labor received a fair slice of the bigger pie, the CSO proposed that *ouvriers coiffeurs* trade their tips for a guaranteed minimum wage.

This became the basis for negotiations between the CSO and the Union intersyndicale, which plowed on even as the new *tarifs* began to go into effect, in early April 1907. Over the course of several months, the patrons made offers and the CSO demands without the two parties arriving at any agreement. In June, even as the spirit of compromise seemed to have seized both sides, the talks collapsed when the groups representing bigger employers pulled out. Luquet and his comrades considered a strike to force the issue, but decided that they did not have the strength to win such a test.

This is not, however, what scuppered the campaign for higher prices. The problem was that, in spite of the conspicuous unity of patronal groups, the majority of salons in Paris did not raise their prices as agreed among their *chefs*. A report to the prefect of police found only one employer in the Gare du Nord *quartier* who had applied the new *tarifs* by the end of May. *L'Humanité* reported barely 50 percent compliance. By mid-July, according to the *Petite République*, of those patrons who had raised their prices, nine out of ten had returned to the old rates.[93]

This episode contains a powerful lesson about the obstacles to improving conditions in coiffure. It also illustrates the peculiar nature of the struggle between employer and employee in *petite enterprise*. There is no question that the unprofitable price structure in the trade was the main source of its misery. The employers' greed or their desire to crush the labor movement, while present in some quarters, played no role in depressing *tarifs*. Indeed, the most politically conservative patrons tended to own the biggest, most profitable salons and to pay the highest wages, just as they had consistently granted their employees a *repos hebdomadaire* even before the law mandated it. Meanwhile, the *petits patrons* of the CSP, despite their sympathy for the employees' demands, could offer them only an equal share of the indigence in which they themselves worked.

If there is a villain in this tale, it is the anarchic and unfavorable market for most coiffeurs. The profession was easy to enter because it required only a modicum of *savoir* to shave and cut hair; hence, an excess of *garçons coiffeurs* depressed wages. *Petits salonniers* found themselves in a similar bind, since a man could open a barbershop with a lot less capital than it took to create a *boulangerie* or almost any other storefront business. Overcrowding naturally followed. And when those who consumed this service cared more about price than quality, it placed an irresistible downward pressure on *tarifs*. The leaders of the profession worked diligently to escape this vicious circle of low prices and low incomes; the ill-fated 1907 campaign was a chapter in that generally unhappy story. As long as the supply of shavers and trimmers exceeded the demand from stubbly chins and messy heads, however, prices were unlikely to climb meaningfully.

Unless the public authorities intervened. The *repos hebdomadaire* demonstrates exactly how the state, acting through legislation or some other form of compulsion, could upend the laws of the market. The *pouvoirs publics* were unlikely, however, to help coiffeurs raise *tarifs* by restricting access to the hairdressing trades or enforcing a price floor. While it sometimes proved willing to regulate working conditions, the fundamentally liberal state balked at obstructing the freedom of commerce. Besides, seen from the other side, the status quo provided cheap shaves and haircuts for millions of French citizens and voters.

Thus, low prices continued to afflict a hairdressing profession, which was changing substantially during the Belle Epoque.[94] The population of hairdressers expanded by almost 25 percent from 1896 to 1911, to over 62,000. At the same time, the proportion of *ouvriers coiffeurs* grew from 36 to 43 percent of the *population active*, which implies that the average salon was getting slightly larger. This trend was predictably more robust in the cities. But the process of concentration should not be exaggerated. Even in Paris, 41 percent of coiffeurs still worked alone. Hairdressing remained overwhelmingly the province of highly dispersed tiny shops and petty proprietors.

And of men. From just over 10 percent of hairdressers in 1896, the proportion of *coiffeuses* crept up to 11.4 percent in 1911: 17 percent of patrons and a scant 5 percent of employees.[95] Ladies' hairdressing establishments remained rare. Following the war, the advance of *coiffure pour dames* revolutionized the profession. Before 1914, however, given their minority role in the working population and their almost complete absence from syndical and professional organizations, *coiffeuses* still cast a small shadow on their trade.

The years leading up to the war also witnessed an improvement of working conditions, albiet slow. Some sources report eighty- and ninety-hour workweeks up to 1914. But these were anomalies. The great majority of hairdressers worked fewer hours in 1914 than they did twenty years earlier, although they still remained very long by the standards of the time. Wages rose in much the same way that work hours declined. Official surveys show that *ouvriers coiffeurs* generally earned more in 1911 than they had at the turn of the century. In Paris in the mid-1890s, the average *garçon coiffeur*, *nourri* and *couché*, earned 25–50 francs a month and worked every day of the year. The 1911 Bordereaux des Salaires reported him working 300 days a year for seven francs a day, which nonetheless left hairdressing behind all the other professions in the survey, save potters.[96]

The training of young coiffeurs remained a dog's dinner. In the Old Regime, apprentice barbers had to demonstrate "good morals," as well as professional competence before they could become master barber-surgeons or master barber-wigmakers.[97] By the end of the nineteenth century, however, the *métier* was recruiting young men who had only the most elementary general education. Most fair-sized cities had some sort of *école de coiffure*, often subsidized by the municipality, but these tended to be undersubscribed. *Faute de mieux*, most training went on in the barbershops themselves. Yet apprenticeship, according to most reports, was in a deplorable state. Working fifteen hours a day, fed scraps from the patron's table, lodged in unsanitary conditions in some closet or room "where the promiscuity threaten[ed] to pervert [them]," *apprentis* were treated more like servants than young professionals.[98]

Apprenticeship and *écoles* probably offered young coiffeurs some tuition in how to conduct themselves in the salon. But the general level must have been pretty low, considering the number of how-to manuals that offered guidance on professional deportment. G. Sorignet bade his readers pay attention to "first principles: cleanliness, politesse, and the deportment of a fellow *bien élévé*." Never speak of politics. Be self-effacing, servile, and avoid the casual intimacy and folksy banter of American salons, which fit badly with French manners. Do not show too much zeal, always call clients by their name, and do not *tutoie* the other coiffeurs in front of them. "It is important," he cautioned finally, "that eagerness not degenerate into obsequiousness."[99]

Hector Ledoux and Elie Etienne advised the beginner *assistant* to make himself presentable, neat, and clean: "His manners must be gentle and thoughtful, his language sober and refined, his attitude amiable without being sycophantic." The patron should welcome clients with courtesy and dispatch, neither ignoring nor fighting over them. "Nothing is more vexing," Ledoux wrote, "than to see a professional, seated in a chair, drag himself to his feet, give up with obnoxious regret the journal he was reading, and welcome the client with the air of being disturbed . . ."[100]

They would have hung their heads in shame at the experiences of an English resident in France. H. Absalom informed readers of the *Hairdressers' Weekly Journal* that the French seemed to spend more money on the "fitting and upkeep" of their salons than the English and that he had never "met a really untidy one, and certainly not a dirty one." Absalom was less impressed by the service he commonly encountered. "I have never once had hot water used for shaving," he averred. "It is seldom more than lukewarm." He saved his most serious criticism, however, for French manners, describing his trip to a middle-class salon in the city where he lived:

> When the service was finished, [the barber] remarked as he brushed my tunic: "I take a tip sir, if you please!" He had not given expression to any English previous to this. He announced the price at the desk, one franc fifty cents, and pocketed my thirty cents tip with no better grace than he had waited on me.

Absalom preferred the treatment he received in a "first-class" establishment, where the barber took great care to keep him free of loose hair and to sterilize his instruments. He was offered an excellent selection of *frictions* at the end, paid for by the quantity used, from sixty-centimes to one-franc's worth. He paid 1.25 francs for the haircut and dropped twenty-five centimes in the *tronc*.[101]

*   *   *

Labor histories usually conjure images of grim, determined men in blue overalls and black-tied, cigar-smoking bosses, backed by politicians and armed force. Its epic set pieces are May Day marches and CGT resolutions, scabs, *flics*, and the occasional bloody encounter.

While this tale may fit the reality in some corners of French society, it does not match the experience of employees and employers in *petits établissements*.[102] In this vast sector of French society that includes the hairdressing trades, strikes were predominantly small and short-lived affairs. The forces of repression were more likely to consist of a solitary *gendarme* rousting a small crowd than a police army of intervention.

A two-day strike involving fifty barber assistants or a rock-throwing group of a dozen vigilantes probably does not rise to the level of national drama.[103] Yet it has something important to teach us about working life and social reform in the early Third Republic. The bottom line is that coiffure had no rich, powerful, reactionary Patronat to stand in the way of a decent living for *ouvriers coiffeurs*. The way was blocked instead by an adverse market. The point is worth reiterating because it was such a fundamental fact of life in coiffure: There were too many barbers. Shops competed by means of price and convenience, which spelled both low incomes and long hours. In this atmosphere of chaotic individualism, looser practices inevitably drove out tighter ones. Time after time—sometimes out of greed, often merely for survival—*réfractaires* pulled prices down and made it harder for their rivals to attenuate their own work hours. Only in that relatively restricted corner of the business that served better-off clients did hairdressers surmount these barriers. Where customers happily paid for hot towels, marble sinks, and superior *tonics*, proprietors could make money and workers enjoy satisfactory conditions.

A perfect professional discipline might have overcome the force of the market, and imperfect coalitions of *patrons* and *ouvriers coiffeurs*, provided they were willing to use force, sometimes succeeded in imposing discipline. On the whole, though, hairdressers' experiences suggest the limits of collective action on behalf of social reform. The campaigns for the *repos hebdomaire* and against the placement offices succeeded primarily because they were reinforced by new laws and the public authorities' determination to enforce them. Even Luquet, committed in principle to revolutionary syndicalism, on a daily basis turned to the state for help, which perhaps points us to a larger truth about revolutionary syndicalism.

An intellectual such as Georges Sorel might be able to pursue ideological consistency to envision political action without compromise. For those engaged in the day-to-day conquest of better working conditions, however, consistency was an unaffordable luxury. In this respect, many of those who have written about revolutionary syndicalism have missed the mark. It is to one degree or another a distortion to speak of revolutionary syndicalism as "a cause without rebels," to use Peter Stearns' well-known phrase, or of anarcho-syndicalists as "practical revolutionaries," or to regret as Kenneth Tucker does the CGT's abandonment of a noble ideal and its subsequent turn to a "productivist discourse." In the trenches of social conflict, as Luquet learned, short- and long-term goals coexisted without treachery or hypocrisy. CSO meetings rang with calls for the overthrow of the "bourgeois" state at one minute and discussions about closing refractory barbershops the next. Luquet and his lieutenants alternated revolutionary rhetoric with letters to the ministries and the police prefect. This was neither a contradiction nor a sellout, just tactical good sense.

Consistent or not, the old debates over revolutionary syndicalism passed into irrelevance as the war shifted the ground from under every element of French society—more than most others, from under the hairdressing profession. The world of barbershops was in eclipse. The future of coiffure belonged to the beauty parlor.

52

Simple de forme, somptueuse par son tissu, l'éclat des ornements qui l'enrichissent et l'idéale couleur dont elle se nuance, la robe de soirée actuelle n'exagère pas le décolleté – mais elle est si légère et moule si parfaitement le corps au moindre mouvement qu'elle en révèle admirablement les lignes, sans pour cela devenir impudique.

The "modern woman" of the 1920s

3

The Bob

The thousands of hairdressers who reported for military service in August 1914 probably did not reflect much on the future of their profession. But the war's reputation as a great turning point is well-deserved, and the social changes it set in motion turned the hairdressing profession upside down, pulling large numbers of barbers and their *assistants* out of the salons while bringing in crowds of young women, both as customers and practitioners. The Great War was a personal tragedy for many coiffeurs, but it had a surprisingly benign effect on the profession.

The war shook up the gendered certainties of the Belle Epoque. Fathers, husbands, and sons went off to fight, and in the absence of male companionship and supervision, women of all classes developed a taste for autonomy.[1] Better wages and government subsidies represented a sizeable payment for lower-class families and gave recipients "the chance to take themselves to the cinema, buy themselves a coffee, a glass of wine" and other small amenities without any male company around to share, or even misspend, the family's money, even if the sight of "masterless" women inevitably made some critics uneasy.[2] Autonomy went hand in hand with independence, which the war fostered by opening up unique economic opportunities to women. Female bus conductors and *munitionettes* became clichés of the war experience every bit as much as trenches and gas masks. Whatever job they were doing, women doubtlessly received a lower wage for it than their male counterparts. But this enduring injustice should not obscure the real gains that the war economy brought *ouvrières*.[3]

For hairdressers, a home front full of women with disposable income and relative autonomy represented a huge new pool of potential customers. The possibilities were hard to discern, however, in the summer and fall of 1914. The declaration of war coincided with a moment of particular prosperity for the trade. But the air of optimism quickly dissipated in August 1914. Mobilization left salons in the hands of inexperienced *assistants* and wives or closed them altogether, while the national emergency dealt the peripheral industries of fashion and leisure a sharp blow. Virtually the whole peacetime economy was suspended while the country geared up for a short, intense conflict. The Paris police closed cafés and the Metro at 8 p.m. They shut down theatres entirely. Horse racing stopped in July, as horses were requisitioned for war duty. The Tour de France was suspended. "While the mobilized men risked their lives and suffered in combat," writes Charles Rearick, "the rest of the people felt obliged to show respect by abandoning normal frivolity."[4]

As life on the home front collapsed to its essentials, those who made a living by the inessentials faced bleak prospects. Under the circumstances, hairdressers asked themselves how they could survive the collapse of their customary business. Emile Long advised them to turn back to fundamentals, to "put their pride in their pockets, lower their prices and resolutely attack the less pretentious tasks . . . ."[5] Long's monthly articles in the *Hairdressers' Weekly Journal Supplement* for late 1914 and early 1915 contained a number of ingenious proposals, but their very ingenuity pointed to the desperate state of affairs in the salons. He advised readers to capitalize on the "infants and juveniles" market. He offered instruction on making dolls' wigs and manufacturing "bracelets, chains, rings" and other mementos for departing loved ones out of customers' own hair. Even where fashion survived, the war brought an end to flamboyance. At first Long applauded the simplification of hairstyles. "The effect of the war," he wrote, "will be to banish the excessive exaggerations of Fashion that were approaching almost to folly." Yet in the next breath he warned against "exaggerations . . . in simplicity" that resembled neglect and that ran counter to women's natural inclination to "look after their hair."[6]

It turned out that Long worried needlessly about the remission of women's natural tendencies. For even as he wrote, the fashion instinct was beginning to reassert itself. As the immediate threat to Paris receded, people became used to the war and began to turn back to other things—to the high cost of living, for example, or even just to recovering some sense of routine. As early as July 1915, Long reported the reopening of a "first-class restaurant" in the Bois de Boulogne, catering to "those blessed with wealth," who were generally reviving

Paris society on behalf, it was said, of war charities. But even in the working-class districts of the thirteenth arrondissement, observers noted that "the cinemas everywhere were full . . . 'of essential workers brought back from the front and employed in munitions factories.' "[7]
The fashion industries also felt the initial jolt of war and the subsequent rebound. As hostilities commenced, even famous designers like Paul Poiret closed their couture houses and went off to join the army, while the "ridiculous toilettes" that had been the rage since 1912— "strange and immense hats" and tight skirts "that prevent all movement"—disappeared in the first flush of patriotic severity and sacrifice.[8] As the initial trauma subsided, however, a certain normalcy returned. The government released Poiret from the army. The *Gazette du Bon Ton* and other fashion magazines returned to publication, if less regularly. Claiming to help the war effort by stirring up interest in French *haute couture*, they presented fashion as a patriotic duty in the struggle against Germany.

On the whole, according to historian Valerie Steele, the fashion system operated with surprising normality during the war. Styles gestured at the fighting, introducing items like the "Marseillaise" dress and the "Bersagliere" hat, after Italy joined the Allies, or employing a photograph of a model posed in front of a military map in "a warlike elegance . . . sportive and easy, leaving every gesture free, either to raise the unhappy wounded, or, if need be, to handle a weapon."[9]

More concretely, the war simplified women's *toilettes*. Hemlines rose and "for the first time in the Western world, trousers became acceptable female attire."[10] Fashionable ladies, *Vogue* magazine wrote in 1918, now changed their clothes only once or twice a day, and even "really chic people" dressed with "relative simplicity."[11] Simpler or not, the clothes displayed in *Vogue* were as carefully tailored as ever, and if stylish ladies exchanged their corsets for brassieres and wore short skirts and V-neck sweaters during the day, it was certainly not for work. "The evidence is inescapable," Steele concludes, "that developments in fashion were *not* primarily a response to changing patterns of work and the need for 'practical clothes.' "[12]

Where the war did affect the fashion system was in accelerating the pace of change and passing previous advances in lightness and comfort down the social scale. Corsets had been on the way out for years, shorter skirts and sweaters on the way in. It is only after 1914 that working-class women got rid of *their* corsets and began to enjoy the *certaine libération du corps de la femme*, that had already swept the upper classes before 1914.[13]

Hairdressers' fortunes too traced this trajectory. Long's columns, so desperate in the first months of the conflict, from the middle of 1915 testified to the "normalization" of fashion life. In February 1916, the first shells fired at Verdun coincided with the return of the highly elaborate "1830s style." As the battle drew to a close nine months later, Long described the young women of Paris wearing "coiffures extremely high, skirts excessively short, dresses decidedly *décolletés*, and faces inordinately painted." The return of hanging curls in front of the ear, Long wrote in October 1918, was a way of showing "how the lady of elegance and position was to be distinctive and different in her appearance from her humbler sister . . . ." His interest in the war itself had long since faded to the occasional platitude.

In spite of attempts to make fashion patriotic, extravagance in the midst of that terrible blood-letting produced a backlash. In December 1916, for example, the government decreed that evening dress could no longer be worn in theatres, "which struck a heavy blow at hairdressers who make a specialty of fancy hairdressing." Long did not disguise his disapproval. No matter how grave the situation may be," he argued, "one ought never to prevent persons who have the money from spending it, and even generously." To do otherwise would deprive "thousands of workers of their means of livelihood." Besides, he added, the suppression of fashion would work a particular hardship on women, if their "innate regard for coquetry remains unsatisfied."[14]

The tenacity of the fashion system and the recirculation of the forms themselves should not conceal the substantial changes that occurred. In particular, the war loosened old constraints on the behavior of even middle-class women, especially with respect to what was acceptable in public. Edmonde Charles-Roux, for example, observed that during the war women managed to crash through a number of old social barriers. "Nothing," she extrapolated, "could prevent the war from bringing women what had always escaped them: freedom." And she pointed to the bar at the Ritz Hotel, which for the first time allowed women to enter that famous male preserve.[15] Charles-Roux exaggerated and "freedom" remained incomplete for most women. Nevertheless, the home front leaves us with an impression of young women suddenly enjoying both disposable income and the liberty to spend it as they liked.

Arthur Marwick has written of the "dining-out girls" of wartime London. We could likewise speak of *les jeunes filles à la mode* of wartime Paris, whose new spending habits and updated notions of hygiene opened up tremendous new business opportunities for hair-dressers.[16] By the time of the Armistice, wrote Long with his usual hyperbole, "Parisian work girls and female employees generally have now all acquired the habit of attending the hairdresser's."[17]

This revolution in social practice had a profound impact on the demographic composition of the hairdressing profession. With demand for coiffure growing and so many coiffeurs either away at the war front or drawn to more lucrative jobs, women flooded the salons. This left a serious gap in professional know-how. The ladies' hair-dresser of the nineteenth century had been required to complete a long apprenticeship. He began by learning *postiche*. Then, after consider-able experience with false hair, he next received tuition in hygiene and technical aspects of living hair, and learned to shampoo, brush, comb, and to apply lotions, pomades, powders, and dyes. Finally, the young *coiffeur pour dames* earned the right to start curling hair and execut-ing simple hairstyles, before graduating to serving sophisticated, paying customers.

How different this was from the war years, when young women poured into the *écoles de coiffure*, where they trained for two months, learning the Marcel wave and earning a diploma that could get them a job in a *salon pour dames*. The wives and daughters of absent coiffeurs comprised a large portion of these students. A minority had no previ-ous connection to the trade and merely saw the opportunity to earn a decent income without having to become factory workers. What struck Long most forcefully about these novice *coiffeuses*, however, was their youth. At least half, he estimated, were between thirteen and twenty years old. Indeed, Long claimed to know of girls of fifteen and under, "with their hair still in plaits," who were earning eight francs a day waving hair for ten or fifteen customers. Older wavers could make twice that in a day.[18]

René Rambaud, who was at the center of these developments, wrote that, by the end of the war Paris had more than 2,000 *maisons dames*, employing nearly 3,000 workers—compared to a dozen *maisons* with hardly fifty workers in 1889, and 300 ladies' *salons* with fewer than 2,000 workers in 1909.[19] Official figures bear him out. By 1921, coiffure had lost almost 10 percent of its *effectifs* in ten years. This without question represented a mass closing of marginal barbershops. Conversely, the number of *coiffeuses* increased by more than 3,000, and they now made up 18 percent of the *population active* in coiffure; 24 percent of *chefs d'établissement*. The change was excep-tionally sharp in the capital, where women now constituted 30 percent of the 11,150 hairdressers. *Coiffeuses* also made up a considerable part of *isolés*, doing hair without actually being able to set up their own *établissements*—probably operating out of their apartments or some other makeshift space.[20]

In addition to the young women who now worked as *coiffeuses pour dames*, thousands of barbers traded in their razors and *tondeuses* for the better sales and more regular work of ladies' hairdressing. The majority of them transformed their already tiny shops into *salons mixtes*, maintaining decorum by drawing a curtain between the two chairs, "in order to spare [ladies] the malign curiosity of the gentlemen."[21]

This new population of ladies' hairdressers, raw recruits and converted barbers, once more received advice from the old guard about how to comport themselves with their female clients. Arvet-Thouvet reminded them that commerce was a war between client and *commerçant*. But do not push it too hard, he warned. Argumentation might win a point, but it would lose the game.[22] Be clean and intelligent, smart but not outrageous, admonished Pierre de Rieucros. Dress neatly but modestly, counseled the *Coiffure de Paris*. If you smoke, wash the nicotine off your hands and take "cachou" bonbons for your breath. Do not talk too much, because *bavardage* with a female client is "infinitely worse than being a bad worker." Especially avoid such volatile subjects as politics or religion. Instead, wrote Hector Malacarne, talk to the client in the same way that a doctor or pharmacist would talk to a patient: When a customer complains about dandruff, for example, use the occasion to sell her a bottle of "special lotion X." Or tell her: "Why keep your hair flat and plastered to your skull when it needs suppleness and lightness to be healthy? A permanent, madame, would flatter your face, permit your skin to breathe, and regenerate your hair?"[23] Ambitious ladies' hairdressers might also consider changing their names, aping their colleagues in the chic *maisons* with a "clientèle snob," where a Joseph or a Léon might rechristen himself Gérard, Roland, or Guy; and Jeanne and Louise might become Arlette, Christiane, or Huguette.[24]

Having been trained so quickly, and lacking technical experience and professional *savoir faire*, the "war-emergency female hairdressers" mostly stuck to waving hair. From an aesthetic perspective, Long was quite critical of the work taught in the *écoles* and performed in the *salons d'ondulation*, as he called them. At the school demonstrations he attended, Long found that the students burned a fair bit of the hair they waved. In the cheap salons, he blanched at "waving [that] has a special character of its own, which can be recognized from afar: a sort of rigid, set, regular groove, very pronounced and so formal that it can be compared to the effect seen in woodcarving."[25] Yet as they gained experience, these young *coiffeuses* expanded their skill and improved their technique. By the end of the war, although they never really mastered the "dressing" of hair, they were learning shampooing, *teinture*, and the placing of *postiche*—because, Long explained, their customers demanded it.

The war did not kill demand for *postiches*, and Long estimated that, by 1918, 75 to 80 percent of French women were wearing some bit of false hair. Traditionally, *postiche* had been where *coiffeurs pour dames* exercised their greatest skill and creativity, and where they earned their greatest profits. At the top of the market, even during the war, elite ladies of fashion could still buy from Cuverville, Jourliac, or Antoine *postiche* that "ha[d] acquired . . . a degree of perfection which can scarcely be surpassed, because it equals the highest natural qualities of artistic attractiveness."[26] But such masterpieces did not come cheaply. A fashionable *dame* might pay 500 francs for such a creation. A step down the scale, a woman of means could find a *postiche* for between 250 and 400 francs. Even the far-from-elite D. Simon, sold his *postiches* for up to 150 francs.[27]

Of course, the vast majority of *françaises* could not afford even Simon's prices. Besides, the mass of newly minted ladies' hairdressers had received no tuition in *postiche*. Both sides found the perfect solution to this dilemma in the *prêt-à-porter postiches* that allowed customers with limited means to buy ready-to-wear *postiches* from their hairdressers. Or they might go to a haberdasher's or a department store, where women on a budget could find mass-produced false hair at low prices—a textbook example of artisanal manufacture surpassed by industrial production.

Long's business side considered the ready-to-wear *postiches* from the "trade houses" and "drapery establishments" to be "rather a convenient idea" for middle-class ladies, but the artist in him recoiled in horror from what he saw on the heads of the masses. He described with palpable distaste the small, frizzy, wavy pieces bought by "many coquettes possessing no personal taste and to whom it would be impossible to sell *postiche* of the latest design and make." They used, he wrote, "common hair" and harsh processes, such as glue diluted in boiling water. This inevitably produced hairpieces that kept their shape but looked terrible, and which, "by their inartistic, inelegant and defective [qualities] create[d] amongst the public a disgust for *postiche* work generally."[28]

As the enduring taste for *postiche* illustrates, while almost everyone acknowledged the need for restraint during wartime, many women from across the social spectrum continued to apply themselves to being stylish—if in a relatively subdued manner. The end of the war, however, released the fashionable classes from whatever inhibitions had held them back. The celebrity galas and "Victory Balls" that followed the Armistice carried caprice to new heights.

Long, whose eminence gave him entrée to many of these affairs, wrote, "Wartime simplicity is commencing to disappear and make way for *grande coquetterie* and luxury . . . ." He described what he called the "Restoration mentality" that he likened to the post-Robespierre days of the *Merveilleuses*, extravagant and *déshabillées*: "Ladies reveal their shoulders; corsets have, so to speak, disappeared; and the habit of applying a depilatory beneath the arms has been acquired." Skirts were short, stockings sheer or even absent, legs made smooth by the safety razors now in every lady's toilette cabinet—and this "in spite of the unheard-of prices of everything."[29] Not everyone was so pleased. Writer Catherine Hartley, to name one critic, winced at the "uncontrollable" behavior and depraved moral condition exhibited at these parties: young women smoking, drinking, and swearing.[30]

Amidst the glitter and activity of these postwar celebrations, several things caught Long's eye. First, whereas prewar society had revolved around *grandes dames*, the new queens of fashion were the "young and very modern ladies of elegance whom the men of wealth dote over." Long watched them "parade the streets with bare arms, bare legs and short hair, frizzed like little school boys . . . in pyjamas, their hair cut short, smoking cigarettes and looking very much like little boys escaped from college."[31] Second, the styles affected by those young women who danced and flirted their nights away at the victory galas differed dramatically from those that had reigned before the war. Expressing the new ideal of slender sensuality, they emphasized the natural, uncorseted figure and linear silhouette that "liberated the body and facilitated movement," in light and washable fabrics such as cotton and silk, and in patterns drawn from cubism and futurism. Dashing, slender, daring, discreet, charming, demure: these were the adjectives that *Vogue* most often employed to describe the fashions of 1920.[32]

Curiously enough, the new styles took the great designers largely by surprise. Most *couturiers* at the war's end immediately reached back to the fashions of the Belle Epoque. Paul Poiret was among those who tried to recapture the past. As Chanel made her clothes simpler, straighter, and blacker, Poiret's became more "audacious," more colorful, more "bizarre": for example, "evening dresses lit up from the inside by miniature electric light bulbs attached to tiny batteries."[33] He criticized Chanel's designs, expensive but not ostentatious, for "making duchesses look like shop girls." "Misérabilisme de luxe," he quipped famously. Yet Poiret, so influential before the war, never got a feel for the 1920s and closed down his *couturier* business in 1929.[34]

The last thing that Long noticed was what he referred to as "this freakish whim" for short hairstyles. When high society gathered at the Opéra in January 1919 to mark the coming of peace, the names were the same as they had been before the war: Polignac, Clermont-Tonnerre, Chabrillan, et cetera. But the queens of French society arrived now with *cheveux courts*.[35]

The subsequent notoriety of the bob—or the "Eton Crop," "Ninon," or "Jeanne d'Arc," it acquired many names—led several individuals to assert their claim to authorship. Antoine took credit for having launched the "coupe à la Jeanne d'Arc" when in 1909 he cropped the hair of Eve Lavallière, in order to fit the forty-year-old actress to the part of the eighteen-year old heroine of *L'Ane de Buridan*. "Something just clicked in my head, and I decided the time had come for *cheveux courts*, he explained."[36] Another legend featured the young Gabrielle "Coco" Chanel. It seems that one evening in 1917, when Chanel was getting ready to attend the opera, her gas heater exploded near her head, leaving her hair singed and smoky. With audacity, for which she soon became famous, Chanel took her nail scissors and cut off her braids. Appearing at the opera with short hair and hip-waisted, short dress, she caused a great stir. The next day, so the fable goes, actresses Misia Edwards and Celia Sorel, who had seen her the previous evening, went to visit Chanel to have their own hair cropped with the now-celebrated scissors.[37] Other genealogies attributed the bob's inspiration to American nurses who brought the style with them to France during the war.

The truth of the matter is that short hairstyles captured the public's fancy in a more gradual and anonymous manner. In 1908 Poiret had already broken dramatically with convention when he chopped his models' hair for that year's collection. And cropped hair had long been the signature of "les marginales, les théâtreuses, les bohèmes." The writer Colette, dancers Irene Castle and Isadore Duncan, and the actress

Iris Storm, were already sporting bobs well before World War I. Its adoption by the young lionesses of Paris society, and especially the publicity it received from the likes of Antoine and Chanel, helped propel the bob to fashion prominence. But it had no author as such.[38]

Long's articles first mentioned "the boy coiffure, so much wished for by some ladies" in March 1911. The subject then disappeared until 1917, when he began to pay short hairstyles serious attention. In May of that year, Long observed that the "smart set" were embracing this "horrible fashion [for] 'masculine women' "—although even so-called short styles remained a foot long and eminently dressable. As late as February 1919, when the bob was attaining "epidemic proportions," Long was still campaigning against a coiffure that he thought made "women, with their overdone make-up and peculiar headdresses, look more like clowns straight from the circus than any category of female."

Several months later, reminding himself that short hairstyles were only "a passing fashion, and one which is already beginning to pass," Long speculated on the genesis of *cheveux courts*. Short hairstyles, he wrote, were rooted in women's recent experiences and political ambitions. Just as "short coiffures appeared after the Terreur [of the French Revolution], Notre-Dame de Thermidor* had short hair, and the beautiful ladies who escaped the guillotine wore their hair *à la victime*, the present taste for *cheveux courts* derived from the trauma of war and the Russian Revolution."[39] In any case, Long could console himself with the reflection that the bob had not succeeded in monopolizing fashionable postwar heads. Not yet.

Between 1918 and 1920, Long's articles chronicled a fabulous variety of hairstyles. Most were high and light but more extravagant than ever. He saw "Grecian" styles with hanging curls, the "Egyptian" style "with its coiffures of Cleopatra and the priestess of Isis," and *coiffures de soir* replete with turbans, pearls, and "feathers [that] appear to come out of the ears, and the horizontal position makes them a source of annoyance to people sitting next to the wearer."[40]

In Deauville, during race week in the summer of 1920, Long unhappily reported the return of the *mode à la chinoise*: pulled back, flattened down, low chignon fastened with a clip. He saw "a dozen eccentric young women" gallivanting about the resort town with "long Oriental pendants [hanging] from the ears; head and arms bare, and a walking stick in their hands," sporting *chinoise* hairstyles. Long remarked with some relief that these *outrées* had failed "in rallying the majority of their sex to their bad example." Still, he fretted:

... they are young and pretty, enjoy an aristocratic following, and are in the front rank of society folk—driving superb automobiles during the day and wearing much jewelry in the evening, besides losing fantastic sums at the casino—the crowd follows them and endeavors to copy their example as far as possible.[41]

The "Chinoise" posed no mortal threat to hairdressers. At worst, it might have hurt coiffeurs for a season or two, until some other, probably more profitable, vogue replaced it. More threatening to the future of hairdressing than any momentary fad was the secular trend toward *cheveux courts* then working its way from the *têtes dorées* of the "Victory Balls" through the rest of *la société féminine française.* Coiffeurs watched with horror as more and more women walked into their salons and demanded short hairstyles, which often dispensed entirely with *ondulations* and the other kinks and forms that had made her hairdresser precious to the woman of style. Even less radical variations of *cheveux courts* seemed to imperil the profession. The Dondels, Dupuys, and others who had reigned in the kingdom of *cheveux longs* worried that without long tresses to coif hairdressers would lose their principal means of artistic expression and commerce. Besides, many of the old-timers did not even know how to use a scissors, only how to arrange large tresses of hair.

The trade journal *Coiffure de Paris*, among others, tried to organize a counterattack: "Coiffure is dying!" admonished the frontispiece of December 1920: "At the theatre, in offices, everywhere women are not longer *coiffées*. Short hairstyles have led to flat styles. The coiffeur no longer styles, no longer waves . . . We must react . . ." And it offered a prize of 5,000 francs for a new coiffure that might "erase every trace of this nefarious fashion."[42]

Hairdressers' disdain for short hairstyles looks pale compared to the ferocious attacks directed at this mode *peu féminine* by religious authorities, natality experts, and social conservatives in general, who looked at cropped hair and saw not bad business but a veritable "civilization without sexes."[43] The refusal "to utter the word 'obey' in the Marriage Service," read an English tract deploring the new styles, "the wearing of men's apparel while cycling, the smoking of cigarettes, and the 'bobbing' of the hair are all indicative of one thing! God's order is everywhere flouted."[44]

The Catholic Church took no official stand on *cheveux courts*, but the *Grande Revue* recounted the story of Gonzague Truc, who went to consult an abbot about the new fashions. "Although the Church only treads with repugnance into the beauty salon," the abbot told Truc, "we will not shorten by a centimeter the skirts and hair of our *pénitentes*," and he quoted Saint Paul himself on the shame of a woman with short hair. The abbot regarded the bob as a stalking horse for women's equality, which he found "unnatural" and "abominable." His fellow prelate, Monseigneur Joseph of the Sarthe, was concerned enough to have a notice posted on all the churches in his diocese, warning the laity against "this despicable style that [was] so prevalent at the . . . time, being inspired by freemasonry and having as its aim, and often for its result, the paganization of the Christian woman."[45]

Doctors of hygiene, aesthetics, and medicine also weighed into the battle against *cheveux courts*. The *Coiffure Française Illustrée* preached the hygienic advantages of long hair: "Hair has as its mission," it cautioned, "the protection of the scalp against the invasion of germs from the outside." An advertising campaign for *Lavona* lotion added that "one of the drawbacks of the current style is its tendency to provoke hair loss." In a similar vein, a "physiologist," who wished to remain anonymous, warned that in cutting their hair short women "violated their nature" and that Nature would have its revenge. He believed that since cutting hair made it fall out more easily, short hairstyles would eventually leave Western women as bald as men. He went on to cite "even more sensational news" from England, where "practitioners have observed that the habit of cutting hair has the effect of stimulating the growth of facial hair," as the "capillary vitality" suppressed by the coiffeur's scissors reasserted itself on other parts of the female body. In other words, cutting their hair would make women more likely to grow beards.[46]

In addition to inducing baldness, facial hair, and eternal damnation, short hair set off legal action and family disputes. *Le Matin d'Anvers* carried a story in 1924 of a local coiffeur who cut a young woman's hair *à la calotte* and was subsequently sued by her mother. Tales abounded of the reactions of outraged husbands and fathers. One husband locked his wife in the house because she had cut her hair; a father allegedly killed his daughter for the same reason. René Rambaud claimed to know two families, who, even after twenty years had failed to reconcile with the young bride, who, feeling that she no longer needed her parents' permission, had cut her hair short after her wedding.[47]

The climax of fear and loathing arrived with the publication in 1922 of Victor Margucritte's novel, *La Garçonne* [*The Bachelor Girl*]. Briefly, *La Garçonne* told the tale of Monique Lerbier, a Beautiful-Idealistic-Young-Woman-Caught-in-a-Hypocritical-Bourgeois-World. On the eve of her arranged marriage, Monique, nineteen years old, discovered that her fiancé had been unfaithful. Bitter and disillusioned, she abandoned the cad, left home, cut her hair very short, dressed in men's clothes, and immersed herself in a life of unbourgeois excess. She even attempted to conceive a child out of wedlock with a succession of handsome *hommes du monde* and indulged in lesbian romances—all in the name of emancipation. Finally, Monique met her soul mate, a young man who believed in women's equality and accompanied her to feminist meetings, and the two of them lived happily ever after.[48]

The public loved the book, and it brought Margueritte a financial bonanza. His earlier work of "engaged" fiction, *Prostituée*, had sold 80,000 copies. But *La Garçonne* truly hit a popular nerve and sold up to 7,50,000 by the time the wave crested. This is not to say that *La Garçonne* pleased everyone, however. Critics dismissed it as "three hundred pages of pretty dull pornography."[49] Literary objections aside, the novel became a convenient lash for flogging a host of partisan causes. The Communist Georges Ponsot claimed to read the "inept monetary policy" of the Bloc National in the story of Monique Lerbier. On the other side of the political aisle, the book's "subversive" message got Margueritte ejected from the Legion of Honor, on the grounds that *La Garçonne* was pornographic, and taken to court by the Ligue des Pères de Famille, which cited the book's deleterious effect on French families. A film version of the book, produced in 1923, was banned for threatening "une déformation déplorable" of public morals.[50]

Neither the wagging finger of Authority nor the coiffeurs' search for alternative fashions had the least effect. French women in the early 1920s, like women across the Western world, continued to visit *salons de coiffure* to have their hair cut. Moreover, as ladies' hairdressers gave in to their customers' wishes and reached for their scissors, their apprehension began to fade, for short hairstyles delivered not misery but unprecedented prosperity. The young *coiffeuse* in Louise Vanderwielen's *Lise du Plat Pays*, complained to her aunt that she could not afford a day off because she was inundated by "all the

women, one after the other, [who] are getting their hair cut."[51] Even in
the countryside, wrote Robert Dieudonné, "young girls can no longer
find a beau if they don't affect city airs and look like movie stars."[52]

If hairdressers had initially opposed cropped hair, it was because
they assumed that women's short hairstyles would come to resemble
men's: simple and low-priced. They did not. Even the market for *postiches* remained vibrant. For the *après-midi*, the *Coiffure de Paris*
noted, the fashionable-young-woman-on-the-go, slipping out of her
tennis clothes and into her evening gown, could use a graceful but discreet bit of false hair to make herself quickly presentable. And a chic
little *postiche*, *Vogue* advised its readers, could lend "dignity" to hair
that was otherwise *trop garçonnier*.[53]

Improvements in permanent-wave technology made an even more
integral and profitable contribution to the vogue for *cheveux courts*.
Permanent waves allowed short hairstyles to remain stylish and feminine. They therefore permitted a woman to be *bien coiffée* with just a
few strokes of her hairbrush.[54] The first *machines à l'indéfrisable*, built
before the war, had been neither reliable nor practical enough to
attract a mass following. Recall French hairdressers' tepid reaction to
Charles Nestlé's clumsy and possibly dangerous apparatus in 1909.
Ingenious and technologically inclined hairdressers, however, continued to tinker with Nestlé's conception, and they made substantial
progress. In 1918, working in London, the entrepreneurial Eugene
Sutter unveiled his own new edition of the permanent-wave machine,
the "Eugene." Like Nestlé's original, Sutter's model still had the flat
cylindrical top and long electric tentacles. But it worked much more
quickly, used less electric current, and left "an absence of steam on the
head [that] obviated the need for fans and other generators of cold
air." Best of all, the "Eugene" replicated the prettiest "marcel" *ondulation*, while its dependability eliminated "the risk of curling like a
poodle dog a head of hair which required only a few large and soft
waves."[55]

The father of the French *machine à l'indéfrisable* was Gaston
Boudou. Born in 1870, son of a coiffeur, Boudou moved to Paris in
1893, following his marriage. Early in the new century, Boudou joined
the small cast of top-flight expatriate *coiffeurs pour dames* in London,
when he accepted an offer to become director of the renowned
Maison Emile. After his patron retired and Boudou took over the
Maison Emile, he built "the largest *maison de coiffure* in London and
without doubt in Europe," where he looked after "toute l'aristocratie
anglaise" and the royal family. In 1908 he launched himself into the

pastiche business and four years later began the research operation that produced "Inecto" hair coloring. During the war, Boudou served as an interpreter attached to the British Expeditionary Force, along with his son Félix. In 1919, he returned to Paris and founded the Parisian edition of the Maison Emile at 400, rue Saint-Honoré, in what had once been Robespierre's apartments.[56]

Impressed with the success of Nestlé and Sutter, Boudou went to work on his own permanent-wave machine, and not long after his return to Paris he introduced the first French *machine à l'indéfrisable*, the *Gallia*. Boudou's *appareil* once again represented a technical step forward. He began by putting rubber into the *Gallia*'s rollers [*bigoudis*], which kept steam from escaping and allowed him to lower the temperature. He developed an *enrouleur automatique* to simplify and speed up the process of rolling the hair into *mèches* and added his secret lotion *boncella* to fortify hair while it boiled and to give it more body afterward. Boudou's most inspired decision, and the one that helped make the *Gallia* the best-selling French permanent-wave machines, was to hire René Rambaud to be the principal spokesman for his company.[57]

The young Rambaud had first unpacked his ambitions in fin-de-siècle Paris, a working-class lad from the Vendée who had left school at eleven. As a *pis-aller*, a last resort, he had found a place as an apprentice barber in a small shop and subsequently spent three "miserable" years in Nantes as barber's assistant before setting off to Paris in search of fortune. Rambaud never noted, nor has anyone else ever recorded, where the eager young man found his first job in the capital. Perhaps his skill and confidence, the foundations of his future celebrity, earned him a desirable post in a bourgeois salon, where he might have made a decent living and shown off his abilities. More likely he took a job in one of the small, grotty barbershops of which the city was so full.[58]

Either way, Rambaud quickly began to make his mark on the profession. His first experiences as a *garçon coiffeur* had led him to the Bourse du Travail, where he entered the orbit of Alexandre Luquet, general secretary of the Hairdressing Workers Federation (FNSOC) and rising star in the CGT. "Hooked" by Luquet, Rambaud quickly became his protégé and threw himself into the syndical movement. The Parisian CSO—"de tendance syndicaliste revolutionnaire"— elected Rambaud its secretary in 1908.

At the same time as he kept an eye on the class struggle, Rambaud devoted himself to the aesthetic and commercial aspects of his profession. Indeed, he believed that art and skill were the foundation of his métier and the building blocks of professional fortune. He considered the days spent as a militant syndicalist of a piece with his evenings at the École parisienne de la coiffure, studying with Emile Long and teaching young coiffeurs the latest fashions and the rudiments of business. Service to the profession was his philosophy: "Renvoyez l'ascenseur" ("Send the elevator back down"), he used to remind his colleagues.[59]

Rambaud served at the front from 1914 to 1917 until he returned home to work with Albert Thomas and Paul Ramadier on provisioning and labor issues. At war's end, Rambaud joined Gaston Boudou at the Maison Emile. There he edited the treacly *Gallia Journal* that Boudou published as publicity for his *machine à l'indéfrisable* and directed the free Gallia clinics that Boudou organized to teach French coiffeurs how to exploit his new invention. By the end of 1928, Gallia had training sites and corporate representatives on four continents and owned the new world-record for an *ondulation indéfrisable*: twenty-nine minutes and thirty seconds, by Jules Agg.[60]

It was while preparing a campaign for the *Gallia* that Rambaud hit upon his own singular contribution to modern hairdressing, the *mise en plis*, or pin-curl. In what quickly became one of the standard techniques of hairstyling, Rambaud took hair that had just been "permed" and was still wet, and set it in little curls [*boucles*] held by pins before drying it. He could thus control the shape of the permanent wave. Performed by a qualified hairdresser, the *mise en plis* took only four to five minutes and saved time on later *ondulations*. More critically, a coiffeur could charge twice as much for a *mise en plis* as for an *ondulation simple*. Rambaud's new procedure turned him from a promising young coiffeur into a professional star.[61]

The *Gallia* made Boudou a very rich man, selling permanent-wave machines that cost over 1,000 francs each at a moment when they were finding their way into virtually every hairdressing salon in Europe. Other manufacturers followed Boudou's lead. Jean Leclabert, who had made his reputation in *postiches*, contacted Alsthom-Thompson, and their collaboration led to the introduction of the Perma Standard in 1925. Franz Stroher brought out the Wella, in 1927. The Schwartzkopf machine appeared the next year, the Regina in 1934. An advertisement for the Gaston quoted prices that ran from 950 francs for a device with six heaters to over 5,000 francs for an instrument with thirty-two *chauffeurs*.[62] All of them promised handsome returns for a substantial capital investment.

Each model incorporated some improvement: lowering the temperature of the acid solution, producing suppler, more attractive waves, reducing the time spent in harness from two-and-a-half hours in 1923 to less than ninety minutes at the end of the decade.[63] Meanwhile, the improved efficacy of the devices allayed women's initial fears of the process, although a session under one of these "electrical appliances" never became completely risk-free, and a badly done "perm" could still cause hair to fall out in "fistfuls."[64]

The technological advance of the permanent wave was undeniable, and it brought women into the salons in unprecedented numbers to pay extraordinary sums to have their follicles violently flattened and twisted. The usual price for a first-class perm was ten francs per *mèche* (curler). Most heads required between thirty and fifty *mèches*, running a customer's cost to well over 300 francs. As hair grew out, of course, it lost its curl, which obliged clients to return for a full treatment under the *machine à l'indéfrisable* about every six months. In the interim, a good "perm" required a weekly visit to the coiffeur for perking up with a "water wave." The process was so highly remunerative that hairdressers toyed from time to time with the idea of introducing "perms" to men's hair, since they figured that fashionable men also wanted to look handsomer, younger, more athletic, and even a bit *coquette*. But the *indéfrisable masculine* never took off.[65]

The permanent wave, by adding an extra element of stylishness to cropped hair, helped to raise the hairdressing profession to unparalleled heights of popularity and affluence. It happened all over the urban, industrial world. French expatriate, R. Louis, wrote from the United States in 1924 that cropped hair, "resolutely and insistently demanded by clients" had made his fortune. His shop had grown from eight assistants (six *coiffeuses*, two coiffeurs) to twenty-eight (ten *coiffeuses*, eighteen coiffeurs) in two years, and they all now earned twice as much as they did before *cheveux courts*.[66] The same was true in France. "Scissors were clicking away profitably," wrote Hector Ledoux, "[and] elegant women did not go two weeks without seeing their hairdresser to freshen up their coiffures, providing ample opportunity to sell our products." The *Coiffure de Paris*, which only a few years before had been offering a reward for their defeat, recognized that *cheveux courts* "brought hairdressers two to three times more business" than *cheveux longs*.[67] Moreover, as Paul Gerbod suggests, the increasing amount of time a woman now needed to spend in the salon provided the perfect opportunity for launching the *soins connexes* of manicures and facials, which had become established in the better salons just before the war.[68]

The woman who entered one of these small "temples d'hygiène et de beauté" in the 1920s to have her hair cropped, colored, and "permed" could well have marveled at the luxury and technology at her disposal. The Paris Archives contain a photograph album belonging to Claude Anthonioz, proprietor of Chez Claude, one of the most elegant of Paris *maisons*, located just off the Boulevard Montmartre.[69] Signs painted on the display windows announced that English, German, Spanish, and Italian were all spoken inside, along with French. The frontage was done in marble and art deco, which also dominated the interior. Inside, customers discovered a sumptuous *salon pour hommes*. Big leather armchairs, each in front of its own mirror and shelved work station and separated by marble pillars, sat in a semicircle on tiled mosaic floors. The waiting area off to the side was furnished with a leather sofa and wrought-iron hat racks. The sinks were in dark marble, with tilted basins and brass faucets. Just above them sat carefully arranged rows of tonics and fragrances for men. The *salon des manicures*—six francs for a manicure, ten for a pedicure—also contained marble-topped tables, leather armchairs, and a spacious display of brushes, razors, and powders. The *comptoir de ventes* on the other side of the *vitrine d'exposition* offered bottles of cologne in all kinds of interesting shapes.

While the men were serviced shoulder to shoulder in a big room, Chez Claude attended to its female clients in a *salon pour dames* that provided each woman with her own *cabine*, replete with velvet armchair, sink, toiletries, brushes, and a gleaming *sechoir* to dry her hair. Outside the *cabines de dames* were more *vitrines d'exposition*, with an array of beauty products for sale. The separate *cabine pour indéfrisables* was equipped like the other stations, but with a permanent-wave machine at the center, all metal dome and dangling electric wires, looking like a prop for a cheap *Frankenstein* movie. Such luxury represented a sizable investment. It was a long way from the cane chairs and straight razors of the turn-of-the-century barbershop.

Whether they emerged from an expensive treatment at Chez Claude or a cheap and cheerful trip to the neighborhood *salon mixte*, *cheveux courts* became the badge of the modern woman. Observers disagreed about the significance of close-cropped heads and hip-waisted dresses, but few failed to recognize their importance. Indeed, we know that women's short hairstyles were exceptional precisely because of the controversy and excitement they stirred up. Most coiffures passed quickly and left the wider society untouched, but cropped hair was a profoundly different matter: "[N]ot simply a fashion," wrote the *haute coiffeur* Léon Agostini, "it is something more tenacious, that has sunk roots in our mores, in the demands of modern life, in the spirit of the modern woman . . . ."[70]

The "flapper" constitutes the most enduring and evocative image of the "roaring twenties." And because the bob played such a fundamental role in shaping and defining the "new woman," the hairdressing profession afforded a privileged view of her. Begin with two basic facts. First, while women's hair became shorter in the early 1920s, it did not become simpler or cheaper. Women consequently began to spend more money on their coiffures. Second, even while each woman was spending more on her *toilette*, vastly greater numbers of women began visiting *salons de coiffure*. All this amounts to saying that the rising fortunes of the hairdressing profession rested on a much larger development: an explosion in the demand for stylish things.[71]

As long as short hair sat only on fashionable heads, nothing fundamental had changed. *Garçonnes* at the races and the seaside resorts might have shocked some stodgy sensibilities. But as shock was the very coin of celebrity in these circles, the craze for *cheveux courts* was just another inning in the old game played by the consuming classes. Only when millions of *françaises* from the middle and lower classes cropped their hair, did a hairstyle become a cultural revolution. The significance of the bob thus lay not in a particular length or shape of hair, but in the collapse of the old social frontiers of fashion.

The new fashion economy certainly did not erase class distinctions, which remained embedded in the differentiated market for stylish hair, yet it emphasized the democratic principal that *every* woman could be well turned out. Ten-franc "marcels," appealing to those women who "have neither the time nor the means of imitating completely their more elegant sisters," off-the-rack *postiches*, cheap but relatively safe *teinture*, mass-market combs, and generic cosmetics: credible versions of fashion became available at popular prices.[72]

Also, the new styles did not directly play to women's desire for practicality and convenience. Women no doubt needed relief from the heavy, formal styles of the fin-de-siècle. Yet it is by no means obvious that cropped hair and the rest of it really answered that need, since even if the social elites who pioneered the fashion wore loose-fitting clothing and short hair, it was certainly not for work. Moreover, the new styles did not really serve utility and sportiness very well: high heels, for instance, or sheer hose, or merely "the psychologically taxing problems of looking comfortable and dressing simply while being rather exposed."[73] Finally, short hair did not in fact deliver much convenience, since time saved in the *corvée matinale* was bought with extra hours at the beauty salon.

If she was not practical, however, the "new woman" was undeniably youthful. Between 1900 and 1920, the "fashionable ideal of serpentine slimness" replaced the hourglass shape and the layers of imprisoning material that had plagued the Edwardian dame. The new fashions, wrote Valerie Steele, minimized "matronly" breasts in favor of "long . . . straight . . . shapely" and nubile legs, producing a figure that was "not so much boyish as the style of a sophisticated schoolgirl."[74] Whereas her mother had done her best to look "mature," the "flapper" worshipped at the altar of youth. She dressed in the "poorboy" designs of the hottest new *couturière* Coco Chanel and wore her revolutionary new perfume, "No. 5." She drove sports cars, played tennis and golf, and danced the night away.[75] Clearly, for the immense majority of *françaises*, life never became a round of morning drives, afternoon golf dates, and evening balls. In the matter of style, however, the ideal of athletic youth exercised a powerful attraction on women, and a close-cropped haircut suggested a sporty, coquettish lifestyle even if it did not correspond to one.

Above all, the new fashions symbolized youth and vigor; that is, young women self-consciously distinguishing themselves from their mothers. "Our mothers' generation," wrote *La Mode Illustrée* in 1922, "was ignorant of sporting activity . . . but how it has taken hold of ours!" Maria Vérone's tribute to her young readers associated vitality with authenticity: "The women who preceded us gave a poor example of false hair, phoney sentiments, marriage without love, homes without intimacy. [Whereas] we wear *cheveux courts* and clothes that don't restrict us, and we want to have careers in order to be independent."[76]

Youth was also the link between the symbolic and the socioeconomic significance of *cheveux courts*, for in cropped hair the ethic of youthfulness met pecuniary opportunity. It might be argued with some conviction that the vogue for women's short hair marks the moment where young women began to replace bourgeois matrons as the chief subjects of fashion. Writing of the "radical democratization of fashion that we owe especially to women," sociologist René Koenig noted that it was not "women in general who [were] responsible for this total revolution but above all the *young women*."[77] With the democratization and "youthification" of fashion, exemplified by the vogue for women's short hairstyles, France said goodbye to the consumer society of the nineteenth century and welcomed that of the twentieth.

None of this was clear to contemporaries, who, taking "fashion to be only the external manifestation of more profound changes," commonly understood the rage for bobbed hair as the climax of a narrative of women's emancipation. They contrasted the 1920s with the "bad" old days of the 1890s, when heavy, confining fashions and long hair served as a kind of metaphor for women's lives. An era when young women of privilege were taught to be vapid and snobbish, and only eccentrics and feminists smoked or cropped their hair; when "no well-bred girl," according to Eugen Weber, "would be allowed to read a novel or go to the theatre without parental censorship and few could go out at all without some kind of chaperone."[78]

This had started to change even before World War I, as elite young women expressed their desire to break out of this "société étouffante," to finish with the tedious morning toilette and some of the other rituals of the well-led life.[79] But it was the war itself that smashed the old structures. It allowed working-class women to escape the *professions féminines* and take jobs that paid decent wages. At the same time, it pulled middle-class women out of the essentially "private" space of the *foyer* and into society's "public" spaces: offices, hairdressing salons, the bar at the Ritz hotel. The relative absence of male authority gave women space to exercise their new autonomy.

The 1920s then completed in fashion what had originated in social fact. Young women who were now free to smoke, drive cars, and go out without chaperones shortened their skirts and cut their hair as an expression of their newfound emancipation. "When I had for the first time to cut off a magnificent head of brown hair," reported Georges Montorgueil, in the French daily *Le Temps*, "I felt a shiver of revulsion and begged pardon of those opulent locks. My client responded with scorn and aggression: "Our long hair was the sign of our ancient servitude.' " Wendy Cooper put the cliché succinctly. "It takes little imagination," she wrote, "to realize that these short dresses, cropped heads, and flat chests were the immediate reaction to emancipation."[80]

The distance that women had supposedly travelled was measured in an article that appeared in the magazine *Coiffures et Modes* in April 1925. "The Moment of Temptation" asked whether a woman who had "outgrown" her marriage and was unsatisfied by her husband, who nonetheless tried his best to please her, had the right to fall in love with another man. In the end, the author advised his unfulfilled readers to resist temptation, arguing less from Christian ethics than from the general principle of contracts. Still, that a popular magazine even thought such an article would engage its readers—rather than, say, horrify them—suggests that women's lives had changed in some substantial way.[81]

In retrospect, however, the easy equation of "freer" styles with freer women looks less compelling. Valerie Steele has often made clear her opinion that while fashion as a system is rooted in its historical context, there exists no simple correspondence between styles and their particular historical moment. So looser clothes and shorter hairstyles would never simply record the fact of women's emancipation. Besides, there was nothing inherently emancipatory about the new fashions. Chanel's emblematic clothes were tailored neither to simplicity nor comfort. While they might have made the rich look young and casual, they were in fact elaborate *haute couture* creations, just like the clothes of other *couturiers*.[82] Anne Hollander agrees that there is no necessary relationship between the formal shape and the symbolic meaning of clothes. "It is not enough to say," she writes, "that women adopted short skirts after the First World War because they symbolized sexual freedom and permitted easy movement of the legs, since these practical and symbolic effects could have been accomplished in other ways."[83]

Moreover, the active, independent woman of the 1920s is by no means a self-evident reality. Françoise Thébaud offers a typically ambivalent assessment: "It was mostly younger women who savored the air of freedom [during the war]. Liberated from parental surveillance, working girls enjoyed each others' company after working hours. Young middle-class women were even more 'transfigured' by their social and intellectual effort." But she stops short of endorsing the idea that the war "liberated" French women. As Anne-Marie Sohn observes, material and social conditions remained poor for the great majority of *françaises*, who went on washing, cooking, and cleaning "much as they had done in the previous century."[84]

Others are more categorical. Steven Hause, for example, rejects the premise that the war liberated French women in any meaningful sense.

Look at the law and economy of postwar France, he suggests. Thousands of women lost their jobs, as employers cleared room in the labor market for the returning *poilus*, while the Senate rejected women's bid for the franchise. Mary Lou Roberts inverts the common assumption that the war somehow liberated women, finding instead a broad cultural assault on the "new woman" that aimed to steady a *phallocratie* deeply shaken by the war's attack on masculinity. At best, she writes, lighter clothes and shorter hairstyles, although they perhaps had some ability to make consumers feel empowered, constituted merely "a visual fantasy of liberation."[85] The most radical critiques turn assertions of "liberation" on their head, contending that *cheveux courts* represented not freedom but an updated form of subjugation—in much the same way that American historian Kathy Peiss reads amusement parks as "cheap amusements" that "lulled women into a state of false consciousness."[86]

These latter assessments tend to imply that there was something inauthentic about the public's powerful taste for *cheveux courts*, as if women had fallen prey to the "irresistible" messages of *couturiers*, cosmetics pushers, and the false-hair industry by way of the subliminal and not-so-subliminal codes transmitted by cinema, literature, and women's magazines.[87] They are the very obverse of Long's faith in women's *innate* need for fashion.

In fact, however, the career of *cheveux courts* suggests that the purveyors of the new fashions of the 1920s did *not* succeed in confidently leading consumers in the intended direction. Hollywood and its French analogues certainly presented fantasized versions of women's lives. The same ideals of femininity appeared in the mass press aimed at women. It is necessary to wonder, though, whether we should take the frequency of an image as proof of its penetration. The hostility provoked by the bob should make it plain enough that those who promoted the "new woman" by no means had the field to themselves. An equal number of voices were raised *against* the breakdown of "traditional" femininity.

In the end, there is no escaping the conclusion that women followed some directions and ignored others. If the House of Chanel prospered after World War I while the House of Poiret went bankrupt, it does not necessarily imply that Chanel was superior in cutting a path for popular taste. Perhaps Coco was only better at anticipating where that path would run. Or maybe she was just lucky that her ideas suited some inchoate and capricious *Zeitgeist*, as Poiret's, which once had, no longer did. In the world of interwar fashion, many were called but few were chosen, and we might as well speak of "fortune's darlings" as of the "captains of consciousness."[88]

Besides, while it is probable that films and magazines played some role in communicating notions of beauty and stoking the urge to buy, it is important not to confuse the media influence of the early 1920s with that of a later period.[89] Of the major women's magazines, *Vogue* and *Fémina* aimed their appeal very strictly at the elite, whose appetite for conspicuous consumption hardly needed whetting. *Harper's Bazaar* had only a small slice of the French market. A number of cheaper publications sought a more popular audience, but none of these achieved a genuinely mass circulation. Of the glossy new entries, *Votre Beauté* began to publish in 1933, and the first issue of *Marie Claire*, "inspired by American examples where optimism, energy, and the battle for happiness triumph," appeared in 1937. The real explosion of the genre arrived after World War II. Before the radio and television era, and without truly mass-market print media for women, therefore, it is hard to see how anyone could have engaged in the mass manipulation of consumer consciousness. Which is all to say that the response of French women to *cheveux courts* and other elements of the new fashions must be considered less fabricated than spontaneous.

What then should we infer about the meaning of the short hairstyles that captivated French women in the early 1920s? In the years following the war, millions of women who had never done so before enthusiastically chose to visit a hairdresser and pay to have their hair "done." Less cumbersome clothes and hairstyles were liberating in a physical sense. But there was more to it than that. The evidence from the beauty salons is that women began to find themselves with the possibility of spending their own money as they liked and creating, in the process, a "feminine public sphere."[90] Whether they also wore *cheveux courts* as a feminist symbol, in the manner of *La Garçonne*, Monique Lerbier, is impossible to know. Specific motivation doubtless varied from moment to moment and woman to woman. Probably, most women found their way to the bob for the same reasons they wore beehives in the sixties and copied Farrah Fawcett in the seventies: they wanted to look trendy.

What is undeniable, however, is that much of the attraction of cropped hair derived less from the cut itself than from the context. In that respect, even if buying a haircut and perm did not amount to a revolution in the female condition, when considered against a history of economic dependence and social constraint, the freedom to march into a salon and order, "Faites-moi couper les cheveux!" *felt* like a kind of emancipation. Critics of the "beauty myth" might be inclined to see fashion as a trick played on the public by those who manipulate signs and dominate discourse. It might be closer to the truth to admit that what looks like repression in logic can feel like liberation in life.

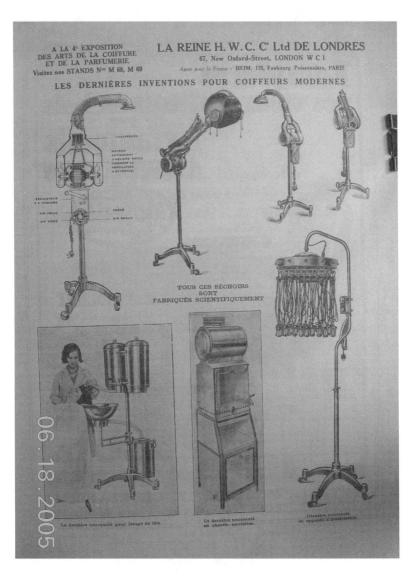

New technology in the salons

4

Back to the Barricades

If the hairdressing profession was poised at the edge of unprecedented prosperity, in the cold gloom of that first postwar winter, it was hard to see. The extravagance of the victory galas profited only the lucky few among the elite ladies' hairdressers. "Take-off" still awaited the arrival of economic stability and the irrepressible taste for *cheveux courts*. For the moment, coiffeurs, like virtually everyone else, faced tough times.

War fatigue and rising prices had already revived the labor movement in 1917. The government had treated the CGT as a partner in the war effort and kept a close eye on wages, fearing that production and popular support for the war would decline in proportion with purchasing power. This solicitude gave workers good cause to think that wartime sacrifice would bring palpable rewards. But victory did not deliver the hoped-for dividend, just inflation, unemployment, and cynicism.[1] Trade union membership, comprising less than 15 percent of the workforce in June 1914, began to climb. The CGT saw its population rise from just under half-a-million in December 1918 to over 1.1 million a year later. Strike activity washed over the country in a swell of labor discontent that seemed to point to "la précarité de l'ordre bourgeois."[2]

It is impossible to fix the precise dimensions of the syndicalist surge in coiffure. The workers' national federation, the FNSOC, claimed to have 2,150 members in forty local unions in 1920, which marked a strong progression from 1914.[3] And there is plenty of evidence of labor troubles in the salons throughout 1919 and 1920. Several elements of these postwar strikes stand out. First, most were short-lived and involved only a handful of *ouvriers coiffeurs*, like the twenty-two who walked out of twenty salons in Angers for two days in June 1919.

The 1920 strike in Paris affected only one salon and twelve workers. Only a few amounted to significant showdowns. The 500 Lyonnais hairdressers who struck for two weeks in July 1919 cost their employers some 3,600 workdays. The 1,000 Marseillais coiffeurs who went out for a week the following month represented 6,000 workdays lost. A strike in Bordeaux lasted two-and-a-half weeks; it touched 300 salons and cost 4,500 workdays.[4]

Second, these postwar strikes were remarkably successful. Before the war, striking hairdressers had been lucky to win even marginal victories—as often as not, they went back to work with nothing to show for their efforts. In 1919 and 1920, on the contrary, workers frequently made substantial gains. In 1919, *ouvriers coiffeurs* in Beziers won a wage rise from nine to thirteen and a half francs a day; in Perpignan, wages more than doubled, from six francs to thirteen and a half; in Marseilles they went from twelve to seventeen francs. Wage settlements in 1920 tended to be a little less dramatic, although workers in Bordeaux signed an agreement that raised wages for certain categories from ten or twelve to eighteen or twenty francs a day, and a collective accord in Nantes recognized a 50 percent wage increase, up to eighteen francs a day at the top of the scale.[5]

Wages, however, were only half the story, maybe less, for the most pressing issue for the French labor movement in 1919 was the forty-eight hour workweek. The CGT had launched its campaign for the eight-hour day in 1906, believing it would reduce unemployment, rationalize production, raise wages, and "rejuvenate family and cultural life." Indeed, it became one of the implicit conditions for labor's cooperation during the war.[6] The government settled its debt to labor with the law of April 1919, which established the eight-hour day in principle but deferred implementation to the near future. *Ouvriers coiffeurs* were not prepared to wait for the state to execute the new rules, however, and immediately set out to impose forty-eight hours on their employers. Subsequent attempts to establish a new workweek in the profession proved to be both contentious and inconclusive.

In Orléans, for example, in February 1920, employers' and employees' syndicats met to work out the operation of the new regime. They signed an accord calling for between fifty-six and fifty-eight hours a week, including an hour-and-a-half mandatory closing for lunch. But not all the local *patrons coiffeurs* accepted the agreement. More than a few continued to demand up to sixty-one hours from their *ouvriers*. The new schedule also disappointed the many workers who wanted two hours for lunch, obligatory Sunday *repos hebdomadaire*, an across-the-board 30 percent pay rise, and the integral application of forty-eight hours. Matters remained deadlocked, and the *syndicats ouvriers* were too weak to force a settlement on their own terms. A strike in June 1920 brought out 300 of Marseille's 1,500 *ouvrier coiffeurs*, mostly Spanish and Italian immigrants working in *salons médiocres*. In the larger, better-off salons, everyone stayed in. The strikers won a pay rise but not the fight for forty-eight hours.[7]

Despite continuing dissension, some sort of agreement on a new work schedule found its way into most collective agreements, with the workers generally demanding forty-eight hours and setting for less. Employers and *assistants* in Marseille, Troyes, Beziers, Paris, and Toulouse actually signed accords calling for the integral application of the April law, although none actually succeeded in putting it into effect.[8] In most cases, leaders of the *patronat* who signed these accords found themselves repudiated by the rank and file of *salonniers*, who were not inclined to be so generous.

If the pending application of the eight-hour day energized *ouvriers coiffeurs*, it likewise drew employers into the *syndicats patronaux* and encouraged the old competitors among them to bury the hatchet. The well-heeled *salonniers* of the Fédération française and the more *petits patrons coiffeurs* of the Fédération nationale had parted company over the modalities of the *repos hebdomadaire* in 1909, but the menace of the eight-hour day led them back into each other's arms, with the creation of the Union fédérale des syndicats patronaux des coiffeurs (UF) in 1919.[9]

The Union fédérale, which first assembled in Strasbourg in early September 1919, saw its task as defending coiffure "against badly thought-out legislation, almost always inapplicable in our profession, and against the often-exaggerated pretensions of the workers' syndicats."[10] Frédéric Schlieffer, the politically ambitious president of the Alsace Chamber of Trades, served as host. René Chauvin, Alphonse Mornot, and Gaston Forestier represented the Fédération nationale. The Fédération française sent its leaders, Robert Maigre and Ulysse Boucoiran. Boucoiran, as director of several trade publications, president of the École supérieure de coiffure de Paris, and founder of the Fédération française, became president.[11]

Edmond Perrin, Emile Long's old friend representing the elite *maisons* of the ICD, explained why his own group *had* granted its employees a forty-eight hour week. Serving women who demanded only excellent service and did not worry about price, his constituents stood above the market forces that confined their less fortunate colleagues. But most of those present opposed the imposition of forty-eight hours, either because they thought it unacceptably skewed to the employees' interests or because they found it "[in]compatible with the needs of the clientele." In the end, the constituent meeting of the UF adopted this statement:

> . . . considering that until now *ouvriers coiffeurs* normally spent seventy or seventy-three hours a week at work, the complete application of the forty-eight hour week would seriously injure our trade; it could easily ruin certain hairdressing establishments which lack the resources to adjust successfully, *asks that hairdressers be accorded an exemption of a minimum of six hours a week.* [Italics mine][12]

Gary Cross aptly calls the 1919 legislation a sort of "enabling act" that still needed to be executed by the administration, in what promised to be a slow and contentious process, precisely because it ambiguously provided for forty-eight hours of "effective work" and permitted *dérogations* for those employed in "intermittent" work.[13] Thus, in the summer of 1920, while the particulars of the new regime in coiffure were still being hammered out, a delegation of hairdressers, employers and employees met with Charles Piquenard of the Labor Ministry to discuss the work schedule in *salons de coiffure*. Representatives of the UF asked for at least fifty-seven hours a week; the workers held the line for forty-eight. Both sides rehearsed their old quarrel over the difference between "presence" and "effective labor." For workers, the latter meant all the time spent on the employer's property. For employers, it meant real productive activity from whistle to whistle.[14]

When the government finally issued its decree of August 26, 1920, applying the eight-hour law to *salons de coiffure*, it split the difference between the two parties. It fixed the work week at fifty-one hours for Paris, fifty-four for cities of more than 25,000 (including the department of the Seine), and 60 hours for cities of under 25,000. It added the possibility of fifty-two paid overtime hours per year and established an across-the-board closing time of 7 p.m. during the week and 1 p.m. on Sundays. The government's judiciousness pleased neither side. Jean Pagès, who had replaced Luquet as FNSOC general secretary in 1920, expressed his disappointment: "There is among the workers," he wrote to labor minister Albert Peyronnet, "the notion that they are always at the mercy of the excessive caprice of the *patronat*; that the law is a fiction and that force is the only reality . . ."[15]

What was too little for the employees was too much for the employers. Rank and file *salonniers* in Paris carried on "an active propaganda" against the decree. Similar conflicts played themselves out across the country. The *Coiffeur-Parfumeur*, voice of Bordeaux's *patrons coiffeurs*, reviled the forty-eight hour law as part of the CGT's strategy of constraining the *patronat* "while awaiting its suppression." Georges Villette, UF general secretary, suggested that salons fire all their workers and wait until their syndicats showed themselves willing to sign "just and very moderate accords" with their bosses.[16]

The August 1920 decree stayed in force for a little more than a year. On October 30, 1921 the government issued a new decree that went a step further in placating the *patrons* and riling their workers. The new decree extended the workweek for salons in Paris and all other cities of over half-a-million to fifty-four hours. It prescribed fifty-seven hours in cities with a population between 100,000 and 500,000; and sixty-hours for all the rest, with a possible thirty-two hours of paid overtime a year.[17]

The workers reacted angrily to this new concession to the employers. Worst of all, they protested, the *patrons* did not respect even the wretched settlement of 1921. *Ouvriers coiffeurs* in Saint-Etienne objected to working fifty-eight or sixty hours a week, while their comrades in Paris, Lyon, and Marseille were working only fifty-four. Workers in Périgueux wrote to the labor minister that they were being forced to work sixty-one hours a week. And so on. The left-wing daily *Le Peuple* in July 1924 protested against gross violations of the forty-eight hour law in Paris, intimidation by the employers, and the "total indifference" of the authorities. The *Coiffeur Confédéré* complained of the state's "excessive benevolence with regard to employers."[18] Yet the evidence suggests that, notwithstanding a certain amount of confusion, the decree of October 1921 was by and large respected.[19]

Evidently, neither broadly advancing wages nor a shrinking work week put an end to the conflict between *ouvriers* and *patrons coiffeurs*. Precision is impossible, given the inadequacy of the sources, but it appears that, throughout the 1920s, *assistants* walked out in a dozen or so cities every year. These strikes remained small, smaller than those of 1919 and 1920. Only a handful involved more than a hundred strikers, and they rarely reached the better-off salons in the city centers, affecting only the workers in the more marginal shops, where work days were longer and wages lower and where, in several of the smaller cities and towns, *garçons coiffeurs* were still *nourris* and *logés* well into the 1920s.[20]

Inevitably, these work stoppages were accompanied by the establishment of *salons coopératifs*—or *salons volants* as they were more commonly known—in cafés and other public venues in the working-class quarters. Here striking coiffeurs invited their neighbors to have their beards shaved and heads trimmed for free—although tips were gratefully accepted. The idea plainly was to generate income for the strikers and pull business away from the salons. The size and duration of most strikes in the 1920s, however, suggest that these *salons volants* could not effectively buttress a long and bitter strike. Even as tokens of class and neighborhood solidarity, they had their limits. After all, the *petits patrons coiffeurs* who owned the salons in the popular quarters also lived there, and most of them were themselves hardly more than working class.[21]

Labor conflict arrived in Paris for Pentecost 1926.[22] The capital had not had a serious hairdressers' strike since the end of the war, despite the ongoing disagreements that divided patrons and employees. Matters changed that spring, however. Unhappy because the *salonniers* had recently raised their prices by 40 percent and were offering employees less than half of that in wages, a group of hairdressing workers, led by Pierre Guny of the CGT-Unitaire, decided that the time was right to assert their claims. On May 3, Guny asked the employers for salaries ranging from forty-five to eighty francs a day, depending on the worker's qualifications. He also demanded two weeks' paid holiday, lunchtime closing of all salons, forty-eight hours, and the *semaine anglaise*. Gaston Forestier, president of the UF, accused Guny of "démagogie révolutionnaire" and made a counteroffer that fell far short of his demands.

A large meeting of hairdressing workers—the *Ouvrier Coiffeur* reported 3,400; the police counted 1,500—gathered at the Salle Ferrer on the evening of May 20 and voted by acclamation to strike the next day. It designated a number of teams of *débaucheurs* to canvass the city's salons and bring out their comrades and told the rest of the crowd to meet at the Bourse du Travail the next morning to receive their *cartes de grève*. The strikers began to prepare the *salons volants* that would sustain them. The *Ère Nouvelle* counted fifty improvised salons in different cafés, each identified by a red banner in the window.[23]

If at the point of combat Guny and his colleagues were optimistic, the employers and the public authorities were strikingly blasé.[24] Forestier and the CSP leadership were concerned to prevent *débauchage* and protect the "liberté du travail." But they agreed with the prefect's assessment that the *grévistes* had only a limited following. As the *Nouveau Siècle* summed up the situation: hairdressing employers were not very authoritarian and workers not very discontent. The strike might have an impact on the *petits patrons* of the working-class arrondissements and the *banlieues*, predicted a report to the Paris prefect of police. It would never exceed five or six hundred strikers, however, and would leave the center of town totally untouched.

The next several days demonstrated the accuracy of the authorities' appraisal, as only a few hundred of the capital's 7,000 hairdressing workers stayed out on May 21. The police reported that only a dozen workers showed up at the Bourse du Travail that morning, and none at all for the *débauchage* meeting at the rue de Bretagne, in front of the mairie of the third arrondissement. There were a few attempts to bring out other workers and some arrests, such as those of two *débaucheurs*, Louis Delaunay and Alexandre Roubaut, collared by police on the rue Tolbiac. *Le Quotidien* told its readers that not a single salon in central Paris shut its doors.[25] After two days, according to *Paris-Soir*, 60 percent of the strikers had accepted some sort of offer and gone back to work.[26] By May 30, only about a hundred workers remained out. In the end, a hundred or so employers signed a new contract with the *unitaires* syndicate; others simply applied the raise recommended earlier by the CSP. Guny declared victory and began to prepare for the next confrontation.

Ouvriers coiffeurs might have caused the patrons more sleepless nights and won more concessions had they put up a united front. On the contrary, by 1926 the French labor movement, and the FNSOC along with it, had split into two hostile camps: the CGT, which tempered its radical doctrine with pragmatic trade unionism; and the new CGT-Unitaire, whose communist leadership remained committed to revolution. The prewar CGT had always managed to contain the divergent tendencies within the labor movement, but its support for the Union Sacrée and participation in the war effort strengthened the practical, reformist party within the confederation.

The confederation's "minimum program" of 1918 proposed an expanded and more thoroughgoing version of wartime codetermination, a system of bargaining among organized interests that would give workers, at least so far as the CGT represented them, an important say in national economic and social life.[27]

Opposition to the CGT's new reformism waxed with the economic crisis and the labor unrest that swept the country between 1919 and 1922. Equally, the French labor movement came apart over its divided view on the Bolsheviks. The split took institutional form with the exile of socialists from the new communist party and, conversely, the CGT's ejection of French Bolsheviks, who formed the new CGT-Unitaire.[28]

As its parent confederation came apart, so did the FNSOC. The division was already manifest at the federation's congress of September 1920, where Alexandre Luquet, the long-time general secretary, came under fire from the more radical among his colleagues. Arthur Roger, delegate from Nancy and Clermont-Ferrand, attacked him and the CGT for their pusillanimous cooperation with the government and the *patronat* during the war. Marcel Cordier, representing the Paris CSO, followed with a motion of no confidence in the bureau confédéral and a call for adhesion to the Third International. The latter gesture failed to carry a majority, but the first vote went against Luquet and his pro-CGT colleagues. Luquet, after working twenty-five years for the Fédération national, resigned as general secretary. Cordier was elected to replace him.[29]

Relations on the bureau fédéral only deteriorated after that. Pagès's resignation shortly followed Luquet's. The new team of Frédéric Doyen and Robert Chauvin took over. Feeling that the CGT had lost its commitment to proletarian revolution, which was certainly true, the renegade coiffeurs led the FNSOC and the majority of its 1,500 members out of the CGT and into the CGT-Unitaire—making the FNSOC only the third federation, after Voiture-Aviation and Enseignement, to make that jump. A violent war of words ensued. Chauvin accused Pagès and the old CGT gang of selling out the working class. The latter replied by saying that the *unitaires* had delivered *ouvriers coiffeurs* to the Comintern. And so on.

The CGT managed to retain the loyalty of most of its trade federations and membership. In coiffure, however, it was the *minoritaires* in the CGTU who seized control of the principal federation. At the FNSOC congress of June 1922 in Saint-Etienne, controlled now by communist elements and attended by thirteen delegates representing two dozen local syndicates, the federation voted to join the Third International. The *unitaires*' second federal congress in August 1924 gave an even clearer indication of changes in the FNSOC. Chauvin called for the elimination of "troublesome" and "petty bourgeois" elements from the CGTU and talked about participating in the new Fédération internationale révolutionnaire d'ouvriers coiffeurs. Joseph Anzalric, the secretary, proposed banning "la presse bourgeoise" from the meeting and proffered a message of "fraternal greetings" to the Kremlin. The anarchist paper *Libertaire* described the congress as a thoroughly Bolshevik "coup de théâtre."[30]

The *unitaires* now controlled the resources and membership of the FNSOC. The old guard, especially Luquet, retained significant support in Paris, however, where they had been important figures for so long. And so, "having left their archives, their money, their journal, and all means of propaganda and action in the hands of the so-called *unitaires*," the former federal leadership began to rebuild an organization of *ouvriers coiffeurs* loyal to the CGT.[31] They succeeded in cobbling together the Fédération des syndicats des ouvriers Coiffeurs Confédérés, whose first national congress in 1925 brought together syndicates from eighteen cities and launched a journal, *Coiffeur Confédéré*. Since the *unitaires* had taken over the venerable École parisienne de coiffure, along with the CSO's other goods, the *confédérés* also set up their own training center, the École de coiffure de Paris. The tireless René Rambaud, an old CGT man who maintained his ties to the labor movement in spite of his growing reputation among elite *coiffeurs pour dames*, became director of the new school, as he had been of the old one. By the end of the decade, the *confédérés* had made up considerable ground on the *unitaires*.[32]

The splintering of the labor movement in coiffure also produced a small anomaly, an association of anarchists, the Fédération autonome des syndicats d'ouvriers coiffeurs. The Fédération autonome was almost entirely the work of Gustave Tixier and Georges Leroy. Long-time members of the FNSOC, but inclined toward anarchism, these two attended the *unitaires* congress of August 1924. They chafed at the Leninist practices of the new bureau, however, and decided to found their own group, at arm's length from both the CGT, "reformists wedded to the bourgeois government of Monsieur Herriot," and the CGTU, "cats paws of Moscow." At its inception, the federation of *autonomes* claimed to have some four hundred members in seven local syndicates. The police were less impressed. They counted only sixteen people at its first meeting at the Salle Freycinet in Paris, in early December 1924. Only a half dozen showed up the following week, but the police report noted that two of them had never heard of the *syndicat autonome*.[33]

Except for their small nuisance value—and more for the other syndicats than for the capitalist order—the *autonomes* were irrelevant. But the *unitaires* and *confédérés* carried sufficient weight to harass the *patronat* and each other. Weight, however, was a relative term. A police report of 1924 counted 600 *unitaires* and 300 *confédérés* among Paris's 7,000 *ouvriers coiffeurs*. Provincial syndicates had no more than a dozen or so members, with the exception of those in the biggest cities, most of which had fewer than a hundred. The FNSOC demonstrated its relative weakness when it organized a *Journée nationale* in October 1928, in support of forty-eight hours. The federation claimed 600 new adhesions as a result, but this was certainly a fabrication. The letters that arrived from the provinces testified to the mediocrity of the event and the enduring difficulties of organizing hairdressing workers. One delegate, from Aix-en-Provence, with eighteen workers at the *réunion* and no new adherents, noted gloomily: "on the whole, few or no syndicalists and no discussion about anything."[34]

Other sources repeated the familiar tale of inertia and apathy. Hairdressing workers were young and passive. The most energetic and ambitious among them either moved up to the *patronat* or left coiffure for better jobs. Virtually everyone hated to pay union dues. G. Fayollet from Nevers complained that even those who belonged to the syndicate did not show up for meetings. A CGTU meeting called to discuss the *repos hebdomadaire*, in May 1924, brought out just eight comrades; and a subsequent rally to pressure Paris *patrons* into boosting wages attracted only forty. The *Coiffeur Confédéré* reminded its readers that "it is by our own forces [and] not by the good will of the patronat, that workers will achieve their aims." Yet, it is hard not to see these forces as weak and undermanned, even while admiring the commitment and stamina of the few syndical leaders.[35]

The halfhearted response to their calls to action did not restrain the *unitaires* and the *confédérés* in their denunciation of one another. François Magnien, a declared Leninst who joined the CGTU in 1923 and quickly rose through the ranks, hurled the communists' favorite insult at Pagès, dismissing him as a "petty bourgeois." The *confédérés*, less vituperative for the most part, nevertheless seldom missed the opportunity to condemn the *unitaires* as "tools of Moscow."[36] Part of this was the understandable product of competition and the residue of a bitter split. But it is also true that the Third International and the new, postwar CGT touted very different versions of the labor movement. In so far as the two groups of *ouvriers coiffeurs* reflected divergent *tendances*, therefore, it is worth asking what these differences amounted to in practice.

The answer would have to be that, on the street, the distance between *unitaire* bolshevism and *confédéré* reformism was less than one might think. When they confronted the *patronat*, the two syndicats of hairdressing workers presented virtually identical *revendications*. For that matter, so did the anarchists in the *syndicat autonome*. All demanded higher wages, the integral application of the eight-hour day and the *semaine anglaise* (the additional half-day off a week). What really separated *confédérés* from *unitaires* was tactics—or rather, temperament. The CGTU was always inclined to action, particularly to strikes, to get their way. The CGT preferred gentler persuasion. *Confédéré* hairdressing workers were ready to strike when pushed into a corner. Mostly, though, they favored negotiation with the employers. This is precisely what happened in the Paris hairdressers' strike of May 1926. Confronted with the same refusal of *patrons coiffeurs* to meet their demands, the *unitaires* decided to call out their troops. The *confédérés*, feeling that the strike would not be big enough to intimidate the employers, wanted to continue to talk. In sum, the *unitaires* talked revolution more freely and generally had nastier things to say about the *patronat*, although the *confédérés* hardly saw themselves as defenders of the capitalist status quo. Between the two approaches, however, it is not possible to say that either paid consistently higher dividends than the other.

The divided movement of hairdressing workers faced a *patronat* that was itself beginning to fracture again. While the workers' organizations split along ideological and tactical lines, the employers fell out over conflicts of commercial interest. For the time being, the Union fédérale remained the only national representative of *patrons coiffeurs syndiqués*. By 1928, the union claimed to have fifty-four member syndicats. More than two hundred delegates attended its national congress in 1933.[37] A few of the local organizations reached a respectable size, at least by the standards of the profession: Lyon had 423 members, Marseille 391, Nantes 278. A half dozen others counted more than a hundred *patrons syndiqués* each.[38] At the other end, a large number of the local affiliates were tiny: fifteen, twenty, or thirty *artisans coiffeurs* in a provincial town or small city, although these small groups increasingly tended to be absorbed by syndicats from bigger cities.

Naturally, the Chambre syndicale patronale in Paris dwarfed all the other local hairdressers' unions. In 1924, a police estimate put the population of the CSP at 2,200, and by 1932 it reported having almost 3,500 dues-paying members.[39] There is no way to verify these numbers. The best one can say is that the Union fédérale had something less than ten thousand members in the early 1930s and that the CSP was by far its dominant local element. The Union's president and general secretary were always Parisians. So were nearly all of its officers at any given moment. There was nothing exceptional in this situation; most national organizations in this most centralized of nations must have been similarly weighted. Nonetheless, as the union's leaders—Hector Ledoux, Georges Villette, Gaston Forestier, Alphonse Mornot, and Joseph Gestalder—traveled around the country looking for new recruits, they encountered understandable hesitation among some of the local and regional groups. Even large syndicats, such as those based in Bordeaux and Toulouse, feared that their regional concerns would not matter enough to the Parisians who ran the UF.[40]

The union's politics made enemies as well as friends. The CSP had always defended *petits patrons coiffeurs*, against both workers and *les gros*; that is, against the forces of big business in coiffure. The implications of this had been muted in 1919, in the bright moment of patronal unity that produced the UF. In the years that followed, however, the business elements of the former Fédération française began to lose interest in the UF, as the CSP took increasing control of the union and made it the voice of artisan-coiffeurs. The UF clarified its position in 1923, when Forestier led it into the Confédération générale de l'artisanat français, which was dedicated to defending the interests of petty craftsmen in a world of industrial concentration and proletarian socialism.[41]

It was not any quarrel over general principles that finally put an end to the uneasy patronal unity. Rather it was substantial disagreements over the operation of the eight-hour law. Recall that the employers had initially opposed this substantial reduction in the workweek but had settled in with the rather favorable compromise imposed by the decrees of 1920 and 1921. Economic recovery and "la folie des cheveux courts" made the new rules easier to live with.

By the mid-1920s, a growing number of workers, particularly in the Paris area, were beginning to enjoy the *semaine anglaise*, which granted employees an extra half-day off per week—ordinarily Sunday afternoon for "lundists" (salons closed on Monday) and Monday morning for "dimanchistes" (closed on Sunday). This was virtually universal in the better salons of the city center and was making substantial progress in the popular neighborhoods and in the salons of the *banlieues*. In 1924, syndicats of *patrons* and *ouvriers coiffeurs* in Paris signed an accord for the formal establishment of the *semaine anglaise* and sent a joint delegation to urge the labor minister to issue a decree to make it mandatory for all salons in the Seine. The decree appeared in February 1925. In its congress of 1928, following a lively debate, the Union fédérale voted in favor of a law that would formally institute the *semaine anglaise* in hairdressing salons across the country.[42]

The motion that carried the UF congress did not merely recommend the *semaine anglaise*, however. It added the priviso that all salons should have to close while their personnel were gone. That is, it attached the *semaine anglaise* to the *fermeture obligatoire*. Replaying the battles over the *repos hebdomadaire*, those who sought to apply the *semaine anglaise* had to confront a number of problems concerning the manner of its implementation: If all workers worked the same *number* of hours, would these be the *same* hours? Could shop owners tailor their schedules to their particular circumstances, as long as they did not exceed the allowable number of hours? Or would all *ouvriers coiffeurs* have to start at the same time, eat lunch at the same time, finish at the same time? Did a salon need to close when its workers were not there? Or could it stay open, staffed by the patron and maybe some "extras"? Opposing responses to these fundamental questions once again split the *patronat* in coiffure.

Advocates of *roulement* wanted a system wherein each employee would work no more than the agreed-upon number of hours, but all employees would not work the same schedule. This would allow, for example, a salon to remain open, say, sixty hours a week and continuously through the day, while each employee worked only fifty-two hours a week and enjoyed the mandatory hour-and-a-half lunch break. Opponents of *roulement* sought to impose a *horaire unique*—that is, a single, mandatory schedule enforced on the profession through *fermeture obligatoire*. This would require employers to grant a *repos collectif*, giving all employees exactly the same hours of work and closing the salons in their absence. It would further mean that the shops themselves could stay open no longer than the fifty-four, fifty-seven, or sixty hours—whatever the schedule in force for any particular locality—during which they were permitted to employ their *ouvriers*.

On these critical issues, battle lines formed according to the logic of self-interest. The workers' organizations generally supported the *horaire unique* because it promised to constrain any employer who was tempted to break the rules. Labor inspectors would have an easy time catching the cheaters; they could simply look for shops that were open when all the others were shut. The *horaire unique* would thereby facilitate the further reduction of the workweek.

Meanwhile, for those patrons who favored it, the *horaire unique* offered "the sole means of battling against the wreckers [*naufrageurs*] of the profession," because it placed all *salonniers* on an equal footing.[43] It saved the conscientious employer who closed his shop on time and respected his workers' rights from having to face "unfair competition" from "blacklegs" or "hairdressing factories" that could stay open when he could not. It also eliminated the temptation, or even the necessity, of self-exploitation by closing down the option for an employer to work by himself when his employees were off—perhaps tossing him back to the bad old days of the 1890s, when *petits salonniers* were spending eighty or ninety hours a week in their shops. For those *patrons coiffeurs* with no competitive edge, the *horaire unique* looked like a guarantee of commercial survival and a decent portion of leisure.

The *horaire unique* and *fermeture obligatoire* appealed especially to small, vulnerable *artisans coiffeurs* of the sort attracted to the CSP, whose president Domède and secretary Joseph Anzalric were both great partisans of restraints on commercial liberties. Anzalric, after all, was another of those coiffeurs who had taken the journey from militant *ouvrier* to patron *engagé*, and who remained committed to the defense of the "little guy." Recall his opposition to "la presse bourgeoise" and fraternal greetings to Moscow in 1924. "Imagine," Domède mocked André Quentin, director of *Cheveux Courts*, founder of the new journal *Reveil des Coiffeurs* and a great advocate of *roulement*, "a schedule for each patron, a schedule for each salon: My God! There's an invention!"[44]

The Union fédérale was more ambivalent about the *horaire unique*. Responding to the workers' demand for more rigor in the application of mandatory opening and closing times, Hector Ledoux, the union's president in 1925, wrote to the labor minister, reminding him of the need for suppleness in applying any regime of *fermeture obligatoire*. He explained that a hairdresser could not simply quit a customer, leaving her with half a perm or a head full of *teinture*, when lunchtime or quitting time rolled around. "We would like the current tolerance [for small transgressions over the work schedule] to be maintained," concluded Anzalric, as long as the time gets made up elsewhere.[45]

Joseph Gestalder, the UF's forceful general secretary, recognized the need for professional "discipline in the face of necessity." He nonetheless saw the inconvenience that the *horaire unique* could present for clients. Besides, as Gestalder told the UF congress of 1931, we call ourselves artisans, and isn't an artisan a man free to work when it pleases him? Gestalder was voted down on this occasion, yet the general secretary's reservations perhaps held the UF back from an all-out endorsement of the *horaire unique*.[46]

Measured as it was, the union's support for the *horaire unique* was the primary cause of division within the ranks of *patrons coiffeurs*. The bigger employers, those who were not artisans but *commerçants*, detested what the journal *Cheveux Courts* called "this *dada* thought up by certain sectarian brains short on popularity."[47] The *gros salonniers* maintained that they had no objection to a shorter workweek and observed that workers in all the important shops *already* enjoyed a forty-eight hour schedule and the *semaine anglaise*. For example, the new salon at the Galeries Lafayette was open for business fifty-four hours a week, but each of its hairdressers worked no more than forty-eight. Coiffeurs in the Maison Ricaud worked a forty-hour week in 1933, but the Maison Ricaud itself stayed open sixty hours, six days a week and gave its *assistants* time off by *roulement*.[48]

The proprietor of this latter establishment, Jean Ricaud, was near the end of an exemplary career. A renowned ladies' hairdresser, Ricaud had followed Emile Long as president of the ICD. He was also, like so many of the best-known coiffeurs, a shrewd businessman. In the 1920s, riding the wave of *cheveux courts*, Ricaud opened several *salons pour dames*, where he offered his valuable name and good service at popular prices. His *tarif* of fifty-seven and a half francs for a whole "treatment," including *indéfrisable*, made his shops the archetypal "hairdressing factories," about which the smaller patrons complained so frequently.

Like so many of his colleagues at the capitalist end of the profession, Ricaud had a political side. He was the leading figure among those *gros patrons* who joined together in 1932 to form the Association des grandes maisons de coiffure de Paris, one of whose chief aims was to fight against the *horaire unique*. He was also close to George Maus and the Fédération des commerçants-détaillants, the organization that worked so hard to protect the prerogatives of small and medium-sized businessmen, which often meant obstructing new labor legislation.[49]

These capitalists of coiffure made no secret of their belief that business was all about making money, and that meant serving clients when and where they presented themselves. They might sympathize with workers' legitimate desire for a humane workweek and yet believe it made no sense for salons to shut their doors on willing customers. The opponents of the *horaire unique* certainly did not seek to return to the brutal regime of the fin-de-siècle. What they claimed to want was a flexible schedule that would allow a reasonable accommodation to customers' habits and convenience. This would make everyone, *assistants* as well as *maîtres*, better off.

The *artisans patrons* of the CSP, however, defended the *horaire unique* precisely because they rejected the logic of the market and put their faith in something more akin to the moral economy. The CSP's monthly *Journal des Maîtres-Coiffeurs* regularly denounced overproduction, automation, and "commercial concentration" as the enemies of "our corporation." J. Cluzel likewise attacked the big salons in the Parisian department stores, while assuring readers of *Commerce des Coiffeurs-Parfumeurs* that clients would always return to the artisanal shops, because the *grands magasins* lacked the essential qualities of the boutique. They were modern, he admitted, but their workers were inferior craftsmen, and their very modernness bred an alienating sense of anonymity.[50] The same reasoning led the *Coiffeur du Sud-Ouest* to deplore the "Americanization" of coiffure, in order not "to lose the taste for knowledge and beauty . . ." "What do we want?" the paper concluded, "To live through our work."[51]

Ouvriers coiffeurs similarly repudiated Quentin's frankly capitalist perspective and used moralistic language to justify their own support for the *horaire unique*. Pierre Guny, now president of the FNSOC, referred to commercial competition as "fratricide" that drove down wages and forced hairdressers to work longer hours, as it had often done before World War I.[52] Guny wanted to replace the anarchy of the market with "a system where everyone was on the same footing, where everyone had to submit to a certain discipline for the common good." He did not agree with those who thought the needs of clients should take precedence over other considerations, such as the work-ers' well being. From his *ouvriériste* point of view, the *métier* of coif-fure—or any true *métier*, for that matter—was not essentially about *service* but about work, and work should not be a commodity. It had an intrinsic value quite apart from satisfied customers and money in the *caisse*. Indeed, Guny argued in the opposite direction that, "It's when we submit to the demands of the client that we are unable to make our work respected."

Extending the labor theory of value from the material to the ethical realm, Guny maintained that a reduction in work hours was desirable not only because exploited workers deserved more leisure, but also because long hours devalued the work itself. He offered as proof the observation that "it's always in the salons where *ouvriers coiffeurs* work the longest that they earn the least, and it's always in the salons that respect the forty-eight hour law that work is most valorized, where wages are highest."[53] Guny did not seem to notice that this way of putting things would align him, not with his fellow *petits*, whose salons were *least* likely to grant forty-eight hours, but with those he castigated as "*des capitalistes . . . le morceau réactionnaire de la coiffure.*"

In any event, the pliability of the forty-eight hour decrees made them a lingering source of discord within the profession. In some cases, public authorities set precise guidelines, for instance, that salons could not open before 8 a.m. or close after 7:30 p.m. or that they had to allow all employees an hour-and-a-half lunch break. More often, the decrees were not definitive and their application was far from consistent. This disorder naturally placed some *salonniers* at a disadvantage. Thus, the CSP received a number of complaints from shop owners that while they were closing for lunch as the law required, their rivals were staying open and thereby stealing precious customers.

At the same time, the decrees pointed a way out of the general con-fusion: If the various organizations of employers and employees could find their way to an agreement on the application of the law, the public authorities were willing to impose it on *all* salons. Accordingly, in the early 1930s, the principal groups of hair-dressers—the CSP, ICD, and *Indépendants* for the patrons; con-fédérés and unitaires for the workers—opened negotiations for a comprehensive regime in coiffure. Along with the *horaire unique*, the parties considered a further reduction in work hours in the Paris region. The CSP and the two workers' unions were prepared to settle on a schedule of fifty-two hours for Paris (fifty-five for the rest of the Seine department) and the *horaire unique*. All parties agreed to accept the *semaine anglaise*, already more or less universal in the capital. The big employers, represented by the Syndicat indépendant, declared themselves ready to give individual workers a forty-eight hour week, which most of them had long since done, and endorsed "all measures likely to ameliorate the workers' conditions, while also protecting the general interests of the corporation." But they bitterly opposed any sort of *horaire unique* that would hamstring their "liberté de commerce."[54] In the end, the *Indépendants* walked out of the negotiations. And in early May 1932 the remaining parties signed a new collective accord without them.

The French administration ordinarily moved slowly in these matters, and the new convention for Parisian coiffeurs was no exception. It sat in limbo for eighteen months, while the authorities prepared a decree and the breach within the profession widened. The workers protested the delay and suspected that the *Indépendants*—"that phantom patronal syndicat [full of] retrograde employers"—were behind it. The signatory groups tried to prod the administration forward and disparaged the convention's opponents as "réfractaires."[55] The "réfractaires," for their part, ridiculed the CSP: "those whom we no longer dare call 'masters,' given the way that the workers organizations chewed them up."[56]

The decree that finally emerged from the Labor Ministry in October 1933 reduced the permissible number of work hours in hairdressing salons across the country: fifty-two *heures de présence* in Paris; fifty-five in the rest of the Seine; fifty-four for cities over 500,000; fifty-seven for those between 100,000 and 500,000; sixty for the rest. It imposed the *repas collectif* in Paris and the suburbs, from 12:30 p.m. to 2 p.m. It took a decisive step toward the *horaire unique* without actually crossing the threshold by giving the authorities jurisdiction to enforce "un régime uniforme de répartition des heures," providing it was the fruit of an agreement between "organizations of employers and employees" and "after consultation with all interested groups."

Gestalder, general secretary of the Union fédérale, expressed his satisfaction that the new regulations would put an end to "la trustialisation . . . des activités artisanales," and discipline "the sinister *gâcheurs* of our trade" who hurt the majority of honest hairdressers by being open all the time. Marcel Bagnaud, leader of the forces opposed to the decree, predicted that it would result in a loss of business and a rise in unemployment.[57] In fact, most of the new rules merely reflected existing practices in the trade, and there is no evidence that they produced any major changes in the operation of hairdressing salons.

The climax of the campaign for the *horaire unique* did, however, lead to a coalescence of those interests in coiffure hostile, not just to the *horaire unique* but to any state restriction of "commercial liberties." Shortly after the collective agreement of May 1932 to which they objected so strongly, a group of *patrons coiffeurs* with considerable business interests and right-wing sympathies joined Jean Ricaud and his newly formed Association des grandes maisons de coiffure de Paris to create the Syndicat des coiffeurs de Paris (SCP). Its first priority, the SCP avowed, was to "suppress the *horaire unique* for every sort of salon in every neighborhood." The like-minded members of the Syndicat indépendant, constituted in 1909 to restrict the application of the *repos hebdomadaire*, soon folded their own little tent and moved in with the SCP. To be precise, the SCP moved into the Syndicat indépendant's offices on the rue Villedo, where it also set up its new placement office. The address had no small significance as an address "predestined" to place hairdressers. A. Spale and Emile Long had passed through it fifty years earlier, before its notorious practices made it the chief target of a drive to outlaw private *bureaux de placement*.[58]

The SCP brought together some of the capital's best-known and politically conservative figures in the hairdressing profession: Adolphe Fried, Victor Touzet, and a host of others. Among the most prominent, Robert Maigre, protégé of Ulysse Boucoiran, had long involved himself in the politics of the *patronat*, as a militant of the Syndicat indépendant and Fédération française. Arvet-Thouvet had served as secretary of the École supérieure de la coiffure and as vice president of the Union Saint-Louis. A brilliant coiffeur, Arvet-Thouvet had won several prestigious international awards, and his salon at 335, rue Vaugirard, was among the capital's most acclaimed.[59] But the chief engineer of this reorganization of patronal forces in coiffure was Marcel Bagnaud, who became one of the two or three key characters within the profession for the next fifteen years.

Bagnaud cut an unlikely figure among hairdressers. Born in 1893, educated at the École Normale Supérieure in the upper-middle-class Paris suburb of St-Cloud, Bagnaud never learned the tonsorial arts. He served in the war, where he was "gravely wounded" at the battle of Labyrinthe in September 1915, and left the army with decorations for bravery and as one of its "plus grands invalides." Since he was an educated man, Bagnaud found work as a journalist, writing for the *Petit Parisien*. He soon moved on to a job as administrator for the journal, *L'Intransigeant*, whose editor-in-chief, Colonel Jean Fabry, was up to his neck in Maurassian friends, including André Maginot, Pierre Taitinger, and Jean Chiappe.[60] Here Bagnaud made connections on the political right and got to know the organizations of *anciens combattants*, these associations he kept up even after he left the paper. In 1921, Bagnaud's career switched tracks when he married a *coiffeuse* and decided to open his own salon. A health crisis forced him into convalescence in the Dordogne for several years. But when he returned to Paris in 1926, Bagnaud bought a new salon on the rue Malakoff, just off the Place Victor-Hugo.

Bagnaud soon proved himself a talented businessman and was invited to join the Club artistique des coiffeurs de Paris, alongside such eminent coiffeurs as René Rambaud, Albert Pourrière, Gabriel Fau, and Guillaume. His "luxurious" Maison Marcel served an "aristocratic, artistic, and grande bourgeoise" clientele and became one of the most successful salons in the city, employing some three dozen *assistants* on its "modern . . . comfortable . . . clean" premises. Even his political nemesis, the labor leader François Magnien, later confessed his admiration for the Maison Marcel. Although at the time Magnien denounced Bagnaud a "speculator" and a "fascist" who drove around in a "sumptuous" car and had married for money—an activity Magnien described as a bourgeois "sport." "The poor," he added, "are above that: we follow our hearts." Magnien followed his three times.[61]

It did not take the SCP's enemies long to mobilize. In September 1932 a group of *ouvriers coiffeurs* showed up at a meeting in the back room of an elegant café on the Place Victor-Hugo to challenge Bagnaud and his new colleagues. The patrons refused to listen and called the *gendarmes*, who greeted the workers when they left the meeting. According to the report in the *Coiffeur Confédéré*, only the workers' *sang-froid* kept a brawl from erupting.[62]

CSP president Domède launched a scathing attack on Bagnaud in February 1933. He compared his own humble career with Bagnaud's privileged entry into the trade and dismissed his rival as the "[l]eader of a group of badly-informed malcontents, who opposed the *repos hebdomadaire collectif* as he had always opposed social progress . . . [Bagnaud] stood for the politics of regression." No wonder he opposed the *horaire unique*.[63]

Domède's criticism aside, Bagnaud's business acumen and political connections earned him an appointment as departmental inspector for

Enseignment technique. Henri Janvier, general secretary of the *confédérés* syndicat in Paris, objected that it was a "scandal" to place the "the worst enemy of the working class in coiffure" in charge of professional education.[64] But the criticism of *ouvriers* and *petits patrons* only helped to push Bagnaud rapidly up the ranks of the Parisian *patronat*. In 1934, he was elected secretary of the Paris Chamber of Commerce; four years later he became one of its vice presidents. It was a career propelled both by Bagnaud's business success and by his commitment to what he considered his primary political task: to block the road to creeping "state socialism."[65]

Bagnaud looked at law and administrative practice in the early 1930s and concluded that free enterprise was being strangled in France. But it is notoriously difficult, even in such a closely administrated country, to infer practice from the hash of labor legislation, decrees, *arrêtés*, and other rulings. If Bagnaud had looked more closely and with fewer prejudices at what was actually going on in the hairdressing salons, he might have imagined fewer Bolsheviks under his bed. He might have taken some comfort, for example, in the frequent complaints that the labor regulations, to which he objected, were *not* being enforced.[66]

In fact, the application of work-hours legislation provides another lesson in the difficulties inherent in reducing the workweek and in satisfying different constituencies. Throughout the 1920s, the Labor Ministry and prefects received a steady stream of reports that the new rules were being flouted. While it is not hard to imagine individual employers pressuring their employees into days longer than the law prescribed, the documents do not on the whole confirm this picture of official laxity. On the contrary, the labor inspectors in the early 1920s unanimously reported that, in spite of having to spread their attention thinly over a number of professions—bakeries, charcuteries, and restaurants, in addition to hairdressing salons—they were busy doing their jobs. Indeed, the evidence points to the state's diligence in enforcing the forty-eight hour week, as it pertained to the hairdressing profession.

In Caen, to take one example, authorities prosecuted Canteux, a shop owner, for attempting to circumvent the labor laws by forcing his employee, Bernard, to sign a contract that made the latter a sort of partner—since laws to protect employees obviously did not cover partners. A labor tribunal saw through the obvious fraud. It found Canteux in contravention of the labor laws, voided the contract, and levied a sizable fine against him.[67]

Confusion inhibited enforcement more than official bad faith because the rules were not always clear to those who had to administer them. Consider this case from the town of Auxerre in 1922. The departmental labor inspector for the Yonne, Albert Drancourt, issued a citation to a Monsieur Décorme, who employed three *assistants* in his salon de coiffure. Décorme's employees had the right to a sixty-hour work week, but the schedule he posted outside indicated that his shop was open seven days a week for a total of seventy-one hours of *ouverture*. He gave his workers time off by *roulement*. Décorme's challenge to his fine set off a revealing exchange within the administration.

Drancourt's action had been based on the understanding that the labor laws treated workers as a *collectivity*, not as individuals. The sixty-hour limit therefore restricted not individual work schedules but the number of hours a salon could employ *any* personnel. Objecting to this interpretation, the prefect of the Yonne wrote to the labor minister, saying that it constituted a constraint on the "liberté de commerce" inconsistent with the eight-hour law of 1919. He read the law as applying to individuals, rather than to the collectivity of workers; it therefore permitted *roulement*.

Peyronnet, the labor minister, disagreed. If the rule for Auxerre was sixty hours, then that was the maximum number of hours a salon could stay open, however many hours the personnel were engaged inside. The prefect's sharp, lawyer-like reply insisted on the minister's wrong headedness and the illegality of his interpretation. In the end, Peyronnet defended his point by basing his position on the 1906 law on *repos hebdomadaire* instead of the eight-hour law of 1919. This seems odd, given that the sixty-hour limit was the fruit of the October 1921 decree that applied the eight-hour law (and not the 1906 law) to coiffure.[68]

In any case, Peyronnet later reversed himself, writing to the divisional inspector of *travail* in Marseille that as long as (a) regular employees did not work longer than the decree allowed; (b) each employee received his *repos hebdomadaire*; and (c) "extras" were not *habituellement* employed by the same employer, then the law was being respected.[69] Above all, however, the dispute attests to the murky legal standing of *roulement*, and to the subsequent difficulty of applying the relevant rules.

Thus labor inspectors could not stop a coiffeur working alone from keeping whatever hours he wanted. And they could not interfere in the work lives of those subject to the authority of the *chef de famille*, for the forty-eight hour law explicitly declined to get involved in the family salon. In other words, the forty-eight hour law, like the *repos hebdomadaire* before it, did not presume to interfere with a proprietor's commercial practices, only with his relations with his employees.

On the other hand, the authorities consistently declined to grant salon owners any dispensation from their strict responsibilities. They refused a *derogation*, for example, to a *mutilé de guerre*, Monsieur Lethoor of Toulouse, a partially blind barber who wanted to keep his *garçon* an hour past the mandatory closing time without exceeding the maximum weekly hours. Likewise, when Monsieur Stoeltzen-Guyot, whose salon was very near the train station in Troyes, approached the administration with a request to bring his workers at 7 a.m., in order to serve customers getting on and off the morning trains, the local inspector turned his request down. The inspectors also kept an eye on congenital *refractaires*, such as Monsieur Blazy, who had received fourteen official visits and three citations in the preceding seven months, when inspector Madame Langlois discovered that he was operating a *salon clandestin* after hours.[70] It seems fair to conclude that the *pouvoirs publics* did their conscientious best to enforce the foggy code of labor regulations.

Denunciations, either by employees or by rivals, often helped lead inspectors to the delinquents. A tip from the Association syndicale des patrons coiffeurs de Lille, for instance, led the authorities to G. Villerval, who still had his employees at work at nine o'clock in the evening, well past the required closing time. The inspector, Madame Keller, first paid Villerval a sneak visit in April 1934, climbing through a small door in the back of the shop at 8:30 p.m., when the salon was officially shut. She found a violation and issued a citation.

In response, Villerval sent the labor minister an indignant letter in which he described Keller's "impertinence" and "aggressiveness." She had, he claimed, found only employees cleaning themselves up, working on each other's hair, or dividing up the day's tips. Keller, in contrast, maintained in her report that she knocked several times at the front door, but that the patron had begun to lock it and to sneak clients in through the back, following a surprise inspection the previous February. It took her twenty minutes to find another way into the shop. Then, when she confronted Villerval with his violations, the shop owner shoved her and her colleague, Mademoiselle Jardin, out the door.[71] Clearly, a labor inspector's work had its hazards.

Such official conscientiousness, if it was insufficiently thorough for the FNSOC and the UF, felt like an administrative dictatorship to the

SPC and other defenders of commercial "liberty." Bagnaud, for instance, accused the labor inspectors of intentionally setting out to entrap shop owners, and he recounted the following, probably apocryphal, incident. On New Year's Day 1933 a hairdresser, who was legally forbidden to work that day, opened his salon in order to sell cosmetics and toiletries, as the law permitted. Suddenly, a woman rushed in. "It's only for a little *friction*," she said. "You can't refuse me that. And call your wife to do my hands. It'll only be for five minutes. Nobody will know anything." Failing, alas, to resist a woman's temptation, the hairdresser relented. So did his wife. The client thanked them, then pulled a card from her handbag: "*Inspectrice du travail*! I am obliged to give you a citation. You have both been very kind in serving me because I have to go lunch in the city. However, duty first, *n'est-ce pas?*"[72]

The SPC also objected when inspectors slapped a Monsieur Lhoummeau of Paris with a 160-franc fine for having his two employees at work at 12:30 on a Saturday afternoon, when they were supposed to be enjoying their lunch.[73] In another case, inspecteur Langlois wrote to her superior, divisional inspector Auribault, about a Madame Moreau, who had been caught more than once making her employees work through their lunch hours. The first time, according to Langlois, Moreau had maintained that the employee was her daughter; hence, not covered by the regulations. But when Langlois paid a second visit, ten days later, she found another girl in the same situation. Again, Moreau explained that "This is my daughter, too. She's from my second marriage." Langlois did not believe her, and found her "hardly very polite" in the bargain.[74]

Of all the aspects of the *horaire unique*, shop owners commonly found the obligatory lunchtime closing, from 12:30 to 2 p.m., the most vexatious, for the obvious reason that, especially in the commercial districts, this was when customers usually wanted to have their hair done. As a Monsieur Varié explained, in the *quartier de l'Opéra*, where he operated a salon, his clientele were principally local employees, who came in overwhelmingly between noon and 2 p.m. "Why not leave the patron the latitude to talk to his *assistants*" and work out an acceptable schedule of *roulement*, he wondered? This same concern led a group of a hundred coiffeurs from nine salons near the Porte Saint-Denis in Paris to ask the labor minister for a *dérogation* that would permit employees to rotate through their lunch hours. This would enable the salons to take care of the crowd of employees from other businesses who had only their own lunch breaks to take care of their coiffures.[75]

Conversely, *ouvriers coiffeurs* were particularly keen to protect their one-and-a-half hour lunch break and keep it collective. The *Ouvrier Coiffeur* explained the workers' thinking in this fictional conversation among patron, client, and *assistant*:

"Why not just be flexible," the client asked the patron. "If the worker stays an hour later today, he can just come in an hour later in the morning."

"That's what I've always said," replied the patron, "but the workers won't let me do it."

The worker explained to the client that this would all be fine if the employers in fact kept their word, which they do not. The only way to be able to check that a worker is not being exploited—because most either do not know their rights or are afraid of the boss—is to have all the salons on the same schedule.

The worker then offered the following rationale for the *repas collectif*: "Take a salon where there are four workers, subject to *roulement*. One day, the first one leaves for lunch at eleven o'clock. The next day, on the pretext that he's taking care of a customer, a second worker takes his lunch slot and the first worker doesn't go off to lunch until one o'clock—if not two o'clock. You see how [with *roulement*] the worker's schedule is likely to change from one day to the next, to the point that his stomach gets upset [l'estomac se fatiguait] and he loses his appetite. This is the reason that so many workers have incurable stomach problems."

"My word," the client concluded, "if it's a matter of the workers' health (and I understand it now that you've explained it to me), I think that you ought to tell all your comrades, because there are some who are abetting their patrons. As for me, I'll no longer go to those salons that play fast and loose with their employees' health."[76]

Charles Desplanques, who had followed the familiar road from young militant syndicalist to middle-aged, professional advocate, considered the question of lunchtime and the "continuous work day" in the pages of the *Gallia* journal in 1929. Desplanques recognized that a hairdresser had to eat. The problem was that a client in a *salon pour dames* usually required two-and-a-half to three hours of his time. Thus, if a coiffeur gave a client an *indéfrisable* at eleven o'clock, he needed to take care of her until one or one-thirty. If the salon closed at noon for the mandatory lunch break, what was he to do? He broke the law if he continued to minister to his customer; he risked ruining her expensive perm if he did not. Desplanques therefore preferred the *journée continue* because it gave hairdressers the chance to do the best work. Moreover, by compressing the work day, it also held out the prospect of "more leisure hours that, employed wisely, are the charm and beauty of life." He dismissed the arguments against *roulement* as "puerile" and thought it made more sense for each salon, depending on its particular situation, to find the most practical and advantageous system of lunch breaks.[77]

It is impossible to say exactly to what extent the system of *repas collectif* operated in the hairdressing salons. The accord of May 1932 and the decree of October 1933 included it among the new regulations. The reports of the labor inspectors and the many requests for *dérogations*, invariably turned down, imply that the *pouvoirs publics* were committed to enforcing it. The *gros salonniers* continued to revile it. Yet there is no record of any fines ever being levied against Bagnaud's Maison Marcel or the Galeries Lafayette or the Maison Emile or any of the other *gros maisons*, while there is substantial hearsay evidence that they continued to practice *roulement* throughout the period.

*   *   *

The battle over the *horaire unique* looks arcane, but in fact it illuminates several interesting issues. First, it illustrates how the French state increasingly found itself caught between its traditional liberal commitment to commercial freedom and its growing obligations to social and labor reform. Hence, its ginger and inconsistent treatment of the *horaire unique* and other restrictions on the rights of patrons. At the same time, the energetic application of the forty-eight hour law and the *repas collectif* makes it clear that the state was becoming both more active and more comfortable with its regulatory responsibilities.

The campaign for and against *roulement* is even more significant for throwing light on the paradox of interest and ideology within the hairdressing profession. On the one hand, militant *ouvriers* often made no distinction between big employers and small *salonniers*. "For me," averred *confédéré* chief Henri Janvier, "There are neither *petits patrons* or *gros patrons*: there are only patrons."[78] On the other hand, support for the *horaire unique* frequently united workers and small *salonniers* behind government intervention and the moral economy.

Ultimately, however, the workers' desire for material advantage usually trumped their sentimental attachment to "smallness" and separated them from their artisanal allies. Thus *confédéré* militant André Langlois rubbished J. Cluzel's preference for artisanal shops over the department-store salons. If anything, Langlois wrote, the coiffeurs were just as good in the *grands magasins*, just as friendly—and probably happier, since they usually had better working conditions. It is the great irony of this three-way tussle that the *gros patrons*, who fought tooth and nail against the *horaire unique* and generally treated the workers' unions as the *avant garde* of Bolshevik revolution, were first to grant their employees a forty-eight hour week and *semaine anglaise*, along with the opportunity to earn superior wages. While *unitaires* and *confédérés* therefore saved their choicest invective for the "bourgeois" *chefs* of the SCP, they could not avoid the uncomfortable fact that the small shops, whatever their sense of solidarity with their employees, paid them less and worked them longer. This remained as true in 1933 as it had been in 1906.

Ladies' hairstyles, 1938

5

Fat Years, Lean Years

The turmoil over the eight-hour day resembles earlier battles for the *repos hebdomadaire*, but there is one fundamental difference. By the middle of the 1920s, economic recovery and the expansion of the market for fashionable commodities, especially the robust demand for short hairstyles, had propelled the hairdressing trades to unprecedented prosperity.

Short hair was the emblem of the "new woman," whose flat tummy, slim hips and bob defined fashion in the age of the flapper. It is the essence of fashion, however, that the climax of a style and its eclipse are never very far apart, and even as the flapper reigned supreme, she was beginning to fade. As the decade wore on and wealth recovered its swagger, the more democratic elements of *la mode*—even if they were strictly formal, like Chanel's "pauvreté de luxe"—started to recede. By the late 1920s, such vulgar displays of class distinction as furs and jewelry had regained their prominence.[1] The new feminine aesthetics were softer and more "sculpturale," their ideal not *le chic* but *la distinction*. In January 1930, *Vogue* reported the return of waists to the female figure and of floor-length skirts. The new fashions still respected the "active" woman—a little curvier, perhaps, a little more likely to be dressed by Schiaparelli and less by Chanel, but still fit and long-legged.[2]

Hairstyles evolved along the same lines. The public's taste for *cheveux courts* crested in 1926 and remained strong to the end of the decade. Plenty of women kept their short coiffures in the 1930s, and others cut theirs for the first time. But the trendiest ladies and their coiffeurs were already looking past the bob. When "waists go up and skirts touch the ground," *Vogue* predicted in December 1929, short hair will strike a false note in the "symphony of the ensemble." Even as hairstyles got longer, they remained short by historical standards, and not even the most "retro" styles sought to resurrect the piles of waves and doodads that had crowned Edwardian heads. After all, observed *Votre Beauté*, "Short haircuts aren't just fashion, they've entered our *moeurs*." Women's hair, it predicted, would never again reach below their shoulders.[3]

Still, the idea that the bob, which had brought so much revenue into the salons, might go out of style roused the hairdressing trades to a vigorous defense of *cheveux courts*. In a perfect turnabout, coiffeurs now argued that *cheveux longs* would be a disaster for feminine beauty. The well-known businessman and journalist André Quentin created a new journal, *Cheveux Courts*, dedicated precisely to preserving this profitable hairstyle. Encouraged by the fashion magazines, Quentin wrote in his first issue, long hairstyles were creeping back into public consciousness. He hoped that his new publication, devoted to the style and stylishness of *cheveux courts*, would parry their nefarious influence. The CSP, for its part, sought to impose a ten-franc annual fee on its members to finance the rescue of short hairstyles.[4]

Once again, coiffeurs' worries were misplaced. Longer styles continued to be as heavily worked as short ones, and fewer haircuts did not necessarily imply fewer trips to the salon. The soft locks that now fell around a woman's shoulders were still full of *boucles* and *ondulations*. The new styles required "perms" and were more likely than ever to use *teinture*. In March 1932, the *Coiffure de Paris* announced that blonde hair was all the rage. "There are no longer any brunettes . . . the Parisienne of 1932 is blonde." Although it added optimistically that, "There remain in Paris more than a million heads to dye." Two years later the journal touted the "platinum blonde" look of Joan [*sic*] Harlow that was bound to bring her "prodigious" success.[5] Clearly, expert opinion differed, since *Vogue* declared at the same moment that platinum blonde was "out" and had been replaced by golden or red highlights.[6]

The point was that longer styles did not mean cheaper styles, and the elaborate coiffures presented by celebrity hairdressers made it eloquently. *Votre Beauté* asked six of them for their predictions for 1936: "Nothing but dyed hair"; "*Vaporeuse* . . . natural, and light"; "curled and *bombé*"; "inspired by Atalante, *cette terrible sportive de la mythologie grèque*." These were some of the responses.[7] Calou's "simple" creation involved a "mass" of little curls; Bruera's were ornamented with jewels, flowers, or feathers. Antoine liked pink and mauve tints. Renée, from Chez Emile, preferred henna, because it was a good *tonique* and left a "blonde rouge" color.[8] The Angel (1932)—without any waves at all, but finished with "flat, soft curls" that created a kind of "aura" around the face—brought Guillaume, one of a new generation of *hauts coiffeurs* working for Rambaud at Chez Emile, his first international exposure. He doubled his fame in 1934, with the Star hairstyle, and celebrated the opening of his own salon on the avenue Matignon with the creation of the Pageboy in 1936 and the Eagle (which returned to shorter and more intensively worked hair) in 1937.[9]

The shift to longer, more *mouvementées*, and more "done" hairstyles evoked the broader evolution towards more "feminine" styles in the 1930s. "Yesterday," ran an advertisement for the oil bath Oléopédal, "the *garçonne* hairstyle sacrificed a woman's most natural finery . . . Today the 1938 woman has again become Woman . . . ."[10] In some respects, the new styles implied a far-reaching change in aesthetic sensibilities, perhaps even a reversal of the movement toward "androgynous" forms that had occurred in the early 1920s.

That this shift appeared to coincide with the very moment when France followed the rest of the industrial world into depression led Rambaud, always the most historically attuned of coiffeurs, to wonder at a possible connection between these two phenomena—as if *cheveux courts* were somehow the expression of optimism, expansion, and proto-feminism, whereas longer hairstyles fit an era of pessimism and retrenchment. Marianne Delbourg-Delphis makes the connection explicit when she writes that the 1930s woman, unlike the *garçonne*, "spoke less of her freedom than of her responsibility."[11]

This pop genealogy raises several problems, however. Leaving aside empirical questions about whether there was any real retrogression in *la condition féminine*, the *garçonne* had already demonstrated the absence of any such easy and reliable correspondence between form and historical context. For another thing, the move away from the *garçonnesque* shapes of the 1920s pre-dated the arrival of the depression in France. Besides, as Cecil Beaton wrote later, the fashion shift was less abrupt than some observers made out: "The boyish bob had vanished, but women's breasts were still flat, and the longer skirts and slightly higher waistlines seem merely mechanical additions to the short, tubular dresses they had displaced."[12] In short, there is no reason to read the 1930s styles as a conservative coup in fashion in general or coiffure in particular.

Notwithstanding the unceasing circulation of fashions, and in spite of the syndical troubles that continued to stir below the surface of the profession, by the second half of the 1920s France had more coiffeurs in more salons attending to more customers and making more money than ever before. The numbers tell an unambiguous and dramatic story. *Population active* in coiffure rose steadily from just under 53,000 in 1921 to 126,000 in 1936. Thousands of barbers converted their shops into *salons mixtes*, exchanging their razors and *tondeuses* for permanent-waves machines and *teinture*. At the same time, *chômage* among coiffeurs virtually disappeared. Even the sector of *coiffeur-hommes* felt the labor shortage, which led the Union fédérale, in an extraordinary turnabout, to encourage barbershops to bring in women to shave their willing customers.[13]

The expanding market for hairdressers aggravated the apprentice-ship crisis that had long troubled the profession, especially since the arrival of technology in the salon made training more technical and complex. "To learn the hairdressing trade," said anarchist and ladies' hairdresser, Gustave Tixier, "it is no longer, as it once was, enough to learn to shave, to cut hair, to use the curling iron haphazardly . . . while talking abut the rain and the sunshine or telling dirty jokes."[14]

The problem, noted Pernellant, CSP president in 1924, was that young people those days lacked patience. It required years of training to become a good coiffeur, while the young would rather go off to a factory, where they could earn money right away.[15] May be. But the young had also been put off by the generally miserable conditions of apprenticeship in coiffure, where *apprentis* were often used as cheap labor and given little of value in return. That was the complaint of Madame Wajnberg, whose son, Benjamin, was taken on as an appren-tice and never taught anything, merely made to clean up.[16] The report of the Office départemental du placement for the Seine expressed a particular concern with the "conditions défectueuses" of female apprentices.[17]

Even under the best circumstances, apprenticeship could be a long, difficult road. Sociologist Bernard Zarca retells the story of a Mademoiselle Frémont. A child of the working class, Frémont was fortunate to find an apprenticeship at age twelve, in a fine salon in the center of town with a distinguished clientele, here she not only learned her *métier* but received an education in life from her worldly cus-tomers. With no apprenticeship contract, Mademoiselle Frémont received no wage at all for the first year and only fifty centimes a day, plus some small tips, for the second. If her third year was a little better, she remembered, that was because of the Popular Front. For the first nine or ten months she stuck to mannequins, mastering the "marcel," learning how to prepare a customer and shampoo her. Frémont then moved on to real heads. The patron introduced her to *teinture* at the end of her second year. In the third year, she began to apply all these techniques together.[18]

Coiffeurs assumed that professional training belonged in the salon, where the experienced patron could pass on professional culture along with technical skill. Yet prominent figures within the trade began to think that the state also had a role to play in *enseignement technique*, not just in promoting apprenticeship, but in organizing, subsidizing, and certifying professional preparation. This had the double advantage of giving coiffeurs professional legitimacy and limiting access to the trade. Progress came slowly, but in 1931 the government created the C.A.P., the Certificat d'aptitude professionnelle. In 1935, following additional lobbying by hairdressers' groups, it added the *brevet professionnel*, a sort of advanced warrant of professional merit. In 1937, the Walter-Paulin law, vested the control over apprenticeship in the artisanal *chambres de métiers* organizing themselves across France.[19]

Young coiffeurs were more dependably trained at the *écoles de coiffure* operated by several Parisian organizations: the École supérieure de coiffure, directed for the Syndicat indépendant by Robert Maigre; the old École parisienne de coiffure, run now by the *unitaires*, which carried on the tradition of *formation professionnelle* by *ouvriers coiffeurs* themselves; and the *confédérés'* new École de coiffure de Paris, under the direction of Gustave Tixier. But these schools were open only to those already *syndiqués* and did not reach enough young coiffeurs to solve the apprenticeship crisis.[20]

A second consequence of prosperity in the hairdressing trades was a substantial rise in the costs of setting up and doing business. Steeply rising commercial rents and the burden of new technology pushed up the price of *installation*.[21] C. Kauffmann and J. Barth, professors at the *école de perfectionnement* in Strasbourg, estimated in 1923 that it cost between two and four thousand francs to set up a hairdressing salon in the countryside, eight to ten thousand in a medium-size city, and fifteen to twenty thousand in a big city, although the particular costs naturally varied according to the size and location of a shop.[22] The real cost of a *situation* rose by more than 400 percent through the 1920s, even discounting inflation (table 5.1). And, although no figures are available for the second half of the 1920s, there is no reason to think that prices reversed direction, at least until the depression sent almost all prices into a tailspin.

Table 5.1 The Sale Price of Salons de Coiffure in Paris, 1915–1935*

Year	No. of Salons	Average Price (Francs)	Inflation Price Index, 1913 = 100	Real Price Index**	Inflation Price Index, 1938 = 100	Real Price Index***
1915	40	2,790	140	199.3	15.6	178.8
1916	35	5,520	190	290.5	19.1	289.0
1917	71	11,329	270	419.6	24.7	458.7
1918	100	21,281	350	608.0	31.8	458.7
1925	519	60,219	560	1,075.3	57.7	1,043.7
1926	466	65,607	720	911.2	71.4	918.9
1935	217	40,730			66.1	616.2

* Information on the price of salons de coiffure bought and sold is in Préfecture de la Seine. Secrétariat général. Statistique départementale et communale, *Annuaire statistique de la ville de Paris, 1915–1918* (Paris: Imprimerie F. Deshayes, 1921), 365; idem, *Annuaire de la statistique de la Ville de Paris, années 1935, 1936 et 1937* (Paris: Imprimerie F. Deshayes, 1942), 745–7. The inflation index based on 1913 and 1914 prices is from *Le mouvement des prix de 1913 à 1950. Recueil des cours et indices des principaux produits industriels, du coût de la vie et des salaires, mis à jour au 1er mai 1950* (Paris: L'Usine Nouvelle, 1950), 1; the index based on 1938 prices is from Jeanne Singer-Kérel, *Le coût de la vie à Paris de 1840 à 1954* (Paris: Presses de la Fondation Nationale des Sciences Politiques, 1961), 239.
** average price of a salon adjusted for inflation (1913 = 100).
*** average price of a salon adjusted for inflation (1938 = 100).

A part of the rising cost of a place in the patronat no doubt reflected the growing importance of expensive *appareils* in the modern salon. It might have also signaled the fact that larger salons were changing hands. There is no direct evidence either way in the sources, yet it is true that, as coiffure grew in the 1920s, the number of larger salons in France multiplied, from 206 *entreprises* with six or more employees in 1921 to 696 in 1936. And their proportion of all hairdressing *entreprises* increased markedly through the prosperous years. Still, they never comprised more than a small part of the profession.

From a different angle, the structure of the profession changed very little, even as the business of hairdressing was transformed. The proportion of *chefs d'entreprise* rose slightly from 1921 to 1936, both in Paris and in the country as a whole. And while the number and proportion of larger salons increased a little bit, the proportion of *chefs* who directed *petits salons* stayed pretty much the same. Salons with one to five employees accounted for 90.7 percent of all *entreprises* and employed 90.5 percent of all employees in 1921. They still made up over 87 percent of shops with 88 percent of the *ouvriers* in 1936. Moreover, these smaller salons were genuinely *petits*, with an average of well under two *assistants*. Only the country's biggest employers got substantially bigger in those fifteen years.[23]

If prices were increasing faster than the size of hairdressing salons, it makes sense to believe that *salons de coiffure* cost more because they were worth more. The rising sale price was therefore a sign of both profitability and the increased cost of doing business. The *salons pour dames* of the 1920s were highly capital intensive, requiring expensive *machines à l'indéfrisable* and hair-dryers, chemicals for *teinture*, custom chairs, porcelain sinks, and a stock of shampoos, tonics, and other beauty products for sale. The Maison Philippe in Marseille offered its pampered clients, up to 250 a day, "thirty *cabines* featuring *toute la perfection du confort moderne*" and affected the style of a medical clinic: "symbol of hygiene, health, and *sécurité totale*."[24]

In her breezy memoir, *Madeleine Grown Up*, Mrs. Robert Henrey described her early career as a young manicurist in the posh salon of the Savoy Hotel in London, although elite culture was so cosmopolitan that she could have easily been depicting one of the luxury hotels of Paris. "Madeleine" found the place intoxicating, "full of glass and perfume," with "its scintillating window of Parisian scent bottles." A small bottle of "Mme. Chanel's Number Five," she observed, "was worth more than a week of my wages." The barbershop, where Henrey gave manicures while customers were being shaved, was downstairs, "with its fascinating mirrors and shining white chairs." But, in fact, early in the morning it was largely empty, since the senior barbers would already have gone upstairs to shave the "various millionaires," staying at the hotel.[25]

The Maison Philippe and Savoy Hotel were clearly exceptional. Even in the middle of the profession, however, Kauffmann and Barth estimated that the price of a hairdressing salon represented almost three years' wages for the average employee. Perhaps that is why, according to Charles Desplanques, the trade was seeing more and more *assistants* in their thirties. Now that the price of becoming a *salonnier* had gone up so sharply, workers more often got struck in wage-earning positions.[26]

Of course, if set-up costs were rising in the hairdressing trade, they could hardly have become prohibitive, since new salons were opening with record frequency. The number of *établissements* in coiffure in Paris jumped from 2,470 in 1921 to 3,989 in 1936, while the population of *employés et ouvriers* leapt from 5,519 to 10,623. Even in the backwater of the Lot department, the number of hairdressing salons doubled from thirty-seven to seventy-seven in these fifteen years. And if more hairdressers were content to spend their careers as *assistants*, maybe it is because the profession was finally giving its workers a living, if not a generous wage and a bearable work schedule.

Table 5.2   Women in Coiffure, 1896–1936: Number of women and percentage of total working population*

Year	France	Paris	Banlieue	Gironde	Lot
1896	4,857 (10.1%)	542 (8.5%)	136 (9.9%)	88 (4.8%)	7 (3.3%)
1911	7,074 (11.4)	977 (10.7)	242 (10.1)	109 (5.1)	14 (6.8)
1921	10,189 (18.2)	3,398 (30.5)	628 (23.8)	257 (14.8)	17 (10.8)
1926	12,131 (19.7)	4,190 (32.4)	774 (23.1)	319 (16.7)	11 (6.8)
1931	NA	6,652 (38.7)	2,037 (34.0)	864 (30.0)	65 (26.1)
1936	45,729 (36.5)	8,664 (43.5)	3,221 (40.6)	1,317 (35.0)	98 (29.9)

* Ministère du Commerce, *Résultats statistiques, 1896, tome I*, 296–7 and 352–3; *tome III* (1900), 473, 497; *tome IV* (1901), 254–5; Ministère du Travail. Statistique générale de la France, *Résultats statistiques du recensement général de la population effectué le 5 mars 1911, tome I* (Paris: Imprimerie Nationale, 1913), 27–8; *tome II* (1915), 8, 21, 575, and 591; idem, *Résultats statistiques, 1921, tome I* (1923), 148–9; *tome II* (1925), 1–8; *tome III* (1926), 74–8; Ministère du Travail, de l'Hygiène, et al, *Résultats statistiques, 1926, tome I* (1931), 158–9; *tome III* (1930), 4, 8, 128, and 136; Présidence du Conseil, *Résultats statistiques, 1931, tome II* (1935), 4 and 8; *tome IV* (1935), 112 and 120; Statistique générale de la France, *Résultats statistiques, 1936, tome I* (1943), 58; *tome II* (1943), 4 and 8; *tome III* (1944), 112 and 120.

To talk merely of numbers, however, is to miss the most extraordinary and profound change that engulfed the profession between the world wars: the influx of young women. The census of 1896 had counted only 4,857 *coiffeuses* in all of France, 10 percent of the *population active*, and these in the great majority would have been wives and daughters helping out in a family enterprise, or *posticheuses*, working in the manufacture of hair pieces.[27]

Table 5.2 paints an unmistakable picture. As demand for coiffure was feminized, the workforce that satisfied this demand itself became feminized. It is a commonplace that World War I produced a lasting impact on the demography of French labor, with a particularly lively leap in the percentage of workingwomen in commerce.[28] The transformation of the hairdressing profession was a particularly striking example of this.

Across the country, the presence of *coiffeuses* grew from one in ten in the 1890s to one in three in the mid-1930s, while the raw numbers of female hairdressers increased fourfold. Paris provided an even more dramatic example of what the modernization of the profession entailed. The *population active féminine* multiplied by a factor of sixteen, while the proportion of *coiffeuses* expanded by 400 percent. Coiffure was on its way to becoming a *profession féminine*.[29]

Louise Vanderwielen's autobiographical novel, *Lise du Plat Pays* (1983) tells the exemplary story of one woman's itinerary as a *coiffeuse*.[30] Fired from her job in a textile factory, Lise came to hairdressing by serendipity. Passing by a shop window one day, she read a sign: "Looking for models for *ondulation Marcel* . . . 1 franc per hour." Needing the work, Lise stepped into the shop and offered her *chevelure* for the training of young *coiffeuses*. The first trainee to touch her, Vanderwielen remembered, was "a fat daughter of rich butcher parents," who almost burned her ear off with a curling iron. Intrigued by what she saw going on around her, however, Lise began to arrive at the *école* early each day and to try out the techniques being practiced on her own head. She did not have the money herself to take these lessons but used these prework mornings to teach herself the rudiments of curling—hardly a unique skill, yet enough to strike out on her own.

After several months of cropping and curling as the opportunity arose, Lise, who by then had a handful of clients, rented a small *deux pièces*. She placed a white table and a mirror in the small parlor and became, in effect, a *coiffeuse à domicile*. On Saturday, the *jour du bal*, clients waited their turn outside, on the staircase. Lise dreamed of having a real shop, on a big street, with a sign and a shop window. In the meantime, she took courses to improve and expand her repertoire of skills. She profited especially from the free lessons on *indéfrisable* offered by all the manufacturers of permanent-wave machines. In the mid-1930s, Lise, who still owed the plumber for the installation of hot water that allowed her to shampoo her customers, could not afford these pricey machines. Finally, however, through perseverance and good luck, Lise succeeded in finding a storefront on a busy street. She bought a couple of hairdryers and a *machine à l'indéfrisable* on credit, hired an employee, and took on an apprentice.

Vanderwielen's tale of social promotion, of the uneducated, unskilled girl from the working class who climbed into the *petit patronat*, undoubtedly captures a certain social reality. Young female recruits to the hairdressing trade must have come overwhelmingly from the popular classes, for whom a career in a beauty salon offered the prospect of a reasonably paid and satisfying professional life. Opportunities for domestic work had largely dried up during the war, and young women without much qualification surely looked at the life of a *coiffeuse* as preferable to the monotony and discipline of the factory, to say nothing of the sweated textile industry. Besides, as the unpromising career of Lise suggests, in coiffure even a young woman without many resources could aspire to become a small shop owner. In 1936, there were over 15,000 female *chefs d'entreprise* in coiffure, 37 percent of the total and more than three times as many as ten years earlier.[31] A place in the petty bourgeoisie was no idle dream.

There is something anomalous in the opportunities that opened to women in coiffure. Labor historians have long made us familiar with the notion that the feminization of a trade marked its decline, as employers shifted from skilled to semiskilled labor and lowered wages dramatically.[32] Yet this decidedly did not happen in the hairdressing trades, where the influx of women between the world wars accompanied a period of unparalleled well-being. Common sense suggests that young women, with less experience and less capital behind them, had a harder time than men breaking into the *patronat*, and that they therefore occupied the most precarious *situations* in coiffure, often working *à domicile*, like Louise Vanderwielen's protagonist. There is also reason to believe that *jeunes filles* monopolized the least remunerated jobs in the big salons, as manicurists and pedicurists, and that, further up the salon hierarchy, women became rarer. It therefore seems fair to assume that the average coiffeur earned more than the average *coiffeuse*.

On the other hand, there is no reason to presume that, even in the finer salons, women earned less than men at the same levels of skill. In fact, the dozens of wage agreements that were signed in the 1930s that set guidelines for different skill levels never distinguished between coiffeurs and *coiffeuses* performing the same tasks. Moreover, so long as a lot of men continued to practice the unprofitable barbering arts while women almost always worked in the more lucrative field of *coiffure-dames*, it is just possible that, on an average, women in coiffure made more money than men.

To be sure, the elite of the profession remained uniformly masculine. Not a single *coiffeuse* was listed among the members of the organizations of elite hairdressers: the Institut des coiffeurs de dames, the Club artistique des Paris, the Association internationale des coiffeurs de dames. This singular fact becomes even more curious when we look at the situation in *haute couture*, where Coco Chanel, Maggy Rouff, and Elsa Schiaparelli more than held their own against Lucien Lelong and the other male designers of the day. There is no obvious explanation for the absence of a parallel group of *hautes coiffeuses*.

At the other end of professional life, women continued to be all but absent from the syndicats of *patrons* and *ouvriers coiffeurs*. Indeed, the invisibility of *coiffeuses* in the labor movement in coiffure becomes all the more confounding when we consider the circumstances. As workers' and patrons' syndicates pursued their struggles over hours and wages, women were streaming into the salons. Yet neither side attempted seriously to recruit them. The FNSOC claimed to have a *Commission féminine*, but it left no significant trace in the federation's archives or its journal, the *Ouvrier Coiffeur*. True, *ouvriers coiffeurs* no longer spoke, as they had at the turn of the century, of the sharp danger from *ouvrières* who would drive down wages; instead, they ignored the issue. In sum, the labor movement in coiffure continued to treat women's work as "an unfortunate accident," in Laura Frader's succinct phrase. It remained an unreconstructedly "male space," and women workers mostly avoided it.[33] It is difficult to avoid the impression of a movement that had a trump card—or, at any rate, an ace—and simply refused to play it. It is even harder to imagine how the *ouvriers* thought they could ever put decisive pressure on their employers without involving the women, who had come to constitute such a sizeable portion of the workforce.

To be fair to the *ouvriers*, patronal groups made equally little effort to appeal to their female colleagues. Two women sat among the hundred delegates to the 1928 congress of the Union fédéral; both were the wives of delegate husbands, and neither spoke during the proceedings.[34] No *petites patronnes* ever made their way onto the *bureau* of the UF or any of the other national groups of employers. The subject never came up at their meetings and congresses. *Coiffeuses*, either as individuals or as a topic for discussion, were equally invisible on the local level. At a moment when the CSP and the SCP in Paris were engaged in a four-way battle—against professional disarray, workers' demands, unfavorable administrative action, and each other—neither of them thought to go looking for allies among the thousands of *salonnières*.

The failure to rally *coiffeuses* to the employers' cause was, if anything, more remarkable than the disinterest of the *organisations ouvrières*, for the simple fact that women comprised a bigger portion of *chefs d'entreprise* than they did of *personnel*. The 1926 census found that a quarter of the *patrons coiffeurs* in France were female, as opposed to 19 percent of *employés*. Women played even a bigger role in the *patronat* in Paris, where they made up 31 percent in 1926. By 1931 women ran 42.5 percent of the capital's 5,179 *établissements*, whereas they accounted for only 33.2 percent of employees.

It was alleged at the time by both workers and employers, and leaders of the profession continue to maintain it today, that the conspicuous absence of women from professional organizations in coiffure reflected women's choice not to participate more than men's reluctance to encourage this participation. Bernard Zarca, in his massive study of the contemporary artisanat, concludes, for example, that women were apt to "interiorize" the values of their trade and to concentrate on social mobility rather than class confrontation.[35] Theresa McBride makes a similar point in her study of "French Women and Trade Unionism," about a female mentality that inhibited union organization.[36] "A boy's career," wrote one British manufacturer, "is bound up with his work, whereas the average woman looks on her work merely as an incident in her career . . . her work is not her life . . . she is merely spending her time usefully until marriage brings her the fulfillment of her life."[37]

Their aversion to confrontation and identification with professional values might elucidate women's reluctance to join the CGT. It would not, however, explain why they avoided the employers' groups and the organizations devoted to *perfectionnement*. Michel Bourlon, the long-time president of the Force Ouvrière's national federation of coiffeurs (FNSOC-FO) who is married to a *coiffeuse*, has come to the conclusion that, while women have often been devoted to their *métier*, they have simply been less attracted than men to collective action.[38] After all, if *coiffeuses* were excluded from the organized ranks of the profession, they never tried to assemble their own troops.

To be honest, the available sources do not allow us to say how feminine culture and personal circumstances worked to keep *coiffeuses* out of trade organizations. They do not even throw much light on the biases of these organizations. These are detectable entirely in the fact that, while the leaders of coiffure gave so much thought and effort to mobilizing hairdressers and straightening out professional affairs, they apparently devoted so little to those female colleagues who had become such an important element of their trade.

Organized or not, women were coming into a profession whose working conditions were improving substantially through the 1920s. Figures on wages in coiffure are sketchy, but they all point to a steady rise from the end of the war to the edge of the depression.[39] In 1923, wage scales in Paris ranged between twenty and thirty francs a day, depending on the quality of the shop and the skill of the practitioner. Elsewhere they settled between twenty and twenty-three francs. Figures from the end of the decade confirm the trend. In Bordeaux, wages reached up to forty-five francs a day in 1927; forty-eight in 1929. Parisian coiffeurs at the same moment were asking for sixty francs a day, half of what the most skilled *assistants* in the best salons were being paid. This privileged portion of *ouvriers* added a percentage, usually 10 or 12 percent, of the business they generated to their paychecks. In a word, real wages more than kept abreast of inflation, doubling between 1919 and 1930.[40]

Even as wages improved, hairdressers continued to count on *pourboires* to make ends meet. According to Marcel Meunier, a vice president of the UF from the Isère, tips accounted for 25 percent of a worker's *salaire*, a fact that, just as it had in the earlier period, pleased some folks and infuriated others.[41] Opinion on *pourboires* did not reliably divide employers and employees, but rather those who worked in fancy shops from those who worked in *salons populaires*. The former, with a more spendthrift clientele, tended to see the gratuity as a way for customers to express their satisfaction. Most others advocated its suppression. The workers' syndicats in particular continued to look forward to exchanging the *pourboire* for a reliable and honorable *salaire minimum*.

Coiffure's new affluence did not kill the old debate. Alphonse Mornot, honorary president of the UF in 1923, predicted that the profession would never be properly respected as long as the *pourboire* remained the basis of the worker's wage. R. Freulon, author of *L'Art de lancer un salon de coiffure*, thought that it distorted the work of the salon by encouraging coiffeurs to treat clients according to their generosity, and allowing them to "blackmail" customers with complaints about low wages. The hairdressing workers of Toulouse condemned tips as "a source of revenue for the patron and humiliation for the worker." Rambaud hated the practice, while his old mentor Luquet accepted that "the tip is ingrained in French habits, and there's nothing we can do about it." Their colleague Ravanier, from Marseille, added his own opinion that "the workers are *against* its suppression." In any case, the *pourboire* survived.[42]

Tips or no tips, a coiffeur's income depended on his salon's revenues, which in turn rested ultimately on prices, which rose throughout the 1920s. In Toulon, in 1918, barbers were still offering their services by subscription. Customers could have two shaves a week for two and a half francs a month; for another franc they could have three shaves a week. Walk-ins paid forty centimes for a shave and fifty for a haircut.[43] Even in 1920, noted the *Coiffure de Paris*, many hairdressers were still working at ridiculous prices: shaves at forty centimes; *ondulations* that could fetch four or five francs, offered for two-francs-fifty.[44] But then, according to the statistics gathered by

Jeanne Singer-Kérel, prices in coiffure began a vertical climb. She does not have precise figures for each year but estimates that prices increased six-fold between 1920 and 1926. They continued to go up thereafter, albeit at a slower pace, until the onset of the economic crisis in 1931. For the whole period from 1913 to 1938, the price of a man's haircut rose by a factor of seventeen, from thirty-five centimes to six francs. The price of a shave climbed from twenty-five centimes to two francs, a mere 800 percent ascent, no doubt restrained by fierce competition from the safety razor.[45]

Prices were already considerably higher in the *salons pour dames* than in the barbershops. For example, in the spring of 1924, the CSP suggested *tarifs* of one franc for a shave and three for a man's haircut, whereas it recommended charging women four francs for an *ondulation*, four more for shampooing, and five for a *coupe*.[46] The real bonanza for ladies' hairdressers, however, lay not in rising prices for these relatively simple services but in the constantly expanding menu of beauty treatments available in the salons: hair "highlighting," gentler shampoos, depilatories.

The most elegant hairdressing establishments added *instituts de beauté*, where they offered pedicures and facials, paraffin baths, epilation for the eyebrows, appointments under ultraviolet lamps to restore "damaged" hair, doublebrush treatments and massage for the scalp to prevent dandruff, and huge body rollers to reduce fat. Elizabeth Arden introduced her line of beauty products in 1920, offering her customers Venetian orange skin food, muscle oil, and *poudre d'illusion*. Helena Rubenstein's followed the next year. Among the French pioneers of this lucrative business, Antoine lent his name to a line of beauty products that came into the market in 1932, and *les produits René Rambaud* were not far behind.[47]

The workhorse of hairdressing profits, however, remained the permanent wave.[48] By the middle of the 1920s, when the technology stabilized and millions of French women acquired the habit of "perming" their hair, a session under the *machine à l'indéfrisable* would cost the customer 150 francs or more, depending on the location and class of her salon. In addition, the client who "permed" her hair required subsequent treatments to keep it "fresh" and products to make it look its best.

Standing near the center of most salons, with its large steel dome and dangling wires, the permanent-wave machine became the material symbol of how much life in the salon had changed in twenty years. It was not only that contemporary coiffeurs or *coiffeuses* now enjoyed a universally recognized right to a *repos hebdomadaire* and *semaine anglaise*, working fifty to sixty hours a week, where the previous generation had worked seventy to eighty; or that better wages had finally lifted most employees into the main part of the working class; or even that most shops were filling up with women. It was above all that the modern salon ran on technology—electrical apparatuses, scientifically developed hair-care products—and commerce.

These new operations naturally altered the work rhythms of the salon. The old barbershop standard, shave and a haircut, took only a few minutes of a hairdresser's time. Except for those occasional moments of frenetic demand on a Saturday night or the eve of an important holiday, when men who were normally pretty casual about their appearance wanted to look neat, work in a hairdressing salon was an on-and-off sort of business. It left ample time to smoke, to gossip, to read the paper, and to keep the place neat and tidy—at least according to the standards of the day. On the contrary, hair coloring was an intense and time-consuming affair, while a permanent wave kept a coiffeur occupied, more or less, for a couple of hours. In addition, the popularity of these techniques "that have seduced feminine coquetry" brought in a lot more customers. Rambaud reminded an audience of this transformation when he referred to the old days of "travail intermittent," that lasted from 6 a.m. to 10 p.m., or even later on the weekends, and where, on a weekday, a barber might serve only half-a-dozen clients. Today's workdays, he told them, are "shorter and fuller."[49]

The cost of higher wages and shorter hours, Rambaud went on, was fatigue. That is, the generally benevolent evolution of *coiffure pour dames* often meant continual work in cramped spaces: hot, poorly ventilated, and filled with noxious vapors. This was particularly true insofar as hairdressing salons, as they multiplied, did not necessarily become more salubrious. Imagine the sinister effect of high rent on commercial space, to say nothing of the thousands of practitioners who worked *à domicile* or in some other *non*commercial lodging. The *Coiffeur Confédéré* complained about the many small, airless, dirty salons, as barbers converted their already tiny shops to *coiffure mixte* and as half-trained young people set up shop in basements and other such places. "How many hairdressers," it asked, "are tubercular, poisoned, dying in the fullness of their youth?"[50] A *unitaire* poster similarly warned of the "noxious emanations from ether, from curling irons, perfumes, hairdryers, and permanent-wave solutions," leading to "the slow murder of thousands of hairdressing workers."[51]

These were no idle accusations. The introduction of machines and chemicals into *salons de coiffure* genuinely increased the risk to those who served and those who came to be served. The evening press of November 29, 1933, for example, published a story about "a young girl electrocuted by a permanent-wave helmet." The *Coiffure de Paris* denied the validity of the story, but its clarification was hardly reassuring. The culprit, it explained, was not *machine à l'indéfrisable*, but a hairdryer in which a faulty maintenance had left a loose wire that triggered the short.[52] Most accidents were not so dramatic, and few were fatal. Less dramatic and nonfatal accidents, however, were common enough. There were the everyday errors, due to inattention and incompetence, like the one that cost Pierre Toché his job at the Maison Charles after he had given a client a horrible cut and burned her for good measure.[53] The most dangerous substance in the salon continued to be *éthère de pétrole*, responsible for a series of reported explosions: in the salon of Monsieur Tagalde in Arcueil, leaving a worker severely burned and blind; in the Salon Tache, in the twentieth arrondissement, seriously burning a client and sending an *ouvrier* to the hospital; at the Salon Chavvot, breaking all the windows on the second floor of the building. Yet another mishap in Paris burned someone alive, while an ether blast in Troyes destroyed a three-story building.[54] Coiffeurs whose own salons escaped trouble often merely passed the hazard along by pouring their used ether down the sink, leading to explosions in the sewers.[55]

In the 1920s, hairdressers discovered that they could reduce the flammability of ether by adding to it a substance called carbontetrachloride. Unfortunately, while "tetra" was less likely to explode, it was highly toxic, and when it suffused the air of a salon it had an effect similar to chloroform.[56] Experts and public officials also worried about the noxious fumes produced by the new system of "cold" permanents. The "système Zoto," introduced in 1932, was a fizzy powder emptied out of a small packet directly on to the rolled wet hair. It gave, according to *Vogue*, "astonishing results" and represented "progress from every point of view."[57] The expert Kling report of 1936, however, noted that the chemical reaction involved emitted highly toxic fumes. It cautioned against the use and sale of this product, which threatened the health of both workers and clients.[58]

Municipal authorities continually sought to regulate the use of dangerous chemicals, but the "grave professional accidents that occur[ed] every day in the hairdressing salons" continued to happen, largely because the authorities lacked the means to police practices in the thousands of small salons, especially when the majority of *patrons coiffeurs* opposed what they saw as an infringement on their professional routines and source of profit.[59]

Throughout the 1930s, medical authorities and *pouvoirs publics*, unable to take effective action, continued to worry about safety in hairdressing salons. Clearly, the specter of burns, allergies, noxious fumes, and the occasional short circuit was never sufficient to scare clients away. As to the long-term toll of *maladies professionnelles* on those who worked in this toxic environment, it remained a matter of speculation.

Within a few years, hairdressers had more to worry about than police regulations and occupational rashes, for the depression that finally reached France in 1931 landed hard on the fortunes of hairdressers. The wives of the working and lower-middle classes no longer had any money, and so had given up the habit of visiting the hairdresser, wrote Lavigne in the *Journal des Maîtres-Coiffeurs*. Robert Maigre complained at the end of 1935 that customers who used to come in every ten or fifteen days now visited the salon only every three to four weeks. Hairdressers in the southwest reported a 38 percent fall-off in business between 1929 and 1935.[60]

One consequence of the crisis was a "vertical drop" in hairdressing prices. In saner parts of the market, wrote Gabriel Fau, solidly trained, proven professionals ought to have enjoyed a competitive advantage. But on the contrary, current conditions favored "les naufrageurs [wreckers] du métier."[61] Poorer customers became more apt to trade quality service for lower cost and to abandon *artisans coiffeurs* for the infamous "hairdressing factories." Even "luxurious" salons got caught in the price vortex: "For you, Madame," advertised one such salon, "haircut, shampoo, *friction ordinaire* and waving—28 francs." The male version of this "boiler-plate special" cost only ten francs.[62] A 1943 report to the Commerce Ministry recalled that barbers had tried to compensate for falling prices by pushing their ancillary business in accessories and toiletries. As a result, it noted, a man who came in for a shave would inevitably find himself "hassled" into accepting a *friction*, and ill-treated if refused.[63]

The pinch had an especially devastating effect on permanent-wave rates. In Saint-Etienne, the cost of some *indéfrisables* fell to seventy francs. In Clermont-Ferrand, they could be found *in extremis* for forty-five francs. Salons that had charged 200 francs a couple of years before, were now asking eighty. By 1932, a woman could treat herself to a permanent for as little as thirty francs.[64] Hairdressers searched in vain for a remedy. The Gallia company, France's largest manufacturer of permanent-wave machines, put up a 10,000-franc prize for any idea that would arrest the price slide, but no one was able to satisfy its jury of eminent coiffeurs.[65]

Conditions in the trade appeared to be regressing to what they had been thirty years earlier. "The number of coiffeurs," wrote *Hebdo-Coiffure*, Robert Maigre's old magazine for his very elite clientèle, now a part of the L'Oréal empire, "surpasses the need [and] prices are plummeting, which explains the many *maisons baissières*."[66] Worse, falling prices were costing hairdressers the respect their trade had only recently earned. "Low prices," wrote CSP vice president Templier, "have dissipated the consideration and esteem that we had earned from our clients . . . When one hasn't the courage to demand that work be compensated at its *juste valeur*," he added, "he loses the respect of both himself and others."[67] Rambaud also scolded his colleagues for having let their customers turn their natural relationship upside down: "She has imposed her prices on you, whereas it's you who should be imposing yours on her!"[68]

Some of the profession's leading figures proposed that coiffeurs brandish quality as a weapon against price-slashers. Marcel Jonca suggested the following line of attack: "Madame," the hairdresser should tell his client, "you may be able to find a permanent wave for forty francs, but that's not possible in my salon, because I guarantee that your hair will retain the suppleness and shine that make it beautiful."[69] What is more, wrote Hector Ledoux, "perms" done "rapide en série" were also likely to pose health risks. "Quality and cheapness rarely go hand in hand," he observed. And he thought that clients would soon recognize that "it was a matter, not of their wallets, but of their health."[70] Clever presentation could not undo the effects of the depression, though, and prices continued to sag.

The structure of hairdressing businesses, small and lightly capitalized, deflected some of the worst effects of the crisis. A *petit patron* who employed two *assistants* in good times could easily enough operate with one when things got tough; if they got tough enough, he could fire all his employees and persevere alone. Conversely, laid-off *assistants* could install themselves in some very modest situation and look for their own customers. This flexibility helped to keep the official unemployment rate among hairdressers comparatively low throughout the 1930s. In 1936, Gabrielle Letellier and her collaborators found 3,183 *chômeurs* in the sector of "soins personnels." That amounted to 6 percent of the *population active*, which meant that unemployment had not risen dramatically since 1930. The authors conceded, though, that in a trade likely to feel the crisis as underemployment rather than unemployment, a study of personal income would probably have shown a steeper fall.[71]

The depression had a less gentle impact on the hairdressers in Paris. In 1936, when the capital had 62 percent of the country's unemployed coiffeurs, *chômage* reached 14.4 percent, more than double the national average. The crash struck the worst-trained and least-established hairdressers hardest. Letellier remarked that it hit young women with particular force—especially the manicurist, a "femme d'appoint," easily replaceable by the patron's wife.[72]

Among the most vulnerable were those young coiffeurs who continued to be trained and dumped into the workforce by the private hairdressing schools. These *écoles privées de coiffure* had proliferated in the bull market of the 1920s. They charged students upwards of 2,000 francs for a three-month training program. In 1930, Paul Gerbod estimated, some 5,000 young men and women were attending hairdressing schools in France, with a lively competition for places. From September to November that year, he wrote, 217 applicants to the *écoles privées* found not a single opening.[73]

As the market for hairdressing constricted, these *écoles privées* attracted increasing censure for cheating clients and ruining the profession. François Magnien summarized the case against the *écoles privées*: A child leaves school at age thirteen or fourteen. His parents want to find him a trade. The child has a preference, but there are no jobs to be had there. Then the parents stumble upon an advertisement for an "*école privée de coiffure*" that promises to train their child in three months and to guarantee him a place thereafter. So the parents pay the tuition.

But it is, remarked Magnien, a kind of confidence trick. One does not become a coiffeur in three months. Indeed, the profession's national convention specified an apprenticeship of eighteen months for "salonniers" and two full years for "coiffeurs-dames." So the "graduate" cannot find a job in a reputable salon. What does he do? (And we are talking of hundreds of "victims," Magnien said.) He sets up at home or in a basement, under the most miserable conditions. He works at cut-rate prices, causing a general calamity for prices and wages. The level of skill suffers, so does business practice. The more competent and honest practitioners are undercut and forced out of business. "Pushed to ruin, our beautiful *métier* becomes the despair of true professionals, who are ashamed of being coiffeurs."[74]

Above all, the *écoles privées* threatened to flood a saturated market
with "bad hairdressers *working at starvation prices.*"[75] Effective
action against them thus became part of the perpetual campaign to
limit access to the trade in order to reduce competition and boost living
standards. "Out of corporate solidarity," the *Artisan Coiffeur* urged
its readers, "coiffeurs must pitilessly refuse [to hire] students coming
out of the *écoles privées.*"[76]

As hairdressers feared, the inevitable corollary of oversupply was
the spread of *travail noir*, as laid-off workers set up in apartments or
basements and tried to pull in customers with below-market prices.
The *Coiffeur-Parfumeur*, carried a typical story about a mining community where out-of-work miners began to open little hairdressing
operations in their houses, cutting their fellow-miners' hair and selling
the accoutrements.[77] An article in the *Coiffure de Paris* condemned a
very different source of *travail noir*, as *coiffeuses*, unable to find work
in reputable salons, offered themselves as "chambermaids who know
how to wave and style hair." Many of these young women, the magazine noted, found places in the richest quarters of Paris and, given the
"servants crisis," they were well-treated.[78]

The various organizations of coiffeurs remonstrated incessantly
about these "blacklegs" who stole business from legitimate hairdressing establishments and paid "not a lick of taxes."[79] They sometimes
compared the performance of the French government unfavorably
with Nazi Germany, where "*travail noir* is punished by prison" and
"the hairdresser who does not respect official prices has his shop
closed for five years."[80] Unfortunately, the French state had no legal
basis for action against most forms of *travail noir*. There was no law
against cutting hair for money, and a person did not need a license to
do it. This was the principal impetus behind the push for a C.A.P. and
brevet professional, which coiffeurs wanted to give the *pouvoirs
publics*—the power to close down illegal practitioners and spare law-
ful ones the ravages of *travail noir*.

The denunciation of *travail noir* occasionally slid into a condemna-
tion of the "flood" of foreigners into the trade. The exact number of
coiffeurs étrangers in France is hard to determine. In 1930, according
to André Armengaud, foreign workers comprised about 7 percent of
the *population active*, exercising in general "the rudest and worst-paid
professions that the French do not want." But he added that this number declined between 1931 and 1936.[81] Paul Gerbod estimated that
the number of *étrangers* in coiffure had increased considerably since
the early part of the century. From under 1,000 in 1911, they became

5,000 in 1926 and 10,800 a decade later, at the depth of the crisis. Still, this amounted to well under 10 percent of coiffeurs. In Paris, where foreign hairdressers concentrated, they accounted for maybe 15 percent of the trade in 1933.[82]

Artisans and small businessmen, the dominant elements in coiffure, were notorious opponents of competition from immigrants, and their organizations duly called for controls on foreign tradesmen and for the application of the restrictive law of August 10, 1932.[83] Hairdressers in the Oise hated foreign workers, "because the majority will end up as disloyal competitors." They flock to the price-shattering "hairdressing factories" or set up mean, dirty little shops, added an angry G. Rouen. Meanwhile, poor, honest *French* coiffeurs "see their modest futures disappear as they abandon to these [Levantine] half breeds the *métier* that they love but that, debased by [these foreigners], no longer affords them a dignified living."[84] The *Reveil des Coiffeurs* sneered at the excess of *artisans étrangers* in Paris: especially Greeks, but also "Jews, Poles, Italians, etc." "I have recently seen," wrote Gaston Bénazet in the *Coiffeur du Sud-Ouest,* "a salon directed by a Portuguese and a Spaniard, with a Polish worker—what you could call a '*salon international.*' There you have it, three rogues who get along perfectly in questions of prices and hours. These are the fellows who are the 'Kings' of France."[85]

Ouvriers coiffeurs were scarcely more hospitable than employers to competition from immigrants. Beneath the masthead reading, "Proletarians of All Countries Unite!" the *Coiffeur Confédéré* demanded, "all entry of foreign workers into our profession be totally prohibited," a demand echoed in a motion passed by the 1935 congress of the Fédération des coiffeurs *confédérés.* Magnien called on his fellow *coiffeurs unitaires* to place the blame for the profession's troubles where it belonged, on the government and the patrons: "*Pas de nationalism,* comrades," he instructed. Yet the mere fact that he felt compelled to call his constituents to order, suggests that xenophobia had already made some headway among them.[86]

*   *   *

The surge in the number of foreign-born coiffeurs was only one of the changes that transformed the working lives of hairdressers in the fifteen years that followed World War I. Given the extent of this transformation, it might be useful to ask two questions about labor process and class relations in the salon: First, did the intimacy of the small shop add to or detract from the tension inherent between boss and worker? Second, as the profession commercialized and employers became more attuned to profits, as work became at once more remunerative and more intense, did it drive patrons and *assistants* further apart or closer together?

With respect to social relations in *petites entreprises*, it seems reasonable to assume that the mobility that carried so many *garçons coiffeurs* into the *patronat* dulled the edge of hostility and mutual incomprehension in most hairdressing salons.[87] Unlike the unbridgeable gap that separated miner from mine owner or navvie from investment banker, *patrons* and *ouvriers coiffeurs* knew each other personally. Save in the *grosses maisons*, they labored and probably resided cheek by jowl in the shop and the neighborhood. The employee could easily enough imagine himself a *salonnier*, while the patron remembered his days as an *ouvrier*. Employers often joined *assistants* in some of the social and sporting organizations the profession sponsored: cycling and football clubs, mutual-aid societies, artistic associations.

Notwithstanding the opportunities for understanding and sympathy, the irreducible tension between profit and wages continued to exist. *Salaires* still had to be paid and the money in the *tronc* shared. Employees clearly understood that the greater part the patron took, the less was left for them. The fact that there was often so little to go around only added to the strain. Moreover, it is perfectly conceivable that, while power is vexatious when it operates at a distance, when the boss is in the same room all day long, occasions for conflict and resentment multiply promiscuously.

It is impossible to say for certain which of these effects was dominant in the *salons de coiffure*. On the one hand, this history of coiffure has already served up innumerable instances of shared interest, mutual sympathy, and common action. On the other, the *procédures* and *jugements* of the Prud'hommes provide eloquent testimony to the quarrels that so often set employers and employees against one another. They are full of stories about workers who hated their bosses, did shoddy work, and left without giving notice, as well as about patrons who tried to cheat their *assistants* out of their due wages and severance pay. The dispute between Marcel Mallet, a CSO militant, and his patron Ignés Armillas, which arrived at the Prud'hommes for adjudication in 1931, was typical. Mallet asked for 720 francs compensation for *renvoi abusif*, after twenty months in the salon, a year under Armillas. The employer denied that he had sacked Mallet without cause, adding that the aggrieved employee had always been paid regularly and received his severance pay when he was fired. Armillas' wife, arguing for her husband, claimed that he had quickly decided that Mallet's work was unsatisfactory and that he would fire him. Mallet said that the reason he was really fired was because one night Armillas asked him to serve a late-arriving client and Mallet told him, "I don't work supplementary hours." Each side produced a couple of supporting witnesses. The client testified that he had waited until 7:30 p.m. and was then turned away. After several hearings over three months, the council ruled against plaintiff and sent him away empty handed.[88]

The most we can say is that while conflict between employers and employees remained endemic in the 1920s, higher wages and a less-murderous work schedule took much of the sting out of it. After the initial tumult of the postwar period, the incidence of strike activity in coiffure diminished, and the street battles disappeared almost entirely. Without overstating the harmony of even a prosperous trade, it seems fair to say that the relative affluence of the 1920s as well as the feminization of the salons made for a less volatile profession. The 1930s were an unlucky decade, however, and hard times rekindled the fires of political passion among hairdressers. Exchanges between rivals became nastier, accusations more scurrilous. It was a reheated profession, in the turbulent summer of 1936, that prepared to apply the new regime ushered in by the Popular Front.

1385

C. G. T.

FÉDÉRATION NATIONALE
des SYNDICATS D'OUVRIERS COIFFEURS DE FRANCE et des COLONIES

MAISON DES OUVRIERS COIFFEURS — 7, RUE DARBOY — PARIS (XI⁼)

L'Ouvrier Coiffeur, organe mensuel fédéral — *Service Juridique, Technique* — *Placement gratuit* — *Sou du soldat*

Téléphone : OBERK. 18.80 — Compte chèque postal : Paris 961-92

LES OUVRIERS COIFFEURS ET COIFFEUSES
manifesteront dans toute la France

LE JEUDI 29 AVRIL 1937, à 21 h.

Assistez tous' avec vos Camarades de travail à la

REUNION GENERALE

qui aura lieu SALLE _____

Au cours de cette réunion, tous les détails vous seront donnés sur l'action générale en cours pour le succès de nos revendications (pourparlers avec le Syndicat Patronal, arbitrage préfectoral, etc.)

NOUS VOULONS :

L'Application des 40 heures et la réglementation des heures d'ouverture et de fermeture des salons ;

Le Rajustement des Salaires (le coût de la vie augmentant constamment);

L'Application obligatoire du Contrat Collectif pour tous les Coiffeurs ;

L'Interdiction du chômage partiel et des licenciements injustifiés ;

La Fermeture des Cours et Écoles privés ;

Le Contrôle syndical et l'application des lois sociales.

Nous ne voulons plus être traités en parents pauvres et gagner moins qu'un manœuvre.

Voilà pourquoi, le même jour, dans toutes les régions, des milliers d'Ouvriers Coiffeurs et Coiffeuses répondront avec enthousiasme et affirmeront leur volonté de lutte.

PAS D'ABSTENTIONS !   Vivent l'Union et la Solidarité ouvrières !

LA FÉDÉRATION.

Imprimerie Chatelain, 15, rue Sedaine, Paris-XI⁼.

A poster summons hairdressers to a mass meeting, April 1937

6

The Failure of the Popular Front

No particular fashion event heralded the arrival of the Popular Front in 1936. The men who trooped to the polls that spring had long since abandoned the *coupe bressant* and the *coupe à l'américaine*. The stylish gent of the mid-1930s wore longer, curled hair, sometimes tapered or dyed, with a patina of gomina gel, in the manner of Caesar Romero.[1] French women, who could not vote, did not cut their hair shorter to mark their support for social justice, as Long thought they had done in 1918, or drape their coiffures in expensive baubles to signal their defiance of policies that elevated the "vile multitude." The accession of the Blum government produced neither *sans-culottes* nor *merveilleuses*, demonstrating once more that fashion was free to acknowledge, or not, history's vicissitudes.

The Popular Front nonetheless produced a substantial ripple in the life of the hairdressing profession. Most obviously, it brought hard-pressed *ouvriers coiffeurs* higher wages, paid vacations, a five-day, forty-hour workweek. Actually, it is more accurate to say that the Popular Front promised *garçons coiffeurs* all these things; what it delivered was something less.

In fact, this gap between promise and fulfillment points to an important truth about the Popular Front. The progressive coalition of radicals, socialists, and communists came to power with the intention of shifting wealth from those who had more than they needed to those who had less. Yet they seem to have had no conception of how to make this policy work, especially in those parts of the economy where wage-payers and wage-earners lived broadly similar working lives. How could the new order ameliorate the lives of *ouvriers coiffeurs* without ruining *petits patrons*? This was the hurdle that Blum's admirable drive for social equity would have to surmount.

The complexity of this task was obscured, at least for *ouvriers coiffeurs*, behind the optimism generated by the recaptured unity of the labor movement. In 1934, the French Communist Party, following the Kremlin's new Popular Front strategy, pushed the CGT-Unitaire toward reconciliation with its old antagonist, the CGT.[2] In coiffure, the FNSOC changed tack and began to talk to the *confédérés* about putting their old disputes behind them and presenting a united front against fascism and associated threats to the working class. The two federations arranged a unity meeting for November 1934, where 500 *ouvriers coiffeurs* heard an amicable exchange of views on subjects ranging from the forty-hour week, to the *salaire minimum*, to the recruitment of foreigners and *coiffeuses* in the syndical campaign.[3] They consummated their reunion at the great "fusion congress" of January 1936, which celebrated the union of the two rival organizations and the amalgam of their respective *écoles de coiffure* under the leadership of François Magnien.

The significance of the event is attested by the participation of leading *patrons coiffeurs*. Even Robert Maigre arrived bearing congratulations from the SCP. Rambaud, always a man above politics, took the podium and saluted "the unity of the working class, especially among coiffeurs." Magnien, perhaps missing the ecumenical spirit of the evening, finished his speech with a tribute to "the country without classes, where the worker is truly master of his destiny: the U.S.S.R." And the meeting concluded with the singing of the *Internationale*. The next day the CSO named a new fusion *bureau*, headed by the old *unitaire* chief, Pierre Guny, and including Magnien as "delegate to the International." The much larger group of *unitaires* received a majority of seats, but the *confédérés* seemed satisfied.[4]

Reunification produced a bounce in recruitment even before the election of the Blum government. The FNSOC grew from about 3,000 *cotisants* in January 1936 to 8,000 by the Toulouse Unity Congress in March and 10,000 by June. By the end of February 1937, the coiffeurs' federation had roughly doubled again in size.[5] In other words, when the moment came to defend their Popular Front victory, *ouvriers coiffeurs* could flex unprecedented muscle.

That moment arrived following the election of the Popular Front coalition in May 1936. A "wave of strikes" washed over coiffure, closing some of the finest shops in Paris. Finally, thought Guny, the patrons would have to listen: "An impetuous wave [of action] is sweeping away all resistance," he wrote, "and the proudest employers' syndicats, who before refused even to talk to their workers' delegates, are now forced to accept their demands . . . ."[6] In cities all across the country, formerly inert groups of *ouvriers coiffeurs* discovered their collective interest. They patched together trade unions where none had existed before and, either directly or by way of the public authorities, compelled the employers to sign collective conventions.

At the moment of the FNSOC's greatest triumph, a small group, led by Robert Solomiac, who had a job in a small salon near the Gare du Nord, began to work in opposition to the Popular Front. We know little about this small band of *gâcheurs*, but we do know something of their umbrella organization, the Syndicats professionnels français (SPF).[7] The SPF, which claimed to offer workers an alternative to "revolutionary marxism," appeared in response to the widespread strikes of May and June 1936. As its initials suggest, the SPF were an arm of Colonel de la Rocque's Parti social français, successor to the outlawed Croix de Feu.[8] Toeing the PSF line, the SPF preached the virtues of the "collaboration des classes." The SPF had only 2,000 members when it was launched, in mid-June 1936, but it picked up support as discontent with the Popular Front spread. The Confédération des syndicats professionnels français appeared in January 1937 and published the first issue of its journal, *SPF* in July of that year. In truth, the SPF played a negligible part in mitigating the troubles that buffeted the hairdressing trades after 1936 and made no imprint on the documents pertaining to coiffure until 1941 when, the political winds having shifted, Solomiac stepped forward to demand a role in professional affairs.

The creation of the SPF corresponded almost exactly to the signing of the first *convention collective* in the hairdressing profession. Concluded less than a week after the Matignon Accords, in June 1936, the new contract extended to *ouvriers coiffeurs* in Paris the benefits of higher wages, paid vacations, and forty-hour work. The contract was signed by Georges Morin, president of the CSP, Bagnaud, chief of the SCP, and Magnien, general secretary of the CSO. The parties agreed to a limit of forty-eight hours in Paris and fifty-two in the surrounding districts, to a *semaine anglaise*, and to the early closing of salons on the eve of important holidays. They set mandatory opening and closing hours—not before 8:30 a.m. or after 7:30 p.m.—and committed themselves to the common struggle against *baissiers* and *travail noir*. The convention also granted workers paid vacations, as provided for in the Matignon Accords and the law of June 20.[9]

Events in Paris were replicated in many provincial cities, where brief strikes ended with the signing of collective contracts. They generally stipulated around fifty hours of work a week and emulated Paris by setting out a sliding scale of *salaires minimums*, based on the experience and skill of practitioners. In Nice, these extended from 159 francs a week for beginning coiffeurs to 219 francs for skilled *coiffeurs dames*. In Lyon, those at the bottom of the scale were guaranteed twenty francs a day, plus 10 percent of their *chiffre d'affaires*; those at the top got forty francs a day and 20 percent.[10] In Paris, the contract provided that apprentices could earn up to ninety francs a month. *Shampooingeuses* began at ninety francs, *débutants* at 120 francs, and on upward through *manucures specialisées* (120f), *salonniers* and *coiffeuses simples* (240f), *coiffeurs mixtes* and *coiffeuses qualifiées* (240f), and *spécialistes* (300f). Wages were slightly lower in the suburbs. Of course, these were wage *floors*, intended to protect the worst-paid, and *assistants* were entitled to earn more. In the better shops they certainly did.[11]

These wage rates still left most hairdressing workers behind the members of other trades. The new contract guaranteed *assistants coiffeurs* minimum wages ranging from 2.50 francs an hour for *débutants* to 6.25 for *specialists*. By way of comparison, a 1936 government survey of wages found tanners, farriers, and cobblers earning around four francs an hour. Cabinet-makers and tailors made 6.50 francs, blacksmiths and plumbers earned 7.25 and 7.50 francs an hour respectively. *Ouvriers coiffeurs* were slightly better off than most *employés* in offices and shops, whose wages dipped below 200 francs a week.[12]

Better off, that is, if the new wage scales were actually applied in coiffure, and there is plenty of evidence that they were not. The SCP considered the new wage agreement a product of extortion. But even the employers of the CSP, ideologically committed to the values of the Popular Front, began to back off their commitments almost immediately. They felt increasingly trapped between the conviction that *ouvriers coiffeurs* deserved better conditions and the belief that small *salonniers* could not afford them, especially now, when business had been so poor for so long.

A glance at prices in the summer of 1936 indicates once again the advantage that *salons pour dames* enjoyed over barbershops (table 6.1). It also suggests that the ladies hairdresser who stuck to the simplest tasks were far from rich. And, of course, prices in the smaller cities, such as Cherbourg and Saint-Nazaire, were even lower.[13]

Jeanne Singer-Kérel's survey of the cost of living in Paris noted that prices in coiffure fell steadily after 1931, although they began to rise

Table 6.1   Prices in Coiffure, 1936*

Coiffure Hommes		Coiffure Dames	
Haircut	5 francs	Haircut	6 francs
Beard trim	5	Ondulation	6
Shampoo	2	Shampoo	5
Shave (no tonic)	1.50	Mis en plis	10
		Permanent wave	70–125

* *Capilartiste* (August 1936), 7.

again in 1937 and 1938. According to one official study of prices between 1913 and 1950, hairdressing *tarifs* held up relatively well, compared to an overall price index that fell by 20 percent between 1931 and 1936.[14] Nevertheless, hairdressers could see that prices were stagnating, and the effect of this was no doubt multiplied by a general fall-off in business. They were feeling poor.

The increase in taxes and other social charges for small businessmen made them feel even poorer. These had multiplied in the early thirties; the Popular Front raised them further.[15] The average sale price of *salons de coiffure* fell by 8 percent between 1935 and 1937, clear sign of a commercial slump, while turnover increased. Workers' expenses alone ate up half a patron's *chiffre d'affaires*, leaving insufficient revenue for the patron. "Only the *grands maîtres*," remarked the syndicat patronal of Saint-Quentin, were making a profit; 90 percent of the profession earned very little.[16] Lucien Eymeric of Toulon asked, "Is it better to be a Patron or a Worker?" The patron, he wrote, worked hard and paid a disproportionate share of public expenses. Yet he did not have the money to take a family vacation and, after thirty years behind the *fauteuil*, was in no position to retire. Employees, on the other hand, enjoyed guaranteed wages, tips, social insurance, paid holidays. Clearly, he concluded, it was better to be an *ouvrier*.[17]

No doubt, most workers would have quarreled with this verdict. They nonetheless accepted the plain fact that a majority of *petits patrons* did not make a lot of money and would find it hard to meet their new obligations to their workers. A joint letter from the CSP and the CSO to the minister of national economy, asking the government to support a policy of higher prices, noted that the average artisan-coiffeur in Paris earned only 10,000 francs a year. His weekly receipts of 350 or 450 francs were not nearly enough to bear the wages guaranteed in the new contract.[18]

The CSO therefore joined the CSP in calling for state action to reinforce the situation of *petits établissements* in order to enable them to fulfill the terms of the collective contract. Morin and the other CSP leaders laid out their plans at a meeting of 5,000 patrons in late June 1936. A month later a huge rally, 10,000 *patrons* and *ouvriers coiffeurs*, met to reassert their solidarity and press for their demands. Socialist deputy Albert Paulin, chairman of the Chamber of Deputies Groupe de défense artisanale, told the crowd that workers had benefited from Matignon Accords and now it was the patrons' turn "to obtain as well a minimum standard of living." He went on to castigate capitalism that, having already ruined much of petty commerce, was now "on the way to expropriating your *petits fonds de coiffure*."[19] And he promised them relief. Two days later, good as his word, Paulin introduced what came to be known as Law 900. "Artisan-coiffeurs," he explained, "are determined to apply the collective contracts, paid holidays, and minimum wages. [But] they'll be able to do it only if the hairdressing profession is stabilized and protected."[20]

It was widely conceded that no collective agreement could hold if coiffure were left to the whims of the market. Law 900 therefore undertook to shelter *petites entreprises* by restricting entry to the profession and cracking down on "the many foreigners who work[ed] at extremely low prices" and other sources of *concurrence déloyale*, in order to buoy up prices.[21] Its structure and logic were clear. They rehearsed a series of ideas that had kicked around coiffure since the beginning of the century but had never before made it through the door of the National Assembly. First, reign in competition. This would permit even marginal salons to be profitable, and thereby allow employers to fulfill their obligations under the *convention collective*. Law 900 also directed the government to enforce the following provisions: *tarifs obligatoires*, standard hours of *ouverture* and *fermeture*, repression of *travail noir*. It aimed, that is, to discipline a profession that could not discipline itself. The CSP and the UF soon made passage of Law 900 the *sine qua non* for their application of the June 1936 *convention*.

The *gros salonniers* of the SCP did not oppose Law 900, which promised to have little impact on the big commercial salons, and Bagnaud's report to the Paris Chamber of Commerce gave it a polite, if not warm, endorsement. On the matter of the *convention collective*, however, the SCP was adamant. They believed that the patrons had signed the June accord under duress, and as soon as the moment of danger had passed they began to direct their efforts toward thwarting it. This seems ironic, in that virtually all the members of the SCP, and certainly those in charge—Bagnaud, Maigre, Victor Touzet, Adolph Fried, Marcel Jonca—ran affluent businesses that already granted their employees the benefits named in the convention. But they were also men of the political right, and their battle against the Popular Front in coiffure looks in many respects more ideological than strictly economic.

Richard Vinen quips that employers generally perceived the events of June 1936 "as symptoms of bolshiness not Bolshevism"; that is, as irritating rather than frightening.[22] Nonetheless, the "indolence laws," as Louis Tison called the Matignon Accords, and the "intrusion of Moscow into professional affairs" spurred *patrons coiffeurs* to action against the "dictature syndicale" currently in power.[23] In order to parry the "economic dislocation and social anarchy" unleashed by the Blum government, the SCP created the Confédération patronale des coiffeurs de France et des colonies (CPC) in October 1936. Bagnaud and his colleagues conceived the CPC as a national rival for the Union fédérale, an extension to the whole of France, in effect, of the Parisian contest between the CSP and the SCP.

Unlike its rival, the UF, which it considered "soft" on the Popular Front, the CPC announced its firm resolution "to defend the general interests of all legitimate hairdressers . . . *whatever the size or structure of their salons.*" At the same time, under the slogan, "Patrons, soyez patrons!" it unashamedly sided with the anti-Blum policies of C.-J. Gignoux and the Confédération générale de la production française.[24] "We do not consider the workers our enemies," said Bagnaud. But he added that the workers, for their part, "must not look at us as adversaries who must be dispossessed."[25]

The CPC could not, at first, match the numbers of the UF. It began by adding the SPC's 800 subscribers in Paris to groups in Strasbourg, Le Mans, Marseille, and Nice; maybe 4,000 members in all, mostly among the *grosses maisons*. But the hard-nosed patronal politics of the confederation had broad appeal across the country, among petty patrons as well as the *gros*. If the CPC and the UF had completely different constituencies in Paris, in the provinces they fished out of the same pond.[26] Apparently, a lot of artisan-coiffeurs took the bait, as the population of the CPC climbed rapidly. By the middle of 1938, the CPC had enrolled between fifteen and twenty thousand *patrons coiffeurs*.[27]

CPC success did not come entirely at the expense of the Union fédérale. Rather, it was part of a mustering of *patrons coiffeurs* in response to the mobilization of their workers that also swelled the ranks of the UF. Once again, it is prudent not to accept at face value the figures put forward. Still, the trend is clear. The UF claimed to have 2,600 members nationally in 1929. At the height of recruitment in 1937, it grouped something on the order of 25,000 artisans-coiffeurs. Its main local syndicat, the CSP, grew by half in the first ten months of 1936, rising to around 7,000 *petits patrons* in 1937: 60 percent of *salonniers* of Paris and the *banlieues*.[28] Clearly, growing antagonism to the Popular Front was driving *patrons coiffeurs* into their syndicates, and this pushed even the CSP and the UF into a tougher line against the workers.

This represented a substantial change. The CSP and UF had not signed the June 1936 agreement solely because they were intimidated. *Petits gens* themselves, they also endorsed the principle of a better deal for all of France's *petits* embodied in the Popular Front. They merely believed that employees should not reap *all* the benefits. "I am *for* the workers' demands," wrote Gaston Bénazet of Montpellier, "but on the condition that we get our share."[29]

In the months that followed, however, *patrons coiffeurs* did not seem to be getting their share. Business had not picked up. "The salons were empty," remembered Magnien. Prices still sagged, *baissiers* and *travailleurs noirs* continued to operate, Law 900 remained stuck in the parliamentary apparatus. The accords of the previous summer, wrote UF officer Léonce Lebègue in January 1937, did not respond to "the spirit" of the law. Across the country, they had been signed too hastily and under the spell of an unfounded optimism. They needed revision.[30]

For different reasons, the CSO and FNSOC likewise voiced their disappointment with the fruits of the June agreement. Many employers were still not applying the new wage schedule. Besides, the workers were coming to believe that the wages they had accepted were too low and wanted to renegotiate an additional 20 percent increase in *salaires*.

On February 10, 1937, the UF and FNSOC signed a second collective convention for coiffure, under the rubric of a national convention concluded on September 19, 1936 between the CGT and the Confédération générale de l'artisanat français, to which the UF belonged. Guny and Magnien affixed their names for the workers' federation, Forestier and Gestalder for the UF. The CPC, unalterably opposed to the terms of the discussion, did not take part in the negotiations or sign the convention. It henceforth made its antipathy to the agreement plain.[31]

The February convention was both more elaborate and less detailed than accords of the previous summer, which makes sense since it was intended to apply all across the country. It did not set a standard for the workweek in coiffure, but handed this ticklish job to individual localities, with the proviso that work would under no circumstances surpass fifty-two hours. It reaffirmed its commitment to the *semaine anglaise* and early closings on special holidays: New Year's Day, Ascension Day, Bastille Day, Assumption Day, All Saints Day, Armistice Day, and Christmas. The new agreement formalized a scale of wages, depending on *qualification*, but once more left the specifics to be worked out locally. The accord further prohibited the use of ether and other dangerous chemicals, committed both sides to work for the suppression of *écoles privées*, and prescribed a minimum training period of eighteen months for coiffeurs. The February convention contained two major innovations. First, the parties agreed that the undecided particulars would be worked out by local *commissions mixtes* of workers and employers. Second, they asserted its validity for *all* salons, whether or not they had employees or belonged to one of the signatory organizations.[32]

Yet the new contract was no more self-enforcing than the last one. It depended ultimately on state action to make it work, since only the *pouvoirs publics* could ensure that recalcitrant coiffeurs obeyed the codes set out in the agreement. This was the point of a letter-writing campaign organized by the UF and the FNSOC, entreating the labor minister to extend the agreement to cover all hairdressing salons and to act decisively against *baissiers* and *travail noir*. A Monsieur Canon, from the Syndicat des coiffeurs of the Saône-et-Loire called the minister's attention to the case of a young colleague whose own custom had disappeared "while a mason . . . stole all his work." Canon went on to denounce the treachery of a local curé. Apparently, his parishioners were angry at the high price of canticles, and the curé suggested that mothers cut their children's hair themselves in order to save enough money to buy the books. In fact, Canon pointed out, the two cases were connected both to each other and to wider political questions. The same curé had caused the young coiffeur's misfortunes by warning his flock away, because the latter "does not go to church and declares his sympathy for [socialist] ideas." But then, Canon finished, what can you expect in a region where "a solid majority of the rural population is solid for [the rural fascism of Henri] Dorgères?"[33]

Long experience had taught coiffeurs that they could not always expect prompt action from the authorities, and so, as they often did under these circumstances, they took matters into the own hands. *Comités de vigilance* once again roamed the neighborhoods. One squad sacked a salon in Belleville, whose patrons flouted the new schedule and wage rates. On February 15,500 patrons and workers circulated along the *grands boulevards*, compelling salons to respect "les accords syndicaux." Things turned nasty when the crowd, which had grown considerably, arrived at the top of the rue Drouot. A bunch of "agitators" and "idlers," to the cry of "collective contract everywhere!" grabbed some coal out of a nearby coal truck and broke the windows of a well-known *baissier*, the Maison Gendre. With the help of police, the leaders of the demonstration succeeded in restoring calm and convincing several *baissiers* to respect the accord henceforth. "Before the fear of starvation," wrote Guillon of the vigilance committee, "nothing will stop artisans and workers defending their livings." He agreed with the CSP's attempts to curb the violence, but warned that the government needed to act quickly, or "we won't be responsible [for the consequences]."[34]

Tactical cooperation between workers and employers could not, however, erase the substantial conflicts of interest that divided them, and the collective agreement of February 1937 did little to ease the tensions or slow the dissolution of their entente. Eight months after the initial *convention*, the workers had to be asking themselves what they had really won, certainly not a livable *salaire minimum* and a forty-hour week. *Patrons coiffeurs* had perhaps even less reason to be satisfied. The CSP and UF maintained their support for the principles of social justice as long as they included *petits proprietaires*. But the fact remained that, after almost six years of economic decline, and now confronted by their employees' demands for higher pay, less work, and other benefits, the great mass of small *salonniers* felt themselves pushed into a corner. The truth is that such evidence as survives about economic conditions in the *petits salons* strongly suggests that they could *not* have fulfilled the terms of the collective conventions without substantially compromising their own chances of survival. Many surely would have confronted the choice between firing their *assistants* and working alone or closing down altogether.

It was precisely to escape this dilemma that the CSP and UF began to qualify their commitment to the February accord and subsequent conventions by tying it to the passage and implementation of Law 900. "We would like to be able to satisfy the workers' *revendications*," wrote the *Semaine de la Coiffure*, "but only on condition that the government gives us the means."[35] In other words, if the government could reverse the "disastrous" conditions in the profession, *petits salonniers* would be delighted to pass along a fair share of this relative prosperity to their workers. Naturally, although the workers seconded the patrons' demand for Law 900, they did not want their own Popular Front benefits held hostage to it. The two disgruntled parties, each determined to yield no further, moved toward a confrontation.

At first, the February convention drove a new wedge between the two factions of *patrons coiffeurs*. The CPC was determined to sign no further accords with the workers, and it bitterly opposed the UF's demand that the government generalize the terms of the convention, particularly those that implied any limit on the *liberté du commerce*. In the days following the signature of the accord, both employers' groups roundly attacked each other. Yet the UF itself rapidly became disenchanted with the new agreement, which neither pushed the government into decisive action to help artisan-coiffeurs nor compelled the workers to withdraw their demands for higher wages and a true forty-hour week. Faced, moreover, with the threat of defections to the more intractable CPC, both the Union fédérale and the CSP began to harden their own positions vis-à-vis the Popular Front. It was then a short step to exploring the possibility of a "front patronal" between one group with "numbers, will, and syndicalist spirit" and another with "pecuniary means."[36] The 7,000 *petits patrons* of the CSP thus joined the 700 employers of the SCP in a defensive battle against the CSO.

April 1937 was the month for mass meetings, as workers and employers pressed their case and lined up their troops. On the evening of April 9, 7,000 *ouvriers coiffeurs* gathered at the Gymnase Japy, where they heard Léon Jouhaux, general secretary of the CGT, reiterate the demand for the forty-hour, five-day week.[37] Although the leadership of the CSO was feeling cautious, strike sentiment was clearly building among the members. It was aggravated by the ministerial decree of April 20 that fixed new guidelines for the application of the forty-hour week in coiffure—forty-five hours in Paris and forty-seven in the *banlieues*—that left *ouvriers coiffeurs* far from satisfied.[38] They set themselves for a show of strength on May Day.

The patrons responded in kind. The CSP held a rally on April 12 to express its "unité d'action" with the SCP and to assail agitators "looking to goad workers into a fight."[39] Two weeks later, a unity meeting of *patrons coiffeurs* saw Bagnaud and Arvet-Thouvet of the SPC sharing the platform with the chiefs of the CSP: Marcel Lamy, Robert Dallant,

Alphonse Mornot. The assembly unanimously voted "to consider worker demands *only* when [Law 900] is passed" and pledged themselves to work together in the event of a strike. In a further gesture of defiance, the employers voted to keep their salons open all day on May 1.[40] The two sides dug in.

Meanwhile, they submitted themselves to arbitration on the principal source of disagreement, wages.[41] The FNSOC was asking for a 20 percent increase above the minimums specified in the June convention. The UF replied that *petits patrons coiffeurs* simply did not have the wherewithal to pay these wages. In his decision of April 30, Piquemal, cabinet secretary to the labor minister, recognized the validity of the demands of both sides and decided on a raise of 10 percent for hairdressing workers. The patrons refused to budge. They would agree to no further wage hikes without Law 900. Magnien complained that the *petits patrons* had fallen under the influence of "the big employers, the fascists, the supporters of Doriot and de la Rocque."[42] But the CSO general secretary was as mistaken in this analysis as Bagnaud was when he attributed the workers' belligerence to "outside agitators." At bottom, the strike was the product, not of clashing political ideologies, but of two desperate parties who felt they had already compromised too much.

The showdown that both sides had prepared for arrived on May 13, the eve of the Pentecost holiday—high season for visits to the coiffeur, the moment the workers had chosen for maximum effect. The strike appears to have had a widespread but spotty impact.[43] On May 14 a headline in *Le Figaro* reported that "In Paris, the majority of *garçons coiffeurs* have abandoned the salons." But this was hyperbole, as even *Le Figaro* realized, since the following day it informed readers that only 20 percent of hairdressing workers had initially responded the CSO's strike call, and that by the second day, many of these had already returned to work. Ninety percent of salons were open and functioning normally. *Le Temps* wrote that of the 8,000 salons in the Seine department, of which 5,000 were in Paris, only a tenth were affected by the strike; only 2,000 of the capital's 15,000 *ouvriers coiffeurs* supported the walkout. Estimates of the exact number of strikers varied. What is certain, however, is that as in 1926 most of the action occurred in the outlying arrondissements and in the suburbs. The center of Paris was virtually unaffected.

As they often did, the workers set up *salons volants* to draw business away from the patrons—the "sovietization" of the trade, the patrons called it.[44] According to *L'Oeuvre*, strikers operated some 300 of these venues, where people could have their hair cut for free, although customers sympathetic to the cause were expected to drop money in the *tronc*.[45] Inevitably, several violent incidents also accompanied the strike. A Monsieur Léaud complained that his salon suffered severe damage and that he himself was "seriously wounded" by a gang of striking workers. In the Opéra district, a group of *ouvriers* broke the windows of salons on the rues Scribe and Daunou. Then, heading to the Place de l'Étoile, singing the *Internationale*, they got into a skirmish with police that finished with three cops hurt and six demonstrators in jail. The unfortunate Robert Jusserand received, as the police delicately put it, "un coup de pieds aux parties sexuelles."[46] Near the Place de la République a crowd of a hundred strikers attacked an open salon, breaking windows and defacing the storefront. Similar episodes in the Halles quarter and in Bagnolet left shopkeepers wounded and led to several arrests. One newspaper reported that patrons were provoking the workers' delegations by receiving them with "revolvers, razors, sabers, and hatchets."[47] All of which did not, by contemporary standards of labor conflict, represent an excessive measure of violence, but it sufficed to keep the police busy and to aggravate the bad feelings on both sides.

As the strike proceeded, the "front patronal" held together better than the "front ouvrier." Maintaining that the walkout was illegal according to the arbitration law of December 1936, the patrons refused to talk to the CSO about a settlement. Indeed, they seized the occasion to pull out of the arbitration talks. The employers were clearly encouraged by the perception that they were winning the decisive struggle with their employees.

Individual *patrons coiffeurs* reacted to the strike in various fashions. The majority, more or less unaffected, probably did little beyond taking a few extra precautions against groups of *saccageurs*. One *gros patron* grumbled that the state of affairs was "catastrophic" for his business. It seems that one of his best clients, an American woman, had received the first part of an oil treatment the day before the strike. Now she was stuck with a head full of oily hair. More common was the case of the coiffeur who told *Le Figaro* that when the *grève* ends he would refuse to take back his two assistants because they "broke" their labor contract by walking out. From then on he would go back to working all by himself. This would enable him to make some money, which he had not done since the new social laws took effect. "For me," he said, "this strike is a liberation." And he added that many of his colleagues would certainly take the same route.[48]

We have seen *ouvriers coiffeurs* lose most of these confrontations over the preceding fifty years, and they lost this one. With support to the strike draining and patrons refusing even to talk to the workers, the leaders of the CSO began to look for a way out. They found it when the interior minister, Max Darmoy, proposed that the parties resubmit themselves, without sanctions, to binding arbitration on the wage question in return for an end to the *grève*. The CSP and SCP were leery of losing in arbitration what they were winning in open battle, but they agreed.

In contrast to the patrons' unity, the discord among hairdressing workers illustrates the turmoil into which the labor movement in coiffure had fallen. On the evening of May 20, a week after the strike had begun, Pierre Guny and François Magnien, the leaders of the CSO and the FNSOC respectively, addressed a meeting of 1,500 *ouvriers coiffeurs*. Guny began by noting the superior solidarity and discipline of the patrons during the strike and told his audience that the interior minister had instructed the parties to settle it. Without acknowledging the strike's failure, Guny offered the opinion that it was time to go back to work. Both catcalls and cheers punctuated his speech. Magnien took the stage next and endorsed Guny's policy. Then, to cries of "sellout!" and "bastards!" he announced that the members of the conseil syndical were resigning. A "weak majority" approved the motion to end the strike, and the meeting broke up "in confusion."[49]

It is easy to imagine that the strike of 1937, which François Magnien had never really wanted and thus added to its failure and his subsequent repudiation at the meeting of May 20, caused a decisive shift in his eventful career. At the very least, it coincided with a refocusing of his considerable energies. From the mid-1930s until his death in 1989, Magnien was probably, next to his patron, René Rambaud, the most important figure in the profession. He was certainly the most controversial. Magnien was not a great coiffeur and did not have the public profile of the likes of Antoine, Guillaume, Alexandre, and the elite of ladies' hairdressers. In fact, the sources provide no evidence that in his long career he ever earned his living cutting hair. Rather Magnien was a professional militant.

Born in 1906, in the Saône-et-Loire, one of six children in a working-class family, Magnien spent the first part of his career more as a communist than as a coiffeur. He began work in a porcelain factory in Chalon-sur-Saône when he was twelve and somewhere along the way acquired the *métier* of coiffeur. He joined the Jeunesses communistes at the age of sixteen. At nineteen he traveled to the Soviet

Union. By the age of twenty he had joined the council of the Fédération des jeunesses communistes and been named a delegate to the fifth congress of the Communist Party. In 1924 he arrived in Paris and in the ensuing years made a couple of unsuccessful bids for electoral office on the PCF ticket while he built a reputation as the fierce leader of the syndicat of *ouvriers coiffeurs unitaires*—the nemesis of both "reformists" and patrons. By 1937, Magnien had shown himself to be passionate and energetic, an admirer of Lenin and hater of "fascists," a man who knew his enemies and was not afraid to name them.

Years later, Magnien declared that he had never really been a communist, only a militant syndicalist interested in improving conditions and raising wages for hairdressing workers.[50] This sounds plausible, despite his long service in communist organizations and many recorded tributes to Bolshevism. Like so many others, Magnien was attracted to communism more by temperament than by ideology; that is, not by his faith in dialectical materialism, but by his taste for action and the fact that the communists looked like the most vigorous and uncompromising defenders of the working man. This explains how Magnien could have become the profession's chief advocate for *formation professionnelle*, even when that required working hand in glove with the patronat. Solid technical training and sound business practice, he reasoned, would improve the working lives of *ouvriers coiffeurs* every bit as much as strikes and political activity could.

Most likely, the collapse of the May 1937 strike, as well as a general sense that the Popular Front was not working out as he had hoped, merely accelerated a process already in progress. Long before this, Magnien had given evidence of his concern for professional *perfectionnement* by taking up the direction of the École parisienne de la coiffure and helping to create the CSO's Centre de formation. In 1936, working ever more closely with Rambaud, the working-class militant who had conquered the world of *haute coiffure*, Magnien founded the Cercle des arts et techniques de la coiffure française (CATC). The CATC henceforth became the material expression of Magnien's conviction that professional skill was a crucial means of social promotion. In 1937, he began to publish the nonpartisan *Tribune des Coiffeurs*.[51]

The more Magnien came to believe that workers had as much to gain from technical training as from militant syndicalism, the more he spoke in favor of *détente* between *ouvriers* and *patrons coiffeurs*. While he led the workers' campaign for the Popular Front, therefore, Magnien expanded his nonadversarial contacts with the patronat and the state. He worked closely with CSP president, Lamy, to implement the *brevet professionnel*, introduced in 1935, and joined the leading patrons, many of whom were his staunch political enemies, as a vice president of the Comité national des concours, which organized professional competitions. In September 1938, the former revolutionary was named inspecteur départemental de l'enseignement technique. Increasingly, Magnien's appearances in the trade press involved black-tie dinners and not fervid speeches to his comrades.

Magnien's migration from militant syndicalist to professional advocate traced a by-now familiar trajectory in coiffure. René Chauvin, Charles Desplanques, and most famous of all, René Rambaud had made exactly the same journey. All began as revolutionaries. All came to believe, first, that their profession had value above and beyond the condition of its proletariat; and, second, that the interests of workers lay primarily in being an intelligent and skilled part of a flourishing trade. They lost faith in the redeeming value of revolution, but none of these men ever let commercial success and the Légion d'Honneur weaken their commitment to improving conditions among the trade's most disfavored elements. In this respect, although these *anciens militants* mixed easily with businessmen and others in the profession's elite, they remained distinct.

Rambaud earned a place among the most eminent *coiffeur des dames* without becoming, like many *coiffeurs artistes*, a poodle to the upper classes—men for whom the Duchess of Windsor was a paragon of femininity and beauty the highest political principle. Magnien, more partisan and combative by nature than Rambaud, never acquired his mentor's "above politics" position. In turning his attention to *perfectionnement*, Magnien did not turn his back on the labor movement. He considered the two perfectly complementary.

Even though Magnien increasingly mixed in the world of *gros patrons* and *hauts coiffeurs*—including the leadership of the CPC, "whom I know well and for whom I have a certain esteem"—he did not cease to reprove "certains gros patrons agents directs du fascisme."[52] Despite the civility of relations suggested by the many photographs of Magnien in the company of Bagnaud and his confederates, their exchanges in the syndical and professional press lost none of their old bite.

Magnien and Bagnaud had been sniping at each other since the formation of the SCP in 1932. Their rhetoric became shriller after May 1936 and even harsher in the period that followed the May 1937 strike, which probably marked the low point in the relations between *ouvriers* and *patrons coiffeurs* between the wars. The CPC Manifesto of March 1938 condemned the anarchism and "aggressive nonsense" of the workers. Louis Tison, Bagnaud's lieutenant and the most right-wing figure in coiffure, called Magnien a tool of the Kremlin and a "born enemy of the artisanat." Magnien responded in kind. Bagnaud's rhetoric, he wrote, "recalled *Mein Kampf*," and the confederation's policies belonged more properly "on the other side of the Alps or the Rhine."[53]

Indeed, the right-wing proclivities of the SPC/CPC hierarchy were well-known. Tison admitted to belonging to the Action française, which also counted among its supporters André Quentin, the businessman behind the *Reveil des Coiffeurs* and notorious enemy of Léon Blum. Bagnaud, whom Touzet touted as "the first [patronal leader] to beat a strike since 1936," never concealed his reactionary politics. One obituary described him typically as a "militant de l'extrême droite," who surrounded himself "with a group of men the labor movement counted as stalwart réactionaries." At the Paris Chamber of Commerce, he earned a particular reputation for hostility to foreigners in France.[54]

As for the "front patronal" that had sustained the employers during the May 1937 strike, it did not much survive the victory. The professional interests and political perspectives of the two groups of *salonniers* were simply too divergent. In addition, the competition for members kept them in a constant state of conflict all around the country. The UF attacked the CPC for representing "those who could not live by their own work or coif a head of hair," businessmen who believed that "only those who had a fancy shop [*pignon sur la rue*] and a bank account were qualified to be hairdressers." Lamy took Bagnaud to task for running a "hairdressing factory . . . which has nothing in common with our modest boutiques." These capitalists of coiffure, implied Lamy, were incapable of understanding either the world of artisan-coiffeurs or the place of the artisanat in French society: "not in the social combat" that the big bourgeois were waging against the workers but, on the contrary, with the "heavy but magnificent responsibility of *disarming* the combattants."[55]

The CPC slung the mud right back. It accused Gestalder and Lamy of being the pawns of "des organisations cégétistes," all too ready to surrender to the workers and guilty of "reinforcing collectivism to the detriment of the middle classes in general and our corporation, in particular."[56] Here, the confederation had a point. The UF remained aloof from the *mouvement des classes moyennes*, which had made so much progress after May 1936 among *petites et moyennes enterprises*.[57] Forestier and his colleagues found the movement's rationale too "glib" and its politics too conservative, and kept their distance. The Confédération des patrons coiffeurs and the Union fédérale thereafter made a few halfhearted attempts to put the "patronal front" back together, "for the common good."[58] Equally, despite the heated words that flew back and forth through the professional press, the factions continued to cooperate in such practical tasks as the organization of competitions and the *brevet professionnel*. A more thoroughgoing reconciliation between the CPC and the UF, however, ran up against the new collective accord that the UF signed with the FNSOC in November 1938.

The patrons' "victory" over the workers in May 1937 had not relieved the distress in the salons. Prices remained too low, competition too sharp, revenues insufficient for a decent middle-class life—in many instances even for a decent working-class life. Besides, when they went back to work on May 21, *ouvriers coiffeurs* did not simply abandon their demands for better wages and forty hours. Both employers and *assistants* continued to search for some solution to their common problems. From May until August they searched by way of arbitration, which had restarted as part of the strike settlement.

The new arbitrator was Ivan Martin, maître des requêtes at the Conseil d'Etat. He issued his decision in early August 1937. After rebuking both sides for their behavior in May, he ruled on the basic issues dividing the UF and the FNSOC. The workers in order to cover the rising cost of living had sought a 20 percent increase above the minimum set in June 1936. The employers had responded by saying that they lacked the revenue to pay higher *salaires*. Martin, recognizing that employers' expenditure had mounted faster than their incomes, split the difference. He granted patrons a 10 percent price rise and allotted *ouvriers coiffeurs* a 10 percent wage increase, provided this figure did not surpass a certain percentage (55–60 percent) of the patron's gross revenues. On the matter of hours, Martin left them more or less where they had been: forty-five in Paris, ranging up to fifty-two hours in cities with under 50,000 people. The administrative *arrêté* that followed on August 13, extended this decision to all hairdressing salons in the country, in effect applying the February convention to all coiffeurs.[59]

A propos Martin's decision, it may be worthwhile to recall Jean-Pierre Le Crom's remark that the implementation of Popular Front reforms involved little collective bargaining and much arbitration. This, he thought, testified both to the primitive state of labor relations in France and to the absolute necessity of government involvement in "la politique sociale," which later guided the efforts of Vichy and the Fourth Republic.[60] Coiffeurs' experiences seem to bear out Le Crom's observations in two respects: first, that hairdressers' fruitless collective bargaining repeatedly gave way to arbitration and, second, that this brought *ouvriers coiffeurs* few tangible benefits.

Martin's decision satisfied neither of those party to the February contract. Magnien and Guny nonetheless advised the workers to live with the 10 percent raise, even though it did not give them all they wanted, and the CSP told its members to pay the new wages and apply the new *tarifs*.[61] The CPC, which had not signed the February accord, challenged the application of the new rules to its own members' salons. Bagnaud argued that the accord had been written explicitly to apply to "artisanal" shops and did not suit conditions in the bigger shops. Perhaps he was thinking primarily of the interdiction of *roulement* that was contained in the accord. No matter. The National Economic Council (CNE), responsible for mediating these questions, judged that the UF was the "most representative group" of *patrons coiffeurs*. According to the laws on collective bargaining, therefore, it had the right to negotiate for the whole profession. The CNE dismissed the CPC's appeal. So did the Conseil d'Etat.[62]

Aside from their determination to fight the Popular Front at every point, it is hard to see why Bagnaud and his cadres put so much energy into obstructing the application of the February convention. As even the left-wing paper *Le Peuple* acknowledged, all the member salons of the SCP already paid the proposed rates. Besides, experience should have led them to anticipate a satisfactory gap between the law and its application. Indeed, no evidence indicates that the Martin ruling made any appreciable difference to the profession. The CSP reported in September 1937 that three-quarters of its members were abiding by the new wage scales. But most of them had likely been respecting the February convention even before the August *arrêté*, maybe even before February.[63] There is no reason to think that those who refused to comply with the new rules ever suffered for it and no sign that the mixed commissions, envisioned in the February convention as the means to settle these issues, ever functioned.

The limited effectiveness of the Martin ruling, and the fact that the 1937 agreement was due to expire in the winter of 1939, pushed the UF and the FNSOC into negotiations for yet another *convention collective*. This time, they aimed for something more comprehensive and durable, a "véritable statut de la profession" that would once and for all establish "a regime of peace and mutual confidence."[64] The two sides appeared to reach an agreement in March 1938. The federal committee of the UF balked, however. It refused to sign the new accord, citing the growing discontent of its rank and file, without decisive action on Law 900, still bogged down in the Senate. The two sides nonetheless pressed on with their discussions, and on November 11, 1938, Armistice Day, they signed a new convention.

"Much more voluminous" than its predecessor, the new agreement looks like a masterpiece of compromise, "with the aim of preventing all conflict and of establishing a prosperous regime for each coiffeur and for the profession." Workers obtained the *repas collectif* but accepted numerous *dérogations*. The Union fédérale granted the principle of a "salaire minimum assuré" for *ouvriers coiffeurs*; the Fédération nationale pledged itself to help establish "tarifs syndicaux minima." Employers promised to respect the new laws on paid vacations, social insurance, and family allowances; employees endorsed the battle against *travail noir*. Each side committed itself to improve the conditions of apprenticeship and rid the salons of dangerous substances. *Commissions mixtes* would assure that the system operated fairly and in the common interest.[65]

The UF hedged its bets by making its formal participation in the convention dependent on a ministerial decree that would subject *all* salons to its terms. The CPC predictably announced its refusal to comply with the new convention, to which it had not been a party. It especially objected to several articles that it considered patently illegal. The signatories, it believed, did not have the statutory authority to set apprenticeship policy or reign in the activity of *écoles privées*, so as to limit access to the trade, or any right to infringe on the *liberté du patron*.[66] Even when addenda of August 1939 removed the problematical articles, the CPC sustained its opposition to the convention, which it considered too favorable to employees and apt only for artisanal salons. In the end, Bagnaud's attempts to obstruct the accord hardly merited the effort, since the Republic never came across with the enabling decree that would have turned the November 1938 convention into a true "statut de la profession."

The state similarly disappointed coiffeurs' hopes for Law 900. The Chamber of Deputies, always receptive to requests from artisans, had passed the bill unanimously at the end of January 1937, spurring the optimism that led to the February convention. In general, the Senate did not share the Chamber's enthusiasm for bailing out *petites situations.* Therefore, when what was by then proposition 900–27 passed on to that more conservative body—"partisans à fond de l'économie libérale," the *Coiffure de Paris* called them—it met with a much colder reception. "The country," remarked Senator Louis Linyer (Loire-Inférieure), "has other concerns."[67]

Linyer's curt dismissal of their interests brought a protest from some of his constituents. "Despite the country's 'other concerns,' " wrote the Syndicat des maîtres et artisans coiffeurs of Nantes, "despite your ignorance, bad faith, and prejudice, our grand cause will triumph because it is logical, just, humane, and because it will contribute to the revival of our beautiful country."[68] Clearly, the majority of senators had felt differently and had voted down Law 900–27 on March 28, 1939, although they supported the principle of obligatory minimum prices and did not rule out another vote on the proposition in the near future.[69] By the summer of 1939, though, the country did indeed have "autres occupations," and the troubles of the hairdressing trades fell off the national agenda.

To be sure, the fate of *petits patrons coiffeurs* and other elements of *petite entreprise* had never been at the center of Popular Front concerns. The Matignon Accords had been negotiated between the representatives of big business and big labor according to their own perspectives and possibilities. This was as reasonable as it was politically expedient. After all, national recovery depended on banking and metallurgy, not on bakeries and hairdressing salons. It meant, however, that like the poor relation who tries to get along in clothes tailored for someone else, *petits établissements* struggled to adapt rules made for others to their own circumstances. The results were understandably uneven.

The labor reforms imposed by legislation in June 1936 and integrated into the hairdressers' collective convention arguably brought some relief to the most unfortunate *ouvriers coiffeurs*. They began to enjoy paid holidays. Their workweek continued to shrink. The decree of April 1937 set schedules of forty-five to fifty-two hours, always depending on location. Sunday closing became more common in the salons, if only because the forty-hour week gave *customers* more time off, so they no longer needed to be served on Sunday. The conventions' most critical innovation was to establish wage minimums across the profession. Unfortunately, the documents do not tell us what proportion of the *salariat* were covered by the minimum wage scale or what percentage of *patrons coiffeurs* applied them. To judge by what the workers did *not* complain about, as well as by what they did, it seems that the minimum wages set in the conventions of 1936 were broadly implemented. It was the ensuing demand to raise them by another 20 percent that caused all the resistance. The documents likewise have little to say about the substantial number of *baissiers*. Logic suggests that those who worked cheap worked mostly by themselves or with family members. They might have been men like the Polish coiffeurs who cut the hair of their immigrant neighbors in their small salon in the twentieth arrondissement. These two *polonais* had no employees and grossed only about 35,000 francs a year. Since net revenue usually amounted to less than half the gross, and in this case needed to be split between two partners, their *petite affaire* hardly afforded them a lush life. They directly exploited no one but themselves, but their business practices likely helped to push down wages in general by depressing prices and hence reducing revenue for a majority of *petits salons*.[70]

Small *salonniers'* laments were perfectly consistent on this score: most shops simply did not make enough money to pay decent wages. The *Hebdo-Coiffure* played a now-proverbial tune: "In the hairdressing trade," it wrote, "the number of coiffeurs exceeds demand, forcing prices down and producing numerous *maisons baissières*."[71] Through their representatives in the Union fédérale, and even in the Confédération patronal, *petits patrons* begged the government to create the conditions that would raise prices and allow them the meet their new wage obligations. As we have seen, the *pouvoirs publics*, particularly the Senate, were not prepared to tinker sufficiently with the free market to make this possible. Similar frustrations across the French economy undoubtedly turned people off the liberal economy and fed the hue and cry for some kind of corporatist solution to these problems.

Failing the passage of Law 900 or something similar, only an economic rebound that sent women back to the salons with money in their purses could have rescued the mass of marginal salons from their commercial difficulties. For the Popular Front as such proposed no remedy for their specific ailments. *Petits patrons coiffeurs* recognized this fully only in the beginning of 1937, when it became clear that the concessions they had granted their employees the previous June would not elicit any compensatory policies from the government. It was this realization that soured the lower middle class of hairdressers on the Blum government and pushed the UF into a hardline against further concessions, leading to the "patronal front" and the strike of May 1937.

The first Blum coalition dissolved a month later, in June 1937. The following year brought what the *Ouvrier Coiffeur* termed the "reprise de combatitivité de la part du Patronat."[72] The failed general strike of November 1938 and the Reynaud decrees that followed brought a definitive end to the Popular Front. Nothing quite so dramatic happened in the hairdressing profession. The search for a workable *convention collective* went on, alongside the never-ending campaign for higher prices, which recovered slowly toward 1939. That summer, as war approached, arbitration over a proposed 18 percent wage rise in Paris faltered "*en raison des difficultés patronales.*"[73] It mattered little. Earlier hopes among both employers and *ouvriers* for a professional renaissance and shared prosperity had all but dissipated. It was a dispirited trade that followed its country to war in 1939.

*   *   *

The troubles that led hairdressers to this gloomy point, from the relative optimism of 1936, together stand as a case study of the unraveling of the Popular Front. They speak hardly at all to the conventionally understood sources of failure: the machinations of the "two hundred families," the macroeconomic shortcomings of Blum's policies, the perfidy of the Radical party, the excessive demands of labor. They provide instead a social history of the process described most fully by Serge Berstein and his student, Jean Ruhlmann; that is, the mutiny of the middle class.[74]

The Rassemblement populaire on which the Popular Front rested had not in principle forgotten France's middling elements. Indeed, observed the general secretary of the PCF, Maurice Thorez, the party accepted that they could "not move faster than the *classes moyennes.*" The Manifesto of January 1936 had committed the coalition to fiscal relief for "les catégories les plus touchées dans leurs conditions d'existence," and this included artisans and *petits commerçants* along with the industrial working class.[75] We have already seen the hopefulness it initially generated among *petits patrons*, as well as their *assistants*.

In the end, however, the Blum experiment let almost everyone down, though for different reasons. If it disappointed *ouvriers* for failing to triumph over the enemies of the working class, it quickly convinced artisan-coiffeurs that it favored workers even against the most *petits patrons*. The Matignon Accords had been worked out without any representation from the *classes moyennes*, and the decrees that issued subsequently from the ministries seemed to take little account of their interests. Under the Popular Front, wrote Ruhlmann, "*les milieux indépendants* felt themselves squeezed between economic *dirigisme* and compulsory legislation on the *durée du travail*."[76] The frustrations that followed fueled the growth of a *mouvement des classes moyennes*, where middle-class opposition to the Popular Front found its voice.[77] This in turn helped to convince the Radicals that their political fortunes lay outside the Rassemblement populaire and to tip them into a new coalition, further *à droite*.

Marcel Rouaix, editor of *Le Front Économique* and one of the self-appointed spokesmen of the middle classes, blamed their predicament on poor organization that allowed the Popular Front to roll on without regard to *their* interests. But the inability of the Blum government to satisfy the claims of both *ouvriers* and *patrons coiffeurs*, which was the cause of continuing turbulence in the hairdressing profession, did not in my view stem from a lack of organization. The failure of the Popular Front in coiffure, and by extension in other sectors of the middle-class economy, lay not in execution but in conception.

Like so many great popular movements, the Rassemblement populaire was sustained largely by a myth, that of *les trusts* who were destroying France through their greedy search for profits and support for the Republic's enemies.[78] The myth, of course, contained more than a grain of truth. The forces of big business and big finance did really oppose the progressive aspects of republican solidarity, and they often made common cause with antirepublican forces. But "the struggle against *trusts* and *cartels*," as Socialist deputy Joseph Rous, founder of the Chamber of Deputies group for the defense of the middle classes, imagined it, did not add up to a plausible political and economic program.[79]

Ideological sympathy and electoral calculation required that the Rassemblement populaire gather France's vast *classes moyennes*—artisans, small businessmen, and *petits agriculteurs*—under its progressive umbrella, to join the working class in its campaign to thwart the "diverse forms of capitalist competition and concentration."[80] It should be abundantly clear by now, however, that the interests of even the most *petits* employers did not harmonize perfectly with those of their *salariés*. An alliance of *les petits* against *les gros* might have made a lot of sense on several levels. It nonetheless necessitated hard thinking about some obvious dilemmas.

The experience of coiffure suggests that the Rassemblement populaire had not worked out these contradictions when it arrived in power, and the consequences did not take long to show themselves.

The Blum government appeared to satisfy the demands of *ouvriers coiffeurs* with the June 1936 collective convention that applied the Matignon Accords to the hairdressing trades. But it could never figure out how to sustain a sector of struggling *petites entreprises* that could support these new charges. It modified the forty-hour law and unsuccessfully tried to arbitrate the other differences between *petits patrons coiffeurs* and their workers. As a result, small employers' continuing distress undermined even the advantages formally given to employees.

There was nothing new in this conundrum, and it would not satisfy the demands of justice to hold the Popular Front responsible for a situation that had plagued coiffure to a greater or lesser degree since the nineteenth century. The Rassemblement populaire, however, made exceptional claims for itself, and its electoral victory excited an exceptional degree of faith that it could make France a substantially better place. It was therefore not the profession's troubles, which were endemic, but the Popular Front's inability to overcome them that was its chief legacy in coiffure.

Working in the sunshine, when there's no electricity

7

Hair in War and Occupation

War, writes Dominique Veillon, whose books on fashion and subsistence in France *à l'heure allemande* are the best guide to everyday life under German domination, turned *la vie quotidienne* upside down, even before the fighting began. Parisians watched workers pile sandbags around the capital's chief monuments, cover the stained glass of Notre Dame, and pack off priceless art treasures to the provinces for safekeeping. The government banned balls and *réunions publiques*, limited theater and cinema hours. It distributed gas masks and sent Parisian children off to school in the *Nièvre* and other French regions so *profondes* that the Germans could not hurt them. Public authorities opened metro stations to the public as air-raid shelters. The Place des Fêtes station, in the outlying nineteenth arrondissement, could accommodate 5,000 people.[1]

The government also stepped into the economy with unprecedented dispatch. In order to protect the livelihoods of those called to the colors, the legislature passed the law of September 9, 1939, which forbade the "creation, extension, and transfer" of businesses without the prefect's express authorization. To hold back inflation, ministerial decrees prohibited any rise in prices or wages without official permission.[2]

The fashion industry reacted as it had in 1914, with a show of seriousness and by attaching its interests to those of a nation at war. The fashion press had given no hint of the coming cataclysm. Rather, in the months before the declaration of war, the *Coiffure de Paris* announced with horror that studies had shown that American women consumed three times more perfume, per capita, than *françaises* and urged hairdressers to stimulate and then exploit the taste for perfume.[3] *Votre Beauté* maintained its sharp interest in large, shapely breasts. As the crisis over Danzig reached a climax in the summer of 1939, *Vogue* offered pictorial essays on high-society masquerade balls, editorials condemning excessive nudity, articles on cosmetic surgery, and a feature entitled "Le Plaisir de Pénélope" that presented the Princess de Faucigny-Lucinge and the Comtesse de Polignac at work on their tapestries.

The war finally reached the pages of *Vogue* several months later. The high-fashion glossy did not publish in October and November, but its December issue carried patriotic messages from all the couturier houses under the heading *Paris Continue*, asserting their determination to keep working. The House of O'Rossen assured clients that "as in 1914–1918, the sober cuts of its tailors will prevail in this year of war." The *maison* Jean Dessès announced that it "remained open, creating models in harmony with *la vie actuelle*." Under the heading "Return to the Land," *Vogue's* April issue looked in on the Comtesse Dulong de Rosnay. A refugee at the Château d'Oursières, the countess was shown doing her bit for the war: planting cabbages, picking fruit, and raking leaves.[4]

The great couturiers were proud to say that they had "responded in exemplary fashion to the government's call." They cancelled their fall shows not only because they could not obtain the necessary materials but also because their "fragile creations [were] meant to embellish happy days and peaceful evenings" and were not appropriate to war. It was nonetheless their patriotic duty to carry on. Second only to metallurgy in importance in the French economy, the clothing industries employed over a million workers, 25,000 in *haute couture* alone.

Fashion's patriotic duty, producers reminded consumers, was reciprocal. Just as manufacturers needed to keep "affirming [France's] indisputable superiority" across the world, *les françaises* also had an ongoing obligation to be beautiful.[5] Women were advised not to waste precious resources in a time of national emergency. Nevertheless, the journal *Candide* averred that "luxury is not a sin but a useful expense and even a form of patriotism."[6] *Votre Beauté* likewise told readers that their beauty was "a reward for the eyes, as for the hearts, of men." *La belle française* was an essential part of "that spiritual capital protected by those who fight for our civilization."[7]

As the Polish campaign gave way to the *drôle de guerre*, the sense of national emergency began to relax, and the country returned to something resembling normal life. Restaurants, theaters, music halls, and cinemas reopened, even if they now operated under certain government restrictions. Despite the official control of prices, inflation began to squeeze the majority of those left on the home front. Veillon estimates that overall expenses for a working-class household rose 35 percent, although wages were frozen.[8] Of course, such money cares scarcely affected the fashionable classes, who promptly returned to their usual watering holes: the Ritz, the Crillon, Maxim's. By the spring, foreign buyers were once again flocking to Paris for the spring collections. The fashions they sampled made no reference to the war.

The months of armed inaction left no particular imprint on hairstyles; there was no *mode drôle-de-guerre*. To be sure, the silliest excesses of the prewar season, such as artificial owls perched on top of ladies' coiffures, disappeared with soberer times, and René Rambaud's new edition of the "Fontange" met with "an unquestionable success" for its suggestion of patriotism and resistance.[9] Some hairdressers sought to turn the war to their advantage by seizing the occasion to resuscitate *cheveux courts*. Long styles with lots of curls, they explained, "would not hold up very long under the straps of gas masks and interruptions of electricity."[10] For the moment, the public resisted, and longish, fluid styles remained the preferred model. The article in the April–May 1940 number of *Vogue* reported that the most up-to-date coiffures emphasized the "suppleness" and "natural lightness" of what it called "la mode d'Hollywood." Although the magazine noted that the leading hairdressers—Guillaume, Rambaud, Fernand Aubry—thought the style too "disordered" for proper evening wear.[11]

The more pressing effect of the war on the far-flung mass of hairdressing salons was social and economic. As it had in 1914, mobilization took thousands of coiffeurs away from their salons and often kept them away for years.[12] The departure of so many men once again left salons in the hands of wives and daughters. "How I Reopened My Husband's Salon," read the title of an article in *Coiffure de Paris* by the wife of the prominent coiffeur, Gabriel Fau. The wife and parents of Marcel Lamy, former and future chief of Paris's *patrons coiffeurs* (but at the time a corporal stationed on the German frontier) contributed the story, "How We Reopened Our Son's Salon."[13] In spite of these perturbations, the profession commonly reported that it was adapting to the circumstances of war: "*C'est la guerre*, but l'Oréal still delivers," read one typical advertisement.[14]

In sum, the first phase of war hurt barbers by sending so many of their customers to the front, while the overall quality of work in the *salons pour dames* suffered from the absence of skilled, experienced hands. Price controls must have displeased both workers and *salonniers*. On the other hand, mobilization pulled a lot of excess labor out of the profession, ameliorating the downward pressure on prices and wages and helping those coiffeurs who remained open for business. Either way, there was no sign that the war brought the hairdressing business, already in a long-term trough, any substantial new troubles.

But it turned syndical politics upside down. The Nazi-Soviet Non-Aggression Pact shattered the hard-won unity of the labor movement, once more setting communist and anticommunist elements at each other's throats. In fact, the Rassemblement populaire had been unraveling for some time, the consequence of deep-seated ideological differences exacerbated by plunging morale. The population of the CGT, a fair measure of labor's *esprit*, declined from five million in 1937 to about one million on the eve of the war.

Social retrenchment under Daladier and Reynaud brought political divisions within the labor movement, buried in a shallow grave during the Popular Front, back to the surface, and international tensions only exacerbated these divisions. In 1938, the CGT split between *munichois* and *anti-munichois* factions. General secretary Léon Jouhaux led the latter, and his ex-second-in-command, René Belin, the former. A second fissure ran between the old *unitaires*, associated with the journal *La Vie Ouvrière*, who continued to work to bring the confederation into the communist camp, and the anticommunist elements behind Belin's journal, *Syndicats*, that accused them of supporting Soviet interests over those of France. Between these bitter rivals sat the confederation's centrists, led by Jouhaux. It was along these lines that the CGT finally cleaved under the pressure of war and official repression.[15]

This same political turbulence broke apart the FNSOC and the CSO. By the late 1930s, the dominant group, composed of former *confédérés* but including a large number of ex-*unitaires* had chosen to follow François Magnien, who had by now completely abjured his old Leninism and set out on the road leading to reformism, *perfectionnement*, and class collaboration. He and his allies more or less controlled the CSO, even though a smaller, more intransigent group of ex-*unitaires*, loyal to the Comintern, still hoped to use the CSO as the agent of proletarian revolution. These two *tendances* had coexisted uneasily within the CSO since the so-called Unity Congress of January 1936, but the disappointments of the Popular Front, especially the failed strike of May 1937, had weakened their sense of common cause. The events of the summer of 1939 blasted the quarreling factions into a frank and bitter hostility that never evaporated.

The Molotov-Ribbentrop treaty imposed a clear choice between loyalty to the Communist Party and loyalty to France, now at war with an ally of the Soviet Union.[16] CGT moderates, led by Jouhaux, joined the Belin faction in spurning any further collaboration "with those who have refused to condemn the Pact," and the confederation voted to force communists out of the leadership. Magnien, who had already broken publicly with "those persons who follow the politics of M. Stalin," abstained, as the CGT aligned itself with the war effort.[17]

As part of its anticommunist campaign, the Daladier government dissolved the CSO, sequestered its goods, and closed down its École parisienne in September 1939.[18] The FNSOC, following the CGT's lead, purged itself. It ejected Marcel Moreau, the CSO general secretary, along with his fellow communists: Arthur Roger, Roger Leclerc, and Georges Philippot. They blamed Magnien, "one of those so-called syndicalists assisting [the premier] in his repressive policies."[19] But, Magnien was nobody's flunky; he had come to anticommunism on his own.

Working through his lieutenants, Paul Petit, René Lhuillier, and Georges Leroy, and despite spending much of the fall in active service, Magnien managed to take full control of the labor movement in the hairdressing trades. In December, the CSO reconstituted itself, minus its communist elements, as the Syndicat des ouvriers coiffeurs de Paris (SOC) and received as its birthright the confiscated goods of the CSO and the École parisienne. Moreau and his colleagues, now underground, never got over their venomous hatred of Magnien and the others who had, as they saw it, hijacked the CSO and betrayed the True Cause.[20]

Defeat and occupation brought these militant communists bigger problems than the loss of the CSO. The new authorities were more diligent than Daladier had been in pursuit of state enemies. Philippot, who combined radical politics with artistic flair—he had won the Meilleur Ouvrier de France competition in 1939, with better results than the celebrated Gabriel Fau—became involved, according to his own account, in "clandestine activities." Arrested in 1943, he spent two years in Dachau. So did his comrade and fellow *ouvrier coiffeur*, Emile Tarrier. Arthur Roger endured two years in an unnamed concentration camp for [his] "syndical activities." Other less visible *coiffeurs communistes* must have suffered a similar fate, or worse.[21]

In the wake of the Armistice, however, active resistance to the new regime still lay in the future. The overwhelming majority of hairdressers, like other *français*, settled in to try to survive what promised to be a difficult situation. For the moment, they could take comfort in the wisdom of the *Coiffure de Paris* that assured them saying, "We have our tools, our hands, our courage. And our clients will always need us."[22] *Petits salonniers* must have been further heartened by what they heard from Marshal Pétain, who famously announced his concern for the "artisanat" and committed himself to preserving what *La Vie Industrielle* called "one of the essential elements of France's economic recovery and of its prestige."[23] The new regime maintained the Republic's restriction on new businesses and guaranteed a crackdown on *travail noir*.

Even *ouvriers coiffeurs* had reason for optimism, despite the evident right-wing bias of the new regime. Whatever grudges it bore against the Popular Front, the Pétain government retained paid holidays and continued to encourage the negotiation of *conventions collectives*. It did not extend working hours beyond Reynaud's reforms of 1938, and in many instances actually cut them back. To be sure, Vichy adjusted the system of social welfare to its political priorities. For example, new rules for *allocations familiales* encouraged larger families, and *allocations de salaire unique* discouraged wives from working. "Anti-French" elements of the population were all but excluded from assistance.[24] But that would not have touched most hairdressing workers.

Whether or not they believed the regime's flattery or took any notice of its social policies, most hairdressers at first seemed willing to grant the new regime the benefit of the doubt and to lend a hand to the task of national regeneration. Not all were as effusive as Hector Malacarne, the old patron coiffeur whose letter to the labor minister pledged that coiffeurs would "do our duty, loyal in sentiments and action, to obey orders from above with discipline and devotion. . . ."[25] More soberly, the *Coiffure de Paris*, when it returned to publication in October 1940, committed coiffeurs both "to work" and "to obey." "We understand," it wrote, "that we will pull through only if the country has order and discipline, and if we are all capable, without murmur or protest, of following the directives and order that are given us."[26] In other words, if coiffeurs did not know exactly what to expect from the National Revolution, they had little reason to be nostalgic for the old Republic and provisionally granted the old marshal their confidence.

Meanwhile, the new government's first order of business was to manage the national crisis that followed the invasion and rapacious German occupation. The law of August 16, 1940, creating *comités d'organisation* (CO) to stabilize and direct the national economy, was its initial response to this predicament.[27] Critics of the CO—and there were many—came to see them as part of some grand and sinister design, although in very different ways. Paul Vignaux, writing in 1943, called the committees "the first victory of anti-syndical corporatism."[28] More typical was the judgment of Pierre Tissier. Noting that the state placed only big employers—"the 'Comité des Forges' of every branch of trade"—in charge of the CO, Tissier concluded that the law of August 16, had delivered France to "the dictatorship of money and plutocracy."[29]

It is probably closest to the truth to say that, while the law of August 16, conformed to the prejudices of the regime, it was less a "design" than a makeshift response to a "situation économique alarmante." There can be no question that the system of CO was both *étatiste and dirigé*, but this was less a matter of principle than of practicality—just as its authors contended.[30] What is more, Vichy's *mainmise* of the French economy represented a mere innovation in scale. The laws of July 11, 1938 that organized the economy for war and the law of September 9, 1939 that required prefectoral authority for the creation or extension of businesses were just the capstone of the Third Republic's considerable intervention in economic affairs.[31] Even the arrangement of the CO largely recapitulated that of the National Economic Council (CNE), established by parliament between the wars. The main difference was that the CNE had awarded big labor a seat beside big business and the state, while the CO were given over lock, stock, and barrel to employers and "experts."[32]

Hairdressers did not at first receive their own organization committee but were placed under the aegis of the CO-Parfumerie. They began to carve out an autonomous place in the system, however, by way of the rationing apparatus. A decree of December 1940 created a Comité national de répartition des produits rationnés aux coiffeurs (CNR-Coiffure) as an arm of the mighty Office central de répartition des produits industriels (OCRPI). Backed with the powers of "control, constraint, and repression," and mixed "incestuously" with the organization committees, the OCRPI monopolized the acquisition and distribution of raw materials in wartime France.[33] It passed a small portion of this power along to the CNR-Coiffure.

To constitute its personnel, the CNR-Coiffure rounded up the usual collection of patronal leaders: Joseph Gestalder, Léonce Lebègue, Amadée Deslongchamps, Edouard Dauvergne, and Gustave Blavy, of the Union fédérale; Robert Maigre, Victor Touzet, Louis Tison, and

Adolphe Fried, of the Confédération des patrons coiffeurs. Marcel Bagnaud, president of the CPC and vice president of the Paris Chamber of Commerce, was the obvious choice as president of the repartition committee.[34] Two facts stand out about this group. First, hairdressing workers were completely absent, since the government reserved the business of *répartition* exclusively to businessmen and technocrats. Second, despite the apparently evenhanded presence of the UF and the CPC, it was the CPC that dominated, both through the authority of Bagnaud and because it represented the better-connected *gros salonniers*.

Not content with the CNR-Coiffure, hairdressers continued to lobby for their own organization committee. They reasoned that full autonomy would bring a fairer portion of resources and provide the opportunity to rehabilitate a trade that had fallen on hard times. Bagnaud and his colleagues gained the support of the Ministry of Production, headed by supertechnocrat of Vichy Jean Bichelonne, and of Pierre Loyer, director of the new Artisanal Service. They managed to overcome the resistance of the German authorities, who thought a proliferation of COs would aggravate the problem of scarce resources. And at the end of 1942, hairdressers finally received their own organization committee, which opened its offices at 88, avenue Kléber, a short walk from the Arc de Triomphe.

The CO-Coiffure was but an expanded version of the CNR, with almost exactly the same membership, mostly Parisians and all patrons. Its mandate was broadened from distributing raw materials to regulating all economic matters concerning the profession, yet the search for hard-to-get *matières primaires* remained its chief preoccupation.[35] Bagnaud slipped naturally into the presidency of the CO-Coiffure and remained without question the most powerful figure in the profession. His position was in many ways an unenviable one, given hairdressers' desperate need for material and his inability to satisfy that need, but he appears to have worked hard at piloting his sinking ship.[36] Over the course of his tenure at the head of the repartition and organization committees, Bagnaud's office turned out thousands of pages of circulars and letters asking his constituents for information and keeping them abreast of a daunting number of official regulations. It also churned out a steady stream of supplications to those in charge of allocating resources.

These *démarches* repeatedly demonstrated that the needs of hairdressers ranked low on the scale of national priorities. For example, at the end of May 1941, Bagnaud wrote to the Directeur des industries chimiques, asking for a supplementary attribution of soap. Several months later he received his reply: "Due to the present shortage of *corps gras*," wrote the director, "I am . . . not able to consider the present request on behalf of hairdressers."[37] This response was neither surprising nor unreasonable, yet the "pénurie organisée" it implied threatened to close the profession down and to leave tens of thousands of coiffeurs without the means to make a living.

In September 1942, Bagnaud called the heads of the departmental organization committees to Paris and laid out the dire situation. *Brillantine* was "introuvable"; cotton "reserved for priority needs." Whereas before the war hairdressers used hairpins worth forty to fifty tons of steel every four months, they had less than five tons available for the beginning of 1942. Hairpins sold for 1,000 francs a kilo on the black market, but even these ran out before long. In 1941 and 1942, hairdressers received only 10 percent of their prewar linen needs. Some were reported to be tearing up their own bedding to make up the difference. The president warned his representatives of even harder times ahead. Coiffeurs could expect to have 50 percent of the shaving powder they required; 26.5 percent of the soap, 15 percent of the shampoo—shortages compounded by the lack of coal, gas, and electricity, which made hot water a rare commodity. The organization committee needed to ration shampoo, but Bagnaud confessed that he could not find the paper to issue the coupons.[38]

The particular shortage of *matières grasses* more or less eliminated beauty products from salon shelves. This was critical because, as we have seen repeatedly, cutting hair itself was extremely unremunerative work, and without this commerce the majority of coiffeurs faced dramatically reduced earnings. Bagnaud urged patience on his departmental agents. Replacement materials are being sought, he told them. But in the meantime, he wondered, "how can we make bricks without straw?"

As the material situation deteriorated, it became increasingly difficult for salons merely to stay open for business. They found their lucrative lunchtime business especially constricted because, in view of the food shortages, workers and customers now required extra time to find lunch or to be served in restaurants. Coal rations fell to a fraction of what they had been before the war, when there was any at all. By 1942, salons received electricity for lighting only between 10 a.m. and 5 p.m., and the supply steadily declined thereafter. This meant, among other things, that even if he had the materials, a coiffeur could not offer his clients a *teinture* or an *indéfrisable* after 2 p.m., because these tasks took three hours to complete. In September 1943, the Production Ministry temporarily cut off all electricity to Parisian salons, eliminating at a stroke drying, perming, and hot water. By the summer of 1944, the *Eclaireur des Coiffeurs* reported, coiffeurs were forbidden to use *any* electricity without special permission.[39] The dearth of power and materiel sometimes produced amazing feats of *débrouillage*. Louis Gervais, for example, solved his electricity problem by hiring two fellows—one had worked as a bicycle deliveryman for Chez Maggi, the other had been an international *footballeur*—to ride a tandem bike that turned a generator eight hours a day, more than 300 miles daily. Albert Pourrière, unable to use his hairdryers as he was accustomed to put his clients out in the sun to dry their hair while they received manicures and pedicures al fresco or wrapped hair that had not quite dried in fabulous scarves. René Garraud organized elegant "drying teas," where his clients' hair could dry at their leisure and in the most exclusive company. Antonio adapted toothpicks and pine needles in place of hairpins, Gauthier made his from common wire. Roger Para acquired the habit of taking off one day a week to collect bone marrow, which he then used to treat his customers' hair.[40] But these were the elite of *hauts coiffeurs*. The mass of hairdressers, whose clientele had neither the money for expensive *foulards* nor the time to sip tea while their hair dried probably had no clever, profitable response to the absence of crucial materials. The more enterprising, or less scrupulous, took to the black market.[41] Others simply became idler and poorer, found another trade, or volunteered for work in Germany.

The government hoped to make up some of the deficit in *matières primaires* through recycling. Thus, in early 1942, the *Coiffure de Paris* carried notices telling its readers that it was no longer sufficient to exchange their empty glassware for full. "We must salvage glassware," it wrote, "by an out and out effort to recycle." In fact, the journal ran its own *bureau de propagande pour la récupération de la verrerie* from the L'Oréal offices at 38, rue Jean Mermoz, off the rue Faubourg Saint-Honoré.

Here public policy met private enterprise. Laws of January and August 1941 on recycling raw material ordered the "récupération des cheveux des salons de coiffure" in order to help industries that suffered from a paucity of raw materials, such as "the manufacture of textiles and carpets, of draught-reducers [*bourrelets*] for windows and doors, slippers, belts, bags, and brushes."[42] Paul Thevenin, who directed the Société de vente et de représentation publicitaire (SVRP), quickly recognized the profitable opportunities and in the fall of 1941 contacted a number of hairdressers' groups, including the CNR-Coiffure, about organizing the collection and resale of cut hair from salons. Simultaneously, he approached the public authorities about obtaining the 40,000 sacks that he thought he would need to hold the hair. He then began to dispatch subcontractors, who combed the cities on bicycles, pulling little trailers and collecting these *déchets* from coiffeurs. The agents paid their suppliers four francs per kilo. They sorted the hair and cleaned it, then sold it to Thevenin for 9.60 francs a kilo. Thevenin then passed it along to interested parties for up to twenty francs a kilo: to the Lelarge company in Reims, which wanted hair to blend with wool and fibranne; to the Établissements Gevelot, who mixed it with felt; to a factory in Calvados, which added it to fibranne to make *piloïta*, used to make slippers, gloves, mittens, sweaters. The Service de la récupération et de l'utilisation of the OCRPI estimated that hairdressers produced over 200,000 kilos of salvageable hair per month, worth four million francs to the SVRP, providing it could get its hands on all these scraps.

The SVRP discovered, however, that hairdressers themselves had no enthusiasm for his scheme—not at four francs a kilo, at any rate. It responded with both blandishments and threats. In Nantes, its subcontractors reminded coiffeurs that recycling was a "national duty" that would compensate for the crippling shortage of resources and help reduce unemployment. Elsewhere, SVRP representatives warned coiffeurs that they would receive no raw materials if they did not save hair for recycling, which was in fact not true. Finally, hairdressers' tepid cooperation led Thevenin to approach Bagnaud. He wanted the president of the CNR-Coiffure to make it mandatory for coiffeurs to collect and hand over their *déchets*. Thevenin even asked Bagnaud to encourage his constituents to cut hair as short as possible, citing "economies of shampoo, hot water, and electricity for drying and coloring." Bagnaud, unconvinced, replied that "if recycling has its *exigences*, fashion has its own." He would not recommend hairstyles of which he did not approve merely to make Thevenin rich. On the other hand, the Service de la récupération was impressed enough by Thevenin's forceful business methods—"patterned after American practices"—to help the SVRP win a monopoly on recycled hair in the Occupied Zone and in most of Vichy France, as well.

There is no evidence that recycled hair made a significant contribution to reducing the deficit in textiles, material for which remained in short supply. Yet fashion proved to be a most resilient social convention, and it bounced back to life in the fall of 1940. Most fashion magazines were forced to suspend publication for the duration, yet the fashionable life went on.[43] Restaurants reopened, although the authorities set their menus and hours of operation. The opera played once again for both the *français* and the *occupants*. Even the fall fashion shows went ahead, as if to "prove to the world that Paris was still the capital of elegance."[44] The lineup of great couturiers had changed, however. Chanel closed her *maison* in September 1939 and soon went into seclusion with her Nazi lover. Schiaparelli fled to the United States. Madeleine Vionnet retired. Still, some twenty fashion houses continued to produce on a limited scale: about 100 models a year "for wealthy collaborators and for export to Germany."[45] Among those who stayed, Lucien Lelong was the man of the hour. President of the Chambre syndicale de la couture parisienne, Lelong became the industry spokesman during the Occupation, burnishing his reputation by allegedly convincing Goebbels to let the fashion industry remain in Paris, rather than move it to Berlin.[46]

Even as the Germans installed themselves in Paris and threatened to deport *haute couture*, those in the *beau monde* found a way to overcome any scruples impeding their desire to dress up. Indeed, high fashion in the early days of the occupation tended to be flamboyant: big hair, huge, decorative hats, garish colors, longer jackets, shorter skirts. The tougher the times, it seemed, the more outrageous the mode, at least until the German crackdown of 1943.

Valerie Steele, in her usual down-to-earth manner, downplays the significance of these conspicuous fashions, proposing that wartime buyers might have preferred this sort of "exaggeration" for reasons that had nothing to do with the occupation. Whatever its "true" meaning, though, ostentatious dress in the midst of foreign occupation struck some observers as singularly inappropriate, if not downright collaborationist. Designers and their followers therefore tried to put a more admirable spin on their activities. Some maintained, as they had after 1914, that a vibrant fashion business was good for France and that favored members of society had a patriotic duty to uphold France's reputation for fashion and taste. Others went further in their defense of *haute couture*, claiming it even as a sort of resistance. After all, they reasoned, saving and rationing only benefited the Germans. The more material that was used in fashion, "the less the Germans would get."[47] A few later bragged that they had promoted ridiculous excess as a way to cock a snook at the occupiers—"a manifestation of insolence that does not pass unnoticed by the Germans."[48]

The height of insolent style arrived with the Zazou fashion. Affected mostly by the young, Zazou constituted a sort of Vichy-era "punk," vilified in the occupation press and public opinion, its wearers were openly harassed. With most of its adherents drawn from the *classes aisées*, Zazou incorporated a jazzy, zoot-suited look in direct contrast to the "natural" and "austere" modes imposed by circumstance and official discourse. Faces excessively painted, wrote Veillon,

> [the women] hide under their furs a collared sweater and a very short, pleated skirt. Their exaggerated square shoulders contrast with the men's drooping shoulders. Their long curls fall about their necks. Their stockings are striped, their shoes flat and heavy, they carry big umbrellas . . . [wear] hair curled and swelled in the front, long on the neck [or] long on the shoulders—never fastened—and very often platinum blonde, like Hollywood stars.[49]

Zazou was self-consciously transgressive, a protest against "the war's absurdity." Yet even conventional wartime fashion brought women into conflict with official ideology. Reactionaries in the Vichy regime especially despised the cosmopolitan "garçonne," but they generally hated *all* forms of the so-called modern woman, whom they blamed for contributing to France's degradation "par cocquetterie ou par égoïsme." Official Vichy counsel on fashion urged women to avoid anything too urbane or too sexy. It attacked what it called "la femme *objet d'art*" and worked to put women back in their homes and in their corsets. It found women in trousers especially provocative and, except for those females engaged in heavy labor, sought to ban them, though without much success. Indeed, *Votre Beauté* explicitly recommended trousers to its readers on holiday by the sea or in the country.

This was surprising advice, given that *Votre Beauté* was part of the L'Oréal publishing empire, whose founder and director Eugène Schueller became notorious for his reactionary opinions during the war, and that its editor Lucien François was renowned for his antediluvian views on fashion and femininity. In his book, *Cent conseils d'élégance*, published in 1942, François lashed out at the "liberated" woman of the *entre-deux-guerres* for modeling her body on "un idéal hermaphrodite" and indulging in "activités viriles." "Today," he preached, "France understands that she owes her defeat in large part to her slackening values." He threw his moral and editorial weight fully behind Pétain's attempt to "reconstruct women's place in the home and in her maternal role." He even believed, he wrote, that when women returned to their "natural" functions, their bodies would return to their "natural" shape: bigger breasts, wider hips, et cetera.

Whatever their feelings about the National Revolution, the majority of fashionable ladies plainly paid no mind to this sort of advice, while the great mass of *françaises* ignored official pronouncements on clothing—being too busy trying to find something clean, neat, comfortable, warm, and not unattractive to wear. For most people, the "système D" [débrouillardise = resourcefulness] dominated such fashion life as survived. Shortages of leather and wool forced women to don wooden-soled shoes and fabrics made from fibranne—a practical "disaster," according to Veillon. In the absence of silk stockings, women had recourse to creams sold by Rambaud and Elizabeth Arden that could be applied to legs to make them look stockinged—in three colors for thirty francs. Because there was no real shampoo to be had, the *Coiffure de Paris* recommended Dopal: "cheaper than soap . . . washes better . . . leaves hair marvelously supple and shiny." L'Oréal introduced a wartime version of its best-selling soap: "Monsavon 30 percent" was not quite the same, but it was economical and long lasting (the advertisement claimed that a bar would last two months).[50] Eventually, as rationing bit harder, even these substitutes became difficult to find.

Bicycles, which became the chief means of local transportation during the occupation, had an important impact on fashion and hairstyles. The practical need to pedal here and there motivated women to circumvent the rules prohibiting trousers by wearing *jupes-calottes*; it also favored the practical benefits of short, loose coiffures. For the less mobile, fancy hats became one of the markers of wartime fashion. All the more so because, with the usual materials in short supply, hats represented a relatively small space for the expression of excess and fantasy that ordinarily took up the whole of a woman's costume. Or perhaps, for ordinary *françaises*, a hat topped with hanging gardens or a bird's nest was just psychological compensation for oppressive deprivation.[51]

Women who could neither find a decent coiffure nor afford a whimsical hat wrapped their hair in turbans, which became increasingly *à la mode* as the occupation dragged on. There could be no clearer evidence of the hard times that fell upon the hairdressing trades. In a society without the means to keep hair clean and make it beautiful, "the turban became the fashion for hiding poorly groomed hair."[52] Compare Long's description of an effervescent hairdressing culture after 1915 to Guillaume's lament that between 1940 and 1944 "the creation of new hairstyles was reduced nearly to zero."[53] It is a measure of how much harsher the home front was in World War II.

Thus coiffure limped along in some faded approximation of its prewar activity. Hairstyles became somewhat shorter and less ornate during the war. Actress Madeleine Sologne popularized a simpler, more natural style of medium-length hair, straight and smooth, with a flip at the bottom. Other fashionable women adopted the Veronica Lake look, their faces half-hidden by their *lisse*, shoulder-length locks.[54] Oddly, comments here and there in the documents go so far as to suggest that hairdressers had *more* business during the war. Gustave Blavy, postwar president of the CSP, alluded to a "high demand" for coiffure under the occupation. And Magnien, in a 1943 pitch for higher wages, called the occupation an "era of prosperity."[55] But it is hard to reconcile a picture of busy, profitable salons with the palpable evidence of general poverty, dirty, unkempt hair, and scarcity of basic materials.

Moreover, conditions for coiffeurs became more and more difficult as the months passed. In December 1940, L'Oréal had organized an evening to celebrate "La Teinture et la Coiffure," with Albert Pourrière as host and star attraction. Almost a thousand people attended and listened to a pitch on the importance of hair coloring to fashion and the bottom line.[56] But *teinture* soon vanished from salon shelves, and gray hair went under cover. *Cheveux courts* made a brief comeback, but principally as a testament to the low expectations of fashion. All in all, short, filthy coiffures and heads wrapped in turbans underline, as Veillon put it, "the degree of precariousness into which the French population had fallen in the space of a few years."[57]

Everyone could see that material shortages derived inescapably from wartime disruptions and German plunder. Nevertheless, hairdressers quickly came to suspect that the allocation of scarce resources was a political as well as a technical matter. Moreover, even assuming that attempts at distribution were somehow honest and unbiased, they were bound to bump into all manner of local disputes over personal and organizational primacy, leading to condemnations of "favoritism." The fact that the chief arbiter of the profession's affairs, Marcel Bagnaud, was the outspoken defender of a very tendentious vision of the New France and coiffeurs' role within it quickly turned turf battles into political squabbles.

For example, in the aftermath of defeat and occupation, a group of *salonniers* from across the Midi had gathered to discuss conditions among artisan-coiffeurs in the southern zone. Led by UF militants from Lyon and Marseille, delegates from eighty-five syndicats of *petits patrons* coiffeurs signed on to a new Union nationale of artisan coiffeurs (UNS) and revived the old syndical journal, *Le Trait d'Union des Coiffeurs.* By the end of 1941, the UNS had united some 135 *syndicats professionnels* in forty-five departmental unions in the Unoccupied Zone.[58]

The UNS involved itself in the full range of professional matters, but its first order of business were the terrible economic problems that followed the military disaster. While the wartime system of organization committees was congealing in Paris, the UNS approached the production minister in the fall of 1940 seeking the authority to allocate resources among hairdressing salons in the Unoccupied Zone. Surprisingly, the minister granted it this authority, which it exercised for over a year "in an equitable and completely impartial manner."[59]

The formation of the CNR-Coiffure a couple of months later, however, called the Union's competence into question and led to an unavoidable skirmish over *répartition.* Bagnaud, of course, believed that responsibility for the distribution of materials to hairdressers belonged exclusively to the CNR that he directed. The UNS, already filling that role in the south, was likewise jealous of its prerogatives and reluctant to cede them to Paris. Pierre Jardelle, a UF officer and president of the UNS, objected that the Parisians who ran the CNR-Coiffure were unable to understand "the needs, the customs, and the mores of each region." What was worse, he charged, when it came to handing out scant resources, Bagnaud and his associates systematically favored *grosses maisons*, "une infime minorité."[60] Jardelle stood four-square against the incursion of these hairdresser-bureaucrats, to whom he derisively referred as "le Ministère de la Coiffure." He advised his constituents not to pay the 4 percent *cotisation* levied by the CNR-Coiffure to support its activities and promised them that they would continue to receive materials just the same. Bagnaud denounced Jardelle's "deplorable" apostasy and complained to the Production Ministry that Jardelle had "caused trouble everywhere by usurping the [task of] allocation in the southern zone."[61]

We might admire Jardelle's bravado and respect his regionalist politics, but it is clear that his challenge to Bagnaud and the CNR-Coiffure never had any chance of succeeding. The UNS had been given some authority in the Unoccupied Zone in a moment of bureaucratic confusion. But it was not an official administrative body, like the CNR-Coiffure, and did not have direct access to *matières primaires* through the official rationing apparatus. Jardelle, the modest *patron coiffeur* from Lyon, had no important contacts in Paris or friends in Pétain's inner circle. Besides, the UNS was only a loose amalgam of hairdressers' syndicates; it was not the sort of organization to which Vichy ordinarily gave its proxy. The new regime was congenitally suspicious of ceding power to grassroot organizations. When it needed collaborators, it tended to reach out to businessmen and "experts," not earnest *petits patrons*. Thus the political winds blew at Bagnaud's back, and by the middle of 1942, the UNS had lost all power to funnel precious resources to its constituents.

Jardelle finally acknowledged his defeat when he came to Paris in November 1942 and accepted Bagnaud's invitation to speak to the regional delegates of the CNR-Coiffure. He told the delegates that he now recognized the CNR's usefulness and would return to the south to urge all his departmental committees to make peace with it. He gave his "formal assurances" that the CNR-Coiffure would henceforth meet not "the least dissension" in the Unoccupied Zone.[62] Jardelle's visit to Canossa marked a clear victory for administrative centralism over regionalist and populist energies released by the collapse of the Republic. It meant that the principal business of the hairdressing bureaucracy would be conducted in Paris and that power would flow in one direction: from the top down.

If the structure of professional decision making changed under the so-called National Revolution and conditions in the salons deteriorated sharply during the war, the outlines of coiffure's problems remained depressingly familiar: too many hands chasing too few heads, leading to low prices, puny profits, measly wages, and widespread distress. The forty-hour standard remained in effect in the profession into 1942. *Ouvriers coiffeurs* still owed their employers forty-five hours in Paris and forty-seven in the *banlieue*. In September 1941, the labor minister finally applied the fifty-hour week to the hairdressing workers of Périgueux. This was not evidence of a Pétainist assault on the working class, however, merely the long-awaited administrative application of the collective accord of 1937.[63]

Circumstances reduced the number of hours that hairdressers could devote to their trade, in any case. Since most coiffeurs had fewer customers with less money to spend, as well as a reduced armory of products and services to sell, they worked less. In addition, the chronic shortage of electricity led the public authorities to compel nonessential services, such as salons de coiffure, to cut back on their hours of operation. This helped to give *ouvriers coiffeurs* the two-day weekend they had long sought, when in December 1943 Labor Minister Jean Bichelonne issued a decree that required every salon to close for forty-eight consecutive hours each week, as a means to save electricity. But since salons already lost their electricity at five o'clock every afternoon, it made the workweek perilously short.[64]

Shorter hours and fewer sales were not compensated by any increase in prices, which remained, as they had always been, the profession's chief concern and the key to any comprehensive improvement in living standards. Price policy continued to animate the hairdressing profession during the war, and it provides another opportunity to gauge the difference between the Third Republic and the Etat Français.

Vichy has a reputation for being eager to intervene in the economy, and it did, in fact, exercise a strict *surveillance* of prices, at least on the formal market. But the war had already led the Republic to abandon its traditional reluctance to control prices.[65] Price controls notwithstanding, inflation accompanied war. Different indexes describe different rates, but all point in the same direction: a 50 to 70 percent rise in the cost of living between 1939 and 1942.[66]

Coiffeurs' incessant requests to the authorities for price increases pointed to the higher cost of materials, of rent, maintenance, laundry, wages, and social charges for their employees, while *tarifs* in the salons had not budged since 1939. Reports by the *pouvoirs publics* and local groups of hairdressers all made the same point. The existing price structure did not allow a *salonnier* to make a profit.[67]

For two years the government refused the coiffeurs' requests until the end of 1941 when it finally authorized a price increase of about 30 percent for *coiffure-hommes* and 25 percent for *coiffure-dames*.[68] Hairdressers were naturally pleased that the new regime was more amenable to officially sanctioned prices than the Republic had been, but they had three specific objections to Vichy price policy. First, the regime was more interested in a price *ceiling* than a price *floor*. Second, there is no evidence that Pétain's government was any more effectual than Blum's or Daladier's at actually imposing its will on a recalcitrant market. Third, the new *tarifs* remained insufficient, and the situation continued to deteriorate up to the end of the war, as small price rises never caught up to the accelerating costs of running a salon. Jeanne Singer-Kérel calculated that hairdressers' prices rose by 30 percent between 1939 and 1944, or at about half the rate of inflation.[69]

One idea that began to gain currency among *patrons coiffeurs* and some public officials sought to combine price controls with market considerations by classing salons according to their costs and clientele and setting maximum prices along a sliding scale. Bagnaud, himself a purveyor of *coiffure de luxe*, was particularly strong for it. As he wrote to De Lavenne, at the direction du commerce intérieur, the best salons, serving *"une clientèle plus riche* that demands more refined care," employed the most skilled workers, used the most expensive products, paid the highest rents, whereas in the cheap shops of the poorer districts, coiffeurs whose talents "leave something to be desired" used inferior products and all but ignored considerations of hygiene. Across-the-board price increases therefore made no sense. They hurt the best establishments. Henri Culmann, director of commerce intérieur at the Ministry of Production, shared Bagnaud's view. He wrote a supporting note to the Paris comité départemental des prix, also advocating a price rise adjusted to the "quality" of the salon.[70]

The authorities ultimately accepted the wisdom of *classement*, and a prefectorial arrêté of April 1944 applied it to the salons of Paris. The prefect established four categories of shop, with prices in the highest category anywhere from 50–100 percent and more above those in the lowest. An *indéfrisable* that cost eighty francs at a small shop in the twentieth arrondissement, for instance, would cost 280 francs at a reasonably smart salon in the center of town. In those few salons listed as *hors classe*, prices were unregulated.[71] Coming right before the Liberation, this system had little impact under Vichy. But it became the foundation of a much more elaborate postwar system of nationwide price controls.

Where salon prices stagnated, wages invariably suffered the same fate. This was as true under the occupation as it had been under the Republic. The Vichy government early on recognized the need to keep wages from falling too far behind the rising cost of living. The law of May 23, 1941 therefore imposed a 200-franc per month *allocation supplémentaire* for France's lowest-paid workers. Initially, this supplement did not apply to *entreprises artisanales*, which deprived 95 percent of *ouvriers coiffeurs* of its benefits. But the follow-up law of October 25 extended the so-called *allocation supplémentaire* to the artisanat and, therefore, to all hairdressing workers.[72] This gave the patrons ammunition in their own campaign for higher prices, yet it hardly represented a significant victory for *ouvriers coiffeurs*, whose meager wages continued to lose ground to inflation.

One interesting solution to the wage problem emerged from a commission appointed by the labor minister to study professional qualifications and wage scales. Chaired by Paul Petit, Magnien's right-hand man at the FNSOC, the commission declared that wages should be tied directly to skill, "the true human competition." The commission proposed a *coefficient professionnel national,* composed of both a "salaire minimum vitale" for all *ouvriers coiffeurs* and a *prime*—a bonus—based on a person's skill.[73] This combination of guaranteed livable wage and reward for talent, separating wages from market forces and linking them instead to the intrinsic values of work and expertise, was the perfect expression of an artisanal moral economy. But it never had much chance of becoming public policy.

Direct negotiations between groups of patrons and workers proceeded as they had before the war. And they proved as fruitless as ever. *Ouvriers coiffeurs* characteristically blamed the "bad faith of the patrons" for the ongoing failure to settle the wage issue and protested that the *salonniers* would not agree to raise *salaires* even after the government had given *them* a price rise in February 1942. Arrêtés issued in January and February 1942 took aim at the "abnormally low wages in the Paris region" and formally endorsed the wage rates set in Martin's 1937 arbitration decision. But these were now far from adequate. At any rate, the patrons continued to balk, so the SOC (formerly the CSO) went back to the Labor Ministry for arbitration, exactly as it had in 1937.[74]

It is not clear whether it was the arbitration that produced the breakthrough. One way or the other, on May Day 1942, *ouvriers* and *patrons coiffeurs* in Paris signed a much-heralded new collective accord, establishing "social peace in the profession."[75] The agreement engendered so much optimism, in part because the SPC, which had resolutely abstained from the collective conventions of 1937 and 1938, now joined the *petits patrons* of the CSP in signing the document. Bagnaud spoke of the "most noble spirit of entente" it represented. Magnien saw it as "the beginning of an era of fruitful collaboration." The *Coiffure de Paris* was so moved by the sight of the president of the CPC and the general secretary of the FNSOC in agreement, that it wrote euphorically of these two old enemies "together leading the good fight" for the profession.[76]

The May 1 agreement was long remembered for establishing the so-called 40 percent; that is, the rule that a worker should earn a salary equaling at least 40 percent of his gross receipts. This would ostensibly protect wages against inflation and give the worker an incentive to perform. The principle derived from the Ivan Martin arbitration decision of August 1937, although the particular percentage to be applied remained a source of dispute. The workers continued to insist that Martin had set the bar even higher, at 60 percent of gross receipts, and indicated that some of the better *salons pour dames* were paying their highly skilled workers 45 or even 50 percent. But the employers replied with equal conviction that few *salonniers* could treat their employees so generously and survive.[77]

More pertinent than the theoretical level of wages was the extent to which agreed-upon rates were paid in practice. While the FNSOC boasted of the "brilliant results" of the May accord, others in the labor movement had their doubts. Arthur Roger, one of the purged leaders of the old FNSOC, blasted the agreement. *Ouvriers coiffeurs*, he noted, had already rejected the percentage principle in 1919, opting instead for the guaranteed minimum wage. After all, he wrote, at 40 percent a patron could hire two or three workers instead of one, and then none of them would earn a living. Furthermore, the "40 percent" was not a hard floor. The agreement of May 1942 formally allowed an adjustment of 10 percent, in either direction, depending on circumstance. René Rambaud, Roger noted, paid his workers only 25 percent of their receipts, "figuring no doubt that [they] earned enough with their tips." In fact, he concluded, the celebrated accord actually amounted to a 10 or 15 percent *reduction* in real wages for hairdressing workers.[78]

Roger's criticism of the May agreement was surely colored by his hatred for Magnien, whom he considered a Pétainist and traitor to the working class. Even so, it remains true that the results turned out to be more uneven than "brilliant." The Paris agreement was never applied to the rest of the country, and wage differentials remained considerable. A FNSOC report from October 1943 observed that *ouvriers coiffeurs* earned minimum salaries that ranged from 600 francs a week in Chambéry and 540 in Paris to 402 in Dijon and only 242 a week in Poitiers, a figure above which they were guaranteed 40 percent of receipts in Chambéry and 36 percent in Paris, but only 10 or 15 percent elsewhere. And, predictably, as Migault wrote to the FNSOC from the city of Niort, even the payment of *official* wages scales depended on the patrons' good will.[79]

So the struggle over wages went on after the May 1942 convention as it had before. *Patrons coiffeurs* in the Allier argued in characteristic fashion that the agreed-upon "30 percent" floor could only be applied in connection with "nouveaux tarifs homologués."[80] All the while, *ouvriers coiffeurs* from across the country reported that employers had been granted price hikes without having to share any of their new income with their employees. Eugène Leduc, president of the Syndicat des ouvriers coiffeurs in Le Havre, wrote to Magnien that local prices had risen "dans une façon fabuleuse," while wages remained "derisory." Similar letters arrived at the FNSOC from local groups in Orléans, Poitiers, and elsewhere.[81] In reality, the May 1942 convention produced precious little evidence of any "spirit of entente" or "era of fruitful collaboration" between hairdressing workers and their employers.

The lag in wages for *ouvriers coiffeurs* may appear to bear out the old wisdom that Vichy made itself the vehicle of patronal revenge against an assertive working class, or at least that the regime was broadly antiworker. Consider the question of wages. Except for some privileged groups of laborers, usually working for the Germans, real wages plummeted during the war. Patrick Fridenson and Jean-Louis Robert, borrowing their numbers from Alfred Sauvy, point to the dramatically lower buying power of French *salaires*, which lost half their real value between 1939 and 1943. The *Tribune des Ouvriers Coiffeurs* painted an even grimmer picture. Citing official statistics, it figured that real wages fell by three-quarters between 1938 and 1944.[82] As communist militant Georges Philippot put it: "No one can deny that the Vichy government was more favorable to the *patronat* than to the working class."[83]

Yet the experience of *ouvriers coiffeurs* suggests that the picture is more nuanced. Jean-Pierre Le Crom is scarcely an apologist for Pétain, but he takes a rather sympathetic view of the regime's wage policies. He notes that Belin, the labor minister, attempted to extend and apply the collective conventions reached before the war, and that Belin and Yves Bouthillier, the finance minister, fought to give workers the "allocation Pétain"—the across-the-board wage increase of May 1941—even in the face of German opposition. Add to this Vichy's maintenance of Republican provisions for *sécurité sociale*, and its selective extension of these benefits, and we discover a regime no less committed to *le social* than the late Republic. Even Fridenson and Robert, who tend to be harsher in their judgment than Le Crom, recognize that Pétainism had its benevolent side.[84] Perhaps François de Wendel was not as mad as he might have seemed to complain that Vichy "continues the work of the Popular Front."[85]

We see the same ambiguity reflected throughout the lives of hairdressers. To be sure, economic circumstances precluded any happy resolution to coiffeurs' problems under the occupation. Rather than a

campaign on behalf of *patrons coiffeurs*, though, the evidence speaks
of the remarkably evenhanded efforts of public authorities to help the
profession out as best they could. They extended the "allocation
Pétain" to artisanal workers, which brought in the vast majority of
ouvriers coiffeurs, and tried to push hairdressers into the sort of collective
agreements, such as that of May 1942, that would generally ameliorate
life in the salons. At the same time, the regime accepted the truth of
the patrons' old argument that decent wages ultimately depended on a
profitable price structure. The archives are full of testimony to the
state's attempts to stabilize prices—not because it favored employers
over employees, but because it saw healthy prices as one of the keys to
prosperity for both parties.

These same archives also attest to the state's failure. If real wages
fell in the salons so did real prices and thus employers' income. Given
the ever-more-catastrophic state of the economy, it is hard to see how
even the best intentions and wisest policies could have brought about
the desired outcome. That being said, Vichy's policy toward
hairdressers was scarcely less solicitous and barely less effective than
the Republic's—presuming, of course, that a coiffeur was not an
"enemy of the state."

Shorn women: The liberation humiliates "horizontal collaborators"

8

Aryanization, Collaboration, Resistance

If Marshal Pétain's France tried to assist large families, pensioners, children, and other "bons français," it also took care to exclude those it considered "anti-French." *Coiffeurs israélites* fell into this latter category, and the Etat Erançais went after them with all energy it could muster. Problems of shortage and falling real incomes, difficult as they were for the majority of hairdressers, paled beside the persecution faced by their Jewish colleagues, who made up a fair proportion of the profession, especially in Paris.[1]

As the Pétain regime settled in power, it began to produce laws, decrees, and other weapons of public policy that aimed to drive Jews out of the French economy. Vichy persecution, which often anticipated German demands, was rooted in the regime's ideological and economic priorities and thus became part of "the regime's search for autonomy"—the invidious process by which the French tried to anticipate German wishes in order to preserve the illusion of independence.[2]

The so-called *aryanisation* of the French economy rested on the law of September 10, 1940 that allowed authorities to name *administrateurs provisoires* for "entreprises privées de leur dirigeants."[3] A German *ordonnance* of September 27, 1940 mandated a census of Jews and Jewish property and was followed shortly by the French law of October 3, which excluded Jews from the "political, economic, and social life" of France. The Pétain government finished off the institutional preparation for aryanization when in December it created the Service de contrôle des administrateurs provisoires (SCAP) within the Ministry of Production and, on March 29, 1941, the Commissariat général aux questions juives (CGQJ), to which the SCAP was attached in June. Since the law prohibited Jews from exercising any profession that involved direct contact with clients, Jews could neither own *salons de coiff*ure nor work therein.[4]

The situation soon became untenable for Jewish hairdressers. Evidence from the dossiers of dispossessed *coiffeurs-juifs* suggests that more than a few of them fled to the Unoccupied Zone or otherwise disappeared. Gabriel A., for example, owned a small shop in Saint-Denis, just to the north of Paris. He had been mobilized in February 1940 and wounded at Amiens at the end of May. After his demobilization and return to Paris, he never reopened his salon. The new provisional administrator for his *biens*, R. Guillois, was informed that he had fled to the south. Nathan A., owner of Chez Albert on the boulevard Saint-Martin, likewise escaped to Marseille.[5]

Other *coiffeurs israélites* prepared to go into hiding. The best known is Albert Grunberg, whose salon was at 8, rue des Écoles, down the block from his apartment in the fifth arrondissement.[6] Grunberg was a Romanian immigrant who had arrived in Paris in 1912, age fourteen, served in the war, married an Auvergnate in 1919 and opened his own salon in 1934. When the persecutions began under Vichy, Grunberg began to take precautions, sleeping in a small room under the eaves of the building where his salon was located. In this way, he managed to evade the *rafles* of the summer of 1942. Two months later, however, Grunberg was eating breakfast with his wife Marguerite, when the police came knocking at his door. Thinking quickly, Grunberg managed to outwit the two French *flics*. He fled the apartment and took up his already-prepared refuge in his 8 m^2 room on the sixth floor of number 8. His brother Sami, on the run after having been released from Drancy, soon came to join him. On the sixtieth day of his confinement, he began to write his journal.

Grunberg avoided discovery and deportation by hiding in his *chambre de bonne* for almost two years. In many ways he was lucky. His two sons were already hidden safely in Chambéry. His wife, a "true *française*," was able to maintain their salon and to visit her husband clandestinely on Wednesday and Saturday nights. The concierge at number 8, Madame Oudard, brought him food and newspapers. Most importantly, she kept his secret. So did Grunberg's new neighbors, who soon learned of his presence but did not give him away. One of them even allowed Grunberg to tap into his electricity, and thus to have light and listen to the radio. Grunberg emerged from hiding with his life, his family, and his property intact. Few of his fellow *coiffeurs juifs* could claim the same good fortune. A large number of Jewish hairdressers ended up, alongside their coreligionists from other professions, on trains to the East, their disappearance marked by an unopened envelope from the Service de Restitution in the back of a dossier, marked: "Residence unknown. *Retour à l'envoyeur.*"

The process of aryanization began with the appointment of a provisional administrator (AP) for an establishment, of whom there were roughly 10,000 at any one time. Formal responsibility for naming AP lay with the prefects, usually in consultation with the SCAP and important people in the profession concerned. Organization committees had no official jurisdiction over aryanization, but they often could not resist the temptation to use it to serve the interests of their directors, or even to promote what they conceived to be the broader interests of their profession. Ordinarily, this meant swallowing or liquidating businesses, to reduce at a stroke the competition for customers and precious raw materials.[7]

In coiffure, the majority of *administrateurs provisoires* seem to have come from the ranks of patrons coiffeurs themselves, especially out of the leadership of the Union fédérale and the Confédération des patrons coiffeurs. That is to say, the same individuals who controlled the CNR-Coiffure and CO-Coiffure, and later served on the *Famille professionnelle*, worked closely with the authorities to make the process of aryanization run smoothly. Dossiers occasionally referred to the fact that Bagnaud or Touzet had given his approval to a certain *vente forcée* or liquidation or recorded their recommendation of likely AP.[8] A significant number of UF and CSP leaders themselves became provisional administrators: Edouard Dauvergne, Léonce Lebègue, Amadée Deslonchamps, among others.[9]

What brought a man—and they were always men—to a career as an AP of hairdressing salons? There is little indication of any ideological commitment to aryanization. The uncatalogued dossiers of *administrateurs provisoires* contain virtually no expressions of anti-Semitic feeling on the part of those who helped empty the French economy of Jews. Those who were already prominent in professional affairs appear to have been motivated by an authentic sense of professional responsibility—a desire to keep good salons afloat, close down *baissiers*, and perhaps even to help *coiffeurs juifs* make the best of a very bad situation. Lebègue, a CSP officer, swore that he had been a thoroughly benign AP never pressuring Jews to sell when they resisted and leaving them, as far as feasible, in control of their old accounts. It is impossible to verify these claims directly, since most of Lebègue's Jews never answered the Service de Restitution's request for information. It can be noted only that the service never accused him of any improprieties. On the other hand, Lebègue did not scruple to alert the CGQJ when he found Monsieur S. to be a "troublesome, uncooperative Jew." Likewise, Lebègue's president at the CSP Amadée Deslongchamps maintained that he had tried to treat the Jews he dispossessed with some consideration. But that did not stop his attaching the notation "attention to the bad attitude [*mauvaise foi*] of the interested party" to the dossiers of Monsieurs M. and K. when they proved less than fully cooperative.

Most coiffeurs drawn into the ranks of *administrateurs provisiores*, passed rather quickly through the process, doing little and receiving modest compensation. Gaston Brissard told a police inquiry in 1947 that he had administered only four *salons juifs* and was never paid for his work. Emile Gelly told the Service de Restitution that he had resigned almost immediately and never received a centime for his services. R. Guillois had asked to be relieved of his duties as AP because, "in view of the diminution of my clientele, I have had to let my workers go, and during my absences I had to close my shop." Jules Lacressonnière claimed never to have sold a single Jewish salon and quit in the spring of 1942, writing that sickness required him to abstain from activity "for a long time."

Henri Coumagnac, a vice president of the UF, told the Service de Restitution that he had become an AP only to defend his own property, and he added ". . . I had sold my business to a Jew, and he still owed me half the money. I thought that if I became the administrator, I could more likely avoid *la spoliation totale*." Coumagnac alleged that he had received 3,600 francs for the sale of Madame K.-A.'s salon and tried to give her the money, but was formally forbidden to do so. "As provisional administrator," Coumagnac concluded, "I lost more in my boutique while I took care of other salons [than I earned for my efforts]." Fernand Ménard noted in his *compte-rendu de fin de gestion* that the sale of the goods of Samuel A., a Bulgarian national, did not cover the salon's accumulated debts and taxes. Ménard complained that he had had to take fifty-three francs out of his own pocket to wind up the affair.[10]

These men, who came to be AP through the CSP, administered Jewish salons as an extension of their professional activities, but others saw aryanization as a pecuniary opportunity. This was likely less true in coiffure than in many other sectors of the economy. Immigrants and foreign nationals comprised a large portion of *coiffeurs israélites*, but they tended to own small, poorly equipped salons in unfashionable parts of Paris. It is not unreasonable to think that many of them had been among the *baissiers* who had helped depress prices and wages before the war. In any case, since AP were paid according to the value of the businesses they administered, coiffure did not offer a very enticing field for profiteers—presuming they even got paid, which many complained they did not.

Nonetheless, in sufficient numbers and as part of a diversified portfolio, hairdressing salons could appeal to those who had chosen to make a living as AP. Maurice Hugot, to take one example, was a photographer and commercial artist by trade. "Being without steady employment since his demobilization," Hugo explained to the Directeur général de l'aryanisation économique that he "absolutely needed to have an occupation." That is why he denounced a photo shop he knew where the current AP was in constant correspondence with the Jewish owner. "It is inadmissible," he proclaimed, "that at this little game continue!" And he wrote often to the CGQJ, boasting of his conscientious work as an AP and asking "to participate more fully in this work of aryanization." The authorities must have been impressed by his performance, because Hugot ended up managing a portfolio of eighty businesses, nineteen of them hairdressing salons.

Jean Bonnefoi was also an AP entrepreneur, with eighty-six businesses in his portfolio, in many different sectors, bringing him thousands of francs a month. The fifty-nine year old, former chief of the gare de Bercy, first approached the CGQJ in November 1941, with an obsequious letter requesting "a position as provisional administrator in numerous Jewish businesses belonging to your Commissariat." Overall, the authorities seemed pleased with his work, expressing disapproval only when he sought to give up thirty-four of his accounts. Bonnefoi told the authorities that he simply could not keep up with his responsibilities, but they suspected that he really wanted to shuck off his more unprofitable businesses and concentrate on those that paid well. Apparently, such cynical profiteering was one thing the authorities could not abide in an AP. Thus when Marcel Cornet, a reserve colonel and officer in the Légion d'Honneur, expressed his desire to be rid of some of his twenty-seven *entreprises juives*, a note from the Services généraux de l'aryanisation économique advised the CGQJ that if Cornet's only motive were monetary he should be stripped of all his AP duties.

It should come as no surprise that the whole dirty process of *spoliation* gave full reign to incompetence and corruption. The job of *administrateur provisoire* was not exactly an honorable one and, for the most part, it did not attract experienced businessmen. If coiffure is an accurate gauge, aside from those hairdressers who became AP *à mi-temps*, the aryanization of *salons juifs* involved some shady characters. To take one example, Léon Janiaud earned a dossier full of complaints against his *gestion*, including one for the embezzlement of 20,000 francs from the *biens* of one Monsieur S., a purveyor of knick-knacks [*marchand de bimbeloterie*]. Someone in the SCAP remarked that Janiaud was "a complete incompetent, negligent in his work, whose sole preoccupation is his fees." He was already in trouble with the CGQJ before the Liberation for having drawn excessive amounts of money from the businesses he administered.[11] Janiaud's dossier contains no hint of any fine or imprisonment for his malfeasance. But it points by implication to the sort of problems that must have plagued the aryanization of even a very poor trade like coiffure.

When the process went smoothly, the new provisional administrator took over a salon whose Jewish owner had either fled or put up no resistance to his expropriation. The AP inventoried the business and checked the books. He weighed assets and liabilities and assessed the tax situation of shops that had frequently closed without settling their debts. If he thought the salon viable, he looked for a buyer. If not, he simply closed it down. The evidence suggests, however, that the AP's job was often not as simple as that. Many of the salons they administered were at best on the edge of viability. They had some value, but not enough to attract buyers readily. Besides, as several administrators noted, Jewish-owned shops tended to have Jewish clients, and these had largely "disappeared."[12]

AP Robert Bouvier was fortunate with the salon of Robert and Albert A., proprietors of a "belle installation" next to the Trocadéro. The salon was owned jointly by several people, one of whom, René B., was "aryan." He agreed to buy the shares that had belonged to his Jewish partners.[13] Other Jewish victims made things difficult for their provisional administrators. Some resisted selling to the end. AP Edouard Pineau reported that the widow Madame A., whose salon was small but in a good location, tried to torpedo the sale of her *biens* to one Marcel Guillement and his wife. When Pineau brought the Guillements by the salon to check out their investment, Madame A. told them that it was not for sale and that she would "throw their money out the window." She then concocted a scheme whereby her accountant, Macret, a "français," would appear to buy the salon from her, while she remained the real owner.[14]

Deslongchamps, president of the CSP, wrote to Melchior de Faramond, director of the SCAP, in June 1941, asking what to do when "*un coiffeur Israélite* . . . refuses to leave his boutique, despite the injunction of the Commissaire-gérant." Simple, responded Faramond: call the police.[15] Thus the police became involved in the case of Charles A., who worked with his wife and an apprentice. A. failed to understand the hopelessness of his situation. When the AP Edmond Dauvergne, another CSP officer, first approached him, A. categorically refused to sell—"because he has no other living for his wife and three children." A. even wrote plaintively to the police, explaining he "was born French of French parents in Algeria . . . with three children . . . a veteran of the first war . . . wounded on May 30, 1918 Croix de Guerre, Carte d'ancien combattant." The police told him that he could not continue with his *métier*, which put him in contact with the public.[16] There followed what the documents refer to as a "vente forcée."

A successful aryanization finished when the assets from the sale or liquidation of the Jewish salon, minus debts and taxes owed, were deposited with the proper authorities. Normally, this would be in an account at the Caisse des dépôts et consignations. Ten percent of the total was set aside in a fund to remunerate *administrateurs provisoires* and as a *fonds de solidarité* to help support indigent Jews.[17] Documents in the dossiers make it clear that when goods were sold off the authorities examined the buyer's resources closely to make sure that he was good for the money, and the SCAP put off eager suitors when it did not trust their finances. Because considerable sums were involved, moreover, the parties to this organized looting often fell out over the spoils. Among the French themselves, the Ministry of Production and the Ministry of Finance fought for control of aryanization, not just for the booty, but because each wanted to dominate French economic policy. And even within the Production Ministry, the secretary general Jean Bichelonne had a very different set of priorities from the chief of the CGQJ.[18] There were other, more powerful hands in the pot since the Germans wanted to grab as many

French assets as they could. That was one reason the French exerted themselves in the aryanization process to such an extent: they wanted to keep French property, even stolen French property, in French hands. The aryanization of the goods of foreign Jews resident in France was particularly complicated. For one thing, the Germans claimed the indisputable right to their property, and in the end the French ceded the point: the net assets of foreign Jews were deposited in the account of the Commissaire général allemand pour les biens juifs. For another, some of these Jewish residents came from countries that still exercised some nominal independence and pretended to protect their nationals resident in France. Polish-born Jews presented no problems, since Poland no longer existed. They were expropriated quickly and their assets handed over to the Germans.[19] The Bulgarian-born Nathan A., however, tried to draw the Royal Bulgarian Legation into his efforts to fend off the aryanization of his salon. The legation even wrote to the SCAP on Nathan A.'s behalf, reminding the service that the goods and rights of its Jewish citizens enjoyed the same status as those belonging to other Bulgarian citizens. Samuel A. also tried to rally the Bulgarian legation to his defense, although there is no evidence in his dossier that the legation took the bait. Leiba A., a Russian immigrant, appealed to the Russian embassy for protection in the weeks preceding Operation Barbarossa.[20] Of course, none of these men managed to save his salon.

Mosau A. similarly approached the Romanian Royal Legation, Romania being a German ally. The Romanians thereupon wrote to the SCAP, saying that it would take several months to verify A.'s citizenship and demanding that the aryanization proceedings be suspended in the meantime. Mosau A. quite unnerved his AP, Deslongchamps, when he showed him the letter from the Romanian legation. But when Deslongchamps then asked the SCAP to relieve him of his responsibilities for Mosau A., the service responded that, under instructions from the Germans, the French made no distinction between French and foreign Jews in this matter. Deslongchamps was instructed to proceed with the aryanization and to call in the police if his victim created any further difficulties. He did not, having been picked up with his wife in the *rafle* of July 1942.

The most striking thing about the dossiers of the *administrateurs provisoires* and *biens aryanisés* is not the gross mistreatment they describe. Rather, it is the tone of bureaucratic normality pervading the documents. Declarations of animosity toward the Jews are as rare as expressions of guilt on the part of the AP. The anti-Semitic comments of Jacques Delaire, in his denunciations of Jews who continued to work secretly in their salons, stand out as a rare exception. (And almost as if Delaire were punished for his frankness, his brother-in-law's letter of January 1944 informed authorities that Delaire had ceased to exercise his functions, since Delaire's note to his brother-in-law included in his file announced that he had "gone off to throw himself . . . into the Seine.")[21]

By the same token, there is not a single recorded instance of shame. It is absent from the letter that L. Guéry wrote to the CGQJ in Toulouse, for example, letting them know that he was interested in acquiring a perfumerie, antique shop, or hairdressing salon, and asking as well for a full list of *fonds juifs* available to buy. Jean Bonnefoi apparently had no qualms about bombarding the postwar Service de Restitution, which was supposed to arrange the return of aryanized properties to their Jewish owners and compensate them for their losses, with letters demanding payment of fees owed for his work in dispossessing Jews. Pierre Roy gave an example, not so much of the failure of conscience, as of its inversion, when he denounced the "deplorable" behavior of those who conspired to fix the bids at the auction of the property of the despoiled Mosau A.

We do not know Guéry, Bonnefoi, Roy, and dozens of others who worked the lower echelons of aryanization. It is easy to believe that, if they did not actually hate Jews and did not want to rid France of their pernicious influence then they were at least morally deficient to have simply seized the chance to make some money without thinking much about the victims. Likewise, what we already know of Bagnaud and Tison readily explains their participation in the process of aryanization. Leaders of their profession, their first priority was to protect their constituents and to make sure that this disagreeable duty was done right. Besides, they were both sympathizers with, if not active members of, the Action française. It is not unreasonable to think they might have supported such a solution to France's "Jewish Problem."

More difficult to understand is the participation of the leaders of *artisans coiffeurs*: Lebègue, Deslongchamps, Dauvergne, et al. They had previously given no evidence of anti-Semitism. Their politics had inclined mildly to the left, and they had demonstrated a reliable ability to distinguish right from wrong. Yet they allowed themselves to be pulled into the aryanization process. To be fair, those who came to it from the ranks of the CSP evinced a marked distaste for the task and tended to resign their commissions early. But not one of them ever uttered a recoverable word against the operation.

Ouvriers coiffeurs had no direct role in the process, since the SCAP naturally preferred experienced patrons to run aryanized salons. It is nonetheless worth noting that the leaders of the FNSOC and other representatives of hairdressing workers, who certainly did not spare other aspects of Pétainism their criticism, failed completely to condemn the policy of aryanization. Even Magnien, a man of forceful opinions, who was himself the target of the extreme right and was hard-pressed to shelter his Jewish wife, never mentioned it. Neither did any part of the postwar professional press in coiffure.

Even the postwar authorities, who set out to reverse aryanization and compensate its victims, were no better at recognizing responsibility. To take only one example, the *ordonnance* of November 14, 1944 on "actes de spoliation," which required all provisional administrators to share their records with the Ministry of Finance, referred to an expropriation "carried out by the enemy and under his control."[22] Thus a procedure that had clearly gone forward under French auspices was immediately absorbed into the general understanding of the occupation, where the Germans and a handful of lackeys were the guilty parties, and everyone else acted under compulsion.[23]

Perhaps that is why no serious action was ever taken against provisional administrators, as such. The Service de Restitution went after those who had committed some kind of fraud or who had shown an unseemly zeal in acquiring Jewish properties. Those who had conscientiously helped to reduce Jews to penury, resisting the temptation to dip into the till and collecting only their official fees, simply melted back into a society that preferred not to ask itself hard questions.

AP, clearly having nothing to fear from public exposure, organized themselves to defend their "rights." They formed the Association française des propriétaires des biens aryanisés in 1943 to shield those who had acquired Jewish property against all "revendications ou recours juifs." The association maintained that it was "independent" and without "*any political or racial agenda.*"[24]

The problem was that all acquirers of aryanized goods were deemed "possesseurs de mauvaise foi" under the ordinance of April 21, 1945 and ordered to return the property or pay damages on it. Even if the expropriated Jew had "consented" to the sale, such consent was "considered to have been given under the threat of violence" and therefore rendered null and void unless the *acquéreur* could prove that he had paid a "fair price." This ordinance no doubt came in response to purchasers of *biens juifs'* continuing attempts to protect their acquisitions.

In October 1944, for example, the new director of the Artisanal Service received a report from a group called the Association internationale intercorporative du commerce, de l'industrie et de l'artisanat, created to protect the interests of "*acquéreurs de biens Israélites* independent of any polemic or anti-Semitism."[25] The extraordinary cover letter from the association's president noted that the "immense majority of buyers" it represented had not "speculated on a German victory." They were POWs, *sinistrés*, or others in distress. Many had continued to employ Jews "despite the risks" and "even to belong to the active resistance." What is more, the president—he obviously had no sense of irony—reminded the director that since all these *acquéreurs* had acted in accordance with French law, their property had as much right to legal protection as any other.

Moreover, the letter continued, those who had bought Jewish property had served the national interest by saving establishments that would otherwise have been dissolved. They had even paid the back taxes that Jews had avoided. And "let us not speak," it noted in an aside, "of the memory of the *évasion des capitaux* that *les Israélites étrangers* had so willingly practiced." The Jews had arrived in France, the president went on, profiting from the country's "legendary hospitality." They attracted more Jews, who engaged in *travail noir* and destroyed the livelihoods of thousands of *français*, exploiting their workers and cheating their employers. He concluded with the opinion that stripping these *acquéreurs des biens juifs* of their property "*would not at all correspond to the will of the French Nation.*" Both parties, Jews and *acquéreurs*, he wrote, "should be seen as VICTIMS OF THE WAR, and both be indemnified."

While the CGQJ concentrated on squeezing Jews out of the economy, other elements within the regime busied themselves with the shape of France's New Order. Pétain had promised that the end of the Republic would be the prelude to national regeneration, based on a new set of principles: more authority in politics and less individualism in social and economic relations. Vichy had taken a step in the direction of economic reform in the summer of 1940, when it created the OCRPI and the organization committees. But the law of August 16 was meant to be a quick fix, not a permanent solution. It illustrates the regime's preference for centralized decision making directed by businessmen and technocrats but does not shed much light on the ambitions and contradictions that existed inside the National Revolution.

More illuminating, in this respect, was the campaign for the Labor charter, which gave full expression to the muddle of grand designs and bureaucratic chaos that might stand as the emblem of a regime that was at once romantic, mean, and inept. The charter itself was a monument to the conflicts that raged within the regime, its passage a black comedy of plodding committee work and midnight raids on the Imprimerie nationale.

There was initially a consensus at Vichy, and probably a broad sentiment throughout France, that social and economic life needed to be restructured in the interests of stability and harmony. In the wake of the military disaster, even the CGT had accepted the need for some reform along these lines. Indeed, a meeting of its national committee in July 1940 offered to support worker–management councils, give up strikes for arbitration, and suppress the language of class struggle in the confederation's statutes—all in the interests of a "French Community of Labor."[26]

The gothic process by which the Labor charter was composed testifies to a split within the regime between those led by labor and production minister René Belin, who wanted a "syndicalist" charter, and those who wanted a "corporatist" one, closer, they said, to Pétain's vision. Sabotage and duplicity set the tone for this administrative melodrama, which finished with Belin watching over the presses at the Imprimerie nationale to make sure that the correct version appeared in the *Journal Officiel*.[27]

Simply put, Belin sought separate syndicalism from class politics and to establish what he called "le syndicat libre dans la profession organisée," according to the "principles . . . of worker–employer collaboration and of professional solidarity."[28] To accomplish this, the charter envisioned a society divided into professional "families," based on syndicates of workers and employers at the local, regional, and national levels. What this amounted to in theory was a kind of codetermination, where the free organizations of workers and patrons in an industry or trade could resolve their disputes short of class war.

Richard Kuisel, whose judgments on Vichy are generally so sure, saw the Labor charter as evidence of the intention to "build a fullfledged corporatist society."[29] But the charter, with its base of trade unions, was closer to syndicalism than corporatism. More precisely, it was largely an empty vessel with its content yet to be determined in practice.

The charter garnered poor initial reviews. Georges Philippot called the charter "a trap for workers, aimed at enslaving them and keeping them on the leash."[30] Historians have likewise dismissed the Labor charter as a cynical attempt to seduce workers into a venture that would ultimately benefit the state and the employers.[31] Yet business interests scorned it, afraid of the "comités d'entreprise" that were supposed to give workers a say in management decisions.[32] Besides, their domination of the organization committees and the rationing apparatus had already left big business in control of the economy, so why tinker?

Those who considered themselves *genuine* corporatists, and the far right generally, greeted the charter even more rudely. Jean Paillard, head of Pétain's Bureau des Corporations, adjudged it the fruit of the "synarchy" conspiracy, the "victoire du syndicalisme de classe." Albert Beugras of Jacques Doriot's Parti populaire français condemned it as conservative and paternalistic. Marcel Déat called it a cold hash of ideas from *Rerum Novarum* that would go nowhere. In the end, even Belin came to see the charter as mediocre, complicated, and ambiguous.[33]

The charter also encountered the contempt of many workers, who feared, as Philippot did, that it would substitute "official" syndicates for a "free and independent" labor movement. Communist elements opposed it vehemently, and *résistant* syndicats denounced it as "an instrument of police repression—a hypocritical comedy." "Workingmen as a whole," wrote John Sweets, "were disgruntled by the dissolution of the trade unions [*sic*] and the attempt by the Etat Français to force a labor charter on all categories of workers."[34] But the reality was more complicated.

For one thing, the government did *not* put an end to trade unions. Its decree of November 9, 1940 dissolved the CGT, along with other workers' and employers' confederations. But trade federations and syndicats remained in business. The FNSOC held congresses throughout the war, and syndicats of *patrons* and *ouvriers coiffeurs* survived, even if circumstances curtailed some of their activities.[35] For another, the labor movement was ambivalent about the principles that underlay the charter. Jouhaux eventually decided that the charter was "worthless," and officially condemned it. Yet, as we have seen, a year earlier the CGT leadership had previously accepted the principle of "free unions in organized professions."

Moreover, even after Jouhaux pronounced his anathema on the charter, several federations opted for a politics of *presence*, which was plausible precisely because the charter did not aim to destroy trade unions, but only to wean them from the politics of class struggle.[36]

Finally, it is imperative not to take the most prominent part of the working class for the whole. Navvies, miners, and for that matter the whole CGT represented only a small portion of French workers. Even after the confederation announced its opposition to the charter, other elements of the labor movement—Christians, anticommunists, and others—continued to believe that something could be made of it.[37]

Whatever its defects, the charter struck a responsive chord among many militant syndicalists in the hairdressing trades. In fact, one group of artisan-coiffeurs had already put forward their own version of a charte corporative in September 1941, which they dedicated to Pétain: "Certain that, in putting their own professional house in order, [coiffeurs] are also preparing the resurrection of WORK, FAMILY and COUNTRY."[38] The coiffeurs' charter promoted the inherent "right of coiffeurs to a living" by giving them the right to set prices, wage rates, and work schedules, "precisely in order to allow each employer to recompense his employees fairly."[39] That is, it followed the lines laid out in Law 900.

President Joseph Gestalder of the UF applauded the charte's provisions for *syndicats obligatoires* and its commitment to the democratic operation of the profession.[40] But it evoked a much more tepid response from the organized ranks of *ouvriers coiffeurs*. General Secretary François Magnien told the FNSOC in December 1941 that although he welcomed a reorganization of the profession, he found this project at once too dreamy and too favorable to employers' interests. On the other hand, he liked the charte's proposal to restrict access to the profession "in order to guarantee workers the indefeasible right to work and the compensation of a *juste-salaire*."[41]

In other words, the FNSOC favored some basic reform of the profession but could not accept the employer control and restriction of syndical liberties embedded in the charte corporative. It believed that the Labor charter, made law two months earlier, would be more to its taste and expressed the hope that the charter would "be more just and more favorable to the 'development of social structures destined to satisfy the legitimate aspirations of the workers, within the framework of the general interest of the Nation.' "[42]

It is crucial at this point not to confuse the FNSOC's cautious support for the Labor charter with a broader Pétainism. "[It] is conditional," wrote Magnien, "upon the maintenance of the *vertical* organization of the syndical movement within the Charter project, as well as upon syndical representation within the corporative councils at the regional and national level."[43] For those who thought like Magnien, *presence* entailed no sacrifice of syndicalist precepts. On the contrary, it "constituted the sole possibility of legal resistance to *la politique vichysoisse*." Meanwhile, the FNSOC secretary advised his colleagues not to dissolve their old unions "as long as the Charter has not taken definitive shape."[44]

Accordingly, hopeful that Vichy sincerely intended to redress their grievances, important elements of the hairdressing profession turned to the Labor charter to revitalize their ancient corporation. This job would have been difficult enough, given the war and occupation. It became virtually impossible when the campaign for the Labor charter entangled coiffeurs in the vicious administrative politics of the regime. The balance of power favored the charter's opponents. But the battle itself is revealing.

Insofar as it sought authority over economic and social affairs, the charter threatened the hegemony of the organization committees. The enabling decree of July 25, 1942 established the Commission provisoire d'organisation (CPO—also known as Commission 77, after the article in the charter that described it) for coiffure. This was the necessary preliminary step to the creation of a *famille professionnelle*, and it gave hairdressers the honor of being among the first professions to comply with the terms of the Labor charter. As he put together the CPO, Hubert Lagardelle, who had succeeded Belin at the Labor Ministry in March 1942, carefully balanced the various interests within coiffure. Parisians dominated, of course. But there was, as the charter demanded, a rough parity between employees and employers. Lagardelle also tried hard to equalize the competing factions, especially on the patrons' side, between the CPC and the UF.[45]

It did not take long for tension to develop between the CPO and the CO-Coiffure. The first source of friction lay in the fact that workers, who had *no* representation on the organization committee, made up half the membership of the CPO; the second in the bureaucratic clash between the Labor Ministry, which controlled the CPO, and the Production Ministry, to which the CO belonged. Consequently, the CPO became the agent of those coiffeurs who wanted a trade organized from the bottom up, autonomous and syndically based, while the CO defended its vision of *étatisme*. Given their stark political disagreements and the looming struggle over jurisdiction, it is hard to see how a battle between the CPO and the CO-Coiffure could have been avoided.

Lagardelle named René Rambaud president of the CPO. A fabulously successful artist and businessman, Rambaud had maintained his old contacts with the labor movement. And unlike so many other *gros patrons*, Bagnaud above all, Rambaud had played no partisan role in the battles over the Popular Front. In a word, there could not have been a more natural figure to stand at the head of a *famille professionnelle* of coiffeurs.

Vice-president was a more controversial choice, for while Rambaud was the embodiment of professional unity, no one stood more forcefully for the militant assertion of workers' rights than the irrepressible François Magnien. Yet odd as the marriage of the ex-Leninist and the doyen of high fashion might seem, Magnien had lately become Rambaud's protégé, and his own career was increasingly coming to resemble that of his friend and colleague. As vice president of the CPO, Magnien stood simultaneously for the principle of syndicalism, the interests of *ouvriers coiffeurs*, and the welfare of the profession as a whole. He himself plainly saw his work for the *famille professionnelle* in exactly the same light.

The CPO, a sort of constituent committee for the *Famille professionnelle de l'hygiène*, held its inaugural meeting in October 1942. Presided over by Rambaud and Magnien, the commission took stock of its responsibilities and its assets. Its main job, as Rambaud explained, was to stimulate the creation of *syndicats uniques* in the localities, either by fusing disparate groups or by inventing a syndicat where none had existed. The *syndicats uniques* would then become the institutional rocks on which to found the *famille professionnelle*. The charter intended the old trade unions to function until they had been integrated into the new system. It did not dissolve them, or indeed make any substantial changes to them.[46]

Conflict with the CO-Coiffure began almost immediately. Bagnaud and his colleagues in the CPC already controlled the organization committee. They had little to gain from the *famille professionnelle* and played almost no active role on the CPO, save the occasional attempt to sabotage it. Bagnaud himself considered the *famille professionnelle* an irrelevancy, if it stuck to its narrowly conceived social mandate, and a nuisance, if it tried to meddle in matters of *répartition* and the economy. On the question of power, the president of the organization committee was categorical: His authority covered all economic aspects of the profession, "en vertu du principe d'économie dirigée." The *famille professionelles*'s domain lay rather in "social" affairs, which for Bagnaud meant things such as accident insurance and bicycle clubs.[47] Those who led the CPO believed, on the contrary, that *they* would eventually control all matters affecting the profession. That is to say, a functioning Labor charter would make the organization committees superfluous. It was difficult to reconcile these views.

A second challenge to the CPO came from the obscure representatives of the Syndicat professionnel français (SPF) group of coiffeurs. The SPF, syndical arm of la Rocque's Parti social français, had emerged in the summer of 1936 and left no discernible imprint on the profession under the Republic. Whether the leaders of the SPF-Coiffure, Paul Vannier and Robert Solomiac received encouragement from friends in the Vichy government or merely decided it was an auspicious moment to stake their claim is not clear. In either case, two days after the CPO's first meeting, Solomiac wrote to Rambaud, demanding "a place within [the CPO] in the sense of the desire of Marshal Pétain, the Head of State." Rambaud at first denied the request, a snub that Solomiac attributed to the fact that "certain people"—he named Rambaud and Gestalder, but could well have included Magnien, Deslongchamps, and others—were Freemasons.[48] But Rambaud soon changed tack and formed a subcommittee to prepare the SPF's integration. Probably, he understood that the CPO could not afford to alienate anyone in the administration who might share Solomiac's politics. Besides, its proponents had always known that the *famille professionnelle* would have to be inclusive, and that meant finding a way to get along with one's enemies.[49]

Old antagonists were making similar accommodations throughout the country, as the CPO set about establishing *syndicats uniques*, the compulsory local bodies (one for patrons, one for workers) that were meant to be the foundation of the *famille professionnelle*. Rambaud and his colleagues set off on this task with their usual energy, but they often found these attempts to invigorate local coiffeurs immensely frustrating.

They had particular difficulty organizing *ouvriers coiffeurs*. The law mandated that local *syndicats uniques* be organized through administrative councils set up by local personalities, assisted by the CPO. It also required members of the councils to be at least twenty-five years old. But that restriction made it virtually impossible to round up enough workers in many localities. There simply were not enough "mature," engaged hairdressing workers to form the administrative councils for the *syndicats uniques*. For example, Paul Petit, FNSOC secretary and member of the CPO, reported from Chalons-sur-Marne, that there were only two apt *ouvriers coiffeurs* in the whole town.[50] Rambaud wrote to the Labor Ministry requesting an exemption that would lower the minimum age for hairdressing workers on the councils to twenty-one.[51] But even a positive response would have had little effect, for additional barriers lay between the *famille professionnelle* and the mass of *ouvriers coiffeurs*.

Reports from all over the country mentioned the indifference and even the hostility of hairdressing workers to the *syndicats uniques*. Jules Guillet, president of the Chambre syndicale ouvrière in Rennes wrote to the CPO: "I am utterly disappointed to report . . . a systematic opposition to the organization of the Charte du Travail—which should be no surprise in view of the workers' mindset in Rennes since 1936."[52] Workers in Clermont-Ferrand wanted nothing to do with the Labor charter: "To them it's collaboration," reported Louis Clauzade, the fiery FNSOC militant.[53] Similar accounts reached the CPO from all parts of the country. G. Puget, president of the *syndicat des maîtres-artisans coiffeurs* in Avignon, wrote that he found it "impossible to find a single worker in the city" interested in the *famille professionnelle*. In the Drôme, a very frustrated Monsieur Leyche informed the CPO that "having organized a meeting on Monday, 28 February [1943], to obtain inscriptions [in the new *syndicat unique*], I found myself, alas, all alone."[54] Where apathy and suspicion were not sufficient to scuttle the local *syndicates uniques*, they were undermined by the labor draft that sent young workers to Germany or by the ordinary havoc of life in occupied France, which left few people with the means or determination to organize *syndicats uniques* of hair-dressing workers.

The CPO had more luck organizing *patrons coiffeurs*, who were usually older, more established in the profession, and more likely to belong to a syndicate already. As a result, the CPO reported the for-mation of several times as many employer as worker *syndicats uniques*.[55] Yet even the constitution of patronal *syndicats uniques* was fraught with problems. Nominees had to be dropped because they no longer practiced the trade or had been bombed out of their salons and forced to move. Jean-Baptiste Charottin had to decline his nomination because he was a POW, Condé Ledieu because he had been arrested by the Gestapo several weeks earlier, André Chabaudy because he had been "conscripted by the *enterprise Todt*." Madame Eugène Masset thanked Rambaud for his confidence in her husband. Sadly, she wrote, he had died the previous February.

In the great majority of cases, the prefects and other *responsables* merely approved the names the CPO proposed, but not always. They rejected some coiffeurs as insufficiently interested in the general welfare—such as Eugène Adriani of the Haute-Saône, who "ha[d] never ceased to give proof of the bitter defense of his personal and family interests." Others failed the test of moral fitness, having been involved in smuggling or, like Albert Sigal of the Tarn, embezzlement. A number of candidates had been implicated in "affaires d'avortement." In the Manche, the prefect scratched Aimé Féral, who had taken up with the wife of a POW, stolen a number of the man's possessions, and then left his own family for his mistress.[56]

The authorities objected to a handful of nominees for political reasons. The prefect of the Meuse expressed reservations about Blanche Gaudry, who professed "des idées de gauche avancées." In the Isère, the prefect struck off Henri Bard for his "marked hostility . . . to the government." The prefect of the Charente-Maritime found René Poussineau unacceptable because he had been a socialist and, although he had overtly done nothing, seemed to hate the regime. Maurice Prieux, who had been removed as president of the Chambre de Métiers in the Aube for having written impolitic letters to Pétain, was considered likely to constitute "an element of agitation" on the *syndicat unique* in Troyes and was therefore blocked by the prefect—although Rambaud succeeded in having this decision reversed.

More striking than the few individuals sanctioned by the authorities for their political attitudes, however, is the relative infrequency of such action. Rejecting several candidates for the *conseils d'administration*, the prefect of the Vosges cited abortion, infidelity, and professional incapacity as reasons for doing so. In the Côtes-du-Nord, the inspecteur divisionnaire du travail, advised the disqualifying of hairdressers for their individualism, indifference, and lack of "le sens communautaire." Otherwise, the regime seemed willing to work with almost anyone, no matter what his politics.

Louis Clauzade had been condemned in 1939 to six months in prison for "interfering [during a strike] with the *liberté du travail* according to a violent and concerted plan and for breaking and entering." It was plain that Clauzade remained an enemy of "Pétainism," in the larger sense. Yet this did not prevent his being nominated to the *syndicat unique* in Clermont-Ferrand and appointed to the CPO.[57] On the Paris *syndicat unique*, former communists Paul Petit, Maurice Poux, and Jean Crapel sat alongside Croix de Feu supporters such as Solomiac. And, of course, Magnien, the most notorious of the bunch, was vice president of the CPO.

Not every former labor militant named to the *syndicats uniques* enjoyed the eminent radical profile of Magnien and Clauzade, but their numbers were legion, and the authorities agreed overwhelmingly to their inclusion in the *famille professionnelle.* Pierre Michaud of Saint-Etienne had spent time in a concentration camp for his political views. Yet the prefect made no fuss about giving him a place on the *syndicat unique* of *patrons coiffeurs,* provided the labor minister was amenable, as he was. Debratagne, divisional labor inspector in the Marne, wrote to his superiors that Marcel Dayart, a nominee to the local administrative council, "was affiliated to the coiffeurs' syndicat (CGT) and took an active part in the defense of the workers' interests." He intended it as a recommendation. And when Torquebiau, a Labor Ministry official, wrote to the prefect in Orléans and asked him to vet nominees to the *syndicats uniques,* he wanted to make sure that they were "really representative of the profession." Torquebiau did not seem interested in their politics.

There is no escaping the conclusion that, when it came to the Labor charter, Vichy had a remarkably low threshold of political reliability. That may seem surprising for a regime that made no secret of its malice towards the political left and displayed no lack of zeal in persecuting its enemies. It dissolved the CGT, hunted down communists and resisters, and put an effective end to the normal operation of the labor movement. It jailed and murdered those too closely associated with the hated Popular Front. Yet it was willing to turn its *familles professionnelles,* the bases of its new socioeconomic system, over to its ideological enemies.

At the same time, the government did not give the CPO the tools and support it needed to achieve even the most modest of its goals. This paradoxical mix of latitude and impuissance points to two critical features of the Pétain regime: first, that it was riven by battles over administrative turf, and second, that those who desired a "National Revolution" often clashed over its substance.

The dispute between the CPO and the CO-Coiffure reproduced the rivalry between their respective ministries, labor and production. Even more than his predecessor Belin, Hubert Lagardelle devoted himself to the construction of the Labor charter. An old advocate of revolutionary syndicalism, the new secretary of state for labor had come to believe that the interests of labor and capital could in fact be reconciled under the proper circumstances, and he considered the Labor charter a blueprint for this social collaboration. Yet something of the old syndicalist remained and, even if he no longer believed in the immutability of class struggle, Lagardelle remained committed to a structure where labor unions played a fundamental role. He always considered them the key component of the Labor charter: "Get rid of the syndicates," he wrote, "and the Charter collapses."[58]

Nothing could have been more foreign to the technocratic and *dirigiste* mentality of the Production Ministry and its chief, Jean Bichelonne. The law actually placed the power to authorize the creation of *syndicats uniques* in the hands of the production minister. And, quite apart from his ideological opposition to syndicalism, Bichelonne had no incentive to extend the administrative reach of a rival ministry. Thus the authorization of *syndicats uniques* proceeded sluggishly.

Lagardelle lashed out at the organization committees, which "could never erase their fundamentally capitalist character," and at the "entourage around the Marshal, *inféodé au grand capitalisme.*" He quarreled increasingly with Bichelonne over the latter's slow authorization of *syndicats uniques.* Yet Lagardelle, "a sixty-eight-year-old relic," had neither the strength nor the resources to prevail in this contest. A resistance report on the Labor charter noted that by August 1943, Lagardelle was "très fatigué" and paranoid. He no longer traveled to Vichy without his bodyguards and refused to go to Paris for fear of being assassinated. In early October 1943, Laval removed him and handed his portfolio to Bichelonne.[59]

Antipathy to Lagardelle's syndicalist vision spilled over into harassment of the CPO leadership. In the spring of 1943, Rambaud lost his post as inspecteur de l'enseignement technique, for being "too Republican." That April, he was prosecuted for his dealings on the black market, sentenced to pay a fine of 800,000 francs, and suspended without pay from the direction of René Rambaud Laboratories.[60] The decision was signed by Bichelonne. At about the same time, Magnien, on CPO business in Moulins, was arrested by the Gestapo, "for political reasons," he surmised. Magnien spent four weeks in prison before he was released, only after Labor Ministry officials intervened on his behalf.[61]

Meanwhile, the fascist press began a campaign to vilify the leaders of the *famille professionnelle de l'hygiène.* In June 1943, *Je Suis Partout* denounced Rambaud as founder of the *"International de la coiffure* [where] all the leaders are Jews and Freemasons" and as director of the workers' école de coiffure, "which is nothing but a bunch of communists who every morning chant 'Vive DeGaulle!' " Magnien, the paper added, was a communist and a Jew-lover.[62] It was at this moment that the president and vice president of the CPO were called to the Labor Ministry and told that a decision of the "Cabinet Civil du Maréchal" had ordered their resignations because they were "two communists and two revolutionaries." Only Lagardelle's solid support returned them to the *famille professionnelle*.

Magnien and Rambaud had no doubts about who was behind these "calumnies" and "manoeuvres dilatoires." It was the work of those who intended, "against the express desires of the Marshal and the French people," to sabotage the Labor charter. They named Bichelonne as the principle culprit, abetted by the CPO's other enemies: Bagnaud, Tison, and Pierre Loyer, director of the Production Ministry's Service de l'Artisanat.

Something at this point needs to be said about Loyer. Loyer was a fascist technocrat, a product of the elite engineering school, the École Centrale, who became involved with several far-right organizations. He belonged to the Croix de Feu and was a member of Action Catholique and the Ligue Anti-judéomaçonnique. As editor of the Ligue's journal, the *Revue Internationale des Sociétés Secrètes*, Loyer specialized in uncovering Jewish and Masonic conspiracies—for example, the alleged Prussian-masonic conspiracy around Alfred Hugenburg that had brought Hitler to power. According to Henry Coston, the house biographer of French fascism, Loyer was also linked to the *Spirale* group of Cagoulards.[63]

Despite his engineering background, Loyer was, like so many on the extreme right, a social romantic, with a particular sympathy for petty production: an "institution naturelle," he wrote, where "the most beautiful family traditions are preserved."[64] These qualities recommended him to Vichy, which named him director of the newly created Service de l'Artisanat at the end of November 1940. During his tenure as director of the Artisanal Service, Loyer worked diligently for his vision of a revitalized artisanat, defending, mostly without success, petty producers in the merciless administrative wars that raged within Vichy.

Loyer's social ideas were as authoritarian as they were romantic, and even as he fought for *matières primaires* for petty craftsmen, Loyer did his best to stamp his personal authority on the artisanat. He was particularly determined to make sure that the artisanal movement did not fall into the hands of "syndicalists" and other agents of social discord. It was in this spirit that he purged the rambunctious Seine Chamber of Trades, naming Tison its new president, and turned the national assembly of presidents of chambers of trades, the APCMF, into a closely monitored subsidiary of the Artisanal Service.[65] Loyer's authoritarian politics and hostility to trade unions made him a natural ally of the CO-Coiffure in the internecine battle seething within the hairdressing profession. He did not conceal his conviction that the *famille professionnelle* of coiffeurs was a den of "militant syndicalists" and champions of "Espagne rouge." Loyer openly attacked the Labor Ministry for its patronage of "particularly suspect groups," like the CPO—a policy that would "put the profession's destiny in the hands of the directors of the Popular Front"—and used his authority and network of agents to impede the creation of *syndicats uniques*.[66]

Loyer made a preemptive strike against the Labor charter in August 1943, with the publication of the Statut de l'Artisanat. The *statute*, a blend of quixotic corporatism and authoritarian *étatisme*, was ostensibly intended to shelter artisans from the harsh winds of modern economic development. It proposed to do this by separating "artisanal" manufacture from the rest of the economy and grouping the various *professions artisanales* into "trade communities" that would run their own affairs under the watchful eye of the Artisanal Service.[67]

This set-up was totally incompatible with the Labor charter. Where the charter rested on autonomous syndicates of employers and employees, the statute envisioned "trade communities" directed by the State. And while the charter provided for parity between workers and employers, the statute fixed the dominance of masters over *compagnons*. Bichelonne liked the statute for its *étatiste* implications and for the territory it promised to seize from the Labor Ministry. He denied that it was "an instrument for dividing the working class, for the return to certain archaic forms of corporatism, and for the battle against syndicalism." It was, he said, inspired only by the idea of the "unité de la profession."[68] Such dissembling, however, did not persuade the members of the *professions artisanales*. Overwhelmingly, they recognized the statute for what it was, half retrograde fantasy and half confidence trick, and rejected it out of hand.[69]

Hairdressers were particularly sharp in their repudiation of the statute. The Union fédérale warned its membership against Loyer's attempt to destroy free trade unions and to "submit our profession to a system of corporative organization." The FNSOC denounced the statute for being "always run by the patrons" and effectively directed from the top by the prefects and the Production Ministry. Magnien announced the federation's plan to defend syndicalism "against all its adversaries . . . who, since 1940, by all sorts of maneuvers inspired by the same political doctrines, have tried to use the hairdressing profession as a guinea pig for their experiments in medieval corporatism."[70]

When the statute forced hairdressers to declare themselves "partisans of a corporation [either] *à base artisanale* or *à base syndicale*," their response was unequivocal. At its meeting in February 1944, the commission of hairdressers that Bichelonne had appointed to oversee the application of the statute to coiffure pronounced itself in favor of a profession organized *à base syndicale*—in other words, against the statute and for the Labor charter. Even Solomiac, a veteran of the Croix de Feu, voted with the majority. Only Tison, who had helped write it, and one other fellow cast their ballots for the statute.[71]

A week later, feelings were still rather raw as the CPO considered its fresh victory over the statute.[72] A number of the coiffeurs recounted their recent meeting with Loyer, the first between the *chef* of the Artisanal Service and members of the CPO. A "frank exchange of views" had not dispelled their differences, but Rambaud thought there might be grounds for an accommodation. Magnien agreed that Loyer now understood the charter better and that this had lessened his opposition to it. However, just so there would be no misunderstanding, the vice president urged his colleagues to pass a plain-speaking proposition to the effect that the syndicalists of the CPO represented the desires of the entire profession against both the organization committee and state authorities. It passed without opposition.

Rambaud next suggested that the CPO, now that it was about to become the Comité national social of an articulated *famille professionnelle*, expand its membership. In particular, he recommended that they ask Bagnaud to join them, in the interests of professional concord. This set off a storm of protest. Pierre Jardelle objected to conciliating a man who "has yet to demonstrate any spirit of conciliation." Clauzade told Rambaud that it would be hard to welcome Bagnaud and his intimates "after what they've done to you and our comrade Magnien,"—a reference to the persecution of the preceding spring—to say nothing of the CO's ongoing campaign to obstruct the CPO. Magnien also accused Bagnaud of orchestrating attacks against the CPO: "He slanders us, he has us put in prison, he drives us to the brink of bankruptcy." Now is the time for a decision, he continued. Either we work together or it is war "jusqu'au bout." It hardly needs saying that Bagnaud refused this invitation to join the *famille professionnelle*. More surprisingly, Bichelonne decided to cede to the CPO, abandon the statute for coiffure, and proceed with the construction of the *famille professionnelle*.[73] Loyer was understandably miffed by his minister's capitulation—"a victory for M. Rambaud against M. Bagnaud" and a gain for satanic political tendencies "that would hurt coiffeurs, encourage other refractory elements and strike a serious blow at the Statute of the Artisanat . . . in its entirety."[74] Loyer tried unsuccessfully to salvage a part of the statute through compromise with the CPO. But the statute was dead as far as it concerned coiffure. Even the appointment of Marcel Déat as labor minister in March 1944 brought no reversion to the statute or appreciable slowdown in the construction of the *Famille professionnelle de l'hygiène*.

Indeed, on the day before the Normandy landing, the government officially created the federations of *maîtres-artisans coiffeurs* and of *ouvriers coiffeurs* that were to become the institutional foundation of the *famille professionnelle*. Several days later Rambaud and Magnien spoke to their troops at the Palais de la Mutualité. Having overcome the "lutte tenace" led by opponents of the Labor charter, Rambaud told his audience, they could be proud that "the syndical principle has been saved" by the *famille professionnelle* that now comprised more than 300 syndicats, comités sociaux, unions régionales, and other *organismes*.[75] The speeches that followed struck an optimistic and self-congratulatory note: "*Eh bien*, my friends," Rambaud told his audience, "if the other [*familles professionnelles*] display the same honesty, the same scrupulous probity, that we have . . . something [important] will have changed in this country." Magnien followed his friend to the podium. "La Charte s'applique. Le syndicalisme continue," he told the crowd. It marked the first step of "a revolution that will put an end to the shameful exploitation of man by man" and lead the way to "social harmony" and the "équitable répartition des richesses."[76]

As the regime limped to its inevitable end, amid the chaos of Liberation, some coiffeurs kept their faith. "I fear," wrote the president of the Syndicat des maîtres-artisans coiffeurs et coiffeuses of the Haute-Marne, "that events are passing us by . . . But the storm will pass and we will meet again to continue our social work, which must live on."[77] Such confidence, alas, was not repaid, and Pétain's fall left most of his projects, among them the Labor charter, unfinished and discredited.

* * *

If the hairdressers' struggle to create a *famille professionnelle* illustrates one thing, it is the fluidity of Pétain's National Revolution, a fluidity that allowed the regime to attract the collaboration even of devoted syndicalists. That those who led the campaign for the Labor charter in coiffure were precisely those who had worked hardest for the Popular Front a few years earlier does not testify to their blindness or corruption, but to both the open-ended nature of the charter and the peculiar shape of the hairdressing profession.

It has often been argued that the charter was an attempt to gull the working class and that it could never have functioned as intended. In truth, it is hard to imagine how the charter ever *could* have been applied in industry or other large enterprises. Where the distance between owners and workers made it impossible to conceive of a "professional family," the charter was an absurdity. Yet conditions were dramatically different in a profession such as coiffure, where most workers toiled in tiny shops, alongside their employers, and where mobility from proletarian to petty bourgeois was common. Here, where the ideal of a *famille professionnelle* did not seem ridiculous or sinister on its face, the Labor charter could appear perfectly reasonable and desirable.

The wartime history of coiffure also calls into question the conventional wisdom that presented Pétainism as the revenge of the propertied classes against the Popular Front and therefore as intrinsically opposed to the interests of labor. Or, as Ingo Kolboom put it, that Vichy represented an "authoritarian alliance between the bourgeoisie and the *classes moyennes* [which] had been prepared ... in the summer of 1936."[78] This premise may or may not hold—and Kolboom's work, in particular, is heavily ideological and sloppy. In either case, it is conceivable that in 1940 workers saw things differently. From labor's perspective the Popular Front was already dead by 1939, but it was Reynaud, not Pétain, who had killed it. Daladier, not Pétain, had driven the Communist Party underground, while the government of 1939–40 had suspended hours legislation, reduced overtime pay, suspended collective bargaining, and shut the CGT out of wartime economic management.[79] Conversely, even the impeccably left-wing *Dictionnaire biographique du mouvement ouvrier français* credits the Vichy regime with a series of laws that were "favorable aux salariés" in 1940 and 1941: unemployment protections, old-age pensions, and the like.[80]

That is not to rehabilitate Vichy, but only to suggest that syndicalists may have been less distraught about the fall of the Third Republic than is normally supposed. Ideologically, there can be no doubt that Vichy was a right-wing regime. From the workers' point of view, however, there was much to be said for trying to get their best deal, whatever the ravings of "extremists" in and around the government. And a Labor charter that performed as advertised was not such a bad deal.

That was precisely the thinking that attracted syndicalists in the hairdressing trade to the *famille professionnelle*, and it answers the question of how an old lion of the labor movement, such as Magnien, could become so deeply implicated in that Pétainist project. Militant coiffeurs were already predisposed by their interests and syndical politics to accept the sort of solution proposed by the Labor charter, which promised both to shield them from the free market and to hand power within the profession to the syndicats of *ouvriers* and *patrons coiffeurs*. This calls to mind the principles embedded in Law 900 or, to go back even further, some of the ideas put forward before World War I for bringing order and prosperity to an anarchic profession. In other words, it seems perfectly plausible that people with impeccable syndicalist credentials and a general leftist perspective, the FNSOC and UF types who ran the CPO, could have offered a doubtful regime their collaboration on this point.

The possibilities implicit in the Labor charter thus launched hairdressers on a campaign that mingled resistance and collaboration in the same actions; that is, they worked with Vichy in pursuit of ends fundamentally opposed to those of the regime. This was not "collaboration" or "Pétainism" in the usual sense. The FNSOC and its general secretary, in particular, remained skeptical, at times openly critical, partners in socioeconomic reorganization. The federation continued to function throughout the war, and while it gave a cautious imprimatur to the Labor charter, it maintained a vocal opposition to the general aims of the regime.

Robert Burba had impeccable *résistant* credentials. A FNSOC activist, he spent two years in a German concentration camp and was later decorated for his resistance activities. Burba nevertheless defended the FNSOC's policy of *présence* as part of "an implacable battle against the reactionary clique at Vichy," against their "chartes corporatives" and "Statut de l'Artisanat."[81] More than anyone else this was true of Magnien who, with his communist past and Jewish wife, was harassed by the regime, arrested by the Gestapo, and reviled in the fascist press. The point is that he, along with Louis Clauzade, Emile Machelon, René Lhouillier, Paul Petit, and their comrades recognized no contradiction between their efforts on behalf of the Labor charter and their militant syndicalism and antifascism.

These ardent trade unionists would never have been drawn into collaboration, moreover, had they not been encouraged by a certain solicitude on the part of the regime, especially from syndicalist elements in the Labor Ministry. Equally, those efforts would have paid bigger dividends without the hostility to syndicalism that existed elsewhere in the Vichy apparatus. John Sweets has argued that "the interminable quarrels at Vichy about particular policies" should not be taken to represent any significant differences over the regime's right-swing agenda.[82] I disagree. The conflict between the Labor Ministry and Production Ministry, visible in the application of the Labor charter to coiffure, indicates rather that such differences *did* exist and that they were both significant and consequential. In the end, a French economy run by organization committees would look very different from one organized into *familles professionnelles*.

It is possible today to see the flaw in the logic of those who lent their energies to the Labor charter. At the end of the day, the principal thrust of Vichy political economy was technocratic and *dirigiste*. Real power in the regime tended to accrue to men like Bichelonne and Bagnaud, "experts" and representatives of economic rationalization within the rationing apparatus and the organization committees. These stubborn realities made the battle for the Labor charter mostly beside the point. Lagardelle's career at Vichy is exemplary, in this regard.

Contemporary judgment on the war needs to be salted with the awareness that what is clear now was perhaps ambiguous at the time, and it is worthwhile distinguishing between misplaced sincerity in the service of decent aims and actual malignity. Marcel Bagnaud, a successful businessman and right-wing activist, was bound by the nature of the regime to be the focus of authority within the hairdressing profession. He was a genuine Vichyist, a collaborator in the usual way. By comparison, Rambaud and Magnien, representing all those old trade unionists, workers and patrons, attached to their profession through a belief in its art and humanity, were chasing a chimera.

Perhaps the antipathy of the possessing classes and the partisan nature of government should have been axiomatic to these two dedicated syndicalists. That they failed to recognize Vichy for what it was proves only that the road to political perdition is often paved not with bad faith or ignorance but with sloppy thinking.

The pop singer Juliette Greco with Alexandre de Paris

9

Dark Days, Bright Future

In the summer of 1944, the economic miracle that carried coiffure to new heights of creativity and prosperity lay in an unimaginable future. Meanwhile, as the Germans left Paris, hairdressers hurried to take their place on the barricades, and the settling of accounts began. The purges mostly ignored those coiffeurs who had become involved in public affairs during the occupation. The expropriation of *coiffeurs juifs* was quickly forgotten, and no one was indicted for the mere act of serving on the CO-Coiffure or the *Famille professionnelle de l'hygiène*. Rambaud, still mourning his wife's recent death after her long battle with cancer, left for the mountains of the Haute-Savoie to write his history of hairstyles. Bagnaud and Magnien stayed in the capital to face their own postwar travails. Other leaders of the CPO and the CO-Coiffure returned to their federations and their salons. Louis Tison, the most Pétainist of coiffeurs, disappeared from the public life of the profession. Eugène Schueller, founder and director of L'Oréal, had a more serious brush with the purge authorities. He was saved, in the end, by a well-timed conversion to resistance causes and the intervention of friends in high places.[1]

If the *épuration* hardly touched them, the coiffeurs could not escape the war's other heavy legacy: penury. Amidst widespread but misplaced expectations that the departure of the *Wehrmacht* would bring a quick return to "normalcy," hairdressers continued to lack the essentials of their trade.[2] Linen, shaving powder, even soap remained difficult to find. Authorities continued to restrict the hours that coiffeurs could light their salons and prohibited the use of electric signs and decorations. Regular power cuts lasted into 1950.[3]

The material hardship of life in liberated France naturally encouraged the resurgence of the labor movement, which generally went forward in a spirit of warmth and comradeship.[4] In coiffure, however, old enmities quickly resurfaced. The strong position that the communists had carved out for themselves in the CGT during the war promised grief for those who had worked too closely with the regime. Magnien was their chief target. He had ruled the FNSOC unopposed during the war, but the Liberation guaranteed a reckoning.

Magnien initially planned to adapt the Parisian *syndicat unique* to the Liberation merely by reintegrating those who had been forced out at the beginning of the war. This would give the communists a presence proportional to their strength among Parisian *ouvriers coiffeur*, and Magnien no doubt hoped that this would mollify the CGT while allowing him to retain control of the former CSO, now the SOC. Instead, Magnien and his allies quickly found themselves under fire from their "comarades communistes," who accused these "sabateurs de la démocratie" of having stolen their syndicat in 1939. The CGT made no secret of its intention to "reconstitute a federation of coiffeurs purged of collaborationist and Vichyist elements."[5]

For the moment, the *ouvrier coiffeurs communists* were led by Marcel Moreau, who believed that Magnien had denounced him to the Germans in 1940, as part of a plot to take full control of the profession. Encouraged by his friends on the CGT executive, who had already assured him that Magnien would be expelled from the labor movement, Moreau proposed that the prewar CSO *bureau* be restored, and that SOC members be required to apply *individually* for readmittance. That would allow "Pétainist" elements to be kept out and guarantee the communists the upper hand. Through the late summer and early fall of 1944, Magnien and Moreau met several times and exchanged polite notes, but their efforts to find common ground came to nothing.[6]

These negotiations were soon preempted by the process of *épuration*. Magnien was summoned to the Commission nationale de reconstitution des organisations syndicales (CNROS) on November 2, 1944 and charged with having written articles praising the Labor charter and the *Maréchal*, served as vice president of the *famille professionnelle*, organized the anticommunist purge of the CSO in 1939, and disobeyed CGT discipline.[7] Six days later the commission excluded Magnien from the labor movement "for life"—a rather *pro forma* verdict, considering his well-known involvement with the *famille professionnelle*.[8]

The CNROS's action was confirmed a month later by the Commission départementale de reconstruction des organisations syndicales (CDROS), which also cast out others who had worked for the *famille professionnelle* and *syndicat unique*: Paul Petit, "le premier lieutenant de Magnien" and former communist, was accused of having expressed "national socialist sentiments"; René Lhuillier, who operated the *centre d'apprentissage* at the École parisienne, was said to have dealt in the black market, while he "followed the directives of the traitor Belin and his accomplices."[9]

Magnien wrote directly to labor minister Alexandre Parodi, asking him to nullify this procedure. It was absurd, he said, to hand the important job of punishing real collaborators over to the forces of "political tyranny," who made no distinction between genuine *collabos* and those who were merely an obstacle to communist ambitions. For the moment, however, the government hesitated to involve itself directly in the *reconstitution des organisations syndicales*—perhaps more out of prudence than sympathy.[10]

When a less partisan body, the Conseil supérieur d'enquête de l'enseignement technique, considered Magnien's case the following May, it took a number of affadavits from those who knew the FNSOC general secretary. A number of witnesses painted Magnien as a courageous resistor. Emile Machelon, member of the Communist Party since 1924 and the "Commission de la CGT clandestine," reported that Magnien had hidden both himself and their colleague Louis Clauzade when the Gestapo was on their trail. Robert Burba, decorated *résistant* and member of the FNSOC council, testified that Louis Saillant, a member of the Conseil National de la Résistance and the CGT Bureau, had approved of Magnien's work on behalf of the Labor charter. René Rambaud, back from the Haute-Savoie, told the conseil that the accused had always been "resolutely hostile *à toute politique vichyssoise*." In 1939, Rambaud went on, there had been only twenty or twenty-five active syndicats in the FNSOC, whereas the federal congress of December 1944 brought together seventy-five unions representing 50,000 hairdressing workers. "In all my experience," Rambaud concluded, "I have never seen a more impressive organization of *ouvriers coiffeurs*."[11]

Those who gave depositions against Magnien adduced almost entirely hearsay and circumstantial evidence. Roger Leclerc, the CSO general secretary who had been arrested in 1941 and spent the rest of the war in hiding, asserted that Magnien had denounced him to the authorities in 1939 and expressed his belief that the Germans would defeat the Soviet Union. Arthur Roger, recently returned from a concentration camp, *was told by a friend* that Magnien had bet a client "that the Germans would be in Moscow in two weeks." Georges Stayanoff, hassled during the occupation for his political opinions, "*had strong suspicions*" that Magnien had traduced him. Pierre Guny, Magnien's mentor in the old days of the CGTU, knew that his old protégé was not pro-German but *had the impression* that he had worked too closely with Vichy.[12]

The council's final report determined that Magnien was *not* a collaborator and saw no reason to relieve him of his duties as director of the Centre de formation professionnelle at the SOC's headquarters on the rue Darboy.[13] The government finally repudiated the entire process when on December 31, 1946 the Conseil d'Etat ruled that the CNROS did *not* have the legal right to lock people out of the labor movement.[14] By then, however, the rift between communist and noncommunist hairdressing workers had become all but irreparable.

So far as these exclusions were part of a CGT effort to chastise a federation that had slipped out of its control, they flopped. Magnien reacted to his excommunication with scorn. Whatever the CGT and his old communist rivals thought of his leadership, Magnien held on to the fierce loyalty of the FNSOC and its Paris arm, the SOC, and these immediately made clear their intention to defy the CGT. Despite warnings that the confederation did not sanction this "special congress" and would not accept its decisions, FNSOC delegates gathered in Paris on December 11, 1944.[15] The federation once more defended its wartime activities, claiming to have gone along with the Labor charter "only in the narrowest sense [and using it only] to reconstruct our *mouvement syndical.*"[16] Magnien, completely in his element amidst the vituperation and political infighting, took the floor and inveighed against the "insinuations by certain elements perverted by *le sectarisme politique* . . . cowards now pretending to be heroes of the French resistance."[17] By unanimous vote the congress demanded that the CNROS rescind its exclusions, and it reelected Magnien secretary general.

Magnien resigned as FNSOC general secretary in mid-January 1945, citing both his fatigue and the "atmosphère impossible" within the labor movement.[18] The new leadership—Albert Jacquelin, from Le Havre, and Emile Machelon, from Clermont-Ferrand—immediately expressed their regret at Magnien's "geste d'unité" and their full confidence in their old *chef*. A referendum on Magnien, carried out by the federation among its member syndicats gave him an overwhelming vote of confidence.[19]

The CGT followed through on its threat not to recognize the actions of the recent FNSOC congress, yet it continued to search for some sort of compromise with its recalcitrant federation. Saillant proposed setting up a *Comité provisoire de gestion* for the FNSOC. This would allow SOC and CSO forces to share leadership of the disputed federation and work out their differences under the tutelage of the confederation until the officially sanctioned congress, scheduled for the summer of 1945, could arrange a full *modus vivendi*. Machelon, for the SOC forces, and Roger, the ex-*unitaire* from Nancy, thereupon took up the job of steering the federation in the direction of internal harmony and obedience to the CGT.[20] The congrès fédéral that met in Paris on August 27–28, 1945 was intended to launch a new era of syndical amity and confederal discipline. But time and the trappings of compromise had not made the FNSOC more tractable. In the meantime, senior CSO leaders—Jacques Célerier, Emile Tarrier, and Georges Philippot—had returned to France from the camps, hardly in a mood to work amicably with those they considered traitors and traducers. To guide the FNSOC back into the CGT's good graces, the confederation sent Julien Racamond and Pierre Neumeyer of its executive bureau to preside over the August congress. But they were unable to impose either order or civility on the proceedings.[21]

Elections to the new executive committee quickly brought simmering resentments back to the surface, as the congress reiterated the federation's loyalty to Magnien. It elected his old comrades to its bureau federal, while consigning Philippot, Roger, and a small handful of CSO men to minor positions in the commission administrative. In a final gesture of defiance to the CGT, the FNSOC restated its opinion that "it was thanks to the action of the federation within the structures of the Labor Charter that Vichy was held in check for three years and that our syndical movement emerged intact at the Liberation."[22]

By the beginning of 1946, Philippot, the blustery leader of the communist faction, had been ousted from the commission and the war of words between the two parties had become more scurrilous than ever. Tarrier attacked the "magnienists" as the enemies of democracy and the "agent des trusts"—still "pursuing," as Philippot put it, "the politics of their old masters: Belin, Lagardelle, and Pétain."[23] His enemies called the CSO *chef* a "fat toady" and a "patented liar."[24] And so on.

The CGT refused to accept the decisions of the FNSOC's August 1945 congress, and convened a Commission confédérale des conflits to mediate between the hostile groups of *ouvriers coiffeurs* and propose a solution. The full CGT then took up the matter at its own April 1946 congress, its first since before the war.[25] With only the FNSOC delegate René Lhuillier opposed, the congress accepted the commission's recommendations. The CGT agreed to rehear the cases of *les exclus* (except for Magnien), implicitly readmitting them into the labor movement. In return, the federation's bureau was obliged to reintegrate the Philippot faction and work for unity *within* the CSO.[26]

The next FNSOC congress was supposed to consummate this shotgun marriage. But the federal congress that met at the CGT offices in Paris in early March 1947 made it perfectly clear that division within the hairdressers' federation was not solely the product of personal rancor. The two sides also disagreed substantially about the future of the labor movement.

Racamond greeted the hairdressers for the CGT. The confederation welcomed differences of opinion, he told them.[27] Nonetheless, such serious times required militants to get past the "maladie infantile" of factionalism and resolve their "difficulties." Lhuillier, the former *exclu* filling in for General Secretary Jaquelin, who refused to sit in the same room with the communists, agreed. "Democracy," he averred, "does not consist in putting everyone in the same uniform and having them raise their hands at the same time." He called for an atmosphere of "tolerance, sympathy, and reciprocal comradeship." Roger Leclerc, general secretary of the CSO, concurred. "There's no 'conflict' [between CSO and SOC forces]," he told his colleagues, "just a lack of understanding."

Yet conciliatory words could not hide the very real disagreements. As the first day's discussion turned to the question of wages and relations with the *patronat*, sharp tactical and philosophical differences emerged. The communists in the CSO took a rather manichean view of social conflict, a struggle, as Leclerc put it, between progressives and "forces réactionnaires," capable of any villainy.[28] They remained committed to a highly politicized and confrontational syndicalism that not only fought the bread-and-butter battles but that always kept its eye on "the liberation [of the proletariat] from the capitalist yoke."[29]

Lhuillier considered this sort of discourse "pure demagoguery." Only a prosperous profession could offer hairdressing workers higher wages and better working conditions. This required not class war, but recognition of the "general situation" and collaboration with *patrons coiffeurs*.

The next day, in a surprisingly harmonious mood, the congress hammered out the details of a *reunion* of the CSO and the SOC, based on the rough equality between the two *tendances*. Elections went forward without any of the bickering that had poisoned the congress of August 1945. The SOC man Machelon became general secretary. Philippot and Tarrier sat alongside Lhuillier and Clauzade as *secrétaires adjoints*. They agreed on a manifesto and a fusion of syndical assets. The congress itself adjourned with smiles and handshakes all around.

But the patina of consensus only obscured the congress's failure to settle a number of crucial issues. It had not found a middle way, for example, between the hard revolutionism of the communists and the accommodationist tactics of Machelon and his colleagues. Moreover, despite some concessions that allowed several second-rank figures back into the labor movement, the CSO forces would never countenance Magnien's return to the federation. Relations between them remained as caustic as ever.[30]

It seems doubtful that any particular arrangement could have reconciled two groups of *ouvriers coiffeurs* with such adverse tactical notions and political loyalties. In any event, the parochial battles within the FNSOC soon melted into the much larger story of the fracturing of the CGT and the formation of the CGT-Force Ouvrière (FO). The confederation had always contained rival approaches to improving the lives of working people. Indeed, the history of *ouvriers coiffeurs* has already traced the jagged path of *scission* and reconciliation that characterized the CGT from the early 1920s to the late 1940s. In the end, however, the fundamental discord between "hard" and "soft" syndicalism remained.

Some sort of showdown between communists and noncommunists had been brewing within the CGT since the Liberation.[31] Relations deteriorated after the congress of April 1946 that sealed the communists' control of the confederation, and the table was already set when the cold war arrived. The strikes of November and December 1947, endorsed by the CGT, following the reversal of Soviet policy but opposed by Jouhaux and his noncommunist associates, were the immediate cause of the split. Funded in large part with American money, the new confederation held its constituent congress the following April. It took a significant chunk of the old one with it—a majority of civil service workers, federations of white-collar, railway and communications workers—leaving the old confederation "as the trade union arm of the Communist Party."[32]

For the Magnienists in the FNSOC it was an easy decision to free themselves from the "*intolérable tutelle*" of the communists by joining the FO.[33] It was a path dictated not just by political affiliations or personal grudges, but by the syndical philosophy of the SOC and its provincial allies. Magnien now disavowed the politics of class struggle. The welfare of *ouvriers coiffeurs*, he believed, depended in the long run not on some sort of "victory" over *salonniers* but on the organization of the profession. "All the rest is so much *blah-blah-blah démagogique*."[34] Magnien's new logic led him to approve the FO's support for "lower prices over an illusory rise in wages," and to welcome the Marshall Plan, which aided both France's battle against "la généralisation de la misère" and labor's attempts to build a more just, democratic society.[35]

Those hairdressing workers who remained loyal to the CGT naturally saw this as further proof that the *équipe magnienne* were and had
always been a bunch of "strikebreakers" in league with "the repressive
governmental apparatus."[36] It was precisely the communists' habit of
treating dissension as treason that had done so much to alienate the
SOC forces in the FNSOC. Now, the adhesion of the Magnien party to
the Force ouvrière inspired them to even greater heights of denunciation. The FO were "enemies of the working class," "accomplices of
International Finance and the *gros patronat*," and hirelings of the
Americans, who were bankrupting France in order to control it.[37]

With the departure of a large portion of the FNSOC, Tarrier and
Philippot began to reorganize the federation, in an attempt to keep
provincial syndicats from defecting to the FO, although it appears they
came away from the secession with the smaller piece of the pie. The
communist remnants of the FNSOC managed to assemble a congress in
September 1949. It lasted two days and divided its energies between
laying out its bread-and-butter program and abusing the FO. The
procès-verbal contains no indication of how many *ouvriers coiffeurs*
attended or from what localities. In 1949, the federation claimed to
have something less than 1,500 members, but this was largely a guess.[38]

The inaugural congress of the new FNSOC-FO met in July 1948 in a
completely different atmosphere. It quickly elected Magnien honorary
president and moved on to business, concerned almost entirely with
formation professionnelle, in cooperation with some of the profession's
leading businessmen and artists: Rambaud, Lamy, Azéma, Marc Ruyer
et al. The bureau fédéral reported on its wage negotiations with the
employers. It never mentioned its rivals in the old FNSOC and the CSO.[39]

From then on, the paths of the two organizations of *ouvriers coiffeurs*
diverged dramatically. The FNSOC-FO steered clear of political
questions. It cultivated its contacts with government ministries and
worked closely with the employers' federation to improve conditions
in the salons. Magnien increasingly occupied himself with issues of
formation, from the top to the bottom of the profession. To increase
its leverage within the profession, the new federation branched out.
It incorporated employees from *parfumerie* and *esthétique* (beauty
treatment) and absorbed the Syndicat national des gérants techniques
de Paris, becoming by the mid-1950s the Fédération nationale de la
coiffure, de l'esthétique, et de la parfumerie-FO (FNCEP-FO), which it
remains today. Machelon replaced Magnien, as the latter expanded his
professional activities, and served as general secretary until 1970,
when he ceded his place to Magnien's other great wartime comrade,

Louis Clauzade. Clauzade retired in 1975, when CGT-FO General Secretary André Bergeron plucked Michel Bourlon from the metallurgists' federation to head the FNCEP.[40]

Membership numbers are both uncertain and rare for the period, but whatever its exact size, the breakaway federation unquestionably emerged out of its divorce from the CGT with the greater organizational clout.[41] Its philosophy of class collaboration and syndical stature made the FNSOC-FO the preferred interlocutor of the government and the employers. It retained its influence in professional affairs that the communist-led rump of the old federation could never approach. In fact, the Magnien forces henceforth ceased almost entirely to take notice of their old colleagues, except when rebuffing the latter's frequent requests for common action.

By way of contrast, the records of the CSO suggest that communist syndicalism struggled to find an audience among *ouvriers coiffeurs*. For a few years, the *Ouvrier Coiffeur Parisien* kept up a steady drumbeat of reproach against the working-class traitors in the Force ouvrière. But then the journal disappeared, probably the victim of fragile finances. Roger Leclerc, the CSO's general secretary, continued to preside over quarterly meetings of the conseil syndical, sprinkling his reports on the group's modest activities with complaints of worker apathy and dissertations on international politics. Tiny and poor, and without a significant role in the collective bargaining process, the CSO faded from sight.

While the organizations of *ouvriers coiffeurs* exhausted themselves fighting one another, the *patrons* quietly buried their old disputes. The CPC and its Paris arm the SPC, never reformed after the war, preferring to fold themselves directly into the Union fédérale and the CSP. The "Unity Congress" of July 1945 sealed the entente among *patrons coiffeurs* at the national level. Two months later, the "historic" meeting of 10,000 hairdressers at the Cirque d'Hiver consecrated the union of Paris *salonniers*. Joseph Gestalder, still president of the UF, told the crowd that similar meetings were bringing hairdressers together all across the country.[42]

The UF marked its renewal by changing its name, becoming the Fédération nationale des maîtres-artisans et patrons coiffeurs de France (FNC). By 1946, the FNC claimed to have 30,000 *cotisants*, representing half the *salonniers* in the country, with sections in every department in France. This was both the legacy of the war, when the need to get materials from the CO-Coiffure and the recruiting efforts of the *famille professionnelle* had pulled *patron coiffeurs* into their local unions, and the consequence of economic difficulties in the early postwar years that stimulated *salonniers*' interest in collective action.[43]

As it grew, the FNC introduced programs in the areas of professional education, artistic promotion, and commercial "creation," along with a host of social services offering members protection against old age, accidents, death. It provided tax information and advice, subsidized vacation colonies and an *orchestre de la coiffure*. To stimulate creativity among coiffeurs and stir up interest in the latest hairstyles among the public, the federation deepened its involvement with *haute coiffure*, and in 1947, its new president Marcel Lamy became the first general secretary of the Confédération internationale de la coiffure.[44]

On the political front, the FNC made common cause with others seeking to defend artisans and *petits commerçants*. Bagnaud, now on the federation's executive committee, led the federation into Léon Gingembre's Confédération générale des petites et moyennes entreprises, where he served on the national executive board.[45] Meanwhile, Edouard Dauvergne, a member of the FNC executive board and president of the CSP, was elected to the Paris Chambre de Métiers in 1946 and became president of the Confédération nationale de l'artisanat, which enjoyed a brief moment of activity defending France's *gens de métiers*, until it more or less dissolved into the Poujade movement.[46]

It was not the resurgence of a stroppy working class that drove *salonniers* into the organized ranks of *petite et moyenne entreprise*, but the new charges imposed on employers and *indépendants* by the burgeoning welfare state.[47] Whether *petites et moyennes entreprises* actually paid more than what social justice demanded is an open question. What is undeniable is that they believed that the government was making small businessmen subsidize a system that would primarily benefit wage-earners. Resistance paid off, as the government responded by restructuring taxes for *petit commerce*. In 1948, the luxury tax ceased to apply to *salons de coiffure*. In 1954, it introduced the VAT, which in effect passed the tax bill along to consumers. Moreover, the smallest businesses were exempt from the VAT. Even so, enough resentment remained to fuel the great "petty bourgeois revolt" of the Poujade movement.

The FNC's affiliation with the new representatives of the *classes moyennes* made sense as a cold political calculation. But there was more to it than that. Dauvergne's politics retained much of the flavor of the moral economy that still ran strong among France's master artisans in the early Fourth Republic. "We are honest men," he wrote, "*bons français* . . . and we have the right to our livelihood like everyone else."[48] At the same time, his attachment to the moral economy made Dauvergne something of an anomaly within the FNC. For while the federation had evolved directly out of the artisanal UF, in its structure and operations the FNC came more and more to resemble the Confédération des patrons coiffeurs. Despite the lingering presence of some of the UF old guard, almost all the federation's new leadership were substantial *commerçants*. Under their direction, the *métier* became the handmaiden of business, and smallness ceased to be a virtue in itself.

The principal architect of the "modernization" of patronal syndicalism was Marcel Lamy, the federation's longtime general secretary and president. Lamy had come up through the ranks of the CSP before the war. Like so many of his colleagues, he left the salon for the army in 1939 and stayed through the occupation in Paris, where his salon at the Gare de l'Est employed thirty workers. For reasons that are not clear, Lamy left no imprint either on the CO-Coiffure or the *famille professionnelle*, yet he emerged out of the Liberation at the head of those who wanted to modernize the Union fédérale.[49]

Lamy applied his business principles to his job as general secretary of the FNC, where his goal was to promote a rationalization of professional affairs that would set coiffure on a steady road to profits and stability. The challenge after 1945 was to accomplish this in the face of unprecedented devastation and economic turmoil. It might be argued that hairdressers were no worse off than many other sectors. They had not suffered any massive destruction of their property during the war. Their shops might have run down a bit, but coiffeurs' capital had not by-and-large been bombed, flooded, or carted off to the Reich. Besides, a hairdresser's greatest assets were his skill and his relations with his customers, and these were undiminished.

Nevertheless, serious impediments to the revival of business in the salons remained. However intact, the salons generally remained empty of the most profitable elements of a coiffeur's trade, and the effects of war and occupation left most women without money to spend on fashionable hair. Beyond these conjunctural difficulties, which looked likely to get better with time, hairdressers fretted about a new flood of recruits into their perpetually overcrowded trade, as thousands of coiffeurs returned to the salons from the prisoner-of-war camps and other points of exile.[50]

As if this prospect were not gloomy enough, on November 6, 1945 the government reestablished "la liberté de création et d'extension du commerce de la coiffure," which was suspended in 1939.[51] "The creation of new salons," warned the CSP, "by the trusts or the profiteers of the black market who, not being able to invest their money in other businesses, are buying up *salons de coiffure*," will bury the real *gens de métier*.[52] Many *salonniers* only made matters worse by taking on too many apprentices, if only to have cheap labor—to say nothing of the *travailleurs noirs*, who paid neither taxes nor social security. This "reserve army" of *ouvriers coiffeurs*, as Magnien called them, produced a disastrous decline in the quality of work being done in the salons.[53]

Hairdressers reached back to a congenial remedy, seeking to reduce the downward pressure on prices, wages, and working conditions by controlling access to the trade. The law of April 26, 1946 granted coiffeurs a part of what they wanted.[54] It required anyone operating a *salon de coiffure* to have some professional certification, either a *brevet professionnel* or a *brevet de maîtrise*, with a *dérogation* for those who had worked at least six years in the profession. A salon whose proprietor lacked these qualifications had to hire a technical director. The law also tightened up the apprenticeship process and entrusted enforcement to the *inspecteurs du travail*. A *salonnier* who failed to comply faced a fine ranging from 2,000 to 50,000 francs and the possibility of his salon being closed down.[55] But the government refused to restrict commercial liberties any further.

There is no evidence that the April 1946 decree produced any salutary effect on the profession. On the contrary, in the years that followed, talk of a "crisis" in the profession became more insistent. Patrons who only a short time ago had employed two or three assistants now worked alone, wrote the *Coiffeur de France* in 1948. A sixth of *fonds de coiffure*—1,500 businesses—had disappeared; half the *ouvriers coiffeurs* had abandoned the trade.[56] Only the top 5 percent of salons could make ends meet, wrote the general secretary of the CSP. The other 95 percent are on the ropes. "The present moment," Rambaud observed, "allows no one, neither employers nor employees, to earn their living [in coiffure]."[57]

Ouvriers and *patrons coiffeurs* soon found themselves in a familiar dance, the former agitating for higher wages and the latter holding out for higher prices—with one important new wrinkle. Whereas the *pouvoirs publics* had always tried to influence this process, now they actually set wages and prices.

The Liberation government, particularly sensitive to the demands of labor, had raised *salaires* across the board in September 1944, giving hairdressing workers an extra five francs an hour.[58] This hardly repaired the damage done to their real income during the war, but it was still more than the employers claimed they could afford. They came back to the government with an urgent request for a rise in *tariffs*.[59] When the government refused to agree, *patrons coiffeurs*, led by Lamy, shut their salons down for a couple of days—to show they meant business.

Labor minister Parodi responded by calling representatives of the FNSOC and the UF together in September 1945 to work out a new agreement on wage rates, and the *arrêté* that followed at the end of October established a scale of minimum *salaries* for Paris ranging from 700 francs per week for the lowest category of *débutants* to 1,225 francs for the highest class of skilled hairdressers. It did away with the 40 percent (of receipts) standard established in the collective agreement of May 1942 in exchange for a new benchmark. Workers now had the right to at least 30 percent of the receipts they generated *or* to a "guaranteed" minimum wage, whichever was larger.[60]

This hardly settled the matter. For one thing, while the noncommunist majority in the FNSOC supported the Parodi *arrêté*, claiming the guaranteed minimum as a great victory and pointing out that the change from 40 to 30 percent would in no case lead to a loss of wages, the communists within the workers' federation attacked the Parodi schedule as a surrender to reactionary salon owners, "made millionaires by war and collaboration."[61] They particularly hated the principle that tied wages to incomes, and therefore to prices. Roger Perrot, CSO general secretary, combined a labor theory of value with a vision of the moral economy when he argued that *ouvriers coiffeurs'* long years of training gave them a right to a relatively high wage, "whatever the volume of their output."[62] For another, *patrons coiffeurs* understood the Parodi *arrêté* in different ways. Some used it as the occasion to reduce the percentage being paid to their employees, which fell to 10 or 15 percent in some localities. Others balked at applying the new wage scale, insisting that it could go into effect only *after* a general price rise.[63]

To clarify its policy, or perhaps to make sure that wages continued to keep up with rising prices, the government returned to the issue of hairdressers' pay in the summer of 1946. Labor Ministry orders of June and July raised the minimum wage for *ouvriers coiffeurs* and restored the 30 percent standard.[64] Once again, *salonniers* responded by demanding a price rise to offset these new costs. The UF congress of August 1946 unanimously voted to raise *tarifs* by 20 to 25 percent, and when the authorities refused to accede, the union again sponsored a two-hour "warning strike." The government responded with a small increase in prices.[65] Thus the profession continued to chase its tail.

Wages went up in small, irregular increments throughout the late 1940s, as the government struggled to keep wages abreast of surging inflation. In 1947, it revised the structure of the *salaire minimum*, giving *ouvriers coiffeurs* a commission of 10 percent on the difference, if real revenues exceeded hypothetical ones. At the lowest level, "salonniers

ou coiffeuses simples" earned 1,700 francs per week, based on weekly
revenues of 6,500 francs, plus 10 percent of anything above that. The
third level of "coiffeur or coiffeuse de dames"—notice the formal equality of men and women—was assured an income of 2,000 francs, plus
10 percent of revenues above 7,500 francs, et cetera. This system promised
assistants both a decent wage and a stake in their own productivity, and
by the end of the decade it applied to virtually all salons, save that
minority of "hors classe," where the most highly skilled practitioners
could work strictly on commission. On the other hand, the complex of
skill levels, geographical zones, and classes of salon comprised an arcane
and cumbersome mechanism for setting minimum wages.[66]

Moreover, because wages depended on a worker's classification,
disputes over qualifications were endemic and often ended up before
the labor inspectors or the Conseils des Prud'hommes. In June 1946,
for example, Roger Leclerc wrote to labor inspector LaVarenne on
behalf of Denise Cariaux, a manicurist at the Maison José, on the
avenue McMahon. Mademoiselle Cariaux, it seems, believed herself
qualified as a *manucure 3e classe*, with a right to 1,000 francs a week,
while her employer paid her only 800 as a second-class manicurist.
LaVarenne eventually convinced her employer to reclassify her. He
complained, however, that "this question is difficult to resolve because
*the arrêté is silent on the means of discriminating between employees
of the second and third class.*"[67] In similar fashion, Emile Machelon
defended Yves Lacheval at the Prud'hommes against his former
employer. Lacheval had been fired after eighteen weeks and was
demanding severance pay based on his classification as "3e catégorie;
3e échelon." His employer maintained that he had been hired as a
"nonremunerated apprentice." The court agreed with Lacheval and
awarded him 52,491 francs in back wages.[68] Little wonder that hairdressers constantly called for a simplification of wage schedules.

The complexity of the system aside, hairdressing workers won two
significant victories in these early postwar years. The first was the
principle of the *minimum vital*, the minimum living wage to which all
assistants had a right, along with a portion of the profit they produced
for the salon. The second, arguably of even greater significance, was
the regularization of the 15 percent tip.

The *pourboire* had long been a contentious issue within the profession,
and arguments against it in 1947 were exactly what they had been fifty
years earlier: it was a degrading practice and an unreliable source of
income.[69] The FNSOC, especially its communist members, sought to
replace it with a genuine *salaire minimum vital*. That is why it rejected

a proposal to integrate a standard gratuity of 10 percent into the price of haircuts and other services to be paid *à la caisse* and then distributed by the patron to his *assistants*. The federation worried plausibly that, if *salonniers* got *their* hands on the tip first, employees would never see their fair share and that customers who had already handed over an extra 10 percent at the register would then not give anything directly to the server. *Assistants* would lose at both ends.[70]

Patrons coiffeurs, on the contrary, thought that a 10 percent *pourboire* added to the price of every service was a splendid plan. It gave them, in effect, exactly the increase in *tarifs* they had been soliciting as the *quid pro quo* for raising wages. Labor minister Parodi also liked the idea. But support for it was not unanimous, even among employers. For one thing, *salonniers* did not have the right to the tip *à la caisse*, which was meant only for employees. They still had to depend on customers' largesse. For another, the *service compris* represented a substantial price rise and hence handed a competitive advantage to those patrons who dragged their feet. In a word, the *pourboire* looked ready to crash against the same market anarchy that had wrecked so many previous efforts to raise *tarifs*.

The authorities decided to go forward nevertheless, and in June 1947 they imposed a tip of 15 percent, integrated directly into the *salaire minimum*, on all hairdressing salons. Both the FNC and the FNSOC-FO praised the new rule, which was, said Machelon, good for both a worker's pocketbook and his honor.[71] Marcel Haggaï, who went on to become proprietor of eight posh salons in Paris and president of the Paris Chamber of Trades, said that the 15 percent *service compris* brought about a fundamental change in the lives of hairdressing workers. Haggaï recalled that when he first entered the profession in the late 1930s, he would never have told any young woman he wanted to impress that he was an *ouvrier coiffeur*, so poor and disdained were they.[72] Whether the new rules made dating easier for young *assistants* we cannot say. Yet they certainly raised incomes, and by the end of 1948, discussion of the *pourboire* had disappeared from the trade press. It never returned.

The goodwill of the labor minister and the regularization of the tip could never overcome the galloping cost of living, however, and there can be little doubt that the wages of *ouvriers coiffeurs* had lost considerable ground since the 1920s. All these figures must be offered with the qualification that different localities had different wage structures, and we can never know what proportion of salons actually applied the agreed-upon *salaires*. Neither can we be sure of the impact of tips on the total wage. Still, the comparisons are striking. Taking the wage agreements concluded in 1920 and 1936, and comparing them in real terms against the wage schedules published for 1948, we can readily see the decline. Prevailing wages of from 13.5 to 20 francs a day in 1920 would translate to between 2,435.77 and 3,608.55 francs per week in 1948. The collective convention that followed the Matignon Accords in 1936 prescribed a *salaire* of 120 francs per week for *débutants* and 300 for the most skilled workers in the best salons. This would equate to wages of 2,586.57 and 6,466.42 francs per week in 1948. (It is not clear whether these earlier figures included tips in their calculations.) The 1948 schedule called for 1,600 francs per week (2,100 including tip) for *débutants* and 2,600 francs per week (3,060 including tip) for the highest category of workers. Plainly, hairdressing workers' pay had taken a considerable tumble, even if its precise dimensions remain vague.[73]

Statistics indicate that hairdressing prices did not suffer the same compression as wages, despite *salonniers*' constant complaints that they could not make a decent profit. Prices roughly doubled between September 1946 and December 1947 and accelerated considerably thereafter, doubling again between 1947 and 1948, adding another 32 percent in 1949, and then doubling again to reach their apex in 1952, when the Pinay government finally began to gain a handle on inflation (table 9.1).[74]

Table 9.1   Index of prices in coiffure and the cost of living, 1938–1954*

	Cost of Living	Percentage Rise on		Hairdressing Prices	Percentage Rise on
Year	Index (1938 5 100)	Previous Year	Year	(1954 5 10,000)	Previous Year
1938	100	—	1938	284.3	—
1945	355	+355.0	1945	582.9	+105.0
1946	580.8	+38.9	1946	1,220	+109.3
1947	913.3	+36.4	1947	1,774	+45.4
1948	1,476.5	+61.6	1948	3,787	+113.5
1949	1,932.4	+30.9	1949	5,001	+32.1
1950	2,116.8	+0.9	1950	6,301	+26.0
1951	2,471.7	+16.8	1951	8,351	+32.5
1952	2,661.5	+0.7	1952	10,000	+19.7
1953	2,609.5	−0.2	1953	10,000**	—
1954	2,564.8	−0.2	1954	10,000**	—

* Singer-Kérel, *Coût de la vie à Paris*, 461.
** Singer-Kérel's price series does not include figures for these years.

The trend appears unmistakable, although it does not trace the lines suggested in the trade press. The hairdressing profession emerged from war and occupation with prices that had fallen substantially below the curve of the cost of living. Set against Singer-Kérel's cost of living index, which climbed by a factor of 3.55 between 1938 and 1945, and 5.81 between 1938 and 1946, prices in coiffure had risen only by a factor of 2.05 and 4.29 respectively. Comparing 1938 prices to 1954, however, yields a very different outcome. While the cost of living jumped by a factor of 25.6, hairdressing prices increased more than 35-fold. Retail prices in coiffure in 1956 were more than double their level of 1949, which was well above the average.[75] We can only conclude that by the early 1950s *salons de coiffure* were more *rentable* than they had been since the 1920s and generally well prepared to profit from France's incipient consumer revolution.

How much of this revenue would patrons pass along to their employees? This remained a persistent source of the frustration and bitterness that characterized negotiations for a new collective agreement between the SOC/FNSOC-FO and the resurgent FNC, led by the tough, determined Marcel Lamy. The collective convention signed by Lamy, Blavy, and Machelon in November 1951 called for minimum *salaires* ranging from 4,000 to 6,630 francs per week, plus the 10 percent *prime* on revenues, which would be more or less proportional to the rise in prices since 1948.[76] The settlement turned out to be too generous for the taste of the FNC congress, which subsequently rejected the accord. But it suggests the acceptable parameters for the *salaire minimum vital*.

On the whole, wages in coiffure neither surged forward nor suffered any notable erosion through the 1950s. They continued to rise through the following decade, while still leaving *ouvriers coiffeurs* among the lowest-paid *salariés*. Statistics published by the Institut national de la statistique et des études économiques (INSEE) in 1952 provide a sense of how hairdressers' wages compared to those of other working men in Paris. In 1951, coiffeurs' hourly wages ranged from seventy-four francs for the lowest category of *assistants* to over 122 francs for the highest. Their average hourly wages surpassed those of watchmakers, navies, roofers, brick makers, glaziers, painters, masons, and stonecutters. They trailed those of quarriers and sculptors, and fell well below the global average wage. Overall, wages in the sector of *hygiène* rose almost sixfold from 1946 to 1956, although this still left hairdressing workers slightly below the average.[77] Between 1958 and 1963, *salaires* increased by another 71 percent. But this once again put *ouvriers coiffeurs* near the bottom of the table.[78] In sum, *ouvriers coiffeurs* do not seem desperately disadvantaged, compared to many of their working-class mates, although that depended heavily on their place in the hierarchy of professional skill.

If the new Republic generally encouraged higher wages, it showed less enthusiasm for reducing the length of the workweek. Wartime difficulties had cut hours in the salons considerably, but public authorities after 1945 were committed to restoring prewar work schedules as soon as the supply of raw materials allowed. As the economy recovered, therefore, salon schedules began to return to the longer hours—from forty-five in Paris up to fifty-two in rural parts of the country—established in the 1937 agreement, which remained formally in force.

Gradually and unevenly, the battle between workers, who called for "forty hours' wages for forty hours' work," and the *patrons*, who did not want to pay employees for *heures creuses*, found its resolution in the progressive "modernization" of the workday. Beginning in the big salons in the cities, where routines had always been more "rational," workers increasingly opted for *la journée continue*. This allowed them to work from 10 a.m. to 6 or 6:30 p.m., with only a half-hour for a light meal at lunch. The slower pace of life made the *journée continue* less practicable in the provinces where, opponents argued, the abbreviated workday "would inconvenience the clientele."[79]

If hairdressing workers lost the abridged schedule of the war years, they nonetheless retained the forty-eight hour "weekend" that the Production Ministry had prescribed in December 1943, as a means to save electricity. As it so often happened, however, new regulations opened the door to disputes over exactly how to apply them. Workers generally favored schedules giving them all day Sunday and Monday off, while many *salonniers* preferred to stay open Sunday morning, and the "grands salons du Centre de Paris" wanted their staffs to work Monday afternoon. In the end, the profession came to a practical resolution that effectively extended the earlier compromise over the implementation of the *repos hebdomadaire*. Depending on clientele and commercial needs, some salons closed all day Sunday and Monday; others from Sunday noon until Tuesday 2 p.m. In either case, from 1954 to 1963, the average work week in the hairdressing profession fell from 42.6 to 42.2 hours, which gave *ouvriers coiffeurs* one of the shortest work weeks among the three dozen sectors surveyed by the INSEE.[80]

In sum, the hairdressing profession gives the impression of decent good health into the 1960s. The number of *effectifs* increased by 22.5 percent between 1954 and 1963, while rising demand provided enough work for everybody.[81] On the other hand, renewed prosperity did little to alter the commercial structure of the profession. In 1959, proprietors in almost 55 percent of the 55,765 *établissements* still worked alone. In another 40 percent, they worked with one or two *assistants*. All in all, 99 percent of *salons de coiffure* had five or fewer employees. Only five *maisons* in the whole country had more than fifty-one.[82]

The dominance of petty commerce points to the stubborn fact that an *assistant*'s wages would never yield a comfortable living, except in the fanciest salons. The surest path to professional satisfaction and economic stability still lay in becoming a *salonnier*. Fortunately, a *salon de coiffure* remained a relatively cheap route into the *petit patronat*. Thus, even as *les trentes glorieuses* transformed the country and the profession itself adapted to the New France, coiffure remained what it had been since the fin-de-siècle: the sheerest part of the fabric that separated the *salariat* from the petty bourgeoisie.

* * *

It should be evident by now that if hairdressers managed to overcome many of their problems and work their way toward a measured prosperity, they remained prisoners of a market defined by *distinction* and the general state of the economy. All the negotiating skill, all the solidarity and political will in the world counted for little when women had no money to spend or when fashion told them not to spend too much of it on their hair.

The perspective for coiffure was grim as hairdressers looked from the Liberation to the future. The hardships of occupation had pushed the art of hairdressing to the brink of extinction. Indeed, if the war had produced any emblematic hairstyle, it was the shaved heads of "horizontal collaborators" and concentration-camp prisoners. Most others merely looked tatty—dressed in old *ersatz*, in wooden-soled shoes and sheepskin overcoats. Hair was in no better condition than clothes. Returning to France after his wartime sojourn in the United States, Antoine was shocked by what he saw: "hair stringy and dirty, ponytails fit only for the bathroom and the sports field."[83] In 1945, several of France's great designers put together a brilliantly conceived and expertly executed exhibition of dolls dressed in miniature couture, to tour the world and propel France "back into the international fashion market."[84] The exhibition was an artistic success, but its scale only emphasized the country's deep impoverishment.

Undeterred, France's most eminent *hauts coiffeurs* greeted the Liberation with efforts to resuscitate hair fashion and reassert their expertise. In 1945, Albert Pourrière founded the Syndicat de la haute coiffure française. Uniting the elite of Paris hairdressers, the Syndicat organized national and international *concours* in order to showcase new talent and popularize the most profitable styles. Pourrière and his colleagues also worked to coordinate efforts among all elements of the fashion business, especially the renascent *haute couture*.

This collaboration bore perhaps its richest fruit when Guillaume coifed the models for Christian Dior's landmark "New Look" collection of 1947. The "conspicuous extravagance" of Dior's clothes, while so much misery still prevailed, offended many. Nonetheless, the long and "froufroutantes" dresses—"a nostalgic voyage back to elegance," Dior called his collection—that graced the runway that February day turned the fashion world on its head.[85] Guillaume's work, meanwhile, made sure that that head was dressed with medium-short, intensely worked hairstyles. *Petite tête*, as the new shape was called, definitively buried the long, relatively *flou* styles of the war years.

Guillaume worked with the House of Dior for the next sixteen years. He also dressed the models for the shows of other great couturiers—Givenchy and Balenciaga, to name two—remaining convinced throughout that the *petite tête* lent women their most elegant and attractive profiles. Guillaume was not alone in this conviction, and *petites têtes* quickly became the new orthodoxy in coiffure. Hairstyles did not return to the ultrashort lengths of the 1920s, and they gave full rein to fantasy. In its February 1947 issue, the same month the "New Look" captured public attention, *Vogue* magazine featured advice from several of Paris's best-known coiffeurs. They recommended medium-short hair, with just enough of a perm to hold a *mise en plis* (pin curls), brushed into long supple waves, with combs to hold stray locks in place for daytime. In the evening, postiches, braids, and chignons, adorned with diadems of flowers or little "plumes" of hair transformed "la petite coiffure en jour" into something special. Fashion and hairdressing magazines repeated these admonitions countless times throughout the 1950s.

The great advantage of the *petite tête* was that it gave women, in Rambaud's phrase, "une allure plus jeune." It was also relatively easy to maintain "at the maximum of [its] healthy and brilliant form."[86] In 1952, the "Amphore" cut was the big hit. It was superceded by the *ligne Panache* with its allusion to the plume of Shako, worn by cadets at Saint-Cyr; then by the "Corolla," shaped like an upside-down tulip, and the "Fronde" and "Nouvelle Fronde," which gave women a "slightly mutinous air."[87]

Têtes became even more *petites* as the decade progressed. The *coupe garçonnière* returned with the short cuts of singer/dancer Zizi Jeanmaire. For his directorial debut, *Breathless* [*A' bout de souffle*], Jean-Luc Godard brought his lead actress, Jean Seberg, to Rosy and Maria Carita. The severe *garçonne* that they gave her reduced Seberg to tears but also helped make her, for a tragically short time, a star.[88] Increasingly, suppler *mise en plis* replaced permanent waves, to achieve a more practical, sporty, and apparently more vegetal effect. The "Artichoke," with its layers of overlapping curls, depended on the new hairsetting technique perfected by the Carita sisters, who set wet hair in horsehair rollers of different sizes, giving their coiffures extra volume. The "Cabbage" looked back to models worn by Mary Queen of Scots and Catherine de Medici.[89]

The *petite tête* did not reign unchallenged through the 1950s, however. The great hairdressing artists also offered their clients the "full-bodied glamour" of longer, more voluminous styles. Jacques Dessange, for one, launched his career with the "Choucroute" cut that he piled high on the head of the nubile Brigitte Bardot. This and other big styles were made possible by the introduction of aerosol hairspray that made it possible to raise natural hair to unprecedented heights— and keep it there—in teased bouffants. The various versions of the "Beehive," which were often stuffed with pads and finished off with wigs, falls, and other bits of artifice, marked the literal apex of Big Hair.

The master of these baroque creations was Alexandre "de Paris."[90] Florentine by background, born in Saint-Tropez in 1922, Alexandre had been hired as an apprentice in Antoine's salon in Cannes at the age of fifteen, at five francs a day. He soon became famous for his "egg shampoos." Beating six or seven eggs, adding a measure of rum and working it in with his fingertips, Alexandre left his customers' hair exceptionally silky and shiny. By 1939, his talent had earned him a place in fashionable Riviera society, whose influential contacts served him well under the occupation. His well-to-do customers often paid him in eggs, milk, and chickens. And it was rumored that, when the STO threatened to deport him in 1943, Alexandre was rescued by Madame de Saint-Julien, who sneaked him into a hospital in Draguignan to work as a nurse.

After the war, Alexandre fell under the patronage of the Duchess of Windsor, who prevailed upon Antoine to bring her protégé to Paris, and the young artist moved quickly into the upper reaches of Parisian society. He worked in the Carita salon until 1957, then opened his own exquisite shop on the avenue Montaigne. As his career took off, Alexandre came to count women such as Elizabeth Taylor, Sophia Loren, Greta Garbo, Jacqueline Kennedy among his celebrated clients, alongside Windsors and Rothschilds, Princess Grace of Monaco, and the queens of Thailand, Jordan, and Morocco. Like his friend and colleague, Guillaume, Alexandre became a perennial at the shows of the premier designers: Carven, Chanel, Saint-Laurent, Givenchy, Dior.

Alexandre was only the best known of a new generation of *hauts coiffeurs* who joined the old timers in restoring French hairdressing to preeminence in the 1950s. Right behind him were Fernand Aubry, who made his reputation with his "Second Empire" styles; Louis Gervais, whose early death only enhanced his legend; and Albert Pourrière, the indefatigable organizer of haute coiffure. Jacques Dessange, who was to revolutionize the business of hairdressing, arrived in Paris in 1946 from a small village in the Loir-et-Cher. He found his first job in the salon of Jules, hairdresser to the National Assembly at the Palais Bourbon. Dessange then moved on, becoming *assistant* then artistic director for Gervais. In 1954 he opened his own salon, capturing *le tout Paris* with his "relaxed, jeans-and-permanent style" of coiffures.[91]

The only women to crack this tight-knit elite of *hauts coiffeurs* were the Carita sisters, Rosy and Maria. Born in Toulouse, of Catalan parents, the sisters began their careers with a salon in their home town, before moving to Paris to join the team chez Gervais and finally opening their own salon on the rue faubourg-Saint-Honoré, which eventually employed more than two hundred people. There, in the heart of fashionable Paris, the sisters created the sophisticated wigs, chignons, and hairdos that became their trademark. They became the favorite coiffeuses of French cinema, working closely with such directors as Vadim, Fellini, Hassein, Resnais, and Bresson, and giving their signature hairstyles to such stars as Mireille Mathieu, Catherine Deneuve, Jeanne Moreau, Simone Signoret, Sabine Azéma, and of course Jean Seberg.[92]

By way of contrast, throughout the 1950s, men's styles remained, as they had long been: short, conservative, and largely barren of profitable opportunities. The long-haired looks of Zazous and existentialists touched relatively few men and passed quickly. For the most part, the men of the Fourth Republic kept their lips and chins clean. They spent hundreds of millions of francs on shaving supplies, but barbershops got only a small piece of this huge commerce. The handful of men's salons that could offer deluxe services at premium prices to an elite male clientele naturally continued to prosper. In the middle of the decade, George Hardy gave *coiffure masculine* a small boost when he introduced the "razor" cut and managed to persuade his clients to accept hair dryers, permanents, and a shampoo with each—although his campaign for *teinture* proved less successful. In the latter part of the decade, some young men began to wear the "Duck's Tail" (pompador), made popular by James Dean, Elvis Presley, and in France, by Johnny Hallyday. All in all, the barbering profession persisted in its long decline.

Even *haute coiffure* saw its fortunes teeter in the 1960s, as the postwar generation began to reject not merely the styles, but the entire ethic of high fashion. It seemed too formal, too "done," too . . . old. Yves Saint-Laurent famously proclaimed the death of haute couture. Brigitte Bardot dismissed it as being "for grandmothers." Elaborate coiffures fell victim to the same turnabout in values and sensibilities: less teasing, less hairspray, less stuff.

Perhaps most vexing to French coiffeurs, the winds of this generational change blew not from Paris but from London, where Vidal Sassoon had authored the "wash 'n blow dry revolution," building his formidable reputation by "redefining the 1920s bob for the 1960s audience."[93] Sassoon's "asymmetric" and "five-point" cuts became part of the "Mod" look associated with Mary Quant's miniskirts. They depended on conceptual audacity and skill with a scissors, not volume and ornamentation. And they became the standard of the 1960s generation, as the bob had been the ensign of the 1920s. From Carnaby Street to the Latin Quarter, and in that inscrutable way that new fashions always capture the public's fancy, the new attitude of casual youthfulness pushed the old formality aside once again.[94]

By the end of that remarkable decade, even though *haute coiffure* survived in certain corners of the fashion world, principally at couture shows and artistic competitions, convenience and practicality had become the hallmark of most women's everyday hairstyles. A second trend finished the process of democratization that had begun before World War I. Where the dominant styles of the Belle Epoque had been determined in the workshops and salons of the great designers, presented to high society, and finally passed down the social scale, modern fashions increasingly got their start in the "street," among the young and hip. The sixties inverted the traditional flow of fashion.

Whether they left with a bouffant *à la Jackie Kennedy* or an up-to-date bob, French women visited the hairdressing salons in almost constantly increasing numbers for the twenty-five years following the war. A trip to the coiffeur was already "anchored in the social practices and consumer habits" of *françaises* by the end of the 1940s. Some frontiers remained to be conquered, of course. In the deepest parts of the countryside, women still wore their hair pulled back in the black "cravate" of the *pays*. Young girls kept their hair in braids, often decorated with velour ribbons and barrettes, or ponytails, with a trip to the hairdresser only on the most special occasions.[95] Yet throughout the "trente glorieuses," estimates Catherine Gavend, French women made ever-more-frequent trips to their coiffeurs—from once every five weeks in 1949 to once every three in 1969—and the supply of salons rose to meet the demand.[96]

An indeterminate mix of factors accounts for this evolution in social practice. For one thing, modern sensibilities led people to pay more attention to personal hygiene, and this dictated clean hair. Every generation of experts in the last 100 years has recommended cleaner hair than the last one, spurred by the multiplication of hair-care products. L'Oréal created the first true shampoos in the 1930s, and in the 1950s, the shampoo practice really took hold in France—although French habits lagged behind British and German. French women not only began to use it more regularly at home, they made *le shampooing* a standard part of their treatment at the beauty salon.[97]

This was possible because rising family incomes allowed women to splurge a bit on their pleasures. A pleasant and sociable morning at the coiffeur became merely one element in a general expansion of consumer spending, along with automobiles, refrigerators, telephones, vacations, televisions, and the like. Women were encouraged in this activity by a growing media, especially by the women's magazines whose stories and images sought to define the up-to-date woman of postwar France. At the high end of the social scale, French *Vogue* restarted publication in 1945, despite very severe shortages of paper and other publishing necessities.[98] More important to the growth of a mass market was the expansion of a *presse féminine* aimed at middle- and working-class young women. The first issue of *Elle* appeared in November 1945. *Elle* conceived itself as a magazine for young women with "more ideas than money," whose taste ran to *prêt-à-porter* rather than couture.[99] Other women's magazines soon emerged, aimed at similar slices of the French market. *Marie-France* was born in 1944 out of the wartime resistance group, "rue de Lille." *Marie-Claire*, launched in 1937 by Jean Prouvost, the publisher of *France-Soir*, reappeared in 1954 as an "inexpensive, prestigious monthly." The monstrous publicity that accompanied this event helped the magazine sell out the 500,000 copies of its first issue within hours. *Mademoiselle*, with its more explicit appeal to trendy young women, began publication in 1962.[100]

Hairdressing salons exploited these developments by offering eager consumers an ever-expanding array of products and services. Predictably, L'Oréal led the field, spinning off its best-selling shampoo, "Dop," into "Dop-crème" (1949) and "Baby-Dop." Its Oréol Régé introduced hair conditioner to France in 1951. "Régé Color," launched in 1952, helped propel the "massification" of hair coloring in France. The company followed with a new setting lotion, "Plix," in 1955. In 1957, it began to sell the hairspray, "L'Oréal Net," through the salons. Three years later it brought out "Elnett," for the general public. "Kérastase," a "beautifying" shampoo, joined the L'Oréal line of beauty-care products in 1964. Each of the French manufacturers— Gallia-Eugène, Perma, and the newly franchised brands—trailed closely behind in the race for this flourishing market.[101]

The authors of *Coiffure 46* noted that more than 80 percent of elegant *françaises* were already coloring, bleaching, or highlighting their hair in 1946.[102] This sounds like a considerable overestimation. In any event, over the next twenty years, the hair-color habit spread across all elements of French society, particularly as youthfulness became more valued and the technology of *teinture* continued to improve. By the end of the 1950s, vegetable-based hair dyes and the dangerous *para*, had all but vanished from the salons. *Analine* became the chemical of choice.[103] Blonde tints were as popular as ever. But while the early 1950s saw a new crop of platinum blondes—Marilyn Monroe, Anita Ekberg, Jayne Mansfield—taste gradually turned to softer colors, like "Dutch blonde" and "heather."

No other new product generated more concern among hairdressers than the "cold" perm that hit the French market after the war. L'Oréal introduced its brand, L'Oréole, in 1945. Perma and Gallia soon brought out their own versions.[104] The advantage of the *permanente froide* was that it cooked hair at a much lower temperature: 100–120 degrees centigrade, as opposed to the 250–300 degrees of the old process. Thus, it was much safer for clients and produced, at least according to those *hauts coiffeurs* who endorsed it, a less frizzy, more natural wave.[105]

Yet hairdressers greeted the "cold" perm with ambivalence. It was *too* easy, *too* safe. Given the right instructions, clients could do it themselves at home, and the loss of the permanent-wave business threatened to cost salons up to 50 percent of their revenue. Pourrière reassured coiffeurs. Women, he predicted, would be put off by the mess and unpredictability of home perms and would soon find their way back to the salons.[106] But the general feeling among hairdressers was less sanguine, and they consistently opposed the sale of cold-perm kits direct to the public. The communist CSO condemned the "permanente à domicile" as the thin end of the American capitalist wedge, aimed at destroying the French economy. But even the usually more sober FNC declared "total war" on this imperialist invasion.[107]

Some of the more enterprising hairdressing establishments took advantage of the unprecedented demand for attractiveness by transforming themselves into *instituts de beauté*, where they offered a gamut of beauty regimens—manicures, pedicures, facials—and often for men as well as women. At the same time, the best-known coiffeurs began to cash in on their reputations by franchising their names. This was not completely new. Between the wars, Antoine had licensed salons under his name in American Department Stores and marketed his own line of beauty products. So had René Rambaud. But the 1960s and 1970s saw a huge expansion in the scale of this practice. Jacques Dessange was the pioneer, closely pursued by Jacques-Louis David, Jean-Claude Biguine, and other operations: Mod's Hair, Vog Coiffure, Saint Karl, Hair Coif. By the mid-1990s, some thirty franchise groups were doing more than five billion French francs worth of business. The Dessange empire alone had 550 salons across the globe, employing 5,200 and coifing 30,000 people a day. If the *quartiers* and *banlieues* remain the province of neighborhood beauty shops, today's *centre villes* are full of sleek, well-appointed salons named Dessange, David, and Biguine.[108]

The evolution of the hairdressing profession in the 1960s also transformed the principal organizations of coiffeurs in profound ways. The FNC now spends considerably less time than the UF and CPC used to wrestling the workers' syndicats. Instead, it devotes the great majority of its energies to promoting new fashions, coordinating *formation professionelle*, and organizing *concours*. These efforts now culminate every year in the Mondial Coiffure Beauté. Heir to the old Fête Marcel first held in 1922, the Mondial, hosted until his death in 1988 by François Magnien, is an international *spectacle* that brings tens of thousands of hairdressers together in Paris with customers and manufacturers, whose money heavily underwrites the event, as it does so much contemporary activity in coiffure.[109]

Workers' syndicalism has likewise lost its partisan edge. By the 1960s, the workforce in coiffure had become overwhelmingly female. Since *coiffeuses* and *syndicats ouvriers* had never shown much interest in one another, the latter became ever smaller and less important. The FNCEP-FO today continues to negotiate with the FNC over wages and working conditions, and thereby to set standards for the trade. But the old spark of class warfare is gone. No one could imagine saying, as Michelle Perrot did about the turn of the last century, that coiffeurs' fiery words and penchant for violence placed them among the most volatile elements of the working class. In this respect, too, the salon de coiffure measures the distance that France traveled in a century.

"The master": Marcel at work

Conclusion

The history of the hairdressing profession illustrates nothing so well as the hard realities of life in petty commerce. At the beginning of the twentieth century, employees in *salons de coiffure* worked pitiless hours for wages that placed them near the bottom of the *métiers masculins*. Most employers were hardly better off. Working alone or with one or two *assistants*, the *patron* had to be in his shop whenever it was open. If he made more money than his *garçons*, it was not much more, and he faced the same desperate need for a bit of leisure.

Sometimes, individual struggles for advantage only added to the general misfortune: barbers who worked long hours at low prices in order not to lose business to competitors; workers who accepted low wages and egregious schedules merely to keep a job. The coalescence of trade unions of both *ouvriers* and *patrons* in the 1890s made the battle for a better life an increasingly collective enterprise. But without much discipline and in the face of a tough market, progress came slowly.

As labor history, there is much in coiffure that is familiar: the collision between those who paid wages and those who earned them, the passion of the few and the apathy of the many, the tension between the language of revolution and the practice of moderation, the back-and-forth from schism to *rassemblement*. Between the two *tendances* of radicalism and reformism, it is hard to say that one was dependably more effective than the other. What is certain is that by the 1960s support for a workers' revolution had all but disappeared among *ouvriers coiffeurs*.

The *petits patrons* who dominated the commerce of coiffure likewise adopted positions and tactics proverbial to students of the petty bourgeoisie. They insisted on the virtues and social utility of "smallness" and attacked the liberal economic system that sanctioned ruinous competition. Hairdressers seldom used the discourse of corporatism, but they borrowed generously from its store of ideas, hatching plan after plan to save their *métier* by restricting access and establishing a price floor.

If *ouvriers* and *patrons coiffeurs* frequently fought one another, their profession was also distinguished by an extraordinary degree of comprehension between them and their frequent collaboration on matters of mutual concern—a consequence both of the common passage from employee to *petit salonnier* and of their shared interest in restraining competition in order to raise the standard of living in the salons. When their own labors came up short, the search for ways to discipline an adverse market often led hairdressers to the halls of government, looking for legislation and administrative action that would close the profession to new entrants, enforce minimum prices, and limit work schedules.

The state satisfied some of these demands and disappointed others. The National Assembly imposed the *repos hebdomadaire* and the eight-hour day, and public authorities repeatedly helped to set wage rates. The government dispatched labor inspectors to keep an eye on small businesses. It is hard to gauge the efficacy of these inspectors, spread thinly across the great number and variety of *entreprises*. The most we can say for sure is that the documents indicate a certain diligence. And workers who could not get satisfaction from the labor inspectors could always take their cases to the Conseils des Prud'hommes for mediation.

On the whole, *ouvriers* received a more sympathetic hearing from the state than *petits patrons*, for while public authorities were ready to regulate relations between employees and employers, they consistently refused to interfere in the *liberté du commerce*. The *pouvoirs publics* might therefore limit the number of hours an *assistant* could work or require his employer to give him Sunday off. But they were not prepared to stop new salons from setting up, tell *salonniers* when they could keep their own shops open, or enforce any minimum prices on *gens du métier*.

The years of national emergency and foreign occupation from 1939 to 1947 provide the principal exception to this rule. The Daladier government forbade the opening of *any* new business without official authorization, as a way to protect those who were called to military service. Likewise, the Laval government imposed a forty-eight hour *repos hebdomadaire* on coiffure in 1943 so as to conserve electricity. Both the Etat Français and the Liberation responded to the shortage of basic goods with wage and price controls.

For the most part, these policies were a response to dislocation and did not represent any deviation in economic philosophy. Yet the Pétain regime also contained elements with an ideological objection to liberal economics, particularly among so-called corporatists, who were more interested in preserving vulnerable parts of the *classes moyennes* than in protecting the commercial freedom. This antiliberal instinct found expression in the *famille professionnelle*, which, even though it was built on a base of syndicates, had ambitions to set itself up as a sort of *corporation des coiffeurs*, by asserting its control over such fundamental matters as training, access, and prices. In the end, what Magnien and his comrades hated about corporatism was not that it favored corporate autonomy, but that it wanted to hand authority within the corporation back to the *maîtres*. In any case, Vichy inclined toward more *étatiste* solutions to the social question.

After the war, the new regime was ready to extend the frontiers of *solidarité*, by granting *ouvriers coiffeurs* a *salaire minimum vital*. But it backed off setting wages and prices as soon as it dared. And while it imposed a minimum level of professional skill on practitioners with the 1946 law on *maîtrises* and *brevets professionnels*, the Fourth Republic was not willing to go much further in suppressing commercial liberties.

Exceptionally, one group of coiffeurs argued not for more state interference in professional affairs but for less. This was the relatively small group of elite *salonniers*, who enjoyed a moneyed clientele with a taste for luxury that made them all but exempt from worries about falling prices. A step down the professional hierarchy from international stars like Antoine and Guillaume, this group included businessmen like Marcel Bagnaud, owner of a fancy salon in the *seizième*, and Jean Ricaud, proprietor of a chain of "hairdressing factories." Coming together over the years in various organizations—the Syndicat indépendant, the SPC, and the CPC—these *gros* patrons worked to keep government *out* of the salons. Not surprisingly, they also comprised the right-wing of coiffeurs, setting themselves against social reform from the *repos hebdomadaire* to the Popular Front and mixing with the likes of the Action française.

It is one of the great ironies of the class struggle, however, that profitable salons run by the enemies of labor invariably offered better working conditions than sympathetic employers with revenue troubles. In the three-way contest between workers, *petits patrons*, and *gros salonniers* ideological affinities often united the first two, while employees' interest in higher wages and shorter schedules attracted them to the richer salons. Conversely, employer solidarity sometimes fell victim to contradictions between those who feared the free market and those who lived by it.

This survey of work and business in coiffure leads to three principal conclusions. First, social struggle in the hairdressing trades bore only partial resemblance to the axiomatic contest between labor and capital, as generations of historians have described it. The normal friction between owners and workers was lubricated in coiffure by the proximity and accessibility of the *patronat*, which was full of people who had once been on the other side of the wage divide. This did not inevitably make them generous bosses, but it did give them a sensitivity to working conditions that employers in *grosses enterprises* were unlikely to share. Conversely, workers who had before them countless examples of social promotion could never consider the barrier between labor and property to be insurmountable. This identification of hairdressing workers with their trade and their patrons, rather than with an oppressed class, looks even more powerful among the *coiffeuses*, who replaced men in the salons as the century proceeded. If the hairdressing profession had its share of revolutionaries, therefore, they did not receive the same sympathetic hearing as in sectors where employers and employees lived in separate worlds. And many of them were simply absorbed into the shopkeeper class.

Second, the period between the 1890s and the 1960s saw an indisputable improvement in working conditions in this poor corner of petty commerce. Wages did not rise steadily. They went up dramatically in the 1920s, hit a long slump between the onset of the depression and the 1950s, then advanced again. Even as *ouvriers coiffeurs* were lifted out of working poverty, their profession never offered them a generous living, save for those highly-skilled *artistes* who worked in the salons *hors classe*. Nonetheless, there can be no denying that life in the salons was vastly better in 1960 than it had been in 1900.

What is true of wages is even truer of the work week. By the 1960s, *ouvriers coiffeurs* were spending half as many hours behind their *fauteuils* as they had during the *fin-de-siècle*, when *assistants* had labored eighty or even ninety hours a week, 350 days a year. By the 1960s, enjoying a more or less forty-hour work week and the whole French array of paid vacations and *fêtes nationales*, hairdressing workers were able to participate fully in society.

Third, these improvements did not stem chiefly from the prodigious energies expended by hairdressers' own organizations and syndicates throughout this period. Yes, their collective efforts attained some modest success in intimidating recalcitrant patrons or stimulating government intervention in professional affairs. At the end of the day, however, conditions within coiffure depended almost entirely on the market for hair care. It was not professional solidarity that rescued coiffeurs from the vicious circle of overpopulation, low prices, low wages, and long hours, but the evolution of fashion and the expansion of modern consumer culture.

The shift from *coiffure-hommes* to *coiffure-dames*, which brought with it an enormous increase in the demand for coiffure and unimagined opportunities for revenue, is the single most important element in the history of the hairdressing profession. It has its roots in a complex series of developments that by the 1920s sent unprecedented numbers of women flocking to the *salons de coiffure*, where they paid considerable sums to have their hair cut, shampooed, frizzed, colored. The habit grew stronger and weaker over the following decades, depending on economic circumstances and, to a lesser extent, on fashion. But once the greater French public acquired a taste for "done" hair, it never lost it.

The rise of *coiffure pour dames* was no isolated process. It was intimately bound up with the femininization, democratization, and "youthification" of consumption that engulfed France as it did other urban, industrial societies in the 1920s and directly linked to the vogue for women's short hairstyles. A careful dissection of the *garçonne*, or any of the other versions of the bob, yields a treasury of insights into the historical moment. Shampoos tell a story of changing standards of hygiene and urban reconstruction that brought hot water into homes and shops. Permanent waves illustrate the progress of chemistry, electricity, industrial manufacture, and commercial distribution. The proliferation of beauty salons implies the existence of women with disposable income and the freedom to spend it. The intensity and reach of the new hairstyles point to the growing influence of magazines and films.

The obvious symbolic richness of fashion, in general, and of hairstyles, in particular, has excited a lot of casual analysis regarding the "meaning" of it all. Recall the glib commentaries that praised or damned the *garçonne* as the expression of women's emancipation. At a more academic level, cultural critics have often tried to go further in their deconstruction and to "read" even deeper meaning into the forms of fashion. Roland Barthes is only the most prominent of those who have deployed quite formal and complex systems for historicizing fashion.[1] But the experience of French hairdressing suggests that such speculative excursions, while they might be stimulating, do not make good history. For while hairstyles are undoubtedly full of information about the women who wear them and the society in which they are worn, the forms themselves appear to be both empty and free floating. They do not contain any reliably deducible *signification*. Just as Emile Long tied *cheveux* courts to the Russian Revolution, Grant McCracken has written that the Big Hairstyles of the 1950s were the embodiment of "subservient, domesticated femininity."[2] Yet it seems to me that in a world where suffragettes wore bulky chignons and *débutantes* sported *garçonnes*, there can be no easy correspondence between the hairstyle and the message.

The capriciousness of popular fashions suggests even more strongly the danger of loading too much meaning on to individual hairdos. To their despair, coiffeurs discovered that they could neither predict nor control women's taste in coiffures. They could sail with the prevailing wind or try to tack against it, but the public soul remained enigmatic. Hairdressers probably worried more about this than they needed to, because what really counted was *not* whether the moment favored long or tight waves, high chignons or low, whether the public pulse quickened for the "Ange" or the "5-points cut." This or that style might make individual fortunes. But what mattered to the profession as a whole was how much money women were spending on their hair. This is what permitted commerce to prosper and incomes to rise. And this is where we find the primary significance of the history of coiffure: not in the changing seasons of fashion but in the steady rise of mass consumer culture.

Notes

Preface

1. See Leo Charney and Vanessa R. Schwartz, *Cinema and the Invention of Modern Life* (Berkeley: Univeristy of California Press, 1995); W. Scott Haine, *The World of the Paris Café: Sociability Among the French Working Class, 1789–1914* (Baltimore: Johns Hopkins University Press, 1996); Priscillia Pankhurst Ferguson, *Accounting for Taste: The Triumph of French Cuisine* (Chicago: University of Chicago Press, 2004); Kolleen Guy, *When Champagne Became French: Wine and the Making of National Identity* (Baltimore: Johns Hopkins University Press, 2003); Stephen Harp, *Marketing Michelin: Advertising and Cultural Identity in Twentieth-Century France* (Baltimore: Johns Hopkins University Press, 2001); Kathleen Kete, *The Beast in the Boudoir: Petkeeping in Nineteenth-Century Paris* (Berkeley: University of California Press, 1994); Philippe Perrot, *Fashioning the Bourgeoisie: A History of Clothing in the Nineteenth Century* (Princeton: Princeton University Press, 1994); Kristin Ross, *Fast Cars, Clean Bodies: Decolonization and the Reordering of French Culture* (Cambridge, MA: MIT Press, 1995); Wolfgang Schivelbusch, *Tastes of Paridise: A Social History of Spices, Stimulants, and Intoxicants* (New York: Pantheon, 1992); Vanessa R. Schwartz, *Spectacular Realities: Early Modern Mass Culture in Fin-de-Siècle France* (Berkeley: University of California Press, 1998); Rebecca Spang, *The Invention of the Restaurant: Paris and the Modern Gastronomic Culture* (Cambridge, MA: Harvard University Press, 2000); and Susan J. Terrio, *Crafting the Culture and History of French Chocolate* (Berkeley: University of California Press, 2000); Christopher Thompson, *Between Myth and Modernity: A Cultural History of the Tour de France Bicycle Race* (Berkeley: Univerisity of California Press, 2006). Although they do not deal with France, also see Elizabeth Haiken, *Venus Envy: A History of Cosmetic Surgery* (Baltimore: Johns Hopkins University Press, 1997); Neil McKendrick, John Brewer and J.H. Plumb, *The Birth of a Consumer Society: The Commercialization of Eighteenth-Century England* (Bloomington: Indiana University Press, 1982); and Kathy Peiss, *Hope in a Jar: The Making of America's Beauty Culture* (New York: Metropolitan Books, 1998).

2. For one of the few studies of petty commerce see Isabelle Bertaux-Wiame, *Transformations et permanence de l'artisanat boulanger en France*, 2 volumes (Paris: Maison des Sciences de l'Homme, 1978).

3. For a small sample: Pierre Balmain, My Years and Seasons (Garden City, NY: Doubleday and Co., 1965); Pierre Boulat, *Yves Saint-Laurent: Naissance d'une légende* (Paris: Martinière, 2002); Jérôme Picon, *Jean Lanvin* (Paris: Flammarion, 2002); and Elsa Schiaparelli, *Shocking Life* (New York: Dutton, 1954).

I   The Rise of *Coiffure pour Dames*

1. Richard Corson, *Fashions in Hair: The First Five Thousand Years* (London: Peter Owen, 1965), 682; Gisèle d'Assailly, *Fards et beauté. Ou l'éternel féminin* (Paris: Hachette, 1958), 331–2; also Robin Bryer, *The History of Hair: Fashion and Fantasy Down the Ages* (London: Philip Wilson, 2000), 59.

2. A. Chantoiseau, *Le coiffeur et la chevelure* (Paris: Ulysse Boucoiran, 1936), 2–3; Wendy Cooper, *Hair: Sex, Society, Symbolism* (New York: Stein and Day, 1971), 165–6; Paul Gerbod, "Les métiers de la coiffure en France dans la première moitié du XXe siècle," *Éthnologie Française* (1983): 39; Jody Shields, "Images," *Vogue* (July 1990), 77.

3. Fernand Braudel, *Capitalism and Material Life, 1400–1800* (New York: Harper, 1973), 241.

4. Cooper, *Hair*, 95; Corson, *Fashions in Hair*, 354.

5. M. Louis, *Six Thousand Years of Hair Styling* (New York: M. Louis, 1939), 57.

6. Bill Severn, *The Long and the Short of It: Five Thousand Years of Fun and Fury over Hair* (New York: David McKay and Co., 1971), 68, 71, 73–4.

7. Severn, *The Long and Short of It*, 112.

8. René Rambaud, *Les fugitives. Précis anécdotique et historique des coiffeurs féminines à travers les âges, des Egyptiens à 1945* (Paris: René Rambaud, 1947), 109–10; also Lois Banner, American Beauty (New York: Alfred A. Knopf, 1983), 210. For a pictorial history of hairstyles see Archives de Paris, D 29 Z 78, *Catalogue illustrée des coiffeurs, exposées par l'Académie école française, au Palais du Costume, du Henri II à nos jours* (Paris: L'Académie de Coiffure, 1900).

9. Rambaud, *Les fugitives*, 203.

10. Eugen Weber, *France: Fin-de-Siècle* (Cambridge: Harvard University Press, 1986), 60.

11. *Hairdressers Weekly Journal. Supplement* [hereafter cited as *HWJS*] (June 1917), 146.

12. Weber, *France*, 97. Also see René Koenig, *Sociologie de la mode* (Paris: Petite Bibliothèque Payot, 1969), 12; Pierre Bourdieu, *Distinction: A Social Critique of the Judgment of Taste* (Cambridge: Harvard University Press, 1984); and Thorsten Veblen, *The Theory of the Leisure Class: An Economic Study of Institutions* (Boston: Houghten Mifflin, 1973).

13. Jane Mulvagh, *Vogue's History of Twentieth-Century Fashion* (London: Viking, 1988), 2–3. On the elite resorts see Charles Rearick, *Pleasures of the*

Belle Epoque: Entertainment and Festivity in Turn-of-the-Century France (New Haven: Yale University Press, 1985), 159.

14. Raymond Rudorff, *Belle Epoque: Paris in the Nineties* (London: Hamish Hamilton, 1972), 83.

15. Antoine [Antek Cierplikowski], *J'ai coiffé le monde entier* (Paris: La Table Ronde, 1963), 87–8.

16. Antoine was celebrated enough to have a play written about his life, later turned into two films, entitled *Coiffeur pour dames* (*French Touch*, in their American release): Charles Graves, *Devotion to Beauty: The Antoine Story* (London: Jarrold's, 1962), 40; and Catherine Lebas and Annie Jacques, *La coiffure en France du Moyen Age à nos jours* (*Paris: Delmas International*, 1979), 278.

17. *Votre Beauté* (April 1933), 31. For a lesson in excessive hairstyles see A. Mallemont, *Manuel de la Coiffure des Dames* (Paris: E. Robinet, 1898), 51.

18. *HWJS* (January 1912), 10; R. Turner Wilcox, *The Mode in Hats and Headdresses* (New York: Charles Scribner's Sons, 1946), 276.

19. Paul Gerbod, *Histoire de la coiffure et des coiffeurs* (Paris: Larousse, 1995), 210–11.

20. Caroline Cox, *Good Hair Days: A History of British Hairstyling* (London: Quartet Books, 1999), 20. For discussions of hairstyles during the Belle Epoque generally see Joyce Asser, *Historic Hairdressing* (New York: Pitman Publishing, 1966), 110–3; and Jean Keyes, *A History of Women's Hairstyles*, 1500–1965 (London: Methuen, 1968), 55.

21. Weber, *France*, 97.

22. Mulvagh, *Vogue's History*, 5–6; Valerie Steele, *Fashion and Eroticism: Ideals of Feminine Beauty from the Victorian Era to the Jazz Age* (New York: Oxford University Press, 1985), 218–22.

23. *Vogue* (September 1924), 16; Valerie Steele, *The Corset: A Cultural History* (New Haven: Yale University Press, 2001); Leigh Summers, *Bound to Please: A History of the Victorian Corset* (Oxford: Berg, 2001).

24. Bonnie G. Smith, *Ladies of the Leisure Class: The Bourgeoises of Northern France in the Nineteenth Century* (Princeton: Princeton University Press, 1981), 80.

25. Antoine, *J'ai coiffé*, 56; Alfred Spale, *Manuel de Coiffeur* (Paris: Librairie J.-B. Baillière et Fils, 1933), 170.

26. *HWJS* (May 1913), 77.

27. *HWJS* (September 1915), 129.

28. *Coiffure de Paris* (January 1923), 1.

29. *Figaro-Modes. A la ville-au théâtre-arts décoratives* (January 1904), 23.

30. *HWJS* (November 1918), 161.

31. See Long's articles in the *HWJS* (August 1913), 114; and (June 1916), 82; *Coiffure Française Illustrée* (June 1914), 10; also 38; Rambaud, *Les fugitives*, 144–5.

32. Theodore Zeldin, *France, 1848–1945*, vol. *II: Intellect, Taste and Anxiety* (Oxford: Clarendon, 1977), 441; also see Marie-Christine Auzou and Sabine Melchior-Bonnet, *Les vies du cheveux* (Paris: Gallimard, 2001), 43–5.

33. A. Coffignon, *Les coulisses de la mode* (Paris: La Librairie Illustrée, 1888), 40–4.

34. *Journal de la Coiffure* (July 1903). Similar scenes can be found in Frances Trollope, *Summer in Brittany*, quoted in Severn, *The Long and the Short*, 110.

35. Weber, *France*, 88.

36. The *Sun* quoted in *Journal de la Coiffure* (September 1903).

37. Pierre-Jakez Hélias, *The Horse of Pride: Life in a Breton Village* (New Haven and London: Yale University Press, 1978), 221.

38. André Bardet, *Technologie de la coiffure* (Paris: Dervy, 1950), 175; *Cheveux Courts* (July 1931), 3; André Gissler, *Technologie de la coiffure pour dames et messieurs* (Paris: Dunod, 1955), 12; Rambaud, *Les fugitives*, 93; and idem, *L'ondulation bouclée. Trois méthodes d'ondulation en une seule* (Paris: Société d'Éditions Modernes Parisiennes, 1949), 46–7.

39. Quoted in Cox, *Good Hair Days*, 141.

40. *Capilartiste* (August 1936), 18.

41. *Guide pratique du coiffeur* (August 20, 1886), 4; Vincent Chenille, *La mode dans la coiffure des françaises: La norme et le mouvement, 1837–1987* (Paris: Harmattan, 1996), 114.

42. *Moniteur de la Coiffure* (October 1892), 6.

43. Emile Long, *Traité complet et illustré de l'ondulation artificielle des cheveux* (Paris: Albert Brunet, 1909).

44. *HWJS* (November 1918), 168.

45. *HWJS* (March 1917), 34; Antoine is quoted in Graves, *Devotion to Beauty*, 37.

46. *HWJS* (March 1916), 33.

47. *HWJS* (March 1912), 33.

48. On Victorian underwear see Judith Flanders, *Inside the Victorian Home: A Portrait of Domestic Life in Victorian England* (New York: Norton, 2004), 306–7.

49. Valerie Steele, *Paris Fashion: A Cultural History* (New Haven: Yale University Press, 1988), 226.

50. Paul Poiret, *King of Fashion: The Autobiography of Paul Poiret* (Philadelphia and London: Lippencott, 1931), 76.

51. Modris Ecksteins, *Rites of Spring: The Great War and the Birth of the Modern Age* (New York: Doubleday, 1989), 37, 48.

52. Poiret, *King of Fashion*, 76–7; and Marcel Haedrich, *Coco Chanel secrète* (Paris: Éditions Robert Laffont, 1971), 114.

53. *HWJS* (February 1910), 23; and (May 1914), 65.

54. *HWJS* (May 1920), 67.

55. *HWJS* (November 1910), 162.

56. *HWJS* (February 1912), 18.

57. *HWJS* (January 1910), 9–10.

58. *Coiffure de Paris* (August 1910), 10.

59. *HWJS* (November 1910), 162.

60. A. Coffignon, *Coulisses*, 33.

61. Quoted in Weber, *France*, 56–60; also Philippe Ariès and Georges Duby, dirs., *Histoire de la vie privée, tome V: De la Première Guerre mondiale à nos jours* (Paris: Éditions du Seuil, 1987), 96.

62. Pauline Laure Marie de Broglie, Comtesse de Pange, *Comment j'ai vu 1900* (Paris: Grasset, 1975), 86.

63. Alain Corbin, *The Foul and the Fragrant: Odor and the Social Imagination* (London: Papermac, 1996), 179–80. In the eighteenth century, powder and bran were used to clean hair: in Georges Vigarello, *Concepts of Cleanliness: Changing Attitudes in France Since the Middle Ages* (Cambridge: Cambridge University Press, 1988), 19 and 83.

64. Cited in Auzou and Melchior-Bonnet, 56.

65. Cox, *Good Hair Days*, 172.

66. Weber, *France*, 60.

67. Antoine, *J'ai coiffé*, 92–3.

68. Cox, *Good Hair Days*, 33–5.

69. *HWJS* (June 1913), 90; also M. Joyeux, "Le gaz chez les coiffeurs: Ce qui nous amène à vous parler des salons de coiffure," extract from *Journal des Usines de Gaz*, April 5–20, 1936, 5–8.

70. Weber, *France*, 80; C. Kauffmann et J. Barth, *Le livret du coiffeur. Technologie* (Paris: Librairie d'Enseignement Technique, 1923), 101; Georges-Lévy, *Hygiène du cuir chevelu et de la chevelure* (Paris: G. Doin, et Cie., 1934), 12.

71. *Coiffure de Paris* (July 1925), 17.

72. Quoted in Corson, *Fashions in Hair*, 494.

73. *Coiffure de Paris* (October–November 1909), 14; *Journal de la Coiffure* (February 1904). On "para" also see Georges-Lévy, *Hygiène*, 100–1; *Journal de la Coiffure* (March 1902); and Edwin Sidi and R. Longeville, *Les accidents par produits capillaires. Étude clinique, expérimentale et medico-légale* (Paris: Éditions Médicales Flammarion, 1958), 25–6.

74. On the beginnings of L'Oréal see International Directory of Company Histories, vol. III, Adèle Hast, *Health and Personal Care Products-Materials* (Chicago, London: St. James Press, 1991), 46; Michèle Ruffat, *175 Years of French Pharmaceutical Industry: History of Synthélabo* (Paris: La Découverte, 1996), 195–6.

75. *Hebdo-Coiffure* (July 22, 1939).

76. *Coiffure de Paris* 119 (January 1920), 6; also Lebas and Jacques, *Coiffure en France*, 310.

77. On hairdryers see Joyeux, *La gaz chez les coiffeurs*, 5; and Spale, *Manuel du coiffeur*, 119–20. On the electric curler see Rambaud, *Les fugitives*, 133.

78. *Figaro-Mode* (May 1904), 17; Spale, *Manuel de coiffeur*, 405; Cooper, *Hair, Sex, Society*, 177.

79. J. Auzary, *Notions de technologie générale pour l'apprenti coiffeur pour dames* (Paris: Éditions Eyrolles, 1954), 69.

80. Mrs. Robert Henrey, *Madeleine Grown Up* (London: J.M. Dent and Sons, 1952), 39.

81. *HWJS* (January 1913), 25.

82. Rambaud, *Les fugitives*, 168–9.

83. *Hairdressers' Weekly Journal* (March 1909), 435, my emphasis.

84. Cox, *Good Hair Days*, 143; also see Esther Picard and Vivianne Jacot-Descombes, *La coiffure à travers les siècles* (Paris: Éditions de l'Artisanat Moderne, 1973), 50.

2   The Poorest of Trades

1. Richard Corson, *Fashions in Hair: The First Five Thousand Years* (London: Peter Owen, 1965), 561.
2. Information on hairdressers' population and demography comes from A. Coffignon, *Les coulisses de la mode* (Paris: La Librairie Illustrée, 1888), 24; Charles Desplanques, *Barbiers, perruquiers, coiffeurs* (Paris: Libriarie Octave Doin, 1927), 215; Ministère du Commerce, de l'Industrie, des Postes et des Télégraphes. Office du Travail, *Les associations professionnelles ouvrières, tome IV* (Paris: Imprimerie Nationale, 1904), 771; idem, *Résultats statistiques du recensement des industries et professions, tome I* (Paris: Imprimerie Nationale, 1896), 296–7; and *tome IV* (Paris: Imprimerie Nationale, 1901), 254–44.
3. Corson, *Fashions*, 561.
4. Paul Gerbod, *Histoire de la coiffure et des coiffeurs* (Paris: Larousse, 1995), 198.
5. *Le Journal*, August 28, 1906. On the city's working geography and its evolution see Anthony Sutcliffe, *The Autumn of Central Paris: The Defeat of Town Planning, 1850–1970* (London: Edward Arnold, 1970), 276–9; and Alain Metton, *Le commerce et la ville en banlieue parisienne* (Courbevoie: Alain Metton, 1980), 269–71.
6. On the history of facial hair see Fernand Braudel, *Capitalism and Material Life, 1400–1800* (New York: Harper, 1973), 241–2; Wendy Cooper, *Hair: Sex, Society, Symbolism* (New York: Stein and Day, 1971), 93; Reginald Reynolds, *Beards: Their Social Standing, Religious Involvements, Decorative Possibilities, and Value in Offence and Defence Through the Ages* (Garden City, NY: Doubleday & Co., 1949), 146; and Charles de Zemler, *Once Over Lightly: The Story of Man and His Hair* (New York: Charles de Zemler, 1939).
7. Bill Severn, *The Long and Short of it: Five Thousand Years of Fun and Fury over Hair* (New York: David McKay Co., 1971), 118.
8. Le Rappel (March 16, 1900), "Chez les Coiffeurs"; *Petit Parisien* (April 3, 1907).
9. Georges Bailly, *Guide pratique pour bien se raser* (Paris: G. Bailly, 1933), 7.
10. Georges Mallet, *Théorie de la barbe, ou comment il faut se raser* (Paris: Editions Midlik, 1928).
11. C. Kauffmann et J. Barth, *Le livret du coiffeur. Technologie* (Paris: Librairie d'Enseignement Technique, 1923), 95, 101; Corson, *Fashions*, 561.
12. Fédération nationale des syndicats des ouvriers coiffeurs, "Compte-rendu complet des travaux du 1er congrès national des syndicats ouvriers des coiffeurs de France," Lyon, September 3–5, 1894, 27–28, manuscript available in the collection of the Institut de l'histoire sociale at the offices of the Confédération générale du travail [hereafter cited as CGT]; also J. Auzary, *Notions de Technologie générale pour l'apprenti coiffeur pour dames* (Paris: Éditions Eyrolles, 1954), 11.
13. Corson, *Fashions*, 561.

14. See the remarks of Dr. Larroussinie, speaking to a group of the Chambre syndicale des patrons coiffeurs, reported in the *Journal de la Coiffure* (May 1903).

15. Alfred Spale, *Manuel du Coiffure* (Paris: Librairie J.-B. Baillière et Fils, 1933), 8.

16. Cited in *Journal de la Coiffure* (April 1904).

17. See the report by M. Baumont, president of the Société de secours mutuels de coiffeurs Saint-Louis, cited in Ministère du Commerce, *Associations professionnelles*, tome IV, 747–8; also A. Lenormand, *Le devoir pour tous: Aux ouvriers coiffeurs de Paris. Première réponse à nos détracteurs* (Paris: Imprimerie du Proletariat, 1889).

18. For information on barbers' wages around the turn of the century see Coffignon, *Coulisses de la mode*, 25–6; Desplanques, *Barbiers*, 215, 241; Gerbod, *Histoire*, 173; Ministère du Commerce, *Associations professionnelles*, tome IV, 771; *Petite République* (November 25, 1896), article by Albert Goullé; Archives of the Prefet de Police, Paris [hereafter cited as PP] Ba 1419, 2000–278A: Police report of March 24, 1904.

19. Ministére du Commerce, de l'Industrie, des Postes et des Télégraphes. Conseil Supérieur du Travail. Commission permanente, *Rapports et documents sur la réglementation du travail dans les bureaux et les magasins et dans les petites industries de l'alimentation* (Paris: Imprimerie Nationale, 1896), 42–3.

20. Other surveys show the same results: see Ministére du Commerce, de l'Industrie, des Postes et des Télégraphes. Direction du Travail, *Salaires et durée du travail dans l'industrie français, tome III: Industries du bois, tabletterie, métaux-travail des pierres et des terres-Ets. De l'Etat ou des communes dans les départements autre que ceux de la Seine* (Paris: Imprimerie Nationale, 1895), 624–5; and idem, *Bordereaux des salaires pour diverses catégories d'ouvriers en 1900 et 1901* (Paris: Imprimerie Nationale, 1902), 162–7.

21. Archives of the Fédération nationale de la coiffure, de l'esthétique et de la parfumerie de France—Force Ouvrière [hereafter cited as FNCEP-FO], Histoire Coiffure, 1894–1934, FNSOC, "Compte-rendu, 1894," 17, 36; Ministère du Commerce, *Rapports et documents sur la réglementation du travail* (1901), 42–43.

22. Archives Nationales, Paris [hereafter cited as AN], F^7 13693, "Coiffeurs: Activité syndicale, 1905–1924," dossier "Coiffeurs, 1913"; FNCEP-FO, Histoire Coiffure, 1894–1934, FNSOC, "Compte-rendu, 1894," 45–6.

23. Coffignon, *Coulisses*, 27–8; *Le Rappel* (March 24, 1900), "Chez les coiffeurs."

24. For wages in coiffure pour dames see Coffignon, *Coulisses*, 33; Desplanques, *Barbiers*, 216; *Petite Republique* (November 18, 1896), article by Albert Goullé.

25. *Le Rappel* (March 16, 1900), "Chez les coiffeurs."

26. *Le Matin* (March 4, 1907); *Humanité* (October 9, 1921).

27. Peter Stearns, *Revolutionary Syndicalism and French Labor: A Cause Without Rebels* (New Brunswick: Rutgers University Press, 1971), 55. Gary Cross suggests that the hairdressers' situation was far from unique. A large segment of the working population, especially in the retail sector and out in the

provinces, remained subject to a sixty- or seventy-hour week into the 1920s, Gary Cross, *A Quest for Time: The Reduction of Work in Britain and France, 1840–1940* (Berkeley: University of California Press, 1989), 147.

28. On the exceptionally long hours in *coiffure* see Ministère du Commerce, *Salaires et durée du travail*, 1895, 624–5; idem, *Rapports et documents sur la reglementation du travail*, 1901, 42–3; and idem, *Bordereaux des salaires*, 1902, 162–7. Also see Desplanques, *Barbiers*, 221–2; CGT, FNSOC, Compte-rendu du Ve congrès national, Orléans, September 1–3, 1903, manuscript, 18; idem, *Compte-rendu des travaux du 7e congrès national des ouvriers coiffeurs, Marseille, 12–15 October 1908* (Bourges: Imprimerie Ouviere du Centre, 1909), 41. Caroline Cox tells a tale of a 12-year old "lather boy" in England driven to attempt suicide by overwork, *Good Hair Days: A History of British Hairstyling* (London: Quartet Books, 1999), 67.

29. *Journal de la Coiffure* (May 1902).

30. *Journal de la Coiffure* (May 1903); Ministère du Commerce, *Associations professionnelles ouvrières*, 760; *Petite République* (November 18, 1896), article by Albert Goullé.

31. See, for example, Richard Butsch, ed., *For Fun and Profit: The Transformation of Leisure into Profit* (Philadelphia: Temple University Press, 1990); Stephen G. Jones, *Workers at Play: A Social and Economic History of Leisure, 1918–1939* (London: Routledge and Kegan Paul, 1986); Kathy Peiss, *Cheap Amusements: Working Women and Leisure in Turn-of-the-Century New York* (Philadelphia: Temple University Press, 1986); and Susan Pennybacker, *A Vision for London, 1889–1914: Labor, Everyday Life and the LCC Experiment* (London: Routledge, 1995).

32. See Albert Goullé's article in *Petite République* (November 22, 1896).

33. Quoted in Catherine Lebas and Annie Jacques, *La coiffure en France du Moyen Age à nos jours* (Paris: Delmas International, 1979), 58.

34. See the police reports for April 27, 1899 and June 30, 1899 in PP B[a] 1419 2000–278.

35. Letter of July 22, 1902, in PP B[a] 1419 2000–278A.

36. On the history of coiffeurs' organizing see A. Chantoiseau, *Le coiffeur et la chevalure* (Paris: Ulysse Boucoiran, 1936), 1–2; Paul Gerbod, "Les coiffeurs en France (1890–1950)," *Le Mouvement Social* 114 (January–March 1981), 71; and Vince Staten, *Do Bald Men Get Half-Price Haircuts? In Search of America's Great Barbershops* (New York: Simon and Schuster, 2001), 45–9.

37. *HWJS* (January 1916), 2.

38. On the formation of the CSO see Desplanques, *Barbiers*, 180–9; Ministère du Commerce, *Associations professionnelles*, 764–81; Lenormand, *Le devoir pour tous*; and an untitled and undated manuscript history of syndical history in coiffure, written by long-time militant Louis Clauzade that undoubtedly dates from the end of his career, in the 1970s, found in FNCEP-FO, Histoire syndicale de la coiffure.

39. On the origins of the Fédération nationale, see CGT, *La Confédération générale du travail et le mouvement syndical* (Paris: Presses de la Fédération syndicale internationale, 1925), no page numbers; Desplanques, *Barbiers*, 191–2; FNCEP-FO, Histoire Coiffure, 1894–1934, FNSOC, "Compte-rendu,

1894," 8; and Ministère du Commerce, *Associations professionnelles*, 788–95.

40. On syndicalism in small business generally see Jeanne Gaillard, "La petite entreprise entre la droite et la gauche," in Georges Lavau, Gerald Grunberg, Nonna Mayer, dirs., *L'univers politique des classes moyennes* (Paris: Presses de la Fondation Naitonale des Sciences Politiques, 1983), 66.

41. PP Ba 1419 2000–278, report of March 27, 1903.

42. Bruce Vandervort, *Victor Griffuelhes and French Syndicalism, 1895–1922* (Baton Rouge: Louisiana State University Press, 1996), 66.

43. For biographies of Luquet see AN F⁷ 13693, "Coiffeurs, 1905–1924," report "Alexandre Luquet (1874–): Police report, 1902–1909"; Jean Maitron, dir., *Dictionnaire biographique du mouvement ouvrier français, troisième partie: 1817–1914, De la Commune â la grande guerre, tome XIII* (Paris: Les Éditions Ouvrières, 1976), 322; Barbara Mitchell, *The Practical Revolutionaries: A New Interpretation of the French Anarcho-Syndicalists* (New York: Greenwood, 1987), 69; and the police note in PP Ba/1686 2000–1095–5: "Au sujet de la CGT," March 1907; and Bᵃ 1419 2000–278, police report of November 28, 1902.

44. On Luquet's rocky relationship with Merrheim see Nicholas Papayanis, *Alphonse Merrheim: The Emergence of Reformism in Revolutionary Syndicalism, 1871–1925* (Dordrecht: Mirtinus Nijhoff Publishers, 1985), 37–8.

45. Stearns, *Revolutionary Syndicalism*, 22.

46. On this episode and Luquet's role in it see Mitchell, *Practical Revolutionaries*, 11–24; Vandervort, *Victor Griffuelhes*, 95–7. On revolutionary syndicalism generally, see the historiographical essay by Steven C. Hause, "The Evolution of Social History," *French Historical Studies* (Fall 1996), 1194–6; also see Katherine E. Amdur, *Syndicalist Legacy: Trade Unions and Politics in Two French Cities in the Era of World War I* (Urbana: University of Illinois Press, 1986), 5–6; Michael Seidman, *Workers Against Work: Labor in Paris and Barcelona During the Popular Fronts* (Berkeley: University of California Press, 1991); and Kenneth H. Tucker, *French Revolutionary Syndicalism and the Public Sphere* (Cambridge: Cambridge University Press, 1996).

47. For an excellent assessment of strike activity in France see Gerald C. Friedman, *State-Making and Labor Movements: France and the United States, 1876–1914* (Ithaca: Cornell University Press, 1998); and idem, "Revolutionary Unions and French Labor: The Rebels Behind the Cause; or, Why Did Revolutionary Syndicalism Fail?" *French Historical Studies*, 20:2 (Spring 1997): 155–81.

48. Ministère du Commerce, *Résultats statistiques, tome I*, 296–7 and 352–3; *tome III*, 473 and 497; *tome IV*, 254–5. Ministère du Travail. Statistique Générale de la France, *Résultats statistiques du recensement général de la population effectué le 5 mars 1911, tome I* (Paris: Imprimerie Nationale, 1913): France Entière, 27–8; *tome II* (1915), Paris, 8; *banlieue*, 21; Lot, 575; Gironde, 591. Also Marcel de Ville Chabrol, "La concentration des entreprises en France avant et depuis la guerre," *Bulletin de la statistique générale de la France et du service d'observation des prix*, XXII (April–June 1933), 439.

254   Notes

49. The phrase comes from an article by René Rambaud in *L'Humanité* (April 1, 1913). On young workers' enthusiasm and indiscipline see Michelle Perrot, *Les ouvriers en grève: France, 1871–1890, tome II* (Paris: Mouton, 1974), 593.

50. FNSOC, *Compte-rendu des travaux du 7e congrès national des ouvriers coiffeurs, Marseille*, October 12–15, 1908 (Bourges: Imprimerie Ouvrière du Centre), 31.

51. Ministère du Commerce, de l'Industrie, des Postes et des Télégraphes. Direction du Travail. *Statistique des grèves et des recours à la conciliation et l'arbitrage survenus pendant l'année 1900* (Paris: Imprimerie nationale, 1901), 264–5 and 451; likewise see Ministère du Commerce, *Statistiques des grèves*, 1904, 356–9; and ibid., 1905, 315.

52. PP B^a 1419 2000–278, police report, June 24, 1899; *Journal de la Coiffure* (May 1903).

53. PP B^a 1419 2000–278, police report, August 8, 1899.

54. PP B^a 1419 2000–278, police report, August 4, 1899.

55. Madeleine Guilbert, *Les femmes et l'organisation syndicale avant 1914: Présentation et commentaires de documents pour une étude du syndicalisme féminin* (Paris: Éditions du CNRS, 1966), 28, 185–89; Sylvie Schweitzer, *Des engrenages à la chaîne: Les usines Citroën, 1915–1935* Lyon: Presses Universitaires de Lyon, 1982; also Marie-Hélène Zylberberg-Hocquard, *Féminisme et syndicalisme en France* (Paris: Éditions Anthropos, 1978), 197.

56. Patricia Hilden, *Working Women and Socialist Politics in France, 1880–1914: A Regional Study* (Oxford: Clarendon Press, 1986), 242. Also see Geoff Eley, *Forging Democracy: The History of the Left in Europe, 1850–2000* (New York: Oxford University Press, 2002), 100.

57. C. Bougle, *Syndicalisme et démocratie: Impressions et réflexions* (Paris: Edouard Cornély et Cie., 1908), 132.

58. The word is Laura Levine Frader's, "Women and French Unions: Historical Perspectives on the Current Crisis of Representation," in Herrick Chapman, Mark Kesselman, and Martin Schain, eds., *A Century of Organized Labor in France: A Union Movement for the Twenty-First Century* (New York: St. Martin's, 1998), 145. On the difficult history of women in craft guilds see Elizabeth Musgrave, "Women and the Craft Guilds in 18th-Century Nantes," in Geoffrey Crossick, ed., *The Artisan and the European Town, 1500–1900* (Aldershot, UK; Brookfield, VT: Scholar Press, 1997), 151–71.

59. On women's hesitation to join unions see Theresa McBride, "French Women and Trade Unionism: The First Hundred Years," in Norbert C. Solden, ed., *The World of Women's Trade Unionism: Comparative Historical Essays* (Westport, CT: Greenwood Press, 1985), 35–56 passim.

60. AN F^7 13693, "Coiffeurs, 1905–1924: Coiffeurs, 1914–1918"; FNCEP-FO, Histoire Coiffure, 1894–1934, FNSOC, "Compte-rendu, 1894," 13–4; Ministère du Commerce, *Associations professionnelles*, 788–90; PP B^a 1419 2000–278, police report on the CSO meeting of March 17, 1896.

61. On the difficulty of characterizing the class politics of artisans see Geoffrey Crossick, "Past Masters: In Search of the Artisan in European History," in Crossick, ed., *The Artisan*, 1–3. Also see useful discussions of "class"

in Ronald Aminzade, "Class Analysis, Politics and French Labor History," in Leonard R. Berlanstein, ed., *Rethinking Labor History* (Urbana: University of Illinois Press, 1993), 92–5; and Gérard Noiriel, *Workers in French Society in the 19th and 20th Centuries* (Oxford: Berg, 1990), xii. For misplaced characterizations of the "petty bourgeoisie's" sense of social inferiority and commitment to Property and Order see Maurice Bouvier-Ajam and Gilbert Mury, *Les classes moyennes sociales en France, tome II* (Paris: Éditions Sociales, 1963), 303; and Roger Price, *A Social History of Nineteenth-Century France* (London: Hutchinson, 1987), 141–2.

62. *Petite République* (November 22, 1896), article by Albert Goullé.
63. On Mornot see *Coffure de Paris* (September 1923), 27; *Journal de la Coiffure* (April 1903) and (June 1903); PP Bª 1419 2000–278, police reports of March 17, 1896; April 27, 1899; May 17, 1899; and September 4, 1900; and Union fédérale des patrons coiffeurs, *Compte-rendu du Xe Congrès National*, Nantes, August 20–22, 1928 (Paris: Imprimerie Parisiennes Réunies, 1929), 5.
64. On Chauvin's life and career see the obituary in the *Capilartiste* (June 1936), 15; and *Coiffure de Paris* (March 1920), 8–9.
65. *Coiffeur Confédéré* (April 1933).
66. *Journal de la Coiffure* (April 1903).
67. Diana de Marly, *Fashion for Men: An Illustrated History* (London: B.T. Batsford, 1985), 97; also G. Sorignet, *Manuel du coiffeur pour hommes* (Paris: E. Robinet, 1894), 79.
68. PP Bª 1419 2000–278, police report on a meeting of coiffeurs, June 23, 1899.
69. Paul Nogues suggested the following treatment for his bourgeois clients: a shampoo and careful cut, followed by the process of "singeing"—burning the end of the hair. The barber rubbed off the burnt ends with bits of antiseptic paper. The treatment continued with recombing, rebrushing, again recombing, this time with a very fine-toothed comb, and brushing off the customer's neck. Then a second friction, wiping, and a "thorough application of *brillantine*." Hair could then be styled *à l'américaine* or curled in a *demi-bombé* (with the brush) or a full *bombé* (with the iron): *HWJS* (April 1911), 53–6. For all the meticulous service, we might as well be in a fashionable *salon pour dames*.
70. Lebas and Jacques, *Coiffure en France*, 254.
71. *Le Rappel*, "Chez les coiffeurs" (March 16, 1900).
72. *Journal de la Coiffure* (May 1902). On prices see Ministère du Travail et de Prévoyance Sociale, *Salaire et coûts d'existence*, 44–5, 53.
73. On the CSP's founders A. Mallemont and Hector Ledoux see Mallemont, *Manuel de la Coiffure des Dames* (Paris: E. Robinet, 1898); also Ledoux's obituary in *Coiffure de Paris* (December 1935), 57.
74. AN²² 364, letter of December 24, 1910; Archives de Paris 1070 W, carton 13, dossier 2534, "Syndicat Indépendant des Patrons Coiffeurs de Paris (1909)"; and *Coiffure de Paris* (October–November 1909), 16.
75. PP Bª 1419, police reports of March 10, 1897 and October 4, 1901.
76. *Le Temps* (October 30, 1903), "Une bagarre à la Bourse du Travail."
77. *Voix du Peuple* (October 30, 1903).
78. Desplanques, *Barbiers*, 204.

79. AN F⁷ 13693, "Coiffeurs: Activité syndicale, 1905–1924," dossier "Coiffeurs, 1905–1912"; PP Ba 1419 2000–278, police reports of November 22 and 24, 1904; *Le Soleil* (November 24, 1904).

80. Cited in Gerbod, *Histoire*, 199. On the Fédération des Commerçants-Détaillants, see FNSOC, *Compte-rendu des travaux du VIIe congrès national des ouvriers coiffeurs, Marseille, 12–15 October 1908* (Bourges: Imprimerie Ouvrière du Centre, 1909), 32; Nonna Mayer, *La boutique contra la gauche* (Paris: Presses de la Fondation Nationale des Sciences Politiques, 1986), 103; and *Petite République* (July 14, 1907).

81. On the Fédération nationale des patrons coiffeurs see Lebas and Jacques, *Coiffure en France, 54, Le Journal* (October 15, 1912); and *Petit Parisien* (September 15, 1911).

82. On Boucoiran and the Fédération française des patrons coiffeurs see *Coiffure de Paris* (October–November 1909), 12; Gerbod, *Histoire*, 199; Hector Ledoux and Elie Etienne, *Méthode pratique de coiffure masculine et d'ondulation. Le parfait salonnier et ondulateur* (Paris: Éditions Ulysse Boucoiran, 1930), frontispiece.

83. This section rests on documents from the following collections: AN F⁷ 13693, "Coiffeurs: Activité syndicale, 1905–1924"; AN F²² 364 and 365, "Repos hebdomadaire, 1906–1935: Coiffure"; and PP Ba 1419 2000–278 and 2000–278A. For a general study of the new law see Gaston Bonnefoy, *Le repos hebdomadaire: Étude théorique et critique de la loi du 13 juillet 1906 avec la jurisprudence la plus récente* (Paris: Imprimerie Typographique A. Davy, 1907); and Ministère du Travail et du la Prévoyance Sociale, *Rapports sur l'application des lois réglementant le travail en 1906* (Paris: Imprimerie Nationale, 1907), ii–iii.

84. Paul Aubriot, *Les dérogations ou repos collectif du Dimanche* (Paris: Librairie Félix Alcan, 1914), 20.

85. *Éclair* (April 26, 1906).

86. *Petit Parisien* (May 9, 1906) and (May 11, 1906); Cross, *Quest for Time*, 102.

87. Letter from A. Reynaud, of the Syndicat philanthropique des patrons coiffeurs de la banlieue to labor inspector Capaduara, August 24, 1909 for Marseille, in AN F²² 365.

88. AN F²² 364, "Repos hebdomadaire, 1906–1935: Coiffure," letter to the labor minister, February 26, 1908; also see *Humanité* (February 20, 1908).

89. AN F²² 364, letters from the prefect of police to the labor minister: May 26, 1908; December 4, 1908; and December 29, 1910.

90. PP Ba 1419 2000–278A, letter of August 28, 1907.

91. Ministère du Travail, *Rapports sur l'application des lois réglementant le travail*, 213.

92. The facts of this story emerge out of several archival collections: AN F⁷ 13693; and PP Ba 1419 2000–278 and 2000–278A.

93. *Journal de la Coiffure* (May 1903); *Humanité* (May 5, 1907) and (November 13, 1907); and *Petite République* (July 10, 1907).

94. The following figures for 1906 and 1911 come from Ville-Chabrol, "La concentration des entreprises," 133; and Ministère du Travail, *Résultats statistiques du recensement général . . . 1911*, 8, 21, 575 and 591.

95. Ministère du Commerce, *Résultats statistiques . . . 1896, tome IV* (1901), 254–5; Ministére du Travail, *Résultats statistiques, tome I* (1913), 28; and Ville-Chabrolle, "Population active," 131.

96. Ministère du Commerce, *Salaires et durée du travail, tome IV*, 1897, 341–7; idem, *Salaires et durée, tome III*, 1895, 624–5; idem, *Bordereaux des salaires*, 162–7; Ministre du Travail et de Prévoyance Sociale, *Salaires et coûts d'existence*, 122–3, 138–9, 146–7, 158–9.

97. Monique Buisson, "Histoire d'un enseignement professionnel et pratiques familiales d'orientation: Le cas de la coiffure à Lyon," in Régis Bernard, Monique Buisson, Jean Camy, Laurence Roulleau-Berger et Guy Vincent, *Education, fête et culture* (Lyon: Presses Universitaires de Lyon, 1981), 148–9.

98. *Bataille Syndical* (October 9, 1911); also Desplanques, *Barbiers*, 156.

99. G. Sorignet, *Manuel du coiffeur*, 1–6.

100. Ledoux and Etienne, *Méthode pratique*, 9–10; Kauffmann and Barth, *Livret du coiffeur*, 7–8.

101. Quoted in *HWJS* (November 1918), 164.

102. Philip Nord, *Paris Shopkeepers and the Politics of Resentment* (Princeton: Princeton University Press, 1986), remains the principle study of conditions and politics in the world of petty commerce in France. Also see Geoffrey Crossick and Heinz-Gerhard Haupt, *The Petite Bourgeoisie in Europe, 1780–1914: Enterprise, Family, and Independence* (London and New York: Routledge, 1998); and Michael J. Winstanley, *The Shopkeeper's World, 1830–1914* (Manchester: Manchester University Press, 1983).

103. See, for example, Pétrus Faure, *Histoire du mouvement ouvrier dans le département de la Loire* (St. Etienne: Imprimerie Dumas, 1956), 9–10.

3 The Bob

1. On women's work before World War I see Judith Coffin, *The Politics of Women's Work: The Paris Garment Trades, 1750–1915* (Princeton: Princeton University Press, 1996); Yvonne Delatour, "La travail des femmes pendant la première guerre mondiale et ses conséquences sur l'évolution de leur rôle dans la société," *Francia* 2 (1974), 482; and Nancy Green, *Ready-to-Wear, Ready-to-Work: A Century of Industry and Immigrants in Paris and New York* (Durham: Duke University Press, 1997).

2. Gabriel Perreux, *La vie quotidienne des civils en France pendant la grande guerre* (Paris: Hachette, 1966), 65.

3. Marilyn Boxer and Jean Quaetart, eds., *Connecting Spheres: Women in the Western World, 1500 to the Present* (New York: Oxford University Press, 1987), 193–5 and 208; Margaret Darrow, *French Women and the First World War: War Stories of the Home Front* (Oxford: Berg, 2000), 169–228; Laura Lee Downs, *Manufacturing Inequality: Gender Division in the French and British Metalworking Industries, 1914–1939* (Ithaca: Cornell University Press, 1995), 1–2; Mathilde Dubesset, Françoise Thébaud, Catherine Vincent, "Les munitionettes de la Seine," in Patrick Fridenson, dir., *1914–1918: L'Autre front* (Paris: Les Éditions Ouvrières, 1977), 192–7; James F. McMillan,

Housewife or Harlot: The Place of Women in French Society, 1870–1940 (New York: St.

Martin's Press, 1981), 117–9 and 157; Françoise Thébaud, *La femme au temps de la guerre de 14* (Paris: Stock, 1986), 172–3; Jay Winter and Jean-Louis Robert, *Capital Cities at War: Paris, London, Berlin, 1914–1919* (Cambridge: Cambridge University Press, 1997), 292–5.

4. Charles Rearick, *The French in Love and War: Popular Culture in the Era of the World Wars* (New Haven: Yale University Press, 1997), 4. On the disruption of amusement and consumption see Jean-Jacques Becker, *The Great War and the French People* (Oxford: Berg, 1985), 9–102 passim; Charles Rearick, *Pleasures of the Belle Epoque: Entertainment and Festivity in Turn-of-the-Century France* (New Haven: Yale University Press, 1985), 214; and William Wiser, *The Crazy Years: Paris in the Twenties* (New York: G K. Hall & Co., 1983), 73.

5. *HWJS* (November 1914), 161.

6. *HWJS* (September 1915), 129.

7. Quoted in Becker, *The Great War*, 95 and 135.

8. Valerie Steele, *Paris Fashion: A Cultural History* (New Haven: Yale University Press, 1988), 236; and Perreux, *La vie quotidienne*, 261.

9. From the *Bon Ton* (June 1915), quoted in Steele, *Paris Fashion*, 237; also Paul de Léon, "La semaine féminine," in *La Femme de France* (May 23, 1915)—or, indeed, virtually any number of the magazine.

10. Christobel Williams-Mitchell, *Dressed for the Job: The Story of Occupational Costume* (Poole: Blandford Books, 1982), 112–4.

11. Jane Mulvagh, *Vogue's History of Twentieth-Century Fashion* (London: Viking, 1988), 45.

12. Steele, *Paris Fashion*, 240–1.

13. On corsets see Béatrice Fontanel, *Corsets et soutiens-gorge: L'épopée du sein de l'Antiquité à nos jours* (Paris: Éditions de la Martilères, 1992), 91; and Valerie Steele, *The Corset: A Cultural History* (New Haven: Yale University Press, 2001).

14. *HWJS* (February 1917), 18–9; and (November 1916), 162.

15. Edmonde Charles-Roux, *L'irrégulière, ou mon itinéraire Chanel* (Paris: Grasset, 1974), 226.

16. Arthur Marwick, *The Deluge: British Society and the First World War* (New York: Norton, 1965), 92.

17. *HWJS* (November 1918), 161.

18. *HWJS* (July 1917), 97–9.

19. René Rambaud, *Les fugitives. Précis anécdotique et historique des coiffeurs féminines à travers les âges, des Egyptiens à 1945* (Paris: René Rambaud, 1947), 204.

20. On the population of hairdressers see Paul Gerbod, *Histoire de la coiffure et des coiffeurs* (Paris: Larousse, 1995), 198; Ministère du Travail. Statistique générale de la France, *Résultats statistiques du recensement général de la population effectué le 5 mars 1911: tome I* (Paris: Imprimerie Nationale, 1913), 28; *tome II* (1915), 8, 21, 575; idem, *Résultats statistique du recensement de la population effectué le 6 mars 1921, tome I* (Paris: Imprimerie Nationale, 1923), 51 and 148–9; *tome II* (1925), 1–8, 76–8.

21. *Coiffure de Paris* (November 1920), 9; FNCEP-FO, Congrès Fédéral, "Fédédration Nationale, 1er congrès national, August 24–26, 1925," intervention by André Langlois (no page numbers); M. Joyeux, "Le gaz chez les coiffeurs: Ce qui nous amène à vous parler des salons de coiffure," *Journal des Usines de Gaz* (August 5–20, 1936), 4.
22. Arvet-Thouvet and Robert D., *De la psychologie dans le salon de coiffure pour dames* (Paris: S.E.I.D., no date), 12.
23. AN F^{22} 1955, "Famille Professionnelle-Hygiène," Hector Malacarne, "L'ère nouvelle et les coiffeurs," an unsolicited book manuscript sent to the labor minister à propos of the Labor charter, May 1942, 38.
24. *Coiffure de Paris* (January 1920), 12–3; A. Mallement, *Manuel de la coiffure des dames* (Paris: E. Robinet, 1898), ii; Pierre de Rieucros, *Comment se faire une clientèle et la conserver* (Paris: Éditions Art et coiffure, 1968), 3.
25. *HWJS* (November 1918), 161–2.
26. *HWJS* (November 1918), 162.
27. On the price of postiches see *La Mode Illustrée* 28 (July 1921).
28. *HWJS* (October 1917), 145–7; and (December 1917), 178.
29. *HWJS* (July 1919), 97–8; and (December 1919), 179.
30. Quoted in Susan R. Grayzel, *Women's Identities at War: Gender, Motherhood, and Politics in Britain and France During the First World War* (Chapel Hill: University of North Carolina Press, 1999), 121–2.
31. *HWJS* (September 1919), 129.
32. On the new styles see Jacqueline Herald, *Fashions of a Decade: The 1920s* (New York: Jacqueline Herald, 1991), 49; Mulvagh, *Vogue's History*, 60–5; François Thébaud, "The Great War and the Triumph of Sexual Division," in Thébaud, ed., *A History of Women in the West, vol. V: Toward a Cultural Identity in the Twentieth Century* (Cambridge: Harvard University Press, 1994), 40–1; and *Vogue* (January 1920), 72 and (March 1923), 36–7.
33. Pierre Galante, *Les années Chanel* (Paris: Éditions Pierre Charron et Mercure de France, 1972), 70.
34. Maylène Delbourg-Delphis, *Le chic et le look. Histoire de la mode féminine et des moeurs de 1850 à nos jours* (Paris: Hachette, 1981), 98.
35. Delbourg-Delphis, *Le chic*, 97.
36. Quoted in Gerbod, *Histoire*, 212.
37. Galant, *Les années Chanel*, 68; Marcel Haedrich, *Coco Chanel secrète* (Paris: Éditions Robert Lafont, 1971), 149.
38. Antoine, *J'ai coiffé le monde entier* (Paris: La Table Ronde), 108; Modris Ecksteins, *Rites of Spring: The Great War and the Birth of the Modern Age* (New York: Anchor, 1989), 259; Catherine Lebas and Annie Jacques quote Colette, *Claudine en Ménage* (1903), in *La coiffure en France du Moyen Age à nos jours* (Paris: Delmas International, 1979, 269–70; Mary Trasko, *Daring Do's: A History of Extraordinary Hair* (Paris and New York: Flammarion, 1994), 109–11.
39. *HWJS* (May 1919), 65.
40. *Livre de la Mode à Paris* (1920); and *HWJS* (April 1919), 49.
41. *HWJS* (October 1920), 145; see also *Vogue* (June 1920), 14.

42. *Coiffure de Paris* (December 1920), frontispiece. See also Esther Picard and Vivianne Jacot-Descombes, *La coiffure à travers les siècles* (Paris: Éditions de l'Artisanat Moderne, 1973), 50.

43. The phrase was coined by the fascist writer, Pierre Drieu la Rochelle and employed by Mary Louise Roberts, *Civilization Without Sexes: Reconstructing Gender in Postwar France, 1917–1927* (Chicago: University of Chicago Press, 1994).

44. From an English tract against bobbed hair, quoted in Richard Corson, *Fashions in Hair: The First Five Thousand Years* (London: Peter Owen, 1965), 615.

45. Gonzague Truc, "De l'Eglise et des Cheveux Courts," *La Grande Revue* (April 1926), 317–8; and the story in Rambaud, *Les fugitives*, 241.

46. Delbourg-Delphis, *Le chic*, 114; *Coiffure de Paris* 181 (June 1925), 17; *La Mode Illustrée* (January 30, 1921).

47. *Coiffure de Paris* (April 1924), 1; Anne Manson, "La scandale de 'la garçonne,'" in Gilbert Guilleminault, ed., *Les années folles* (Paris: Denoël, 1958), 153.

48. Victor Margueritte, *La Garçonne* (Paris: Flammarion, 1922), published in English as *The Bachelor Girl* (New York: Knopf, 1923). On *La Garçonne* see Mary Louise Roberts, "This Civilization No Longer Has Sexes: *La Garçonne* and the Cultural Crisis in France After World War I," *Gender and History* 4 (Spring 1992), 49–69; also Georges Bernier, "La Garçonne," in Olivier Barrot and Pascal Ory, eds., *Entre Deux Guerres: La Création Française, 1919–1939* (Paris: Éditions François Bourin, 1990), 154; Anne-Marie Sohn, "La garçonne face à l'opinion publique: Type littéraire ou type social des années 20," *Le Mouvement Social* 80 (1972), 3–27; Wiser, *Crazy Years*, 74. "The novel provided a stereotypical image with which various kinds of transgressive behavior by girls or young women could be aligned": Siân Reynolds, *France Between the Wars: Gender and Politics* (London and New York: Routledge, 1996), 62.

49. Manson, "La scandale," 159.

50. Manson, "La scandale," 161.

51. Louise Vanderwielen, *Lise du Plat Pays* (Lille: Presses Universitaires de Lille, 1983), 125.

52. Robert Dieudonné, "Le village des tondues," in *L'Oeuvre* (May 29, 1925). Lois Banner cites the effect of the bob on coiffure in the United States in Lois Banner, *American Beauty* (New York: Knopf, 1983), 271; also Julie A. Willett, *Permanent Waves: The Making of the American Beauty Shop* (New York: New York University Press, 2000), 35.

53. *Vogue* (March 1920), 60; also (December 1924), 16 and (February 1927), 21.

54. *Gallia Journal* (March–April 1926).

55. *HWJS* (June 1917), 88 and (March 1919), 34–5.

56. For a biographical sketch of Boudou see *Coiffeur de France* (May 1948).

57. On the Gallia see *Coiffure de Paris* (March 1925), 17; *Gallia Journal* (February 1926); Volo Litvinsky, *Toute la permanente. Tous les procédés et tours de mains* (Paris: Société d'Éditions Modernes Parisiennes, 1958), 13–4; Rambaud, *Les fugitives*, 211.

58. *Éclaireur des Coiffeurs* (July 25, 1947), 6–8, for a short biographical summary of Rambaud's career upon the occasion of his election as Officier de la Légion d'Honneur.
59. For Rambaud's biography see: AN F^7 13693, "Coiffeurs, 1913"; *Coiffure de Paris* (February 1934), 34–5; Lebas and Jacques, *La Coiffure en France*, 55 and 64; Confédération générale du travail, *La Confédération générale du travail et le mouvement syndical* (Paris: Presses de la Fédération Syndicale Internationale, 1925), no page numbers; *Éclaireur des Coiffeurs* (July 25, 1947); FNCEP-FO, Histoire Coiffure 1894–1934, "Rapports de travaux du conseil de 1902 au 3e trimestre 1917" and "1933"; Jean Maitron, dir., *Dictionnaire biographique du mouvement ouvrier français: Troisième partie: 1817–1914, De la Commune à la Grande Guerre, tome XIV* (Paris: Les Éditions Ouvrières, 1976), 338–9; and René Rambaud "Les qualités nécessaires à un coiffeur pour dames: Physiques, morales, psychologiques, techniques et artistique," conference held on November 24, 1933 at l'École de coiffure de Paris, 3.
60. *Gallia Journal* (November–December 1926); (January–February 1927); (January–February 1928); and (May–June 1928).
61. On the *mise en plis* see Fermo Corbetta, *Notions élémentaires de coiffure pour dames* (Paris: Société d'Éditions Modernes Parisiennes, 1941), 54.
62. Alfred Spale, *Manuel de Coiffure Paris*: Librairie J.-B. Baillière et Fils, 1933), 1.
63. See *Art et Coiffure* (February 1, 1928), 9; (June 1928), 5; (January 1929), 12.
64. Georges-Lévy, *Hygiène du cuir chevelu et de la chevelure* (Paris: G. Doin et Cie., 1934), 40.
65. On men's permanents see *Coiffure de Paris* (April 1932), 40; and *La Mode Illustrée* (January 16, 1921).
66. R. Louis, "Bobbed Hair," in *Coiffure de Paris* (April 1924), 17.
67. *Coiffure de Paris* (January 1935), 19; (September 1924), 17.
68. Paul Gerbod, "Les métiers de la coiffure en France dans la première moitié du XXe siècle," *Éthnologie Française* (1983), 40.
69. Archives de la Seine 16 (unclassified), Album, "Un magasin de coiffeur-parfumeur" (10, rue du faubourg Montmartre, B. Horn & J. Curtz architects/ DPLG), n.d. My thanks to archivist Philippe Grand for finding this album for me.
70. Agostini was Director of the Société Eugène, the manufacturer of the *machine à l'indéfrisable*, and winner of the *Grand Prix Marcel*. He is quoted in *Coiffure de Paris* (May 1925), 17.
71. The "embourgeoisement des apparences," Philippe Perrot called it, in *Refashioning the Bourgeoisie: A History of Clothing in the Nineteenth Century* (Princeton: Princeton University Press, 1995), 8–9.
72. Mulvagh, *Vogue's History*, 85; Kathy Peiss, "Culture de masse et divisions sociales: Le cas de l'industrie américaine des cosmétiques," *Le Mouvement Social* (July–September 1990), 15.
73. Hollander, *Seeing Through Clothes*, 339.
74. The first quote is from Valerie Steele, *Fashion and Eroticism: Ideals of Feminine Beauty from the Victorian Era to the Jazz Age* (New York: Oxford University Press, 1985), 239; the second from idem, *Paris Fashion*, 246.

75. On the American experience of "Flapper fashions" and "a carefree lifestyle," see Jane R. Plitt, *Martha Matilda Harper and the American Dream: How One Woman Changed the Face of Modern Business* (Syracuse, NY: Syracuse University Press, 2000), 103.
76. *La Mode Illustrée* (May 14, 1922); Vérone quoted in Rambaud, *Les fugitives*, 253.
77. René Koenig, "La diffusion de la mode dans les sociétés contemporaines," *Cahiers Intenationaux de Sociologie* 63 (July–December 1967), 40; also idem, *Sociologie de la mode* (Paris: Petite Bibliothèque Payot). On the dominance of older women during the Belle Epoque see *Figaro—Modes. A la ville—au théâtre—arts décoratives* (February 1904), 23.
78. Eugen Weber, *France: Fin-de-Siecle* (Cambridge: Harvard University Press, 1986), 92.
79. On consumerism among middle-class Victorians see Lori Ann Loeb, *Consuming Angels: Advertising and Victorian Women* (New York: Oxford University Press, 1994), 4.
80. *Le Temps*, October 20, 1923; Wendy Cooper, *Hair: Sex, Society, Symbolism* (New York: Stein and Day, 1971), 106. On parallel developments in the United States see Joanne J. Meyerowitz, *Women Adrift: Independent Wage Earners in Chicago, 1880–1930* (Chicago: Chicago University Press, 1988), 124–5.
81. *Coiffure et Mode* (April 1925), 15.
82. Steele, *Paris Fashion*, 247.
83. Hollander, *Seeing Through Clothes*, 313. Jean Baudrillard, one of the most frequently cited authorities in studies of culture, said that "the signs of fashion are free-floating and not grounded in the referential," which is of course a more lugubrious way of making the same point as Steele and Hollander: quoted in Shari Benstock and Suzanne Ferriss, eds., *On Fashion* (New Brunswick: Rutgers University Press, 1994), 5; also Elizabeth Wilson, *Adorned in Dreams: Fashion and Modernity* (Berkeley: University of California Press, 1985), 8–9.
84. Thébaud, "The Great War," 43; and Anne-Marie Sohn, "Between the Wars in England and France," in Thébaud, ed., *A History of Women*, 103.
85. Steven C. Hause, "More Minerva than Mars: The French Women's Rights Campaign and the First World War," in Margaret Randolf Higgonet, Jane Jensen, Sonya Michel, and Magaret Collins Weitz, eds., *Between the Lines: Gender and the Two World Wars* (New Haven: Yale University Press, 1987), 101–2; McMillan, *Housewife or Harlot*, 99; Roberts, *Civilization Without Sexes*, 84–7.
86. Kathy Peiss, *Cheap Amusements: Working Women and Leisure in Turn-of-the-Century New York* (Philadelphia: Temple University Press, 1986), 6. For similarly inverted readings of popular culture see Herbert Marcuse, *One-Dimensional Man: Studies in the Ideology of Advanced Industrial Society* (Boston: Beacon Press, 1964). Stuart Ewen lays out an analogous argument in *Captains of Consciousness: Advertising and the Social Roots of Consumer Culture* (New York: McGraw Hill, 1976). On the fashion system see W. Godfrey

Cobliner, "Feminine Fashion as an Aspect of Group Psychology: Analysis of Written Replies Received by Means of a Questionnaire," *Journal of Social Psychology* 31 (May 1950), 283–9. Also see Roland Barthes, *The Fashion System* (New York: Hill and Wang, 1983), xi–xii; idem, "Le bleu est à la mode cette année: Unités signifiantes dans le vêtement de mode," *Revue Française de Sociologie* (April–June 1960), 147–8; and Rosalind Williams, *Dream Worlds: Mass Consumption in Late Nineteenth-Century France* (Berkeley: University of California Press, 1982), 12. For a fine study of real department stores see Michael B. Miller, *The Bon Marché: Bourgeois Culture and the Department Store, 1869–1920.* For a solid discussion of consumerism for the interwar period see Ellen Furlough, "Selling the American Way in Interwar France: *Prix Uniques* and the Salons des Arts Ménagers," *Journal of Social History* (Spring 1993), 491–519. On consumers' ability to resist attempts to manipulate them see Stephen G. Jones, *Workers at Play: A Social and Economic History of Leisure, 1918–1939* (London: Routledge and Kegan Paul, 1986). He writes that, "It is clearly wrong to depict the working class as impotent consumers, having little or no say in the form and content of the leisure product," 6. We have no reason to believe that women as a group were any more impotent in this regard. For another perspective on the process of maintaining social relations, of which fashion was supposedly a key strategic element, see Pierre Bourdieu, Luc Boltanski, Monique de Saint-Martin, "Les stratégies de reconversion: Les classes sociales et le système d'enseignement," *Social Science Information*, 12 (October 1973), 61–2.

87. Kathy Peiss, "Making Up, Making Over: Cosmetics, Consumer Culture, and Women's Identity," in Victoria de Grazia, with Ellen Furlough, eds., *The Sex of Things: Gender and Consumption in Historical Perspective* (Berkeley: University of California Press, 1996), 324.

88. Nancy Green writes of the "dépotisme capricieux" of women's taste that made it difficult for manufacturers to know what they wanted: Nancy L. Green, "Art and Industry: The Language of Modernization in the Production of Fashion," *French Historical Studies* 18 (Spring 1994), 735.

89. Samra-Martine Bonvoisin et Michèle Maignien, *La presse féminine* (Paris: Presses Universitaires de France, 1986), 19–20. On the effect of cinema see Larry May, *Screening Out the Past: The Birth of Mass Culture and the Motion Picture Industry* (New York: Oxford University Press, 1980).

90. Victoria de Grazia, citing film historian Miriam Hansen, in "Empowering Women as Citizen Consumers," in De Grazia, *Sex of Things*, 281.

4   Back to the Barricades

1. On the labor movement in war Niall Ferguson, *The Pity of War: Explaining World War I* (London: Basic Books, 1999), 271–5; John H. Horne, *Labour at War: France and Britain, 1914–1918* (Oxford: Clarendon Press, 1991), 265–7. On the CGT's cooperation with the state see Jean-Pierre Le Crom, *Syndicats, nous voilà! Vichy et le corporatisme* (Paris: Les Éditions Ouvrières, 1995), 23–4.

2. John Barzman, *Dockers, métallos, ménagers: Mouvements sociaux et cultures militantes au Havre, 1912–1923* (Rouen et Le Havre: Presses de l'Université de Rouen et du Havre, 1997), 187–8.

3. See Luquet's report in FNCEP-FO, congrès fédéral, May 25–27, 1920.

4. See Pagès's correspondence with local syndicats in December 1919, in FNCEP-FO, Histoire Coiffure, 1894–1934; for the official report on strikes see Ministère du Travail, *Statistique des grèves et des recours à la conciliation et l'arbitrage survenu pendant l'année 1919* (Paris: Imprimerie Nationale, 1920), 320–3; and idem ... *pendant l'année 1920* (Paris: Imprimerie Nationale, 1921), 252–5.

5. See the various reports for 1920 in AN F^7 13866, "Coiffure."

6. On the promise of the eight-hour day see Gary Cross, *A Quest for Time; The Reduction of Work in Britain and France, 1840–1940* (Berkeley: University of California Press, 1989), 130; also Charles S. Maier, *Recasting Bourgeois Europe: Stabilization in France, Germany and Italy in the Decade After World War I* (Princeton: Princeton University Press, 1975), 77–9.

7. On the Marseille strikes see AN F^7 13866, "Coiffure"; and Ministère du Travail, *Statistique des grèves*, 1920, 254–5. Their descriptions do not quite tally on the details.

8. AN F^7 13693, "Coiffeurs, 1914–1924: Grèves"; and FNCEP-FO, Histoire Coiffure, 1894–1934, congrès fédéral, May 25–27, 1920.

9. On the founding of the Union fédérale see Congrès national des syndicats patronaux de coiffeurs-parfumeurs et industries qui s'y rattachent de France et des colonies, *Compte-rendu. Statuts de l'Union fédérale. Appel du comité, Strasbourg, 1–3 September 1919* (Paris: Imprimerie de la Coiffure Française Illustrée, 1919); also Charles Desplanques, *Barbiers, Perruquiers, coiffeurs* (Paris: Librairie Octave Doin, 1927), 150–2; Paul Gerbod, "Les coiffeurs en France (1890–1950)," *Le Mouvement Social* (January–March 1981), 78; Catherine Lebas and Annie Jacques, *La coiffure en France du moyen âge à nos jours* (Paris: Delmas International, 1979), 54.

10. *Coiffure de Paris* (February 1920), 16, quoting Georges Villette, the UF's general secretary.

11. On Boucoiran see Hector Ledoux and Elie Etienne, *Méthode pratique de coiffure masculine et d'ondulation. Le parfait salonnier et ondulateur* (Paris: Éditions Ulysses Boucoiran, 1930), frontispiece.

12. UF, *Compte-rendu du congrès*, 1919, 22. My emphasis.

13. Cross, *Quest for Time*, especially chapter six, "Labor Insurgency, International Reform, and the Origins of the Eight-Hour Day, 1917–1924," 129–49.

14. FNCEP-FO, Congrès fédéral, "1920."

15. For the workers' reaction see AN F^{22} 421, "Loi de huit heures: Coiffure"; FNCEP-FO, Histoire Coiffure, 1894–1934, "1921."

16. Villette's remarks are in *Coiffure de Paris* (December 1920), 14; also see AN F^7 13693, "Coiffeurs, 1914–1924: Grèves"; and *Coiffeur-Parfumeur* (February 15, 1923).

17. Confédération générale du travail, *Confédération générale du travail et le mouvement syndical* (Paris: Presses de la Fédération Syndicale Internationale, 1925), no page number.

18. *Coiffeur Confédéré* (December 1923).
19. See in general AN F^{22} 421 and 422, "Coiffure: Loi de huit heures"; and AN F^{22} 364, "Repos hebdomadaire, 1906–1935: Coiffure," from a letter from the labor minister to Georges Villette, February 11, 1924.
20. For official accounting of strikes in coiffure see AN F^7 13866, "Grèves en coiffure, 1919–1931"; and Ministère du Travail, de l'Hygiène et de l'Assistance et de la Prévoyance Sociale, *Statistique des grèves et des recours à la conciliation et l'arbitrage survenu pendant l'année* (Paris: Imprimerie Nationale . . . series from 1923 to 1925).
21. AN7 13693, "Coiffeurs, 1914–1924: Grèves"; and 13866, "Coiffure"; *Ouvrier Coiffeur* 49 (May 1925).
22. The following information on the strike comes from AN F^7 13866, "Paris, May 1926"; *Ouvrier Coiffeur* (May 1926) and (June 1926); and PP Ba 1419, 12.000–111.
23. *Ère Nouvelle* (May 24, 1926).
24. *Petit Journal* (May 21, 1926).
25. *Le Quotidien* (May 23, 1926).
26. *Paris Soir* (May 22, 1926).
27. On the Minimum Program see Horne, Labour at War, 217, 357–8; and Kenneth H. Tucker, *French Revolutionary Syndicalism and the Public Sphere* (Cambridge: Cambridge University Press, 1996), 198.
28. Barzman, Dockers, *métallos, ménagers*, 187–8; Bruce Vandervort, *Victor Griffuelhes and French Syndicalism, 1895–1922* (Baton Rouge: Louisiana State University Press, 1996), 219–20.
29. FNCEP-FO, Congrès fédéral, September 21, 1920, Paris.
30. On the FNSOC's adhesion to the CGTU see AN F^7 13693, "Coiffeurs, 1914–1924: Grèves"; FNCEP-FO, Histoire Coiffure, 1894–1934, "1923" and "1924–1925"; and *Libertaire* (August 26 and 28–29, 1924).
31. From the Fédération nationale des syndicats confédérés, "Compte-rendu du 1er congrès, 24–25 août 1925: Circulaire et ordre du jour du congrès," in FNCEP-FO, *L'Ouvrier Coiffeur*, 1939–1947.
32. On the creation of the Fédération des confédérés see AN F^7 13693, "Coiffeurs, 1914–1924: Grèves"; *Le Coiffeur Parisien-Syndicaliste* (October 1928); *Coiffure de Paris* (January 1923), 16; CGT, *La Confédération générale du travail*, no page number; FNCEP-FO, Congrès fédéral, Fédération nationale des syndicats des ouvriers coiffeurs confédérés, 1er congrès national, August 24–26, 1925.
33. On the *Syndicat autonome* see AN F^7 13693, "Coiffeurs, 1914–1924: Grèves"; PP 316p, 2000–278, report on the Syndicat autonome des ouvriers coiffeurs; and PP, Bureau des Affaires Réglementaires-Dossiers des Syndicats, dossier #4217, Fédération autonome des syndicats d'ouvriers coiffeurs et parties similaires de France et des colonies.
34. FNCEP-FO, Histoire Coiffure, 1894–1934, "1928." The police report is in AN F^7 13693, "Coiffures, 1914–1924: Grèves."
35. On syndical weakness see AN F^7 13693, "Coiffeurs, 1914–1924: Grèves"; also the reports of local syndicats in FNCEP-FO, Histoire Coiffure, 1893–1934, "Syndicats": the president of the syndicat in Angers wrote to the

federation that his people rejected national affiliation because of the dues it entailed; also *L'Artisan Coiffeur* [Moulins] (February 1934); *Coiffeur Confédéré* (November 1932).

36. For a taste of this see FNCEP-FO, Histoire Coiffure, 1894–1934, "1923"; and *Le Coiffeur Parisien-Syndicaliste* 19 (February 1930).

37. Union fédérale des maîtres-coiffeurs de France, d'Algérie et des Colonies, *Xe congrès national, Nantes, 20–22 August 1928* (Paris: Imprimerie Parisiennes Réunies, 1929), 9–10; also the report on the fifteenth congress, in Saint-Etienne, in *Bulletin des Maîtres-Coiffeurs de l'Oise* (September 1933).

38. Union fédérale, *Compte-rendu du XIVe congrès national, Tours, 21–25 August 1932* (Paris: Éditions de l'Union Fédérale, 1932), 18.

39. AN F⁷ 13693, police report of June 26, 1924; Union fédérale, *XIVe congrès national*, 1932, 20.

40. *Coiffeur du Sud-Ouest* (June 1932); also *Coiffeur-Parfumeur* (April 15, 1934) and (July 15, 1934).

41. Steven M. Zdatny, *The Politics of Survival: Artisans in Twentieth-Century France* (New York: Oxford University Press, 1990), 26; also see *Coiffeur-Parfumeur* (September 15, 1925).

42. *Coiffeur Confédéré* (March 1925); *Ouvrier Coiffeur* (January 1925); Union Fédérale, Congrès nationale, 1928, 53–7.

43. *Le Trait d'Union des Coiffeurs* [Lyon] (November 1935).

44. AN F²² 422; also see *Cheveux Courts* (April 1931), 3–4; *Coiffure de Paris* (December 1933), 16–17.

45. AN F²² 421, letter from Ledoux to the labor minister, February 11, 1925.

46. *Coiffure de Paris* (December 1933), 15–16; *Le Trait d'Union des Coiffeurs* (November 1935).

47. Cited in *Revue Nouvelle des Coiffeurs et Parfumeurs* (May 1932).

48. AN F²² 422, booklet put together by the FNSOC, "Le problème des heures de travail dans la coiffure"; and "Association des Grandes Maisons de Coiffure de Paris." Also see F²² 509, "Sécurité des travailleurs," which has an excerpt from the *Ouvrier Coiffeur* (November–December 1931) attesting to the application of forty-eight hours "in certain hairdressing salons, in particular in the department stores." On the Galeries Lafayette see Pierre Guny's article in the *Capilartiste* (March 1927): FNCEP-FO, Histoire Coiffure, 1894–1934, "1927."

49. On Ricaud, see FNSOC, "Le problème des heures"; and, "Association des grandes maisons de Coiffure de Paris"; Archives de Paris, 1070, "Statuts des syndicats professionnels," carton 10, #1704: Institut des coiffeurs de dames de France; *Coiffure de Paris* (December 1933), 17; PP, "Bureau des Affaires Réglementaires—Dossiers des Syndicats," dossier #5321: Association des grandes maisons de coiffure de Paris.

50. *Le Coiffeur Parisien—Syndicaliste* (October 1928); also see *Ouvrier Coiffeur* (January 1935), where the *unitaire* paper makes the same point.

51. *Coiffeur du Sud-Ouest* (February 1933).

52. Unless otherwise noted, Guny's remarks are in FNSOC, "Le problème des heures," 17, 19.

53. FNCEP-FO, Histoire Coiffure, 1894–1934, "1927."

54. *Revue Nouvelle des Coiffeurs et Parfumeurs* (May 1932).

55. FNCEP-FO, Histoire Coiffure, 1894–1934, "1933"; also *Coiffeur Confédéré* (February 1933).
56. *Capilartiste* (January 1933).
57. *Coiffure de Paris* (December 1933), 15–17.
58. The quote is from *Coiffure de Paris* (June 1933), 54. On the SCP also see Archives de Paris, 1070W, "Statuts des syndicats professionnels," Carton 13, #2534: Syndicat indépendant des coiffeurs de Paris; *Coiffeur Confédéré* (November 1932); PP, "Bureau des Affaires Réglementaires-Dossiers des Syndicats," dossier #5368: Syndicat des coiffeurs de Paris.
59. AN F^{12} 11999, "Organisation des matières primaires: Coiffure," biographical note on Arvet-Thouvet.
60. Claude Bellanger, Jacques Godechot, Pierre Guiral, Fernand Terrou, dirs., *Histoire générale de la presse française, tome III: De 1871 à 1940* (Paris: Presses Universitaires de France, 1972), 366.
61. On the life and career of Marcel Bagnaud see the police dossier compiled for Bagnaud's promotion to Officier in the Légion d'Honneur that can be found in CCIP: I 2.55. Also see the obituaries in the *Coiffeur de France* (May 1964); and *Éclaireur des Coiffeurs* (May 4, 1964).
62. *Coiffeur Confédéré* (December 1932).
63. *Journal des Maîtres-Coiffeurs de Paris et de la Région Parisienne* (February 1933).
64. *Coiffeur Confédéré* (March 1934); also *Coiffure de Paris* (February 1934), 46.
65. Bagnaud, cited by Janvier in *Coiffeur Confédéré* (January–February 1934).
66. See, for example, *Coiffeur Confédéré* (August 1928), which complained that "it is impossible in our trade to close the shop on time"; or the request that the authorities finally enforce the regulations on *repos hebdomadaire* in Bordeaux, *Coiffeur-Parfumeur* (October 15, 1935).
67. AN F^{22} 365, "Repos hebdomadaire, 1906–1935."
68. This exchange of letters is in AN F^{22} 365, dossier "Documents par localité."
69. AN F^{22} 365, letter from Peyronnet to the divisional inspector in Marseilles, May 11, 1923.
70. AN F^{22} 422, letters of April 13 and June 29, 1934.
71. AN F^{22} 422, "Huit heures en Coiffure."
72. Quoted in *Coiffure de Paris* (February 1933), 1.
73. *Coiffeur Confédéré* (July 1925).
74. AN F^{22} 364, "Repos hebdomadaire, 1906–1935: Coiffure."
75. Varié's plea is in *Coiffure de Paris* (January 1934), 32; the letter from the Porte St. Denis hairdressers is in AN F^{22} 422.
76. *Ouvrier Coiffeur* (May 1926).
77. *Gallia Journal* (March–April 1929), 3.
78. *Coiffeur Confédéré* (February 1932).

5 Fat Years, Lean Years

1. Jane Mulvagh, *Vogue's History of Twentieth-Century Fashion* (London: Viking, 1988), 85.

2. See Bruno Villien, "Schiaparelli," in Olivier Barrot and Pascal Ory, dir., *Entre deux guerres: La création française*, 1919–1939 (Paris: Éditions François Bourin, 1990), 491.
3. *Votre Beauté* (September 1933), 32.
4. On the defense of *cheveux courts* see *Cheveux Courts* (March 10, 1930), 1–2; Union fédérale, *Compte-rendu du XIIe congrès national, Paris, 17–21 August 1930* (Poitiers: Société Française d'Imprimerie, 1931) 88; *Artisan Coiffeur* (March 1933); *Coiffure de Paris* (April 1937), 37; *Coiffeur du Sud-Ouest* (November 1933).
5. *Coiffure de Paris* (March 1932), 1; and (January 1934), 2.
6. *Vogue* (February 1933), 18.
7. *Votre Beauté* (August 1936), 41.
8. *Vogue* (December 1933), 26–9.
9. Guillaume, *Guillaume raconte . . . la coiffure et ses métamorphoses* (Argenton-sur-Creuse: Imprimerie de l'Indre, 1982), 53–61; and Vincent Chenille, *La mode dans la coiffure des françaises: "La norme et le mouvement," 1837–1937* (Paris: Harmattan, 1996), 11.
10. *Votre Beauté* (February 1938), 6.
11. René Rambaud, *Les fugitives. Précis anécdotique et historique des coiffeurs féminines à travers les âges, des Egyptiens à 1945* (Paris: René Rambaud, 1947), 269; Marylène Delbourg-Delphis, *Le chic et le look. Histoire de la mode féminine et des moeurs de 1850 à nos jours* (Paris: Hachette, 1981), 148.
12. Quoted in Valerie Steele, *Paris Fashion: A Cultural History* (New York: Oxford University Press, 1988), 265–6.
13. Fédération nationale de la coiffure, "Au service des métiers de la coiffure française, 1896–1987," (1967), report available at the FNC, no page numbers. On the population of coiffure see Ministère du Travail. Statistique générale de la France, *Résultats statistiques du recensement de la population effectué le 6 mars 1921, tome I* (Paris: Imprimerie Nationale, 1923), 148–9; and Ministère du Travail, de l'Hygiène, de l'Assistance et de la Prévoyance Sociale. Statistique Générale de la France, *Résultats statistiques du recensement général de la population effectué le 7 mars 1926, tome I* (Paris: Imprimerie Nationale, 1931), 158–9. On the shortage of hairdressers see A. Chantoiseau, *Le coiffeur et la chevelure* (Paris: Ulysse Boucoiran, 1936), 8; *Coiffeur-Parfumeur* (July 15, 1923); and FNCEP-FO, Congrès Fédéral, "1921": Compte-rendu of the 11th Congrès National, June 23–25, 1922, "Rapport sur le chômage et le placement" (Masia).
14. FNCEP-FO, Histoire Coiffure, 1894–1934, "1931"; *Syndicalism* (September 1938).
15. *L'Intransigeant* (January 9, 1924); also see the article by C. Grillon, President of the Syndicat des maîtres-coiffeurs de Bordeaux, in *Coiffure de Paris* (March 1924), 15–16.
16. Archives de Paris, Procédures des Prud'hommes, Tissus, dossier 1183: Mme. Wajnberg v. M. Gerszonowiez. The widow Wajnberg received 200 francs compensation.
17. Office départemental du placement et de la statistique du travail de la Seine, *Le fonctionnement de l'Office départemental du placement et de la statistique*

du travail et l'organisation des secours de chômage dans le département de la Seine pendant l'année 1923 (Paris: Imprimerie Municipale, 1924), 56.

18. Bernard Zarca, "Survivance ou transformation de l'artisanat dans la France d'aujourd'hui," tome II, thèse en sociologie, Institut d'études politiques, 1983, 864–5.

19. On the Walter-Paulin law see Edgar Hector, *La législation actuelle de l'artisanat: Commentaire et jurisprudence* (Paris: Librairie du Recueil Sirey, 1939), 326–7; and Steven M. Zdatny, *The Politics of Survival: Artisans in Twentieth-Century France* (New York: Oxford University Press, 1990), 124–5. On the C.A.P. and the *brevet professionnel* see Guy Billon, *La coiffure pour dames et messieurs aux examens du CAP-BP, CFA et BM. Cours préparatoire* (Nancy: L. Stoquert, 1962); Monique Buisson, "Histoire d'un enseignement professionnel et pratiques familiales d'orientation: Le cas de la coiffure à Lyon," in Régis Bernard, Monique Buisson, Jean Camy, Laurence Roulleau-Berger and Guy Vincent, *Education, fête et culture* (Lyon: Presses Universitaires de Lyon, 1981), 150; Catherine Gavend, "Les coiffeurs de Lyon (1848–1975)," Centre Pierre Lyon d'histoire économique et sociale, *Métiers et Statuts. Bulletin* (1999), 138; and Catherine Lebas and Annie Jacques, *La Coiffure en France du Moyen Age à Nos Jours* (Paris: Delmas International, 1979), 62.

20. See *Coiffure de Paris* (March 1933), 33; FNCEP-FO, Histoire Coiffure, 1894–1934, "1931"; and Histoire Coiffure, 1935–1942, "1937."

21. AN F⁷ 13693, "Coiffeurs, 1914–1924: Grèves" and *L'Intransigeant* (January 19, 1923). Also see *Coiffure de Paris* (February 1920), 7; Nonna Mayer, "Small Business and Social Mobility in France," in Robert Goffee and Richard Scase, eds., *Entrepreneurship in Europe: The Social Processes* (London, New York: Croom Helm, 1987), 45.

22. C. Kauffmann and J. Barth, *Le livret du coiffeur. Technologie* (Paris: Librairie d'Enseignement Technique, 1923), 10.

23. Ministère du Travail, *Résultats statistiques du recensement, 1921: tome I*, 148–9; *tome II*, 1–8; idem, *Résultats statistiques du recensement, 1926: tome I, 158–9; tome III*, 4; Présidence du Conseil. Statistique générale de la France, *Résultats statistiques du recensement général de la population effectué le 8 mars 1931* (Paris: Imprimerie Nationale, 1935), *tome II*, 4; Statistique générale de la France, *Résultats statistiques du recensement général de la population effectué le 8 mars 1936* (Paris: Imprimerie Nationale, 1943): *tome I*, 58; *tome II*, 4. On the commercial geography of Paris see Alain Metton, *Le commerce et la ville en banlieue parisienne* (Courbevoie: Alain Metton, 1980), 269–71.

24. Paul Gerbod, *Histoire de la coiffure et des coiffeurs* (Paris: Larousse, 1995), 313.

25. Mrs. Robert Henrey, *Madeleine Grown Up* (London: J.M. Dent and Sons, 1952), 2–4.

26. Charles Desplanques, *Barbiers, perruquiers, coiffeurs* (Paris: Librairie Octave Doin, 1927), 241; Kauffmann and Barth, *Livret du coiffeur*, 10.

27. Ministère du Commerce, de l'Industrie, des Postes et des Télégraphes. Direction de l'Office du Travail, *Résultats statistiques du recensement des industries et professions, tome IV* (Paris: Imprimerie Nationale, 1901), 254–5.

28. Annie Fourcault, *Femmes à l'usine en France dans l'entre-deux-guerres* (Paris: François Maspéro, 1982), 216.
29. On the parallel trend in the United States see Dewey Anderson and Percy E. Davidson, *Occupational Trends in the United States* (Stanford: Stanford University Press, 1940), 2; also Julie A. Willett, *Permanent Waves: The Making of the American Beauty Shop* (New York: New York University Press, 2000), 29–30.
30. Louise Vanderwielen, *Lise du Plat Pays* (Lille: Presses Universitaires de Lille, 1983).
31. Ministère du Travail, *Résultats statistiques, 1926: tome I*, 158–9; Statistique generale, *Résultats statistiques*, 1936: *tome I*, 58.
32. See, for example, Laura Lee Downs, *Manufacturing Inequality: Gender Division in the French and British Metalworking Industries, 1914–1939* (Ithaca: Cornell University Press, 1995), passim; and idem, "Women's Strikes and the Politics of Popular Egalitarianism in France, 1916–1918," in Leonard R. Berlanstein, ed., *Rethinking Labor History: Essays on Discourse and Class Analysis* (Urbana: Illinois University Press, 1993), 116–8. Also see Judith Coffin, *The Politics of Women's Work: The Paris Garment Trades, 1750–1915* (Princeton: Princeton University Press, 1996); and Nancy L. Green, *Ready-to-Wear and Ready-to-Work: A Century of Industry and Immigrants in Paris and New York* (Durham, NC: Duke University Press, 1997). On women's unemployment see Gabrielle Letellier, Jean Perret, H.E. Zuber, and A. Dauphin-Meunier, *Le chômage en France de 1930 à 1936* (Paris: Librairie du Recueil Sirey, 1938), 157.
33. Laura Levine Frader, "Women and French Unions: Historical Perspectives on the Current Crisis of Representation," in Herrick Chapman, Mark Kesselman, and Martin Schain, eds., *A Century of Organized Labor in France: A Union Movement for the Twenty-First Century* (New York: St. Martin's Press, 1998), 146–53; also Siân Reynolds, *France Between the Wars: Gender and Politics* (London and New York: Routledge, 1996), 119.
34. Union fédérale, *Compte-rendu du Xe congrès national, Nantes, 20–22 août 1928* (Paris: Imprimeries Parisiennes Réunies, 1929), 9–10.
35. Zarca, "Survivance ou transformation," II, 878–90.
36. Theresa McBride, "French Women and Trade Unionism: The First Hundred Years," in Norbert C. Solden, ed., *The World of Women's Trade Unionism: Comparative Historical Essays* (Westport, CT: Greenwood Press, 1985), 48–9.
37. Quoted in Downs, *Manufacturing Inequality*, 5; also Mary Jo Maynes, *Taking the Hard Road: Life Course in French and German Workers' Autobiographies in the Era of Industrialization* (Chapel Hill: University of North Carolina Press, 1995), 159.
38. This observation is based on my several conversations with Michel Bourlon.
39. Ministre du Travail et de Prévoyance Sociale. Statistique générale de la France, *Salaires et coûts d'existence à diverses époques, jusqu'en 1910* (Paris: Imprimerie Nationale, 1911), 122–3, 138–9, 146–7, 158–9.
40. See AN F[7] 13693, "Coiffeurs, 1914–1924: Grèves"; and 13866, "Coiffure"; Archives de Paris, Jugements des Prud'hommes; *Bulletin des Maîtres-Coiffeurs de l'Oise* (October 1932); *Coiffure de Paris* (February 1925), 1 and

(March 1925), 19; FNCEP-FO, Syndicats (by department); Histoire Coiffure, 1894–1934; Ministère du Travail, *Statistique des grèves et des recours à la conciliation et l'arbitrage survenu pendant l'année 1919* (Paris: Imprimerie Nationale, 1920), 320–3; and idem, . . . *pendant l'année 1920* (Paris: Imprimerie Nationale, 1921), 252–5; (1923), 136–7; (1924), 136–7; and (1925), 122–3.

41. *Coiffure de Paris* (January 1935), 30–2.
42. The debate on the tip can be followed in the forum organized by the *Coiffure de Paris* spanning 1934 and 1935. For Mornot's and Freulon's comments see respectively *Coiffure de Paris* (September 1923), 17 and (March 1925), 20. Also see Frédéric Doyen's remarks in *Humanité* (October 9, 1921); *Le Peuple* (July 2, 1923); Luquet's and Ravanier's exchange is in FNCEP-FO, Congrès Fédéral, September 1920; and the clippings in Histoire Coiffure, 1894–1934, "1933."
43. Price information can be found scattered in AN F⁷ 13693, "Coiffeurs, 1914–1924: Grèves."
44. *Coiffure de Paris* (June 1920), 7.
45. Singer-Kérel, *Le coût de la vie*, 239 and 407; and *Reveil des Coiffeurs* (March 7, 1935).
46. Information on prices in *Coiffure de Paris* (May 1923), 19; (September 1923), 1; (June 1924), 1.
47. On the avalanche of beauty products see Gisèle d'Assailly, *Fonds et Beauté. Ou l'éternel féminin* (Paris: Hachette, 1958), 203; Caroline Cox, *Good Hair Days: A History of British Hairstyling* (London: Quartet Books, 1999), 60; *Gallia Journal* (January–February 1932), 7.
48. For an interesting essay on the perils and virtues of permananent waves see the chapter entitled, "Permanent Waving," in Hazel Leonie Koslay, ed., *Beauty Shop Problems* (New York: H.R. Howell, 1935), 17–28.
49. René Rambaud, "Les qualités nécessaires à un coiffeur pour dames. Physiques, morales, psychologiques, techniques et artistiques," *conférence held on November 24, 1933* at l'École de coiffure de Paris, 6–7.
50. *Coiffeur Confédéré* (November 1932).
51. AN F²² 422.
52. *Coiffure de Paris* (January 1934), 46–7; Georges-Lévy, *Hygiène du cuir chevelu et de la chevelure* (Paris: G. Doin, 1934), 39–40.
53. Archives de Paris, "Procédures des Prud'hommes," carton #230.
54. *Ouvrier Coiffeur* (January 1935); also see Alfred Spale, *Manuel du coiffeur* (Paris: Librairie J.-B. Baillière et fils, 1933), 122–3.
55. *Avocat des Coiffeurs* (May–August 1926).
56. On carbon-tetrachloride see Pierre Breteau, "Interdiction du commerce, de la détention et de l'emploi des liquides inflammables ou toxiques destinés au lavage de la chevelure," *Bulletin de l'Académie de Médecine*, séance du May 5, 1931, 729–30; and P. Cazaneuve et Gabriel Bertrand, "Communication: Sur les liquides inflammables ou toxiques utilisés dans les salons de coiffure," *Bulletin de l'Académie de Médecine*, séance du March 31, 1931 (Paris: Masson et Cie, 1931), 542–3. These can be found in AN F²² 509, "Securité des Travailleurs: Proposition de loi 'Tendant à interdire l'emploi des éthers

dans les salons de coiffure.' " On the use of poisonous paraphenylene-diamine, see Edwin Sidi and R. Longueville, *Les accidents par produits capillaires. Étude clinique expérimentale et medico-légale* (Paris: Éditions Médicales Flammarion, 1958), 25–6.

57. *Vogue* (February 1933), 18; also on the Système Zoto see M. Joyeux, "Le gaz chez les coiffeurs: Ce qui nous amène à vous parler des salons de coiffure," extract from *Journal des Usines de Gaz*, April 5–20, 1936, 7; and Spale, *Manuel du coiffeur*, 241.

58. Conseil d'hygiène publique et de du département de la Seine, "Au sujet d'un produit pour salons de coiffure," *Compte-rendu des séances*, 1935 (Paris: Imprimeries Chaix, 1936), 186 8. Also Dr F Bordas, "L'emploi de liquides inflammables ou toxiques dans les salons de coiffure," *Annales d'Hygiène Publique, Industrielle et Sociale* (1935), 171; Conseil d'hygiène publique et de salubrité du département de la Seine, "Emploi dans les salons de coiffure de liquides émettant des vapeurs inflammable ou toxiques," *Compte-rendu des séances*, 1936 (Paris: Imprimerie Chaix, 1937), 73–6.

59. *Coiffure Française Illustrée* (April 1924).

60. *Hebdo-Coiffure* (December 1935), 2; also *Coiffeur du Sud-Ouest* (March 1938). According to Julian Jackson, shopkeepers' income fell by 18 percent: Jackson, *The Popular Front in France: Defending Democracy, 1934–1938* (Cambridge: Cambridge University Press, 1988), 20.

61. *Coiffure de Paris* (January 1933), 42.

62. *Coiffure de Paris* (January 1932), 1.

63. AN F^{12} 10250, "Note sure les prix bas dans la coiffure," May 12, 1943.

64. AN F^{22} 422, dossier on the Association des grandes maisons de coiffure de Paris; FNCEP-FO, Syndicats, dossiers for St. Etienne and Clermont-Ferrand.

65. *Gallia Journal* (January–February 1931), 3; and (April–May–June 1932), 3.

66. *Hebdo-Coiffure* (April 1, 1939).

67. *Journal des Maîtres-Coiffeurs* (October 1933), 3.

68. *Cheveux Courts* (February 1931).

69. *Cheveux Courts* (March 1931).

70. *Coiffure de Paris* (January 1933), 21.

71. Letellier, et al., *Chômage en France*, 81–3, 103–4; also *Journal des Maîtres-Coiffeurs* (June 1933), 19.

72. Letellier, et al., *Chômage en France*, 156–7.

73. Paul Gerbod, "Les métiers de la coiffure en France dans la première moitié du XXe siècle," *Éthnologie Française* (1983), 46n.

74. *Ouvrier Coiffeur* (July 1939).

75. *Artisan Coiffeur* (November 1932), my emphasis.

76. *Artisan Coiffeur* (September 1935).

77. *Coiffeur-Parfumeur* (May 15, 1934).

78. *Coiffure de Paris* (February 1932), 65.

79. A. Dumont, in Union fédérale, *Compte-rendu du XIVe congrès national, Tours, 21–25 août 1932* (Paris: Édition de l'Union Fédérale, 1932), 107.

80. Georges Morin in *Coiffure de Paris* (May 1935), 35–7.

81. André Armengaud, "La démographie française du XXe siècle," in Fernand Braudel and Ernst Labrousse, eds., *Histoire économique et sociale de la*

France. tome IV, L'ère industrielle et la société d'aujourd'hui (siècle 1880–1980); tome II, Le temps des guerres mondiales et de la grande crise (1914–vers 1950) (Paris: Presses Universitaires de France, 1982), 615–20.

82. Paul Gerbod, "Les coiffeurs en France (1890–1950)," *Le Mouvement Social* (January–March 1981), 73; Magnien's comments are in AN F²² 422, in the CGTU booklet, "Le problème des heures du travail dans la coiffure," 44.

83. *Le Trait d'Union des Coiffeurs* (August 1935). For the attitude of lower-middle class elements see Vicki Caron, "The Anti-Semitic Revival in France in the 1930s: The Socioeconomic Dimension Reconsidered," *Journal of Modern History* 70:1 (March 1998), 33–6. Caron deals with the phenomenon more extensively in idem, *Uneasy Asylum: France and the Jewish Refugee Crisis, 1933–1942* (Stanford: Stanford University Press, 1999), especially chapter 2, "Refugee Policy and Middle-Class Protest During the Great Depression," 13–42.

84. *Journal des Maîtres-Coiffeurs* (February 1933), 15.

85. *Bulletin des Maîtres-Coiffeurs de l'Oise* (August 1933); *Reveil des Coiffeurs* (March 7, 1935); *Cheveux Courts* (March 1931); *Coiffeur du Sud-Ouest* (July 1936).

86. *Coiffeur Confédéré* (February 1933), reprinted a letter from Maurice Baugé, the general secretary of the *confédérés*, to the labor minister.

87. See Alfred Aversa, Jr.'s study of American salons: "The Barber: A Sociological Analysis of an Occupation," PhD Thesis in Sociology and Labor Relations, New York University, 1973, 103.

88. Archives de Paris, Jugements des Prud'hommes, case #453, May 30, 1931.

6   The Failure of the Popular Front

1. Paul Gerbod, "Les métiers de la coiffure en France dans la première moitié du XXe siècle," *Éthnologie Française* (1983), 41.

2. Jean Brethe de la Gressaye, "Le mouvement syndical depuis 1936," *Droit Social* (1938), 224. Also see Jean Bouvier, et al, dirs., *La France en mouvement, 1934–1938* (Seysel: Champ Vallon, 1986); and Maurice Larkin, *France Since the Popular Front, 1936–1986* (Oxford: Oxford University Press, 1988), 47.

3. *Coiffeur Confédéré* (December 1934); PP 316p 2000–278–4, "Syndicats des ouvriers coiffeurs unitaire, confédéré, autonome."

4. *Capilartiste* (February 1936), 3 and (April 1936), 7; *Coiffure de Paris* (February 1936), 1; FNCEP-FO, Histoire Coiffure, 1935–1942, "1936."

5. On the growth of the FNSOC see *Capilartiste* (May 1936), 7; FNCEP-FO, Congrès fédéral, "Congrès confédéré/unitaire, Toulouse, 2–5 mars 1936"; Catherine Lebas and Annie Jacques, *La coiffure en France du moyen âge à nos jours* (Paris: Delmas International, 1979), 57; *Ouvrier Coiffeur* (June 1936); PP Ba 300p 2000–1100, "Unité syndicale."

6. *Ouvrier Coiffeur* (June 1936).
7. The following information on the Syndicats professionnels français comes from AN F^{12} 11971, "Études divers, Service de l'Artisanat," which contains an essay by Edmond Verdun, "Le mouvement syndicalist français," published by the Institut d'études corporatives et sociales, no date; also Brethe de la Gressaye, "Mouvement syndical," 227; Gérard Dehove, "Le mouvement ouvrier et la politique syndicale," *Revue d'Économie Politique* (November–December 1947), 1559–60 note; *Éclaireur des Coiffeurs* (July 7, 1941), 5; Philippe Machefer, "Les syndicats professionnels français (1936–1939)," *Le Mouvement Social* (April–June 1982), 91–112 *passim;* Parti social français, *Le Parti social français et la semaine de 40 heures* (Paris: Service du Propagande, 1937), 1; Robert Soucy, *French Fascism The Second Wave, 1933–1939* (New Haven: Yale University Press, 1995), 130–1; and Paul Vignaux, *Traditionalisme et syndicalisme. Essai d'histoire sociale* (1884–1941) (New York: Éditions de la Maison Française, 1943), 77.
8. See William D. Irvine, "Fascism in France and the Strange Case of the Croix de Feu," *Journal of Modern History* (June 1991), 272.
9. On congés payés generally, see Gary Cross, *A Quest for Time: The Reduction of Work in Britain and France, 1840–1940* (Berkeley: University of California Press, 1989), 222–3; idem, "Vacations for All: The Leisure Question in the Era of the Popular Front," *Journal of Contemporary History* (1989), 599–621; and Henri Noguères, *La vie quotidienne en France au temps du Front populaire* (Paris: Hachette, 1977), 97–8; On Morin's opinion see *Semaine de la Coiffure* (Septement 4, 1936).
10. For the provincial collective conventions see AN F^{22} 1689 and 1690, "Conventions Collectives, 1936–1938."
11. Summaries of the collective contract of June 12, 1936 can be found in the Archives des Yvelines, 16 M 69; *Capilartiste* (July 1936), 32; *Coiffure de Paris* (July 1936), 13.
12. "Tableau I—salaires horaires moyens de certains catégories d'ouvriers dans la région parisienne," in Présidence du Conseil, Direction de la statistique générale et de la documentation, *Annuaire statistique, 1936* (Paris: Imprimerie Nationale, 1937), 168; also Noguères, *Vie quotidienne*, 103–4
13. Surveys of prices are scattered through AN F^{12} 102502, "Homologation des Prix, 1945–1946"; and F^{22} 1689.
14. Jeanne Singer-Kérel, *Le coût de la vie à Paris de 1840 à 1954* (Paris: Presses de la Fondation Nationale des Sciences Politiques, 1961), 461; and *Le mouvement des prix de 1913 à 1950. Recueil des cours et indices des principaux produits industriels, du coût de la vie et des salaires, mis à jour au 1er mai 1950* (Paris: L'Usine Nouvelle, 1950), 1.
15. From the report of the Commission spéciale sur l'artisanat, cited in *Semaine de la Coiffure* (November 1938).
16. Quoted in *Coiffure de Paris* (December 1938), 45.
17. *Hebdo-Coiffure* (April 1939). On the *rentabilité* of salons, see Paul Gerbod, "Les coiffeurs en France (1890–1950)," *Le Mouvement Social* (January–March 1981), 77; and Préfecture de la Seine. Secrétariat général. Statistique départementale et communale, *Annuaire statistique de la ville de Paris*.

Années 1935, 1936 et 1937, "Ventes de fonds de commerce assujeties à la taxe municipale pendant l'année . . ." (Paris: Imprimerie F. Deshayes, 1942), 745–7. On the class of shopowners generally, see François Gresle, *L'univers de la boutique: Famille et métier chez les petits patrons du Nord (1920–1975)* (Lille: Presses Universitaires de Lille, 1981).

18. AN F^{22} 1690.
19. *Semaine de la Coiffure* (August 7, 1936).
20. *Coiffeur du Sud-Ouest* (November 1936).
21. CCIP, III 4.13, "Divers: Salons de coiffure."
22. Richard Vinen, *The Politics of French Business, 1936–1945* (Cambridge: Cambridge University Press, 1991), 69.
23. Cited in *Hebdo-Coiffure* (March 12, 1938); *Reveil des Coiffeurs* (March 3, 1938).
24. AN F^{22} 1689, "Avis du CNE [Conseil National Economique]," minutes of the meeting of June 16, 1937 of the 17th *Section Professionnelle* (Section des Commerces autres que ceux de l'alimentation, du commerce d'importation et d'exportation), report by Arvet-Thouvet, CPC president; PP. Bureaux des Affaires Réglementaires-Dossier des syndicats, #7096 Confédération patronale des coiffeurs de France et des colonies.
25. *Reveil des Coiffeurs* (March 3, 1938).
26. AN F^{22} 1689.
27. AN F^{22} 1689.
28. On the UF's population see AN F^{22} 1689 and 1690, report from divisional inspector of labor, Gelé, to the labor minister, August 4, 1939; *Semaine de la Coiffure* (June 24, 1936); Union fédérale des syndicats et groupements patronaux des maîtres-coiffeurs de France et des Colonies, *Annuaire général de la coiffure* (Poitiers: Société Française d'Imprimerie, 1929), 145–61.
29. Bénazet in *Coiffeur du Sud-Ouest* (July 1936).
30. *Semaine de la Coiffure* (January 15, 1937) and (January 22, 1937).
31. Archives des Yvelines, 16 M 69; *Reveil des Coiffeurs* (April 24, 1938).
32. The text of the convention can be found in AN F^{22} 1689; and *Semaine de la Coiffure* (February 12, 1937).
33. The folder of letters is in AN F^{22} 1689.
34. *Semaine de la Coiffure* (February 19, 1937) and (March 12, 1937).
35. *Semaine de la Coiffure* (April 9, 1937).
36. Alphonse Mornot in *Coiffure de Paris* (April 1937), 21.
37. *Ouvrier Coiffeur* (April 1937).
38. Dessirier, Dieterlen, Dugé de Bernonville, et al., *La France économique de 1937. Annuaire de la vie économique française* (Paris: Sirey, 1938), 504–5.
39. *Capilartiste* (April 1937).
40. *Coiffure de Paris* (June 1937), 34; *Semaine de la Coiffure. Numéro spécial* (May 3, 1937); *Le Temps* (May 1, 1937).
41. Joel Colton, *Compulsory Labor Arbitration in France, 1936–1939* (Columbia University Press, 1951).
42. *Le Populaire* (May 15, 1937).
43. The hairdressers' strike was front-page news in the Parisian papers throughout. PP Ba 12.000–111, dossier "Grève des coiffeurs, 1937," contains relevant

articles from a collection of Paris dailies for the period of the strike and its aftermath.

44. *Le Temps* (May 21, 1937).
45. *L'Oeuvre* (May 15, 1937).
46. PP Ba 12.000–111, police report of May 14.
47. Quoted in Archives des Yvelines, 16 M 69, dossier from May 17, 1937.
48. *Figaro* (May 14, 1937).
49. PP Ba 12.000–111.
50. Interview with François Magnien, July 10, 1988.
51. On the CATC see Paul Gerbod, *Histoire de la coiffure et des coiffeurs* (Paris: Larousse, 1995), 224; Lehas and Jacques, *Coiffure en France*, 64. For a hagiographic look at Magnien's career see the video, "Il s'appelait François Magnien," directed by Jacques de Closet, director of the CATC and available there.
52. *Humanité* (May 12, 1937).
53. These vituperative exchanges can be found in CCIP, "Protestation de la Chambre de Commerce de Paris contre un article paru dans l'*Hebdo-Coiffure* (1938)"; *Coiffeur-Parfumeur* (May 15, 1938); *Humanité* (May 12, 1937); *Hebdo-Coiffure* (March 12, 1938) and (April 2, 1938); *Ouvrier Coiffeur* (May–June 1939).
54. *Éclaireurs des Coiffeurs* (May 4, 1964), 8; CCIP, I 2.55, "Marcel Bagnaud, décédé le 21 avril 1964," concerning Bagnaud's promotion to Officier of the Légion d'Honneur; and "Procès verbal de la séance du 23 novembre 1938," à propos Bagnaud's report to the Chamber of Commerce on "Situation des étrangers en France."
55. The quotations in this paragraph come from *Coiffure de Paris* (January 1937), 17; *Union des Syndicats de Coiffeurs* (April 1939), "Lettre ouverte à M. Bagnaud," and (January 1939), "M. Bagnaud à Cannes"; Lamy's comments are in *Semaine de la Coiffure* (March 11, 1938).
56. The charges come from an article by C. Bideau, of the Syndicat des petits artisans coiffeurs de Clermont-Ferrand et du Puy-de-Dôme, cited in *Artisan Coiffeur* (April 1939).
57. Nonna Mayer, *La boutique contre la gauche* (Paris: Presses de la Fondation Nationale des Sciences Politiques, 1986), 108–11. Also on the classes moyennes see Ingo Kolboom, *La revanche des patrons. Le patronat français face au Front populaire* (Paris: Flammarion, 1986), 324; Jean Ruhlmann, *Ni bourgeois ni prolétaires. La défense des classes moyennes en France au Xxe siècle* (Paris: Seuil, 2001), 73–5.
58. *Union des Syndicats des Coiffeurs* (June 1939).
59. On the Martin's decision see AN F²² 1690; Archives des Yvelines 16 M 39, report of the Reconciliation Committee, November 5, 1937, and 11 M 47, "tarifs des coiffeurs"; FNCEP-FO, Histoire Coiffure, 1935–1942, "1937"; *Ouvrier Coiffeur* (August 1937); *Semaine de la Coiffure* (August 27, 1937).
60. Jean-Pierre Le Crom, *Syndicats, nous voilà! Vichy et le corporatisme* (Paris: Les Éditions Ouvrière, 1995), 41–6; also see Jean-Pierre Rieux, "La conciliation et l'arbitrage obligatoire des conflits du travail," in René Remond and Janine Bourdin, dirs., *Edouard Daladier: Chef du gouvernement, avril 1938–septembre 1939* (Paris: Presses de la Fondation Nationale des Sciences Politiques, 1977), 114–15.

61. *L'Oeuvre* (August 14, 1937); *Le Populaire* (August 14, 1937).
62. AN F^{22} 1689; *Coiffeur du Sud-Ouest* (March 1938) and (August 1939); *Reveil des Coiffeurs* (May 18, 1939).
63. *Le Peuple* (September 18, 1937).
64. *Capilartiste* (January 1939), 13; AN F^{22} 1690.
65. From the "2e Convention collective nationale," published March 31, 1939, between the UF and the FNSOC, in FNCEP-FO, Histoire de la Coiffure, 1947–1949, "1948."
66. See the letter from Bagnaud to the Labor Minister, May 16, 1939, in AN F^{22} 1690; and FNCEP-FO, Textes officielles: conventions collectives nationals— coiffure, November 11, 1938.
67. *Coiffure de Paris* (May 1939), 1.
68. *Capilartiste* (May 1939), 12.
69. AN F^{12} 102502, "Notice sur les prix bas dans la coiffure, May 12, 1943," carries excerpts from the Senate report of March 18, 1937.
70. AN AJ38 2318, salons de coiffure aryanisés, dossier # 4.185.
71. *Hebdo-Coiffure* (April 1, 1939).
72. *Ouvrier Coiffeur. Édition de Paris* (February 1939).
73. *Hebdo-Coiffure* (July 22, 1939). On prices see for example AN F^{12} 102502, Groupement artisanal professionnel des coiffeurs de l'Orne, "Étude sur une homologation des tarifs dans le cadre régional," Alençon April 15, 1943, which compares prices in 1939 and 1943.
74. Serge Berstein, "Les classes moyennes contre la gauche," *Histoire* (1984), 6–21; idem, "Les classes moyennes devant l'histoire," *Vingtième Siècle, revue d'histoire* (January–March 1993), 3–12; and Jean Ruhlmann, "Un corporatisme sans doctrine? Les commerçants, le corporatisme, et la defense des classes moyennes dans la première moitié du XXe siècle," in Steven L. Kaplan and Philippe Minard, dirs., *La France, malade du corporatisme? XXIIIe– XXe siècles* (Paris: Belin, 2004), 315–26.
75. Louis Joxe, "Le Front populaire," *Sciences Politiques* (May 1937), 132–4; also Julian Jackson, *The Popular Front in France: Defending Democracy, 1934–1938* (Cambridge: Cambridge University Press, 1988), 226.
76. Ruhlmann, *Ni bourgeois, ni prolétaires*, 121.
77. Georges Izard, *Les classes moyennes* (Paris: Éditions Rieder, 1938), 7; Gaston Lecordier, *Les classes moyennes en marche* (Paris: Bloud et Gay, 1950), 9.
78. Julian Jackson, *The Politics of Depression in France, 1932–1936* (Cambridge: Cambridge University Press, 1985), 133.
79. Henri Mougin, "Notes sur les mouvements des classes moyennes," in Raymond Aron, ed., *Inventaires III, les classes moyennes en France* (Paris: Félix Alcan, 1939), 327, emphasis added.
80. Ruhlmann, *Ni bourgeois, ni prolétaires*, 128.

7   Hair in War and Occupation

1. Dominique Veillon, *Vivre et survivre en France, 1939–1947* (Paris: Payot, 1995), 17–19.

2. Jacques Lehoulier, "L'évolution des salaires depuis 1938 (jusqu'en juin 1946)," *Revue d'Économie Politique* (November–December 1947), 1530; *Union des Syndicats de Coiffeurs* (November 1939).

3. *Coiffure de Paris* (March 1939), 25.

4. *Vogue* (April–May 1940), 62.

5. *Vogue* (December 1940), 10–21.

6. *Candide* (October 25, 1939), cited in Veillon, *Vivre et survivre*, 27.

7. *Votre Beauté* (April 1940), 12; and (February–March 1940), 36.

8. Veillon, *Vivre et survivre*, 38.

9. Paul Gerbod, *Histoire de la coiffure et des coiffeurs* (Paris: Larousse, 1995), 238.

10. Dominique Veillon, *La mode sous l'Occupation: Débrouillardise et coquetterie dans la France en guerre (1939–1945)* (Paris: Payot, 1990), 26.

11. *Vogue* (April–May 1940), 26.

12. AN F^{22} 1955, "Procès-verbal de la réunion de la sous commission de la charte corporative," December 16, 1943; "Rapport moral, Commission administrative fédérale, XXe congrès national, FNSOC, March 7, 1944: Deux années d'activité syndicale," in FNCEP-FO, Histoire Coiffure, 1943–1946, "1944."

13. *Coiffure de Paris* (January 1940), 22–5.

14. *Hebdo-Coiffure* (October 28, 1939).

15. Gérard Dehove, "Le mouvement ouvrier et la politique syndicale," *Revue d'Économie Politique* (November–December 1947), 1557–9; Peter Novick, *The Resistance Versus Vichy: The Purge of Collaborators in Liberated France* (New York: Columbia University Press, 1968), 131–3.

16. For a very tendentious account of this episode see Jean Bruhat and Marc Piolot, *Esquisse d'une histoire de la CGT (1895–1965)* (Paris: CGT, 1966), 169–70.

17. Denis Peschanski, "Le régime de Vichy a existé. Gouvernants et gouvernés dans la France de Vichy. Juillet 1940–Avril 1942," in Peschanski, dir., *Vichy 1940–1944: Archives de guerre d'Angelo Tosca* (Paris: Éditions du CNRS, 1986), 323–5. On Magnien's anticommunism see AN F^{22} 1955, "Famille Professionnelle-Hygiène," meeting of the Comité provisoire d'organisation, July 19, 1943.

18. CGT, carton 14, "Correspondance relative à l'Affaire Magnien," dossier "Ordre de Réquisition, November 15, 1940."

19. Roger Leclerc, from his report to the Conseil syndical of the CSO, October 30, 1944, in CGT, carton 9, "Rapports moraux du conseil syndical de la CSO."

20. CGT, carton 14, "Correspondance relative à l'Affaire Magnien." Also see AN F^{22} 1965, "Syndicats uniques des ouvriers coiffeurs: Correspondance"; *Éclaireur des Coiffeurs* (December 30, 1940), 4 and (July 10, 1945), 2; and *Ouvrier Coiffeur Parisien* (March 1946).

21. On the persecution of Philippot, et al. see *Coiffeur de Paris* (November 1946), 35; *Éclaireur des Coiffeurs* (May 20, 1945), 1; FNCEP-FO, 22e Congrès Fédéral, Paris, 1945, letter from Roger to his "chers camarades," November 21, 1945.

22. *Coiffure de Paris* (October 1940), 3.

23. *La Vie Industrielle* (April 4, 1941). On Pétain's love of the artisanat see Philippe Pétain, *Message adressé aux artisans, ouvriers, technicians et patrons: 1er mai 1942* (Vichy: Imprimerie Jacques Haumont, 1942), 4; "M. Pierre Loyer, chef du Service de l'Artisanat annonce la création prochaine d'un statut et de communautés de métiers artisanales," in *Paris Soir* (February 17, 1943), included among the clippings in AN AJ72 1849, "Artisanat—Chambres de Métiers, 1941–1943."

24. On Vichy's politics of social protection see AN AJ72 1856, "Diverse législation du travail, 1941–1943"; Henri Bartoli, "La législation sociale," *Revue d'Économie Politique* (November–December 1947), 1594–1630; Patrick Fridenson and Jean-Louis Robert, "Les ouvriers dans la France de la Seconde guerre mondiale: Un bilan," in Robert, dir., *Le Mouvement Social: Syndicalismes sous Vichy* (January–March 1992), 131–8; and Jean-Philippe Hesse and Jean-Pierre Le Crom, dirs., *La protection sociale sous le régime de Vichy* (Rennes: Presses Universitaires de Rennes, 2001), 355–60.

25. AN F²² 1955, letter to Belin, June 2, 1941, in the dossier that contains Malacarne's book manuscript: "Pour la Charte du Travail: L'ère nouvelle et les coiffeurs. Rapport des réformes et modifications à apporter à la Corporation des coiffeurs" (Dédié: A la Commission compétente chargée d'édifier les nouveaux réglements à appliquer dans la Charte du Travail, concernant le métier de coiffeur et ses branches annexes), May 1942.

26. *Coiffure de Paris* (October 1940), 3.

27. On the organization committees see Claude Gruson, *Origine et espoirs de la planification française* (Paris: Dunod, 1968), 30; Julian Jackson, *France: The Dark Years, 1940–1944* (Oxford: Oxford University Press, 2001), 162–5; Adrian Jones, "Illusions of Sovereignty: Business and the Organization Committees in Vichy France," *Social History* (January 1986), 1–31; Richard F. Kuisel, *Capitalism and the State in Modern France: Renovation and Economic Management in the Twentieth Century* (Cambridge: Cambridge University Press, 1981), 142; Jean-Guy Mérigot, *Essai sur les comités d'organisation professionnelle* (Paris: Librairie Générale de Droit et de Jurisprudence, 1943), 85–100; Henry Rousso, "L'organisation industrielle de Vichy," *Revue d'histoire de la deuxième guerre mondiale* (October 1979), 27.

28. Paul Vignaux, *Traditionalisme et syndicalisme. Essai d'histoire sociale (1884–1941)* (New York: Éditions de la Maison Française, 1943), 115.

29. Pierre Tissier, *The Government of Vichy* (Westport, CT: Greenwood Press, 1974 [1942]), 66, 75.

30. On the motives of the law's authors see René Belin, *Du secrétariat de la CGT au gouvernement de Vichy (Mémoires, 1933–1942)* (Paris: Éditions Albatross, 1978), 148–55; Yves Bouthillier, *Le drame de Vichy, tome II: Finances sous la contraint* (Paris: Plon, 1951), 273–8; and the report to Pétain by Belin, Bouthillier, François Pétri, General Maxime Weygand, General Colson, General Pujo, Admiral Darlan, Pierre Caziot, and Raphaël Alibert, in CCIP III: 4.111 (1), "Organisation professionnelle, corporatisme, économie dirigée, 1936–1946." Also see Kathryn Amdur, "Paternalism, Productivity, Collaborationism: Employers and society in Interwar and Vichy France,"

International Labor and Working-Class History 53 (Spring 1998), 149; Raymond Aron, *The Vichy Regime, 1940–1944* (New York: Macmillan, 1958), 178; Jean-Pierre Le Crom, *Syndicats, nous voilà! Vichy et le corporatisme* (Paris: Éditions Ouvrières, 1995), 106; Jean Marcou, "Le corporatisme contre le corporatisme," in Dominique Colas, dir., *L'Etat et les coporatismes* (Paris: Presses Universitaires de France, 1988), 77. On the operation of organization committees across the country and the economy see Hervé Joly, ed., *Les Comités d'organisation et l'économie dirigée du régime de Vichy* (Caen: Centre de recherche d'histoire quantitative, 2004).

31. G. Liet-Veaux, "L'organisation professionnelle, 1939–1946," *Revue d'Économie Politique* (November–December 1947), 1274–7.

32. Bouthillier, *Drame de Vichy*, 276. Also see the report on the CO in AN AJ72 1849, "L'organisation de l'industrie française," containing clippings from the Agence française d'information de presse; Pierre Pucheu, then minister of industrial production, answered his critics: AFIP. Service économique, May 15 and 19, 1941.

33. The quotes are from Marcou, "Corporatisme," 77; and Richard Vinen, *The Politics of French Business, 1936–1945* (Cambridge: Cambridge University Press, 1991), 142. On the OCRPI generally see Robert Catherine, *Économie de la répartition des produits industriels* (Paris: Presses Universitaires de France, 1943).

34. *Coiffure de Paris* (June 1941), 3–4; also the letter from Bagnaud to Lebègue, December 11, 1940, in AN F²² 1958, "Famille Professionnelle," dossier "Personnel des syndicats locaux."

35. AN F¹² 11993, "Comités d'organisation dans l'artisanat," letters exchanged between Loyer and Culmann, November 12 and 19, 1941.

36. *Éclaireur des Coiffeurs* (October 21, 1940), 3.

37. *Coiffure de Paris* (July 1941), 19 and (September 1941), 28.

38. See *Coiffure de Paris* (April 1941), 41; and (August 1942), 2–3; AN F¹² 11993, "Procès-verbal du comité d'organisation de la coiffure et de professions annexes, 1er février 1943."

39. *Éclaireur des Coiffeurs* (June 5–20, 1944), 1. On the electricity shortage in the salons see AN F²² 1955, note from Pierre Jardelle of Lyon to the departmental presidents of the UNS, September 1942; AN F¹² 11999, letter from Henri Culmann to the Comité départemental des prix for Paris, November 20, 1941; Alain Beltran and Patrice Carré, *La fée et la servante. La société française face à l'électricité, XIXe–XXe siècles* (Paris: Belin, 1991), 280.

40. Jean Camus, "Les coiffeurs pendant la guerre," in *Coiffure* 46 (Paris: Imprimerie Curial-Archereau, 1945), 55–6.

41. Lynne Taylor, *Between Resistance and Collaboration: Popular Protest in Northern France, 1940–1945* (New York: St. Martin's [London: Macmillan], 2000), 127.

42. For the story of hair recycling see NA AJ68 515, "Cheveux." Also *Coiffure de Paris* (May 1942), 23; and Veillon, *Mode sous l'Occupation*, 144–5.

43. See Samra-Martine Bonvoisin and Michèle Maignien, *La presse féminine* (Paris: Presses Universitaires de France, 1986), 20.

44. Veillon, *Vivre et survivre*, 97.

45. Valerie Steele, *Paris Fashion: A Cultural History* (New York: Oxford University Press, 1988), 266–7.

46. Veillon, *Mode sous l'Occupation*, chapter VI, "La haute couture à l'heure allemande," 141–75 *passim*.

47. Steele, *Paris Fashion*, 267; the same idea appears in Jane Mulvagh, *Vogue's History of 20th-Century Fashion* (London: Viking, 1988), 129.

48. Veillon, *Mode sous l'Occupation*, 122.

49. The first part of the quote comes from *L'Illustration* (March 28, 1942); the second from Emmanuelle Rioux: cited in Veillon, *Mode sous l'Occupation*, 236–7. Also on Zazous see Steele, *Paris Fashion*, 271.

50. Veillon, *Vivre et survivre*, 155; *Coiffure de Paris* (January 1941), 49; *Votre Beauté* (November 1940), 29.

51. On Vichy hats see René Rambaud, *Les fugitives. Précis anécdotique et historique des coiffures féminines à travers les âges, des Egyptiens à 1945* (Paris: René ed., Rambaud, 1947), 297; Steele, *Paris Fashion*, 271.

52. Dominique Veillon, "La mode comme pratique culturelle," in Jean-Pierre Rioux, ed., *Politiques et pratiques culturelles de la France de Vichy: Cahiers de l'Institut d'Histoire du Temps Présent* (June 1988), 241.

53. Guillaume, *Guillaume raconte . . . la coiffure et ses métamorphoses* (Argenton-sur-Creuse: Imprimérie de l'Indre, 1982), 69.

54. Marylène Delbourg-Delphis, *Le chic et le look: Histoire de la mode féminine et des moeurs de 1850 à nos jours* (Paris: Hachette, 1981), 178; also Gerbod, *Histoire*, 239; and Rambaud, *Les fugitives*, 297–8.

55. AN F[12] 11999, "Organisation des matières primaires. Coiffure," note "à tous les syndicats fédérés," November 25, 1943, signed by Magnien; and *Cahiers de la Coiffure* (March 1946).

56. *Coiffure de Paris* (January 1941), 43.

57. Quote is in Veillon, *Vivre et survivre*, 162. On short haircuts, see the interview with M. Desca, whose salon sat on the Champs-Elysées, in *Éclaireur des Coiffeurs* (January 10, 1943), 2.

58. *Le Trait d'Union des Coiffeurs*, organe de l'UNS (September 1942), in AN F[22] 1955.

59. *Éclaireur des Coiffeurs* (April 25, 1943), 3.

60. AN F[12] 11993, letter to the production minister from Jean Paillard, chargé de mission au vice-présidence du Conseil pour les corporations, and Marcel Rouaix, November 3, 1941.

61. AN F[12] 11994, "Comité d'organisation: Artisanat," letter from Loyer to Jardelle, September 5, 1942, and notes from Loyer to his regional delegate in Marseille and to Henri Culmann.

62. *Éclaireur des Coiffeurs* (December 10, 1942), 2.

63. AN F[12] 11994; also AN AJ72, 1856, "Diverse législation du travail, 1941–1943." For the position of labor minister Marcel Déat on the 48-hour week see AN F[22] 1957, "Hygiène-correspondance du commissaire du gouvernement: Ministère du Travail-Sécretariat général à la main d'oeuvre."

64. *Éclaireur des Coiffeurs* (April 5–20, 1944); and FNCEP-FO, Histoire de la Coiffure, 1947–1949, "1948": letter from the labor minister to the general secretary of the FNSOC, April 5, 1948.

65. Jean Ruhlmann, *Ni bourgeois ni prolétaires: La défense des classes moyennes en France au XXe siècle* (Paris: Seuil, 2001), 152–3. Also see AN F[12] 11999, report from the Comité national de répartition d'augmentation de tarifs to the Contrôle national de surveillance des prix, November 20, 1941, M. Abrial reporter.

66. *Le mouvement des Prix de 1913 à 1950. Recueil des cours et indices des principaux produits industriels, du coût de la vie et des salaires, mis à jour au 1er mai 1950* (Paris: L'Usine Nouvelle, 1950), 38; R. Rivet, "L'évolution des prix depuis la guerre," *Revue d'Économie Politique* (September 1947), 865–6, 871.

67. AN F[12] 102502, "Notice sur les prix bas dans la coiffure," report prepared by R. Barthoull for M. Lehoulanger, délégué à l'artisanat, May 12, 1943.

68. *Coiffure de Paris* (February 1942), 25.

69. Jeanne Singer-Kérel, *Le coût de la vie à Paris de 1840 à 1954* (Paris: Presses de la Fondation National des Sciences Politiques, 1961), 461.

70. AN F[12] 11999, letter of November 20, 1941.

71. *Coiffure de Paris* (May 1944), 1.

72. *Coiffure de Paris* (August 1941), 37; *Éclaireur des Coiffeurs* (July 28, 1941), 2 and (November 17, 1941), 1; Lehoulier, "L'évolution des salaires," 1530.

73. AN F[12] 1956, report from Paul Petit, June 30, 1944.

74. AN 72 AJ 1856, from Agence française d'information de presse, April 24, 1942.

75. AN F[22] 1963, "Famille professionnelle," dossier "Seine."

76. *Coiffure de Paris* (June 1942), 3–4.

77. "Rapport sur la situation des salaires des ouvriers coiffeurs de France au 15 octobre 1943, déposé au Ministère du Travail, 28 octobre 1943," in FNCEP-FO, Histoire Coiffure, 1943–1946. Also see the debate between Paul Petit of the FNSOC, and Gustave Blavy and Edouard Dauvergne of the CSP in the *Éclaireur des Coiffeurs* (August 18, 1941), 5.

78. Letter from Arthur Roger to "cher camarades secrétaires," à propos of "les attaques vénimeuses dont j'étais l'objet," in FNCEP-FO, 22e Congrès fédéral, Paris, 1945.

79. FNCEP-FO, Histoire de la Coiffure, 1943–1946, "1944"; also see the discussion of wage differentials in the Famille professionnelle of hairdressers, AN F[22] 1955, process-verbal de la sous-commission, April 26, 1944.

80. AN F[22] 1962, "Syndicats uniques des maîtres-artisans coiffeurs: Correspondance," dossier "Allier."

81. Letters to Magnien from Leduc, February 1, 1944, and to Petit from Robiney, president of the Poitiers SOC, in FNCEP-FO, Histoire de la Coiffure, 1943–1946, "1944"; also see AN F[22] 1955, passim.

82. Fridenson and Robert, "Ouvriers dans la France," 129–31; and *Tribune des Ouvriers Coiffeurs* (May 1948).

83. CGT, carton 1, FNSOC, Procès-verbal du XXIIe congrès national, March 3–4, 1947 (no page numbers).

84. Fridenson and Robert, "Ouvriers dans la France," 137–8; Le Crom, *Syndicats*, 337–44; and Hesse and Le Crom, *Protection sociale*, "Conclusion," 355–64. On Vichy's progressive social policy also see Paul V. Dutton, *Origins of the French Welfare State: The Struggle for Social Reform in France,*

1914–1947 (Cambridge: Cambridge University Press, 2002), 189–202; and Timothy B. Smith, *Creating the Welfare State in France, 1880–1940* (Montreal: McGill-Queen's University Press, 2003).
85. Quoted in Vinen, *Politics of French Business*, 99.

8 Aryanization, Collaboration, Resistance

1. The Association professionnelle des maîtres-coiffeurs israélites de Paris shared its offices on the rue Albuoy with the SCP: see PP "Bureau des Affaires Réglementaires-Dossiers des Syndicats," dossier #8157, March 1939.
2. AN AJ38 1148 (extrait 32JA), "Service de législation et des cotentieux. Professions, 1941–1943"; also Henry Rousso, "L'aryanisation économique-Vichy, l'occupant et la spoliation des Juifs," YOD. *Revue des Études Hébraïques et Juives Modernes et Contemporaines* (1982), 58; and Philippe Burrin, *La France à l'heure allemande, 1940–1944* (Paris: Seuil, 1995), 161.
3. Michael R. Marrus and Robert O. Paxton, *Vichy France and the Jews* (New York: Basic Books, 1981), 152–60.
4. Julian Jackson, *France: The Dark Years, 1940–1944* (Oxford: Oxford University Press, 2001), 355–7; André Kaspi, *Les Juifs pendant l'Occupation* (Paris: Seuil, 1991), 112; and Leni Yahil, *The Holocaust: The Fate of European Jewry* (Oxford: Oxford University Press, 1991), 172–3; Susan Zuccotti, *The Holocaust, the French and the Jews* (New York: Basic Books, 1993), 60. Also see the notes from Melchior de Faramond, head of the SCAP, to Pierre Loyer, March 25, 1942, in AN AJ38 405, "Comités d'organisation professionnels artisanaux" and from Loyer to Xavier Vallat, AJ38 1148.
5. AN AJ38, carton 2304, dossier #1513; and carton 2369, dossier #35950.
6. Albert Grunberg, *Journal d'un coiffeur juif à Paris sous l'Occupation* (Paris: Éditions de l'Atelier, 2001).
7. See Jacques Adler, *The Jews of Paris and the Final Solution: Communal Response and Internal Conflicts, 1940–1944* (New York and Oxford: Oxford University Press, 1987), especially chapter 2, "The Politics of Expropriation," 15–31.
8. CCIP I 2.55, dossier "Marcel Bagnaud, décédé le 21 avril 1964."
9. AN AJ38 493, "Etats se rapportants à la gestion des maisons israélites de la coiffure."
10. AN AJ38, carton 2386, dossier #15260.
11. AN AJ38, dossiers des administrateurs provisoires non-côtés [hereafter cited as AP], dossier de Léon Janiaud.
12. See, for example, AN AJ38, carton 3966, dossier #3996; and carton 4525, dossier #4525.
13. AN AJ38, carton 2391, dossier #30657.
14. AN AJ38, carton 2318, dossier #3992.
15. AN AJ38, 405.
16. AN AJ38, carton 2320, dossier #4732.
17. Kaspi, *Juifs pendant l'Occupation*, 112.

18. Rousso, "Aryanisation économique," 63–4. For a sympathetic account of Bichelonne see Guy Sabin, *Jean Bichelonne, Ministre sous l'Occupation: 1904–1944* (Paris: Éditions France-Empire, 1991).
19. AN AJ38, carton 2318, dossier #4185; and carton 2375, dossier #2307.
20. AN AJ38, carton 2369, dossier #35950; carton 2386, dossier #15260; and carton 2374, dossier #367.
21. AN AJ38, AP, "dossier Jacques DELAIRE."
22. See the letter from AP Roger Barthouil to the finance minister, November 21, 1944, in AJ38, AP, dossiers of Barthouil and René Davion.
23. See Jean-Pierre Bertin-Maghit, "Le comité interprofessionnel régional d'épuration de Paris," *La Gazette des Archives*, nouvelle série, no. 136, 1987), 29–30.
24. AN AJ38 1075, "Aryanisation économique [my emphasis]."
25. AN F¹² 11967, "Courrier. Service de l'Artisanat."
26. Roderick Kedward, *Resistance in Vichy France: A Study of Ideas and Motivation in the Southern Zone, 1940–1942* (Oxford: Oxford University Press, 1978), 105; Jean-Pierre Le Crom, "Le syndicalisme breton face à la Charte du Travail," in Claude Geslin, dir., *La vie industrielle en Bretagne. Une mémoire à conserver* (Rennes: Presses Universitaires de Rennes, 2002), 227; idem, *Syndicats, Nous Voilà! Vichy et le corporatisme* (Paris: Éditions Ouvrières, 1995), 112; and Robert Paxton, *Vichy France: Old Guard and New Order, 1940–1944* (New York: Norton, 1972), 213.
27. On the tortuous history of the charter see Philippe Bauchard, *Les technocrats et le pouvoir: X-crise, Synarchie, C.G.T., Clubs* (Paris: Artaud, 1966), 135; René Belin, *Du sécretariat de la CGT au gouvernement de Vichy (Mémoires, 1933–1942)* (Paris: Albatros, 1978), 162–3; Paul Farmer, *Vichy: Political Dilemma* (New York: Columbia University Press, 1955), 233–4; and Jean Paillard, *1940–1944: La révolution corporative spontanée* (Annonay: Éditions du Vivarais, 1979), 103–5.
28. Robert Aron, *The Vichy Regime, 1940–1944* (New York: Macmillan, 1958), 294; *Paris Soir* (October 31, 1941).
29. Richard F. Kuisel, *Capitalism and the State in Modern France: Renovation and Economic Management in the Twentieth Century* (Cambridge: Cambridge University Press, 1981), 144.
30. *Ouvrier Coiffeur Parisien* (July 1946).
31. For historians' criticisms see Jean-Pierre Le Crom, "Le syndicalisme ouvrier et la Charte du Travail," in Jean-Pierre Azéma and François Bédarida, eds., *Le régime de Vichy et les français* (Paris: Fayard, 1992), 435; Henri Bartoli, "La législation sociale," *Revue d'Économie Politique* (November–December 1947), 1603; Herrick Chapman, *State Capitalism and Working-Class Radicalism in the French Aircraft Industry* (Berkeley: University of California Press, 1991), 248–9; Jacques Julliard, "La Charte du Travail," in Fondation Nationale des Sciences Politiques, *Le gouvernement de Vichy, 1940–1942: Institutions et politique* (Paris: Éditions de la Fondation Nationale des Sciences Politiques, 1972), 161; Peter Novick, *The Resistance Versus Vichy: The Purge of Collaborators in Liberated France* (New York: Columbia University Press, 1968), 135; John Sweets, *The Politics of Resistance in*

France: A History of the Mouvements unis de la Résistance (DeKalb, Ill: University of Northern Illinois Press, 1976), 23.

32. Richard Vinen, *The Politics of French Business, 1936–1945* (Cambridge: Cambridge University Press, 1991), 105–12.

33. Paillard, *1940–1944*, 110; AN AJ72 1856, "Diverse législation du travail, 1941–1943." The Beugras quote comes from an article, "La Charte devançant les révolutionnaires nationaux," in *Je suis partout* (n.d.); on Beugras also see Confédération Générale du Travail, *Compte-rendu des travaux de la Commission nationale de réconstruction des organisation syndicales des travailleurs* (Versailles: Imprimerie Coopérative "La Gutenberg," 1946), 23. Déat's quote is from *L'Oeuvre* (November 8, 1941); also see Marcel Déat, *Mémoires politiques* (Paris: Edtions Denoël, 1989), 817; and Belin, *Mémoires*, 163.

34. Sweets, *Politics of Resistance*, 23; the second quotation is from Novick, *Resistance*, 134. On communist workers' opposition see Kedward, *Resistance*, 110–13; also Georges Ribeill, "Le chantiers de la collaboration sociale des Fédérations légales des cheminots (1939–1944)," *Le Mouvement Social* (January–March 1992), 102–16.

35. Gérard Dehove, "Le mouvement ouvrier et la politique syndicale," *Revue d'Économie Politique* (November–December 1947), 1571.

36. Jean-Pierre Le Crom, "La fédération du livre face au régime de Vichy: Entre réalisme et opportunisme," *Le Mouvement Social* (October–December 1999), 7.

37. Robert Aron, *Le monde de la presse, des arts, des lettres . . . 1944–1953*, vol. II of *Histoire de l'épuration* (Paris: Fayard, 1975), 311–3. Also see Rény Handourtzel and Cyril Buffet, *La collaboration . . . à gauche aussi* (Paris: Librairie Académique Perrin, 1989), 14–5.

38. *Le Trait d'Union des Coiffeurs* (September 1942).

39. See the comments of Marcel Rouaix, militant patron-coiffeur, in AN F[22] 1955, minutes of the meeting of the Commission provisoire d'organisation (CPO), July 19, 1943.

40. *Coiffure de Paris* (May 1942), 7.

41. FNCEP-FO, Histoire Coiffure, 1935–1942, "1941."

42. F[22] 1961, "Famille professionnelle," dossier "Seine Inférieure."

43. AN F[22] 1955, "Famille professionnelle—Hygiène, process-verbal de la réunion de la sous-commission de la charte corporative tenue le 12 janvier 1943 à Paris." My emphasis.

44. Magnien's letter of May 4, 1944, in CGT, carton 14, "Correspondance relative à l'affaire Magnien, 1944–50."

45. Only one woman, Odette Wadoux, a worker in *soins de beauté*, was named to the commission.

46. AN F[22] 1955, minutes of the CPO meeting of October 6, 1942.

47. *Coiffure de Paris* (October 1942), 1; and *Éclaireur des Coiffeurs* (December 10, 1942), 2; also Henri Culmann's circular to the heads of the organization committees of January 29, 1944, in AN F[12] 102512 "Groupements artisanaux professionnels."

48. AN F[22] 1957: Comments about "certaines personnes" are in a letter from Solomiac to Nicolas, director of organisation sociale at the Labor Ministry, December 4, 1942.

49. On the contentious negotiations over the SPF's inclusion in the CPO, see AN F²² 1955, minutes of the CPO meetings of 10, 16, and November 24, 1942 and February 22, 1943; AN F²² 1957, letter from Solomiac to Rambaud of November 25, 1942 and Rambaud's undated response; AN F²² 1961, letter from the prefect of the Seine department to the labor minister, September 11, 1943, and the dossier, "Re: Recrutement des syndicats uniques ouvriers: Seine"; and AN F²² 1965, "Syndicats uniques ouvriers coiffeurs: Correspondance," dossier Paris (Seine).

50. AN F²² 1955, minutes of the CPO subcommittee for *syndicats uniques* meeting of March 23, 1943.

51. AN F²² 1957, letter from Rambaud to Henri Pouillot, directeur de l'organisation sociale, secrétaire d'état au Ministère du Travail, March 3, 1943.

52. AN F²² 1961, "Recruitement des syndicats uniques ouvriers," dossier Ille-et-Vilaine.

53. AN F²² 1955, minutes of the meeting of the CPO, May 31, 1943.

54. AN F²² 1955, reports about Orléans and Brittany in the proceedings of the FNSOC, 20e Congrès National, Paris, March 7, 1944; and the minutes of the CPO subcommission for *syndicats uniques* meeting of January 18, 1944. For the Drôme, see AN F²² 1964, "Famille professionnelle de l'hygiène, Syndicats uniques ouvriers—Correspondances," letter of March 4, 1944.

55. Two to three hundred patronal syndicats and sixty to seventy workers' is a reasonable guess. See AN F¹² 11999, minutes of the CPO meeting of March 30, 1944; F²² 1955, minutes of the CPO meetings of October 19 and November 10, 1942, February 2 and May 17, 1943; and 1958, "Déclaration des organismes syndicaux."

56. All these cases can be found, by department, in AN F²² 1958–1967.

57. On Clauzade, see AN F²² 1961, dossier for the Puy-de-Dôme; and F²² 1967, "Unions régionales et fédérales," minutes of the general assembly of the Union régionale des ouvriers coiffeurs de Paris; and *Ouvrier Coiffeur* (October–December 1938).

58. *Éclaireur des Coiffeurs* (May 10, 1943), 3–4; and (October 25, 1943), 2. On Lagardelle generally, see Zeev Sternhell, *The Birth of Fascist Ideology* (Princeton: Princeton University Press, 1994), 99; and idem, *Neither Right nor Left: Fascist Ideology in France* (Princeton: Princeton University Press, 1996), 267–68.

59. On Lagardelle's fading battle for the charter and his fall see AN F¹² 11999, letter from Bichelonne to Lagardelle, June 28, 1943; and the letter from Magnien to "tous les fédérés of the FNSOC," November 25, 1943. Also see AN F²² 2029, "Charte du travail-Comité français de la libération nationale," dossier II-A-3, note from A. Tixier, *commissaire aux affaires sociales*, to Henri Hauck, in Algiers, December 29, 1943; the report, "La situation dans les milieux syndicalistes en octobre 1943 (source collaborationiste)," dated October 12, 1943; and a report by M. Bigiauoui, "La Charte du Travail," February 14, 1944.

60. AN F¹² 11999.

61. AN F²² 1957; also see Magnien's letter from prison to Foullet, Secretary of the Union des syndicates parisiennes, in CGT, carton 14 "Correspondance relative à l'affaire Magnien, 1944–1950."

62. *Je Suis Partout* (July 2, 1943).

63. On Loyer's prewar politics, see the *Revue internationale des sociétés secrètes: Bulletin mensuel de la Ligue anti-judéomaçonnique;* and Henry Coston, *Partis, journaux et hommes politiques d'hier et d'aujourd'hui: Lecture française* (1960). On Coston himself see Jean Defrasne, *Histoire de la collaboration* (Paris: Presses Universitaires de France, 1982), 50; Dominque Rossignol, *Vichy et les francs-maçons: La liquidation des sociétés secrètes, 1940–1944* (Paris: Éditions J.-C. Lattès, 1981), 167. For Loyer's remarks on the destruction of France see Pierre Loyer, "Vue d'ensemble sur la politique intérieure," *Conférence faite le 23 novembre 1935 à la réunion des membres de l'Union Croix de Feu-Centraux;* and "Les affinités françaises: La maison des producteurs: Réunion octobre 1936," *Les dessous maçonniques du radicalisme* (Paris, 1936).

64. Quoted in Bernard Zarca, "Survivance ou transformation de l'artisanat dans la France d'aujourd'hui," thèse en sociologie, Institut d'Études Politiques, Paris, 1983, 412.

65. Steven M. Zdatny, *The Politics of Survival: Artisans in Twentieth-Century France* (New York: Oxford University Press, 1990), 139–40.

66. AN F^{12} 11999, letters from Loyer to the director of organisation sociale at the Labor Ministry, December 24, 1942; and to the general secretary at the Organisation industrielle et commerciale, May 31, 1943; and AN F^{22} 1955, minutes of the CPO meeting of July 19, 1943.

67. On the Statut de l'Artisanat see Jean Bichelonne, *Le Statut de l'Artisanat: Extrait du Journal Officiel du 25 août 1943* (Clermont-Ferrand: Imprimeries Paul Vallier, 1943); Pierre Loyer, *Les incidences sociales du Statut de l'Artisanat: Conférence* (Vichy: Éditions du Centre d'Information et de Documentation Artisanales, 1945); idem, *Le Statut de l'Artisanat* (Paris: Dunod, 1944).

68. AN F^{22} 2029, Bigiaoui report on the Charte du Travail, Bichelonne speech of October 11, 1943.

69. AN F^{12} 10135, "Note sur l'artisanat."

70. AN F^{12} 11999. Benzenger, an Artisanal Service delegate from Nantes, alerted Loyer to the circular from Gestalder to UF adherents, December 31, 1943. The declaration of the FNSOC administrative council, authored by Magnien, is in *Éclaireur des Coiffeurs* (December 1943), 6; also see his circular to all the *syndicats fédérés*, November 24, 1943, in FNCEP-FO, Histoire de la Coiffure, 1943–1946.

71. On the activity of Commission 13 see AN F^{12} 11999, note from Loyer to Bichelonne with regard to the committee's personnel, December 31, 1943; minutes of the committee's meeting of February 2, 1944; and *Artisan Français* (July 1944).

72. AN F^{22} 1955, minutes of the CPO meeting of February 10, 1944.

73. AN F^{22} 1955, note from Gérard Bardet, vice president of the Conseil Supérieur du Travail, to Bichelonne, February 11, 1944.

74. AN F^{12} 11999, see Loyer's note, "Décision de M. Bichelonne," February 11, 1944; and his letter to Bardet, "suite à la décision verbale du Ministre en date du 11 février [1944]."

75. Éclaireur (June 5–20, 1944), 1.

76. AN F^{22} 1956; FNCEP-FO, Histoire Coiffure, 1943–1946, dossier "1944."

77. AN F²² 1957, "Famille professionnelle de la Coiffure," dossier "Courrier reçu depuis la dissolution."

78. Ingo Kolboom, *La revanche des patrons. Le patronat français face au Front populaire* (Paris: Flammarion, 1986), 351. See also Guy Bourdé, *La défaite du Front Populaire* (Paris: F. Maspéro, 1977); Patrick Fridenson, "Le patronat français," in *La France et les Français, 1938–1939*, ed., René Rémond and Janine Bourdin (Paris: Presses de la Fondation Nationale des Sciences Politiques, 1978), 139–58. John Sweets, *Choices in Vichy France: The French under Nazi Occupation* (New York: Oxford University Press, 1986), 31. Vinen, *Politics*, 2, claims emphatically that this was not true.

79. Val Lorwin, *The French Labor Movement* (Cambridge, MA: Harvard University Press, 1954), 86–7.

80. Jean Maitron, dir., *Dictionnaire biographique du mouvement ouvrier français, Quatrième partie: 1914–1939, De la première à la seconde guerre mondiae, tome XVIII* (Paris: Les Éditions Ouvrières, 1982), 348.

81. *Éclaireur des Coiffeurs*, special Liberation edition, 1945, 6.

82. Sweets, *Choices*, 31. On the regime's "contradictory tendencies" see Kim Munholland, "Review Article: Wartime France: Remembering Vichy," *French Historical Studies* (Spring 1994), 811.

9   Dark Days, Bright Future

1. On Schueller see Raymond Abiello [Georges Soulès], *Ma dernière mémoire III: Sol invictus, 1939–1947* (Paris: Editions Ramsey, 1980), 213–7 and 268–9; Philippe Bourdrel, *La Cagoule: 30 ans de complots* (Paris: Albin Michel, 1970), 83; Philippe Burrin, *La France à l'heure allemande, 1940–1944* (Paris: Seuil, 1995), 393; Ingo Kolboom, *La revanche des patrons. Le patronat français face au Front populaire* (Paris: Flammarion, 1986), 273, 279–80; Pascal Ory, *Les collaborateurs, 1940–1945* (Paris: Seuil, 1976), 99; Henry Rousso, *La collaboration: Les noms/les thèmes/les lieux* (Paris: MA Editions, 1987), 130–1.

2. On the unrealistic expectations of the population see Megan Koreman, *The Expectation of Justice: France, 1944–1946* (Durham, NC: Duke University Press, 1999), 258. On postwar hardships see Dominique Veillon, *Vivre et survivre en France, 1939–1947* (Paris: Payot, 1995), 289–301.

3. *Cahiers de la Coiffure* (March 1946) and (April 1947); *Coiffeur de France* (November 1946) and (January 1950); *Éclaireur des Coiffeurs* (January 25, 1946).

4. Gérard Dehove, "Le mouvement ouvrier et la politique syndicale," *Revue d'Économie Politique* (November–December 1947), 1574. Jean-Daniel Reynaud, *Les syndicats en France* (Paris: Armand Colin, 1963), 90; Jean-Pierre Rioux, *The Fourth Republic, 1944–1958* (Cambridge: Cambridge University Press, 1987), 76.

5. FNCEP-FO, Histoire Coiffure, 1943–1946, letters of September 26 and 28, 1939. Also see *Ouvrier Coiffeur Parisien* (March 1946); and the unsigned letter to the Paris Prefect of Police, October 21, 1944, denouncing Magnien

for having seized CSO goods illegally in 1939 and threatening to have his opponents sent to a concentration camp: in CGT, carton 14.

6. CGT, carton 14, "Résumé de l'affaire Magnien sur le plan syndical": letters from Magnien to Reynaud September 24, 1944, from Moreau to Reynaud, September 27, 1944, and from Reynaud to Moreau, September 30, 1944; also Procès-verbal of the CSO General Assembly, October 30, 1944.

7. The CNROS, which was more or less an arm of the CGT, took its legal mandate from the *ordonnance* issued by the provisional government from Algiers on July 27, 1944, which empowered all syndical organizations to pronounce sanctions, covering participation in the labor movement "against anyone who . . . had served the enemy's purposes, directly or indirectly" and contributed "to the destruction of *la liberté syndicale*." See Confédération générale du travail, *Compte-rendu des travaux de la Commission nationale de reconstitution des organisations syndicales des travailleurs* (Versailles: Imprimerie Coopérative "La Gutenberg," 1946), 3–5, 23.

8. FNCEP-FO, 22e Congrès Fédéral, Paris, 1945, letter from Arthur Roger to "chers comarades," November 21, 1945. Also CGT, carton 14, letters from Julien Racamond, of the CGT executive board, to the FNSOC executive, February 23, 1945; and from the CDROS to the CSO, February 8, 1946; and *Le Peuple* (November 11, 1944).

9. CGT, carton 14, letter from the CSO to the CGT Executive Board, September 18, 1944; FNCEP-FO, Histoire Coiffure, 1943–1946, "1945," letter to Albert Jacquelin, FNSOC President, December 21, 1945.

10. Letter from Magnien to Parodi, December 6, 1944, in CGT, "Dossier: Affaire Magnien François." See also the letter from Henry Hauck, Directeur des relations professionnelles et des questions sociales, at the Labor Ministry, to Jayat, a member of the CNROS, telling him, in effect, that the commission is free do as it likes, December 20, 1944.

11. The report of the Conseil supérieur d'enquête and testimonies can be found in CGT, carton 14. See also Machelon's letter to "Comarade Aurèche," of Annecy, in FNCEP-FO, Histoire Coiffure, 1943–1946.

12. The depositions against Magnien, taken on April 9 and May 29, 1945, are also in CGT, carton 14 [my emphases].

13. CGT, carton 14, report by the Conseil supérieur d'enquête, May 11, 1945.

14. *Front Syndicalist* (January 1948); also see Magnien's gloating essay, "Fin du scandale de l'épuration syndicale," in *Tribune des Ouvriers Coiffeurs* (December 1947).

15. CGT, carton 14, note from Burba to Gautereau, January 4, 1945; letter from Racamond, of the CGT executive committee, to the FNSOC *bureau*, February 23, 1945; also the report from the CSO in Paris to its provincial members, February 19, 1945.

16. FNCEP-FO, 21e Congrès fédéral, "Rapport moral du bureau et de la commission administrative; also the report on the congress in Histoire Coiffure, 1943–1946, "1944."

17. *Éclaireur des Coiffeurs* (Number 4 [n.d. but surely early 1945]), 1.

18. See Magnien's letter of resignation to the FNSOC, CGT, carton 14, January 18, 1945.

19. The vote was 61–7 for Magnien, FNCEP-FO, 22e Congrès fédéral, Paris, 1945, circular, February 13, 1945.
20. On the Comité provisoire de gestion see CGT, carton 14, Magnien's letter of resignation, January 18, 1945, Racamond's letter of February 22, 1945 and Saillant's letter of March 15, 1945 to the federation. Also FNCEP-FO, Histoire Coiffure, 1943–1946, "1945," circular from the federation to its members, March 19, 1945. On Roger see Éclaireur des Coiffeurs (August 10, 1945), 1 and (October 10, 1945), 2; Front Syndicalist (July 1946).
21. FNCEP-FO, 22e Congrès fédéral, Paris, 1945 contains the process-verbal of the proceedings.
22. Éclaireur des Coiffeurs (September 10, 1945), 1.
23. These insults come from the Ouvrier Coiffeur Parisien (March 1946) and (August 1946). But similar comments could be found in every number of the CSO journal.
24. Front Syndicalist (July 1946); Tribune des Ouvriers Coiffeurs (December 1947).
25. CGT, carton 14, "Décision de la Commission confédérale des conflits," Feburary 4, 1946.
26. Confédération générale du travail, XXVIe Congrès national de Paris, 8–12 August 1946. Compte-rendu sténographique des débats (Paris: Éditions de la CGT, 1946), no page numbers.
27. For the fullest account of the congress see CGT, carton 1, FNSOC: XXIIe [sic] congrès, March 3–4, 1947.
28. Ouvrier Coiffeur Parisien (January 1, 1946).
29. CGT, carton 9, rapports moraux of December 1946 and July–September 1947.
30. This also focused on Magnien's refusal to return CSO property that had passed to the SOC during the war: CGT, carton 14 and carton 9 passim.
31. The first issue of the journal Force Ouvrière appeared in January 1946. This "organe de réflexion syndicale des minoritaires et de nombreux socialistes," replaced the journal Résistance Ouvrière, which had first appeared in November 1944: Jacques Girault, Benoît-Frachon: Communiste et syndicaliste (Paris: Presses de la Fondation Nationale des Sciences Politiques, 1989), 245.
32. Val Lorwin, The French Labor Movement (Cambridge: Harvard University Press, 1954), 127; also see Girault, Benoît-Frachon, 248; Reynaud, Les syndicats en France, 91–2. For a highly tendentious view of the split see Jean Bruhat, and Marc Piolot, Esquisse d'une histoire de la CGT (1895–1965) (Paris: CGT, 1966), 201.
33. In addition, the SOC officially changed its name to recall its roots in the 1920s, now calling itself the Syndicat confédéré des ouvriers coiffeurs de Paris: Tribune des Ouvriers Coiffeurs (December 1947).
34. Tribune des Ouvriers Coiffeurs (January–February 1948).
35. Tribune des Ouvriers Coiffeurs (December 1947).
36. CGT, carton 9, Rapport moral du conseil syndical de la CSO, October 1947–January 1948.
37. See the remarks in Combat Syndicalist (October 20, 1950); Leclerc's comments in Le Peuple (September 20, 1947); FNCEP-FO, Histoire de la Coiffure,

1950–1953, letter from Leclerc to all syndical personnel (CSO), November 3, 1947; *Ouvrier Coiffeur Parisien* (February 1948).

38. CGT, carton 4, "Circulaires fédérales, 1948–1949," circular of December 29, 1947; dossier also contains a samizdat edition of the *Ouvrier Coiffeur* (March 1949), dedicated to the activity of the "XXXe congrès, 27–28 September 1948," in Paris. On the FNSOC's new population see CGT, carton 3, "Procès-verbaux du bureau fédéral, conseil fédéral, et commission administrative," réunion January 24, 1949.

39. FNSOC-FO, 23ème Congrès Fédéral, Paris, July 4–5, 1948.

40. FNCEP-FO, Histoire de la Coiffure, 1950–1953, "1950," Rapport d'activité: Syndicat national des gérants techniques de Paris; "1953," circular July 18, 1953; and Historique Syndicale de la Coiffure, which contains Clauzade's manuscript history of the federation. Also see Catherine Lebas and Annie Jacques, *La Coiffure en France du Moyen Age à Nos Jours* (Paris: Delmas International, 1978), 62.

41. The federation claimed to have grown, between August 1945 and May 1946 from 9,000 to almost 20,000 adherents: *Ouvrier Coiffeur Parisien* (April–May 1946).

42. *Cahiers de la Coiffure* (December 25, 1945); *Coiffeur de France* (August 1946); *Coiffure de Paris* (January 1946), 17.

43. *Coiffeur de France* (June 1946); *Coiffure de Paris* (February 1946), 5.

44. Catherine Gavend, "Les coiffeurs de Lyon (1948–1975)," Centre Pierre Lyon d'histoire économique et sociale, *Métiers et Statuts, Bulletin* (1999), 137; *Coiffeur de France* (June 1947).

45. See Bagnaud's obituary in *Coiffeur de France* (May 1964); also Nonna Mayer, *La boutique contre la gauche* (Paris: Presses de la Fédération Nationale des Sciences Politiques, 1986), 270.

46. *Cahiers de la Coiffure* (July 1946); *Coiffeur de France* (June 1947). On the CNA see Gaston Lecordier, *Les classes moyennes en marche* (Paris: Bloud et Gay, 1950), 152–54; Noël Metton, *Brève histoire de l'artisanat en France, 1925–1963* (Lyon: L'Artisan de la Métallurgie du Rhône, 1964), 11; Henri Mourier, "L'artisanat, sa structure et son intégration dans l'économie moderne," Thèse en droit, Paris, 1952, 178–9.

47. Nonna Mayer writes that *petits commerçants* were very frustrated with their economic and social circumstances and resented greedy employers, "priviliged" larger businesses, and the state: "Small Business and Social Mobility in France," in Robert Goffee and Richard Scase, eds., *Entrepreneurship in Europe: The Social Processes* (London: Croom Helm, 1987), 53–5.

48. *Cahiers de la Coiffure* (September 1946).

49. *Ouvrier Coiffeur Parisien* (April and June 1946); and *Coiffeur de France* (May 5, 1946).

50. *Cahiers de la Coiffure* (March 1946).

51. AN F^{12} 10147, letter from Lamy to the minister of industrial production, November 8, 1945.

52. *Cahiers de la Coiffure* (January 1946).

53. Ministère des Finances et des Affaires Économiques. INSEE. Direction de la Statistique Générale. *Résultats statistiques du recensement général de la*

population effectué le 10 mars 1946 (Paris: Imprimerie Nationale, 1952): vol. III, "Population Active," 282.

54. FNCEP-FO, Histoire de la Coiffure, 1946, "Report: Assemblée Nationale Constituente, 1946: Projet de loi portant réglementation des conditions d'accès à la profession de la coiffure," April 20, 1946.

55. The requirement of a *gérant technique* did not apply in communes with populations under 2,000: Gavend, "Coiffeurs de Lyon," 135–7.

56. *Coiffeur de France* (June 1948); *Tribune des Ouvriers Coiffeurs* (May 1948).

57. Rambaud's quote is in *Coiffeur de France* (March 1948).

58. CGT, carton 9, "Rapport moral: 15 April 1946"; and Jacques Lehoulier, "L'évolution des salaires depuis 1938 (jusqu'au juin 1946)," *Revue d'Économie Politique* (November–December 1947), 1531.

59. AN F^{12} 102502, "Homologation des prix, 1945–1946."

60. The wage scale is in AN F^{12} 102502; *Cahiers de la Coiffure* (December 25, 1945); *Éclaireur des Coiffeurs* (October 25, 1945), 4.

61. CGT, carton 9, "Rapport moral, October–December 1945."

62. CGT, carton 4, Circulaires fédérales, 1945, 1948.

63. *Cahiers de la Coiffure* (March 1946).

64. On the *arrêté* of June 8 and the decree of July 29, 1946 see CGT, carton 9, "Rapport moral: juin–novembre 1946"; and *Coiffeur de France* (August 1946).

65. *Éclaireur des Coiffeurs* (September 10, 1946), 6; *Coiffeur de France* (October 1946).

66. CGT, carton 4, "1945": The Commission nationale des salaires produced the following schedule in 1945:

Category	Coefficient	Definition
1st	100	*manoeuvre*
2nd	115	*manoeuvre spécialisé*
3rd	130	*ouvrier spécialiste*
4th	155	*ouvrier qualifié*
5th	185	*ouvrier hautement qualifié ou ouvrier d'art*

The arrêté of March 24, 1948 set the following schedule for minimum *salaires*:

1st category–1,600 francs/week
2nd category–1,700 francs/week
3rd category–1,850 francs/week
5th category
   1st rank–2,200 francs/week
   2nd rank–2,300 francs/week
   3rd rank–2,500 francs/week
   4th rank–2,600 francs/week

However, guaranteed tips raised these wages from a minimum of 2,100 francs for the lowest category of *débutants* to 3,060 francs for a worker of the

4th category, third rank. Guaranteed minimums for manicurists, pedicurists, and workers in *soins de beauté*, including tip, ranged from 2,100 francs to 2,675. These wages pertained only to the first zone of the Région parisienne: *Tribune des Coiffeurs* (March 1948).

67. CGT, carton 13, Correspondance du Ministre du Travail au Syndicat des ouvriers coiffeurs, letters of June 27 and July 17, 1946 [my emphasis].

68. FNCEP-FO, Histoire de la Coiffure, 1950–1953, "1950," Rapport: Jugement des Prud'hommes, June 9, 1950.

69. CGT, carton 1, FNSOC, 22e congrès, March 3–4, 1947, comment by Fournier, delegate from Nice/Monaco.

70. CGT, carton 4, Comité de gérance, report to the congrès national, August 27–28, 1945; *Le Peuple* (August 25, 1945).

71. *Coiffeur de France* (August 1947).

72. Interview with Marcel Haggaï, May 7, 1992.

73. Jeanne Singer-Kérel, *Le coût de la vie à Paris de 1840 à 1954* (Paris: Presses de la Fondation Nationale des Sciences Politiques, 1961), see her table "Indices du coût de la vie en France de 1913 à 1954 (1938 = 100)," 235. The table contains fourteen different indexes. I have used the first one: "213 articles reconstitués," but they are all more or less proportional. For other calculations on prices over this period see *Le mouvement des prix de 1913 à 1950. Recueil des cours et indices des principaux produits industriels, du coût de la vie et des salaires, mis à jour au 1er mai 1950* (Paris: L'Usine Nouvelle, 1950), 38. For the period of the Liberation see Institut national de la statistique et des études économiques, *Mouvement économique en France de 1944 à 1957* (Paris: Presses Universitaires de France), 108; and R. Rivet, "L'évolution des prix depuis la guerre," *Revue d'Économie Politique* (September–October 1947), 871.

74. *Cahiers de la Coiffure* (September 1946) and (December 1947).

75. An index of 203 for Coiffure, as against a general index of 147.7 (1949 = 100): Ministère des Affaires Économiques et Financiers, INSEE, *Annuaire statistique de la France, 1956* (Paris: Imprimerie Nationale, 1956), XIV.

76. FNCEP-FO, Histoire de la Coiffure, 1950–1953, "1951."

77. INSEE pour la Métropole de la France d'Outre-Mer, *Annuaire statistique, 1951: Résumé rétrospectif* (Paris: Imprimerie Nationale, 1952), 251. I calculated hairdressers' wages by extrapolating from the 1951 settlement, accounting for inflation of 16.8 percent, as indicated by Singer-Kérel. For the *indices des taux des salaires horaires* for 1956 see Ministère des Affaires Économiques *Annuaire statistique*, 1956, IX: The index for wages in *hygiène* was 585, while the average index was 609 (1946 = 100).

78. INSEE, "Bulletin mensuel de statistique," (May 1964), 51.

79. FNCEP-FO, Histoire de la Coiffure, 1950–1953, "1953," from the *process-verbal* of the 25e FNSOC congress, July 6–7, 1953.

80. INSEE, "Bulletin mensuel," (May 1964), 50.

81. INSEE, "Bulletin mensuel," (May 1964), 51.

82. Ministère des Finances et des Affaires Économiques. INSEE, *Annuaire statistique de la France 1959* (résultats de 1958) (Paris: Imprimerie Nationale and Presses Universitaires de France, 1959), XI.

83. Quoted in Paul Gerbod, *Histoire de la coiffure et des coiffeurs* (Paris: Larousse, 1995), 263.
84. Janet Flanner (Genêt), *Paris Journal, 1944–1955* (New York: Harcourt, Brace Jovanovich, 1965), 16.
85. Anthony Beevor and Artemis Cooper, *Paris After the Liberation: 1944–1949* (London: Penguin, 1994), 312–6, describe the excitement and outrage that greeted the "New Look"; and Stanley Karnow, *Paris in the Fifties* (New York: Times Books, 1997), 267, 274. Also see Guillaume, *Guillaume raconte . . . la coiffure et ses métamorphoses* (Argenton-sur-Creuse: Imprimerie de l'Indre, 1982), 69; Mary Trasko, *Daring Do's: A History of Extraordinary Hair* (New York, Paris: Flammarion, 1994), 120; and *Votre Beauté* (June 1948), 18.
86. On the advantages of shorter hairstyles see *Vogue* (February 1949); and *Votre Beauté* (October 1949).
87. Gerbod, *Histoire*, 265; also see Joyce Asser, *Historic Hairdressing* (New York: Pitman Publishing, 1966), 122; and Jean Keyes, *A History of Women's Hairstyles, 1500–1965* (London: Methuen, 1967), 63.
88. Richard Corson, *Fashions in Hair: The First Five Thousand Years* (London: Peter Owen, 1965), 662–3; Trasko, *Daring Do's*, 122.
89. Gerbod, *Histoire*, 268.
90. On Alexandre's career see Alexandre, *Sous le casque d'Alexandre* (Paris: Presses de la Cité, 1972); and Giselle d'Assailly, *Fards et Beauté, ou l'éternel féminin* (Paris: Hachette, 1958), 259–65.
91. Gerbod, *Histoire*, 245.
92. Gerbod, *Histoire*, 257.
93. Trasko, *Daring Do's*, 128–9.
94. Caroline Cox, *Good Hair Days: A History of British Hairstyling* (London: Quartet Books, 1999), 119.
95. Jean Fourastié, *Les Trentes glorieuses, ou la Révolution invisible de 1946 à 1975* (Paris: Fayard, 1979), 23; Dominique Veillon, *Nous les enfants (1950–1970)* (Paris: Hachette, 2003), 133–5.
96. Gavend, "Coiffeurs de Lyon," 134.
97. On the dangers of too much shampooing, see the warnings of Dr. Jean H., in Maguelonne Toussaint-Samat, *La Femme de quarante ans* (Paris: Centurion/Grasset, 1973), 103.
98. See *Vogue* (January 1945), "Numéro de Libération."
99. Colombe Pringle, *Telles qu'Elle: Cinquante ans d'histoire des femmes à travers le journal* Elle (Paris: Grasset, 1995), 14.
100. Samra-Martine Bonvoisin and Michèle Maignien, *La presse féminine* (Paris: Presses Universitaires de France, 1986), 20–2. For a more in-depth treatment of *Elle* and *Mademoiselle* see Susan Weiner, *Enfants Terribles: Youth and Femininity in the Mass Media in France, 1945–1968* (Baltimore: Johns Hopkins University Press, 2001), especially chapter 1, "From *Elle* to *Mademoiselle*," 21–66.
101. Gerbod, *Histoire*, 297–324 *passim*.
102. *Coiffures 46*, 41; André Gissler, *Technologie de la coiffure pour dames et messieurs* (Paris: Dunod, 1955), 12. According to Gerbod, the number of

tinted *françaises* went from half a million in 1950 to seven or eight million thirty years later: *Histoire*, 301.

103. J. Auzary, *Notions de technologie générale pour l'apprenti coiffeur pour dames* (Paris: Édition Eyrolles, 1954), 107; Edwin Sidi and R. Longueville, *Les accidents par produits capillaires. Étude clinique, expérimentale et medico-légale* (Paris: Edtions Médicales Flammarion, 1958), 11.

104. Marie-Christine Auzou and Sabine Melchior-Bonnet, *La vie du cheveux* (Paris: Gallimard, 2001), 90–1; and Volo Litvinsky, *Toute la permanente. Tous les procédés et tours de mains* (Paris: Société d'Édition Modernes Parisiennes, 1958), 15.

105. *Votre Beauté* (April 1946), 24; and (November 1949), 12–13.

106. "La permanente à froide aux coiffeurs," in *Coiffure de Paris* (December 1948), 1.

107. *Coiffeur de France* (November 1948) and (December 1948); *Tribune des Ouvriers Coiffeurs* (September 1948): Manifesto from the FNSOC's 23e congrès national.

108. Gerbod, *Histoire*, 242.

109. The Second International Congress of Haute Coiffure, held in Paris, 13–October 15, 1946, listed the following sponsors: Bonaz, Coty, Gallia, Houbigant, Lancôme, Nina Ricci, L'Oréal, Perma, Roger et Gallet, Worth, and Lanvin: FNCEP-FO, Histoire de la Coiffure, 1946; the 1950 Championnat de France de la Coiffure was sponsored by Gallia, Eugène, Komol, Perma, and L'Oréal: *Coiffeur de France* (April 1950).

Conclusion

1. Roland Barthes, *The Fashion System* (New York: Hill and Wang, 1983).

2. Grant McCracken, *Big Hair: A Journey into the Transformation of the Self* (Woodstock, NY: Overlook Press, 1995), 36–7. His much-cited book is full of this sort of thumbnail semiotics.

Select Bibliography

Archives and Government Publications

National Archives, Paris

AJ38 Commissariat Générale aux Questions Juives (CGQJ) et Services de Restitution des Biens Spoliés

AJ72 Papiers du Comité de l'Histoire de la Deuxième Guerre Mondiale et Fonds Privés Relatifs à la Période, 1939–1945

F^7 Ministère de l'Intérieur

F^{12} Ministère du Commerce et de l'Industrie

F^{22} Ministère du Travail

Other Archives

Archives de Paris
    Jugements des Prud'hommes
    Procédures des Conseils de Prud'hommes
    Versements de la Préfecture de Police
Archives Départementales des Yvelines
Chambre de Commerce et d'Industrie de Paris
Fédération Nationale de la coiffure, de l'esthétique et de la parfumerie—Force Ouvrière
Institut d'Histoire Sociale, Confédération Générale du Travail, Paris
Préfecture de Police, Seine

Journals and Newspapers

Art et Coiffure (Paris)
Artisan (Paris)
Artisan Coiffeur (Moulins)
Ártisan Français (Paris)
Avocat des Coiffeurs (Paris)
Bulletin des Maître-Coiffeurs de l'Oise (Beauvais)
Cahiers de la Coiffure Parisienne
Capilartiste (Paris)
Cheveux Courts (Paris)

Coiffeur Confédéré (Paris)
Coiffeur de France (Paris)
Coiffure de Paris
Coiffeur du Sud-Ouest (Montauban)
Coiffeur Nantais (Nantes)
Coiffeur-Parfumeur (Bordeaux)
Coiffeur Populaire (Paris)
Coiffure Française Illustrée (Paris)
Combat Syndicalist
Commerce des Coiffeurs-Parfumeurs
Eclair
Éclaireur des Coiffeurs (Paris)
Ere Nouvelle
Femme de France
Figaro-Modes
France Coiffure (Paris)
Front Syndicaliste
Gallia Journal
Hairdressers' Weekly Journal Supplement
Hebdo-Coiffure (Paris)
Humanité
Intransigeant
Je Suis Partout
Journal de la Coiffure (Paris)
Journal des Maîtres-Coiffeurs (Paris)
Libération
Libertaire
Livre de la Mode à Paris
Mode Illustrée (Paris)
Nouveau Siècle
Oeuvre
Ouvrier Coiffeur (Marseille)
Ouvrier Coiffeur Parisien
Paris Coiffures
Paris Soir
Petit Journal
Petit Parisien
Petite République
Populaire
Quotidien
Rappel
Reveil des Coiffeurs (Paris)
Reveil des Figaros (Paris)
Revue Internationale des Sociétés secrètes. Bulletin bi-mensuel de la Ligue Anti-judémaçonnique: "Le franc-catholique"
Revue Nouvelle des Coiffeurs et Parfumeurs (Paris)
Semaine de la Coiffure (Paris)

Soleil
Syndicalisme
Trait d'Union des Coiffeurs (Lyon)
Tribune des Ouvriers Coiffeurs (Paris)
Union des Syndicats de Coiffeurs (Paris)
Vogue
Voix du Peuple
Votre Beauté
W (vu). Journal de la Semaine (Paris)

Books, Articles, and Theses

Alexandre. *Sous la casque d'Alexandre*. Paris: Presses de la Cité, 1972.

Amdur, Kathryn E. "Paternalism, Productivity, Collaborationism: Employers and society in Interwar and Vichy France." *International Labor and Working-Class History* 53 (Spring 1998): 137–63.

———. *Syndicalist Legacy: Trade Unions and Politics in Two French Cities in the Era of World War I*. Urbana and Chicago: University of Illinois Press, 1986.

Andrews William. *At the Sign of the Barber's Pole: Studies in Hirsute History*. Cottingham: J.R. Tutin, 1904.

Antoine [Czierplikowski]. *J'ai coiffé le monde entier*. Paris: La Table Ronde, 1963.

Aron, Robert. *The Vichy Regime, 1940–1944*. New York: Macmillan, 1958.

———., ed., *Inventaires III, les classes moyennes en France*. Paris: Félix Alcan, 1939.

Assailly, Gisèle d'. *Fonds et beauté, ou l'éternel feminine*. Paris: Hachette, 1958.

Asser, Joyce. *Historic Hairdressing*. New York: Pitman Publishing, 1966.

Auzou, Marie-Christine and Melchior-Bonnet, Sabine. *La vie des cheveux*. Paris: Gallimard, 2001.

Azéma, Jean-Pierre and Bédarida, François, eds., *Le régime de Vichy et les français*. Paris: Fayard, 1992.

Banner, Lois. *American Beauty*. New York: Alfred A. Knopf, 1983.

Barrot, Olivier and Ory Pascal, dirs. *Entre Deux Guerres: La creation française, 1919–1939*. Paris: Éditions François Bourin, 1990.

Barthes, Roland. *The Fashion System*. New York: Hill and Wang, 1983.

Barzman, John. *Dockers, métallos, ménagers: Mouvements sociaux et cultures militantes au Havre, 1912–1923*. Rouen et Le Havre: Presses Universitaires de Rouen, 1997.

Becker, Jean-Jacques. *The Great War and the French People*. Oxford: Berg, 1985.

Beevor, Anthony and Cooper, Artemis. *Paris After the Liberation: 1944–1949*. London: Penguin, 1994.

Belin, René. *Du Secrétariat de la CGT au gouvernement de Vichy (Mémoires, 1933–1942)*. Paris: Albatros, 1978.

Berlanstein, Leonard R., ed., *Rethinking Labor History*. Urbana: University of Illinois Press, 1993.

Berstein, Serge. *Histoire du parti Radical, tome II: Le temps des crises et des mutations, 1926–1939*. Paris: Presses de la Fondation Nationale des Sciences Politiques, 1982.

Bodiguel, Jean-Luc. *La réduction du temps du travail: Enjeu de la lutte sociale*. Paris: Éditions Économie et Humanisme: Les Éditions Ouvrières, 1969.

Bonvoison, Samra-Martine and Maignien, Michèle. *La presse feminine*. Paris: Presses Universitaires de France, 1986.

Bordé, Guy. *La défaite du Front populaire*. Paris: François Maspéro, 1977.

Bourdieu, Pierre. *Distinction: A Social Critique of the Judgment of Taste*. Cambridge, MA: Harvard University Press, 1984.

Bouvier, Jean, et al. *La France en mouvement, 1934–1938*. Seysel: Champ Vallon, 1986.

Braudel, Fernand. *Capitalism and Material Life, 1400–1800*. New York: Harper, 1973.

Braudel, Fernand and Labrousse, Ernst, eds., *Histoire économique et sociale de la France, tome IV: L'ère industrielle et la société d'aujourd'hui (siècle 1880–1980)*. Second volume, *Le temps des guerres mondiales et de la grande crise (1914–vers 1950)*. Paris: Presses Universitaires de France, 1982.

Broglie, Pauline Laure Marie de (Comtesse de Pange). *Comment j'ai vu 1900*. Paris: Grasset, 1975.

Bryer, Robin. *The History of Hair: Fashion and Fantasy Down the Ages*. London: Philip Wilson, 2000.

Buisson, Monique. "Histoire d'un enseignement professionnel et pratiques familiales d'orientation: Le cas de la coiffure à Lyon." In Bernard, Régis, Buisson, Monique, Camy, Jean Roulleau-Berger and Vincent, Guy. *Education, fête et culture*. Lyon: Presses Universitaires de Lyon, 1981.

Caron, Vicki. *Uneasy Asylum: France and the Jewish Refugee Crisis, 1933–1942*. Stanford: Stanford University Press, 1999.

Chapman, Herrick, Kesselman, Mark, and Schain, Martin, eds., *A Century of Organized Labor in France: A Union Movement for the Twenty-First Century?* New York: Saint Martin's, 1998.

Charles-Roux, Edmonde. *L'irrégulière, ou mon itinéraire Chanel*. Paris: Bernard Grasset, 1974.

Chenille, Vincent. *La mode dans la coiffure des français: "La norme et la mouvement," 1837–1987*. Paris: Harmattan, 1996.

Coffignon, A. *Les coulisses de la mode*. Paris: À la Librairie Illustrée, 1888.

Coffin, Judith. *The Politics of Women's Work: The Paris Garment Trades, 1750–1915*. Princeton: Princeton University Press, 1996.

Coiffures 46. Paris: Imprimerie Curial-Archereau, 1945.

Connelly, Ida. *Beauty Operator on Broadway*. Fresno: Academy Library Guild, 1954.

Cooper, Wendy. *Hair: Sex, Society, Symbolism*. New York: Stein and Day, 1971.

Corbin, Alain. *The Foul and the Fragrant: Odor and the Social Imagination*. London: Papermac, 1996.

Corson, Richard. *Fashions in Hair: The First Five Thousand Years*. London: Peter Owen, 1965.

Cox, Caroline. *Good Hair Days: A History of British Hairstyling*. London: Quartet Books, 1999.

Cross, Gary. *A Quest for Time: The Reduction of Work in Britain and France, 1840–1940*. Berkeley: University of California Press, 1989.

Crossick, Geoffrey, ed., *The Artisan and the European Town, 1500–1900*. Aldershot, UK, and Brookfield, VT: Scholar Press, 1997.

Crossick, Geoffrey and Haupt, Heinz-Gerhard. *The Petite Bourgeoisie in Europe, 1780–1914: Enterprise, Family, and Independence*. London and New York: Routledge, 1998.

Darrow, Margaret. *French Women and the First World War: War Stories of the Home Front*. Oxford: Berg, 2000.

De Grazia, Victoria and Furlough, Ellen, eds., *The Sex of Things: Gender and Consumption in Historical Perspective*. Berkeley: University of California Press, 1996.

Delatour, Yvonne. "Le travail des femmes pendant la première guerre mondiale et ses consequences sur l'évolution de leur role dans la société." *Francia* 2 (1974): 1482–1501.

Delbourg-Delphis, Marylène. *Le chic et le look: Histoire de la mode féminine et des moeurs de 1850 à nos jours*. Paris: Hachette, 1981.

Desplanques, Charles. *Barbier, perruquiers, coiffeurs*. Paris: Librairie Octave Doin, 1927.

Downs, Laura Lee. *Manufacturing Inequality: Gender Division in the French and British Metalworking Industries, 1914–1939*. Ithaca: Cornell University Press, 1995.

Dutton, Paul V. *Origins of the French Welfare State: The Struggle for Social Reform in France, 1914–1947*. Cambridge: Cambridge University Press, 2002.

Ecksteins, Modris. *Rites of Spring: The Great War and the Birth of the Modern Age*. New York: Anchor, 1989.

Ewen, Stuart. *All Consuming Images: The Politics of Style in Contemporary Culture*. New York: Basic Books, 1988.

Flanner, Janet (Genêt). *Paris Journal, 1944–1955*. New York: Harcourt, Brace, Jovanovich, 1965.

Fondation Nationale des Sciences Politiques, travaux et recherches de science politique. *Le gouvernement de Vichy, 1940–1942: Institutions et politiques*. Paris: Armand Colin, 1972.

Fontanel, Béatrice. *Corsets et soutiens-gorge: L'épopée du sein de l'Antiquité à nos jours*. Paris: Éditions de la Martilères, 1992.

Fourastié, Jean. *Les trentes glorieuses, ou la revolution invisible de 1946 à 1975*. Paris: Fayard, 1979.

Fourcault, Annie. *Femmes à l'usine en France dans l'entre-deux-guerres*. Paris: François Maspéro, 1982.

François, Lucien. *Cent conseils d'élégance*. Paris: Société d'Éditions Modernes Parisiennes, 1942.

Friedenson, Patrick, dir. *1914–1918: L'autre front*. Paris: Les Éditions Ouvrières, 1977.

Friedman, Gerald C. *State-Making and Labor Movements: France and the United States, 1876–1914*. Ithaca: Cornell University Press, 1998.

Galante, Pierre. *Les Années Chanel*. Paris: Éditions Pierre Charron et Mercure de France, 1972.

Gavend, Catherine. "Les coiffeurs de Lyon (1948–1975)." Centre Pierre Lyon d'Histoire Économique et Sociale. *Métiers et Status, Bulletin* (1999): 133–46.

Georges-Lévy. *Hygiène du cuir chevelu et de la chevelure*. Paris: G. Doin et Cie., 1934.

Gerbod, Paul. *Histoire de la coiffure et des coiffeurs*. Paris: Larousse, 1995.

Graves, Charles. *Devotion to Beauty: The Antoine Story*. London: Jarrold's, 1962.

Grayzel, Susan R. *Women's Identities at War: Gender, Motherhood and Politics in Britain and France During the First World War*. Chapel Hill: University of North Carolina Press, 1999.

Green, Nancy L. *Ready-to-Wear and Ready-to-Work: A Century of Industry and Immigrants in Paris and New York*. Durham, NC: Duke University Press, 1997.

Grunberg, Albert. *Journal d'un coiffeur juif à Paris sous l'Occupation*. Paris: Éditions de l'Atelier, 2001.

Guilbert, Madeleine. *Les femmes et l'organisation syndicale avant 1914*. Paris: Éditions du CNRS, 1966.

Guillaume. *Guillaume raconte . . . la coiffure et ses metamorphoses*. Argenton-sur-Creuse: Imprimerie de l'Indre, 1982.

Haedrich, Marcel. *Coc Chanel Secrète*. Paris: Robert Laffont, 1971.

Hélias, Pierre-Jakez. *The Horse of Pride: Life in a Breton Village*. New Haven and London: Yale University Press, 1978.

Henry, Mrs. Robert. *Madeleine Grown Up*. London: J.M. Dent & Sons, 1952.

Herald, Jacqueline. *Fashions of a Decade: The 1920s*. New York: Jacqueline Herald, 1991.

Hesse, Jean-Philippe and Le Crom, Jean-Pierre, dirs. *La protection sociale sous le régime de Vichy*. Rennes: Presses Universitaires de Rennes, 2001.

Higgonet, Margaret Randolf, Jensen, Jane, Michel, Sonya and Weitz, Margaret Collins, eds., *Between the Lines: Gender and the Two World Wars*. New Haven: Yale University Press, 1987.

Hilden, Patricia. *Working Women and Socialist Politics in France, 1880–1914: A Regional Study*. Oxford: Clarendon, 1986.

Hollander, Anne. *Seeing Through Clothes*. New York: Viking, 1975.

Horne, John N. *Labour at War: France and Britain, 1914–1918*. Oxford: Clarendon, 1991.

Jackson, Julian. *France: The Dark Years, 1940–1944*. Oxford: Oxford University Press, 2001.

———. *The Popular Front in France: Defending Democracy, 1934–1938*. Cambridge: Cambridge University Press, 1988.

Joly, Hervé, ed., *Les comités d'organisation et l'économie dirigée du régime de Vichy*. Caen: Éditions du Mémorial du Caen, 2004.

Jones, Adrian. "Illusions of Sovereignty: Business and the Organization of Committees in Vichy France." *Social History* 11 (January 1986): 1–31.

Jones, Stephen G. *Workers at Play: A Social and Economic History of Leisure, 1918–1939*. London: Routledge and Kegan Paul, 1986.

Karnow, Stanley. *Paris in the Fifties*. New York: Times Books, 1997.

Kedward, Roderick. *Resistance in Vichy France: A Study of Ideas and Motivation in the Southern Zone, 1940–1942*. Oxford: Oxford University Press, 1978.

Kent, Susan Kingsley. *Making Peace: The Reconstruction of Gender in Interwar Britain*. Princeton: Princeton University Press, 1993.

Keyes, Jean. *A History of Women's Hairstyles, 1500–1965*. London: Methuen, 1967.

Koenig, René. *Sociologie de la mode*. Paris: Petite Bibliothèque Payot, 1969.

Kolboom, Ingo. *La revanche des patrons. Le patronat français face au front populaire*. Paris: Flammarion, 1986.

Korman, Megan. *The Expectation of Justice: France 1944–1946*. Durham, NC: Duke University Press, 1999.

Koslay, Hazel Leonie, ed., *Beauty Shop Problems*. New York: H.R. Howell, 1935.

Kuisel, Richard F. *Capitalism and the State in Modern France: Renovation and Economic Management in the Twentieth Century*. Cambridge: Cambridge University Press, 1981.

Lavau, Georges, Grunberg, Gerald, and Mayer, Nonna, dirs. *L'univers politique des classes moyennes*. Paris: Presses de la Fondation Nationale des Sciences Politiques.

Lebas, Catherine and Jacques, Annie. *La coiffure en France du Moyen Age à nos jours*. Paris: Delmas International, 1979.

Le Crom, Jean-Pierre. *Maréchal, nous voilà! Vichy et le corporatisme*. Paris: Éditions Ouvrières, 1995.

Lenormand, A. *Le devoir pour tous: Aux ouvriers coiffeurs de Paris. Première réponse à nos détracteurs*. Paris: Imprimerie du Proletariat, 1889.

Loeb, Lori Anne. *Consuming Angels: Advertising and Victorian Women*. New York: Oxford University Press, 1994.

Long, Emile. *Traité complet et illustré de l'ondulation artificielle des cheveux*. Paris: Albert Brunet, 1909.

Louis, M. *Six Thousand Years of Hair Styling*. New York: M. Louis, 1939.

Loyer, Pierre. *Le Statut de l'Artisanat*. Paris: Dunod, 1944.

Lurie, Alison. *The Language of Clothes*. New York: Random House, 1981.

Machefer, Philippe. "Les Syndicates professionnels français (1936–1939)." *Le Mouvement Social* 118 (April–June 1982): 91–112.

Manson, Anne, ed., "La scandale de 'la garçonne.'" In Guilleminault, Gilbert, *Les Années folles*. Paris: Denoël, 1958.

Marly, Diana de. *Fashion for Men: An Illustrated History*. London: B.T. Batsford, 1985.

Marrus, Michael and Paxton, Robert. *Vichy and the Jews*. New York: Basic Books, 1981.

Marwick, Arthur. *Women at War, 1914–1918*. London: Fontana, 1977.

May, Lary. *Screening Out the Past: The Birth of Mass Culture and the Motion Picture Industry*. New York: Oxford University Press, 1980.

Mayer, Nonna. *La boutique contra la gauche*. Paris: Presses de la Fondation Nationale des Sciences Politiques, 1986.

McBride, Theresa. "French Women and Trade Unionism: The First Hundred Years." In Solden, Norbert C. *The World of Women's Trade Unionism: Comparative Historical Perspectives*. Westport: Greenwood Press, 1985, 35–56.

McCracken, Grant. *Big Hair: A Journey into the Transformation of the Self.* Woodstock, NY: 1995.

Mcmillan, James F. *Housewife or Harlot: The Place of Women in French Society, 1870–1940.* New York: Saint Martin's, 1981.

Metton, Noël. *Brève histoire de l'artisanat en France, 1925–1963.* Lyon: L'Artisan de la Métallurgie du Rhône, 1964.

Miller, Michael B. *The Bon Marché: Bourgeois Culture and the Department Store, 1869–1920.* Princeton: Princeton University Press, 1981.

Mitchell, Barbara. *The Practical Revolutionaries: A New Interpretation of the French Anarcho-Syndicalists.* New York: Greenwood, 1987.

Le mouvement des prix de 1913 à 1950. Recueil des course et indices des prinicipaux produits industriels, du coût de la vie et des salaries, mis à jour au 1er mai 1950. Paris: L'Usine Nouvelle, 1950.

Mulvagh, Jane. *Vogue's History of Twentieth-Century Fashion.* London: Viking, 1988.

Noguères, Henri. *La vie quotidienne en France au temps du Front populaire.* Paris: Hachette, 1977.

Noiriel, Gérard. *Workers in French Society in the 19th and 20th Centuries.* Oxford: Berg, 1990.

Nord, Philip. *Paris Shopkeepers and the Politics of Resentment.* Princeton: Princeton University Press, 1986.

Paillard, Jean. *1940–1944: La révolution corporative spontanée.* Annonay: Éditions du Vivarais, 1979.

Papayanis, Nicolas. *Alphonse Merrheim: The Emergence of Reformism in Revolutionary Syndicalism, 1871–1925.* Dordrecht: Martinus Nijhoff, 1985.

Paxton, Robert. *Vichy France: Old Guard and New Order, 1940–1944.* New York: Norton, 1972.

Peiss, Kathy. *Cheap Amusements: Working Women and Leisure in Turn-of-the-Century New York.* Philadelphia: Temple University Press, 1986.

———. *Hope in a Jar: The Making of America's Beauty Culture.* New York: Metropolitan Books, 1998.

Perreux, Gabriel. *La vie quotidienne des civils en France pendant la grande guerre.* Paris: Hachette, 1966.

Perrot, Michèle. *Les ouvriers en grève: France, 1871–1890.* 2 vols. Paris: Mouton, 1974.

Perrot, Philippe. *Fashioning the Bourgeoisie: A History of Clothing in the Nineteenth Century.* Princeton: Princeton University Press, 1994.

Peschanski, Denis, dir. *Vichy, 1940–1944: Archives de guerre d'Angelo Tosca.* Paris: Éditions du CNRS, 1986.

Picard, Esther and Jacot-Descombes, Vivianne. *La coiffure à travers les siècles.* Paris: Éditions de l'Artisanat Moderne, 1973.

Plitt, Jane R. *Martha Matilda Harper and the American Dream: How One Woman Changed the Face of Modern Business.* Syracuse, NY: Syracuse University Press, 2000.

Poiret, Paul. *King of Fashion: The Autobiography of Paul Poiret.* Philadelphia and London: Lippencott, 1931.

Pringle, Colombe. *Telles qu'Elle: Cinquante ans d'histoire des femmes à travers le journal* Elle. Paris: Grasset, 1995.

Rambaud, René. *Les fugitives. Précis anécdotique et historique des coiffures féminines à travers les ages, des Egyptiens à 1945.* Paris: René Rambaud, 1947.

Rearick, Charles. *The French in Love and War: Popular Culture in the Era of the World Wars.* New Haven: Yale University Press, 1997.

———. *Pleasures of the Belle Epoque: Entertainment and Festivity in Turn-of-the-Century France.* New Haven: Yale University Press, 1985.

Rémond, René and Bourdin, Janine, eds., *La France et les français, 1938–1939.* Paris: Presses de la Fondation Nationale des Sciences Politiques.

Reynolds, Reginald. *Beards: Their Social Standing, Religious Involvements, Decorative Possibilities, and Value in Offence and Defence through the Ages.* Garden City: Doubleday & Co., 1949.

Reynolds, Siân. *France Between the Wars: Gender and Politics.* London and New York: Routledge, 1996.

Robert, Jean-Louis, ed., *Syndicalismes sous Vichy. Le Mouvement Social* 158 (January–March 1992).

Roberts, Mary Louise. *Civilization Without Sexes: Reconstructing Gender in Postwar France, 1917–1927.* Chicago: University of Chicago Press, 1994.

Rousso, Henry. "L'aryanisation économique—Vichy, l'occupant et la spoliation des Juifs." *YOD. Revue des études Hébraïques et Juives modernes et contemporaines* 15–16 (1982): 51–79.

———. "L'organisation industrielle de Vichy." *Revue d'histoire de la deuxième guerre mondiale* 29 (October 1979): 27–44.

Rudorff, Raymond. *Belle Epoque: Paris in the Nineties.* London: Hamish Hamilton, 1972.

Ruhlmann, Jean. *Ni bourgeois ni prolétaires. La défense des classes moyennes en France au XXe siècle.* Paris: Seuil, 2001.

Sabin, Guy. *Jean Bichelonne, Ministre sous l'Occupation: 1904–1944.* Paris: Éditions France-Empire, 1991.

Sauvy, Alfred. *Histoire économique de la France entre les deux guerres.* 3 vols. Paris: Fayard, 1965–1972.

Schweitzer, Sylvie. *Des engrenages à la chaîne: Les usines Citroën, 1915–1935.* Lyon: Presses Universitaires de Lyon, 1982.

Seidman, Michael. *Workers Against Work: Labor in Paris and Barcelona during the Popular Fronts.* Berkeley: University of California Press, 1991.

Severn, Bill. *The Long and Short of It: Five Thousand Years of Fun and Fury over Hair.* New York: David McKay Co., 1971.

Singer-Kerel, Jeanne. *Le coût de la vie à Paris de 1840 à 1954.* Paris: Presses de la Fondation Nationale des Sciences Politiques, 1961.

Smith, Bonnie. *Ladies of the Leisure Class: The Bourgeoises of Northern France in the Nineteenth Century.* Princeton: Princeton University Press, 1981.

Smith, Timothy B. *Creating the Welfare State in France, 1880–1940.* Montreal: McGill-Queen's University Press, 2003.

Sohn, Anne-Marie. "La garçonne face à l'opinion publique: type littéraire ou type social des années 20." *Le Mouvement Social* 80 (1972): 3–27.

Soucy, Robert. *French Fascism: The First Wave, 1924–1933.* New Haven and London: Yale University Press, 1986.

———. *French Fascism: The Second Wave: 1933–1939.* New Haven: Yale University Press, 1995.

Staten, Vince. *Do Bald Men Get Half-Price Haircuts? In Search of America's Great Barbershops.* New York: Simon and Schuster, 2001.

Stearns, Peter N. *Revolutionary Syndicalism and French Labor: A Cause Without Rebels.* New Brunswick: Rutgers University Press, 1971.

Steele, Valerie. *The Corset: A Cultural History.* New Haven: Yale University Press, 2001.

———. *Fashion and Eroticism: Ideals of Feminine Beauty from the Victorian Era to the Jazz Age.* New York: Oxford University Press, 1985.

———. *Paris Fashion: A Cultural History.* New York: Oxford University Press, 1988.

Stéphane. *L'art de la coiffure féminine. Son histoire à tavers les siècles.* Paris: Édition de *La Coiffure de Paris,* 1932.

Sternhell, Zeev. *The Birth of Fascist Ideology.* Princeton: Princeton University Press, 1994.

———. *Neither Right nor Left: Fascist Ideology in France.* Princeton: Princeton University Press, 1996.

Summers, Leigh. *Bound to Please: A History of the Victorian Corset.* Oxford: Berg, 2001.

Sweets, John. *Choices in Vichy France: The French Under Nazi Occupation.* New York: Oxford University Press, 1986.

———. *The Politics of Resistance in France: A History of the Mouvements unis de la Résistance.* DeKalb, IL: University of Northern Illinois Press, 1976.

Thébaud, Françoise. *La femme au temps de la guerre de 14.* Paris: Stock, 1986.

Trasko, Mary. *Daring Do's: A History of Extraordinary Hair.* New York and Paris: Flammarion, 1994.

Tucker, Kenneth H. *French Revolutionary Syndicalism and the Public Sphere.* Cambridge: Cambridge University Press, 1996.

Vandervort, Bruce. *Victor Griffuelhes and French Syndicalism, 1895–1922.* Baton Rouge: Louisiana State University Press, 1996.

Vanderwielen, Louise. *Lise du plat pays.* Lille: Presses Universitaires de Lille, 1983.

Vanier, Henriette. *La mode et ses métiers: Frivolities et luttes des classes, 1830–1870.* Paris: Armand Colin, 1960.

Veillon, Dominique. *La mode sous l'Occupation: Débrouillardise et coquetterie dans la France en guerre (1939–1945).* Paris: Éditions Payot, 1990.

———. *Nous les enfants (1950–1970).* Paris: Hachette, 2003.

———. *Vivre et survivre en France, 1939–1947.* Paris: Payot, 1995.

Vigarello, Georges. *Concepts of Cleanliness: Changing Attitudes in France Since the Middle Ages.* Cambridge: Cambridge University Press, 1988.

Vinen, Richard. *The Politics of French Business, 1936–1945.* Cambridge: Cambridge University Press, 1991.

Weber, Eugen. *France: Fin-de-Siècle.* Cambridge, MA: Harvard University Press, 1986.

Weiner, Susan. *Enfants Terribles: Youth and Femininity in the Mass Media in France, 1945–1968*. Baltimore: Johns Hopkins University Press, 2001.

Wilcox, R. Turner. *The Mode in Hats and Headdresses*. New York: Scribner, 1946.

Willet, Julie A. *Permanent Waves: The Making of the American Beauty Shop*. New York: New York University Press, 2000.

Williams, Rosalind H. *Dream Worlds: Mass Consumption in Late Nineteenth-Century France*. Berkeley: University of California Press, 1982.

Wilson, Elizabeth. *Adorned in Dreams: Fashion and Modernity*. Berkeley: University of California Press, 1985.

Winstanley, Michael J. *The Shopkeeper's World, 1830–1914*. Manchester: Manchester University Press, 1983.

Winter, Jay and Robert, Jean-Louis. *Capital Cities at War: Paris, London, Berlin, 1914–1919*. Cambridge: Cambridge University Press, 1997.

Wiser, William. *The Crazy Years: Paris in the Twenties*. New York: G.K. Hall and Co., 1983.

Wolf, Naomi. *The Beauty Myth: How Images of Beauty are Used Against Women*. New York: William Morrow & Co., 1991.

Zarca, Bernard. "Survivance ou transformation de l'artisanat dans la France d'aujourd'hui." 3 vols. Thèse en sociologie, Institut d'études politiques de Paris, 1983.

Zdatny, Steven, ed., *Hairstyles and Fashion: A Hairdresser's History of Paris, 1910–1920*. Oxford: Berg, 1999.

Zemler, Charles de. *Once over Lightly: The Story of Man and his Hair*. New York: Charles de Zemler, 1939.

Index